French Music
from the
Enlightenment
to
Romanticism

Jean Mongrédien

French Music
from the
Enlightenment
to
Romanticism
1789–1830

Translated from the French by
Sylvain Frémaux

Reinhard G. Pauly, General Editor

Amadeus Press
Portland, Oregon

Translation of this book into English was made possible in part by a grant from the French Ministry of Culture.

Copyright © 1986 as *La Musique en France des Lumières au Romantisme* by Flammarion, Paris. Text published in cooperation with the Centre National des Lettres.

Translation copyright © 1996 by Amadeus Press (an imprint of Timber Press, Inc.) All rights reserved.

ISBN 1-57467-011-5

Printed in Singapore

AMADEUS PRESS
The Haseltine Building
133 S.W. Second Avenue, Suite 450
Portland, Oregon   97204, U.S.A.

ML
270.4
M6513
1996

Library of Congress Cataloging-in-Publication Data

Mongrédien, Jean.
  [Musique en France, des lumières au romantisme. English]
  French music from the enlightenment to romanticism : 1789–1830 / Jean Mongrédien ; translated from the French by Sylvain Frémaux ; Reinhard G. Pauly, general editor.
    p.   cm.
  Translation of: La musique en France, des lumières au romantisme.
  Includes bibliographical references (p.   ) and indexes.
  ISBN 1-57467-011-5
    1. Music—France—19th century—History and criticism. 2. Music—France—18th century—History and criticism. 3. Romanticism in music.   I. Pauly, Reinhard G.   II. Title.
  ML270.4.M6513   1996
  780' .944'09033—dc20   95–49766
                                                                         CIP
                                                                         MN

Contents

Foreword 7

Chapter 1   Music Instruction 11
The founding of the Conservatoire and the standardization of
music education during the French Revolution.

Chapter 2   Revolutionary Hymns and Songs 35
The role of music as a political and propaganda tool.

Chapter 3   Musical Theater 49
The influence of the political climate on the leading theaters of
the day and its effect on the evolution of French musical theater.

Chapter 4   Sacred Music 159
The spiritual transformation of France as evidenced by the repertoire of the Tuileries Chapel.

Chapter 5   Public and Private Concerts 205
The changing musical tastes reflected in concert programs presented by music societies and associations and private salons.

Chapter 6   Instrumental Music 261
The impact of shifting political events and aesthetic sensibilities
on the development of French instrumental music.

Chapter 7   Influence of the German School in France 315
The slow and reluctant acceptance of the German masters in
France.

Afterword   An Evolution Without Revolution 343
The French Revolutionary Calendar 347
Notes 349
Bibliography 365
Index of Names 373
Index of Music 389

Illustrations follow p. 192.

Foreword

Out of the great divide that separates the Age of Enlightenment from romanticism, the names of only a few truly inspired works by famous French composers emerge. It may, therefore, seem curious to devote an entire volume to such an unproductive period in the history of French music. Most of today's historians tentatively mark the end of the Enlightenment with Gluck's masterpieces in 1780 and the beginning of romanticism with the *Symphonie fantastique* in 1830. Nothing or nearly nothing comes between. Could there have been a great void from Gossec to Berlioz and from Gluck to Meyerbeer? What was there besides Rouget de Lisle's "La Marseillaise" and Méhul's "Le Chant du Départ"? In musical anthologies, catalogs, and recordings, this half-century is either ignored or condescendingly labeled a "transitional period," as if romanticism did not gradually develop but blossomed suddenly and spontaneously.

This volume is aimed at correcting this misconception. It does not, however, claim to uncover and revive unknown masterpieces. That research has already been done and done well. After all, this period spans the years between the death of Mozart and the death of Schubert and roughly corresponds to all of Beethoven's career; what important French musical work

7

could compete with the perfection of some of the German School's output? *Habent sua fata libelli!*

All the same, it is time to acknowledge that music history is not solely comprised of masterpieces. Historians do not necessarily share the opinion of professional musicians or music lovers who believe that the intrinsic value of a work is of utmost importance, and its ability to withstand the test of time proves its worth. From this perspective, works that successfully resist the erosion of the centuries are the only ones worth studying. Historians take a different view. In an effort to reconstruct all of the elements of a society's or a nation's musical life, they examine every clue. They are interested not only in the works of music, but also in their history, the institutions that promoted them, and the reasons for their success or failure. They are alert for every sign of a change in mentality and taste. With this in mind, the approximate forty years between the beginning of the French Revolution in 1789 (followed by the fall of the French kings on 10 August 1792) and the temporary return of French kings in the July Monarchy of 1830 seem particularly fascinating to me. Feverish musical activity spread in all directions—not only in the French capital—in the midst of an especially unstable political climate and despite repeated changes of regime, both of which tend to hinder the development of institutions and talents by imposing either unwilling silence or shameless retractions.

Consider, for example, the decade between 1795 and 1805, roughly the period of the Directoire and the Consulate. The Paris Conservatoire, which was to have a profound and enduring influence on French musical life, was created in 1795. In 1799, the famous concerts of the Rue de Cléry were launched, following the trend of the great eighteenth-century Paris concert societies and destined to gain an unsurpassed reputation throughout Europe for their interpretation of symphonic music, particularly that of Haydn. The year 1801 saw the establishment in Paris of a permanent company for Italian opera that would feature the works of Mozart and Rossini, among others. That same year, a German theater introduced *Singspiel,* and though it failed to dazzle French audiences, it did set wheels in motion. In 1802, the newly built Tuileries Chapel opened and enjoyed unparalleled prestige until 1830. Works that premiered there revealed a profound transformation of spiritual life and religious feeling at a time when the rites of Christian worship were officially reinstated in France and the first generation of romantics emerged. What other ten-year period in the history of French music produced so many fruitful and far-reaching innovations?

In the aftermath of the revolutionary upheaval, composers and musicians were seized by an almost messianic inspiration. On 20 October 1801, the French violinist Baillot wrote to a friend who was on an extended visit to Italy:

> What news do you wish to hear from here? The newspapers must have reported the general peace, which seems to fall from the skies. Everything is transformed. The arts are encouraged more than ever; our manufacturing competes with that of the English. Bridges, columns, and statues are being erected in Paris—work has already begun. Trade is returning to life, and our ports are like the dying suddenly brought back to health and happiness by the hand of God. Authors and poets are hard at work. Cries of joy and thanks rise up everywhere.

Something comparable to the immense hope felt by certain Renaissance humanists inspired these musicians. They may have worked in humble obscurity, but a great, slow process of maturation was taking place, and each of them contributed to its development. Their generation tirelessly prepared the way for the great adventure of modern times.

This book is an attempt to prove the validity of these ideas.

Chapter 1

Music Instruction

A state of utter confusion best characterizes the methods of music education under the French monarchy. There was tremendous disparity between what was taught in the cathedral choir schools, what was taught in the countless private schools established in Paris and in the provinces during the period, and private instruction imparted from master to pupil. Although a great number of vocal and instrumental methods developed by experienced artists were published in the eighteenth century, these treatises are often difficult to decipher today. Musical techniques—especially those pertaining to the voice—are not easily described in writing. They do not necessarily reveal what daily musical teaching must have been like, nor do they recreate the true dialogue between master and pupil.

On the eve of the Revolution, music education in France was essentially provided by the century-old choir schools attached to the chapters of cathedrals or collegiate churches. These choir schools—over five hundred of them before the Revolution—offered the considerable advantage of being located throughout France. Girls, of course, had no access to the schools, so private instruction provided their only opportunity for music education.

A systematic analysis of church archives provides a glimpse into what life was like in some of these choir schools. They were boarding schools entirely under the clergy's authority, and children blessed with clear voices and the ability to sing in tune were admitted at an early age, even as young as seven or eight. The chapters provided general education, often with the help of resident grammar and Latin teachers. Music was taught by the *maître de chapelle*. A contract from 6 August 1780 was recently found in the Dijon archives.[1] It is signed by the chapter of that city's *Sainte-Chapelle* and by a certain Laurent Dupuy, stipulating that the latter's duties include teaching the children "plain-chant, music, counterpoint, or singing from a book, as well as music composition." Such an ambitious program was not always realized, either because the pupils were unable to assimilate studies of such breadth or because the master himself had but limited knowledge. In any case, when the pupils' voices changed, they were expected to leave the school and begin their own careers as independent musicians, often to become *maîtres de chapelle* themselves. Most were ill equipped, since their experiences were confined to the narrow repertoire heard and studied during their choir school years. Pupils were exposed to *solfège*, singing, harmony, and the rudiments of composition. In addition, they studied the organ, the bassoon, the serpent, and under the best circumstances, the violin or the cello.

Imperfect as it was, this training allowed some of the more talented young provincial musicians, after completing their education through private instruction, to embark on fairly decent careers. Le Sueur is one of the last famous examples of a provincial composer from a humble peasant family. The early talents of Le Sueur and others like him would never have been brought to light without the help of this free education.

With the development of opera in the eighteenth century, the instruction given by the choir schools proved insufficient to train operatic singers and actors. Moreover, since women were excluded, young ladies wishing to become opera singers or concert artists did not have a chance unless they belonged to a well-to-do family that could offer them high-caliber private instruction. In order to improve this situation, a school was opened in January 1784, during the monarchy's final years. It was located in the *Hôtel des Menus-Plaisirs* (The House of the King's Entertainment) under the direction of Gossec. The main objective of this Royal School for Voice and Drama was to train the singers in the king's service for his chapel, his chamber, and especially the Opéra. There was little emphasis on the study of instrumental music, but voice students were extremely well taught. In 1788 there were no fewer than twenty-one masters (among them the famous

Piccini) for thirty students![2] The school was quick to achieve positive results and just as quick to draw criticism. In a 1790 study entitled *De l'organisation des spectacles à Paris ou essai sur leur forme actuelle* (On the Organization of Performances in Paris or Essay on Their Present Form), Framery proposed to close the school in favor of a broader form of training: "It would be useful if another school existed," he wrote. In 1791, there was talk of closing down. In a letter from the National Archives signed on 26 April, the Baron of La Ferté, administrator of the king's entertainment (*Menus-Plaisirs*), pleads in favor of maintaining the school with an annual budget of 12,000 French livres

> to preserve the only institution created by His Majesty to promote the arts with the chief purpose of training composers and performers for the service of His Chapel as well as His Chamber . . . and to reduce at the same time the expenses in written music and avoid the considerable cost of bringing in high voices from Italy.

The last words clearly show how difficult it was at the end of the eighteenth century to recruit female voices.[3]

Such was the very poor state of official French music education before the Revolution, a situation that became even more precarious after all the choir schools of France were closed down, beginning in 1792. It fell to the Revolutionary government to take some action—action of the greatest importance, since it led to the foundation in 1795 of the *Conservatoire national supérieur de musique* of Paris.[4] Ironically, the man who was chiefly responsible for its creation was not a musician. Bernard Sarrette, born in 1765 to a Bordeaux shoemaker, was a simple accounting clerk prior to 1789. Like many young people of the time, Sarrette was swept up by the new ideals, and after the takeover of the Bastille, he agreed to organize a band of musicians within the newly created National Guard. Until 1792, this band performed in Paris at various public festivals, including the last grandiose religious ceremonies of the Monarchy: a Te Deum sung in Notre-Dame in thanksgiving for the king's recovery (20 March 1791) and again at the funeral of Mirabeau (4 April 1791). The National Guard band, modeled after a traditional military band, included piccolo flutes, oboes, clarinets, French horns, bassoons, drums, and trumpets. Sarrette added a *tuba corva* and a *buccin*, which were heard for the first time during the ceremony of glorification honoring Voltaire and were allegedly imitations, the former of a Greek instrument, the latter of a Hebrew one.

In 1792 Sarrette cleverly submitted to the government a project aimed at transforming the National Guard band into a "Military Music School that would supply players to the whole battle-line army," and his project was approved. Band musicians became instructors and agreed to teach free of charge 120 students, themselves the sons of citizens serving in the National Guard. The instruction consisted of two *solfège* lessons and three instrument lessons per week. Thus the first French wind instrument school was created.

The school began operations in July 1792 under the administrative direction of Sarrette and the music direction of Gossec. Its chief purpose was to train musicians for the army. The *Chronique de Paris* of 10 January 1793 explains that thirty-two graduates from this institution had already "been assigned to the 102nd, 103rd, and 104th regiments of the national voluntary battalions." The same article that praised Sarrette's enterprise also deplored France's lack of "institutions where the art of singing and string playing could also be perfected."

This opinion was obviously shared by Sarrette, who was eager to extend the activities of his music school. In November 1793 he went in person to the Convention and made a speech requesting that his school be transformed into a National Music Institute in order to train the hundreds of artists, including choral singers, needed for the great national celebrations that would be taking place in Paris as well as in the newly created départements. According to the new revolutionary philosophy, music had to be taken out of the salons and the churches and be made accessible to all by way of outdoor performances: "Vast arenas and public squares will become concert halls for a free people." To be carried out, this program required a considerable number of performers who could be trained only by a music institute worthy of the French Republic.

Throughout his astonishing speech, Sarrette expresses a nationalistic bias directed chiefly against Italy and Germany. For instance, he proposed that the creation of a French music education system would forestall having to borrow from "subservient and weak Italy the austere and masculine mode of singing required for the sacred worship of liberty." Sarrette also advocated putting an end to the necessity of having to call on German instrumentalists to fill in certain parts in the better French orchestras for lack of a decent national education:

Our despots did not know how to put the spirit of France to good use, so they called on artists from Germany instead. Under the new reign of liberty these must be found among the French.

Sarrette's eloquence was well suited to his audience, and it paid off. He obtained permission from the Convention to change his music school into a National Music Institute. The government authorized the creation of new classes and the addition of thirteen new artists, including two composers, Méhul and Le Sueur; three violin teachers including Kreutzer; and one cello teacher, Levasseur.

The institute developed quickly and became better known by participating in national celebrations and even presenting a series of concerts in the Feydeau theater to which the members of the Convention received standing invitations. On 4 July 1794, the entire National Institute was to give an important concert in the National Gardens. To increase its numbers, seventy-eight additional choral members and thirty instrumentalists were recruited from the main Paris theaters. Several hymns were heard that evening, including Gossec's *Hymne à la Liberté* and the first performance of Chénier and Méhul's "Le Chant du Départ."

The momentum of Sarrette's influence was briefly interrupted when he was incarcerated at *Sainte-Pélagie* in March 1794 due to a partisan struggle between opposing clans during the Reign of Terror. His colleagues from the National Music Institute testified on his behalf and requested the removal of the seals from his personal effects so that they could have "access to the musical scores to be used at the national celebrations and concerts ordered by the *Comité de Salut Public* (the Committee of Public Welfare)." One month later, Sarrette was paroled and resumed his active training of the various music bands for the army.

The celebration of the *Fête de l'Être Suprême* (the Festival of the Supreme Being) at the Champ-de-Mars in Paris on 8 June 1794 was to showcase the teachers and students of the National Music Institute. It is likely that the teachers themselves traveled to different Paris districts ahead of time to teach the hymns and refrains to be performed at the upcoming celebration to the citizens and schoolchildren. In fact, the teaching staff of the Institute sent a letter to the Committee of Public Welfare to propose their services in this capacity so that everyone could participate in the singing of the revolutionary hymns:

Simple songs will be composed. The members of the Institute in every district will go into each primary school: thus the people and especially its most important group, the hope of our Nation, will learn the hymns to be performed at the celebrations.

After the *Fête de l'Être Suprême*, it seems that this practice was in fact abandoned.

Meanwhile, Sarrette knew how to take advantage of every occasion to increase the number of permanent teachers for his institute. For every revolutionary celebration requiring the Institute to participate, he was granted permission by the Committee of Public Welfare to recruit outside musicians, sometimes in large numbers. For instance, there were no less than 240 outsiders recruited for Bastille Day 1794. The eighty students registered in the National Music Institute at that time would not have been enough to satisfy the demands of the organizing committee for such a large event, and voice training was not yet offered. Out of the sixty classes taught at the time, twenty-two were devoted to *solfège*, eleven to the clarinet, six to the French horn, and only three to the violin. Four inspectors—Gossec, Méhul, Le Sueur, and Cherubini—supervised all the teaching.

At the Feydeau theater on 7 November 1794, the National Music Institute performed two *sinfonia concertantes* by Devienne and Kreutzer, in addition to some patriotic hymns. The concert was particularly successful, and Sarrette seized the opportunity to take another step forward. The Convention had just created the *École Polytechnique* on 28 September, the *Conservatoire des Arts et Métiers* (the Conservatoire for Crafts and Engineering) on 10 October, and the *École Normale* (the National Education School) on 30 October. It was, therefore, no surprise to find the following entry in *Annonces, Affiches et Avis Divers* (Previews, Proclamations, and Various Announcements) dated 9 November:

> This superb concert leads us to believe that the Institute deserves to become one of the first secondary schools for public education and will attract the attention of the Committee for Education, which spares no effort to be useful to the arts, talents, and virtues.

Sarrette's hand in this announcement is obvious. On 13 November, the same periodical took a strong stand on the state of music education in France. It particularly cited the success of the German and the Italian conservatories, which had produced excellent results for many years, and attacked the training provided by the old choir schools.

> In the past, we used to have around six hundred secondary schools in operation, but what were they? Cathedral schools, with their usual archaic tastes, their marked and heavy singing style, their

choral singing devoid of melody or expression, where there was more interest in self-protection than in true talent, in short, where good taste and admirable progress were excluded.

After the choir schools were closed down, Gossec's old Royal singing school remained in a diminished capacity as the only such school in France. "There was not one *lycée* left where the art of music had its teachers and its students." Fortunately, the National Music Institute had been created to put an end to this unacceptable situation, but it had to go further to be transformed into a conservatory in the Italian tradition. A large press campaign took place at the end of 1794, and several articles stressed the eminent role that the musicians of the former National Guard had played over the past five years. All was ready for Sarrette to make his decisive move with the help of his friend Marie-Joseph Chénier, the author of a large number of revolutionary lyrics. Chénier volunteered to address the Convention on 28 July 1795, reporting on the reorganization of the National Music Institute in order to obtain its new status as a conservatory. The main thrust of his speech was to show that music is an integral part of patriotic celebrations and is essential in stimulating the soldiers' courage. His long presentation ended artfully with the word *peace*. Here is its conclusion:

> How glorious it will be for you, Representatives, after the Republic has won an uninterrupted succession of triumphs in an immense war, while containing anarchist and monarchist terrorism at home, and enacting for the next centuries a wise and republican constitution—how glorious it will be for you to prove to all Europe that you can yet devote a little time to the encouragement of an art that has won victories and will be at the sweet service of peace.

On 3 August 1795, the Convention was persuaded to reorganize the National Music Institute and adopted a law creating the Conservatoire. Gossec's Royal School for Voice and Drama had survived the Revolution but since 1789 had steadily declined in importance. Now it was by law required to merge with the new institution.

The government named five inspectors of instruction to run the Conservatoire: Méhul, Grétry, Gossec, Le Sueur, and Cherubini. The number of teachers grew from 70 to 115, and the student capacity of the new school grew to 600. Every musical discipline was represented, and every musical

leader of the time was included in the faculty. Initially, Sarrette was not assigned a position, and two long months went by before he regained the administrative direction of the school that had been his idea in the first place.
Now he proudly declared it "the largest of its kind in all Europe."

The creation of the Conservatoire undeniably began a new page in the
history of music education in France. It was the first time that the country
had a public school of this importance. In addition, new regulations ended
sex discrimination, and the school became co-educational. At last, women
were able officially to receive music training in a national school. The initial
guidelines did caution, however, that "students of each sex meet in separate
classrooms and cannot mix except during stage rehearsals sung with or
without orchestral accompaniment." Women remained a minority in instrumental and composition classes for a long time, but the ratio in voice
classes was just the reverse. An 1816 report stated that 90 men, as opposed
to 227 women, had graduated from the voice classes since the creation of
the institution. This disproportion resulted from the difficulty in finding
men with exceptional voices and also from "the war, which continuously
took the students away from their studies."[5] When the school opened in
1795, pianist and composer Hélène Montgeroult was appointed to teach a
piano class, a position she held for three years. Her salary was 2500 livres,
the same as that of her male colleagues of equal rank. In contrast with all
other professional schools created in Paris at the end of the eighteenth century, the Conservatoire was the only one that allowed women on its faculty
and admitted women students.

The opening of such a brilliant school in Paris also reinforced the cen-
tralization of French music education. As shall be seen, several institutions
in the provinces sought a new status comparable to that of the Paris Conservatoire at the turn of the nineteenth century, but they were considered to
be its subsidiaries and never gained much influence. The change that took
place in 1795 moved in the opposite direction. The better students who
came from the départements to take the entrance examinations each year
were attracted to the Paris Conservatoire. Going through the minutes of
municipal councils in various local archives, I frequently found agreements
to pay for a provincial music student's travel expenses to Paris in order to
allow him to try his luck with the prestigious school. When it first opened,
the Conservatoire already included students from forty-six départements.
The third article of the 3 August law creating the new school specified that
it would dispense free education to "six hundred students of both sexes pro-
portionally chosen in all the départements."

At the opening of the second academic year on 22 October 1796, Sarrette made a long speech that helps to clarify some of the founders' underlying intentions. In the field of instrumental music, they were hoping to improve wind instrument instruction in particular. Up until then, students were trained almost exclusively in the military music schools. There existed no decent manual to enable the most gifted to rise above a reasonably average level, which may explain the lack of good repertoire for these instruments, since most of the eighteenth-century German baroque music was still unknown at that time. Composers were asked to "write more often for this useful medium of their art," and wind instrumentalists were required to study a stringed instrument in order "to gain from it a feeling for good music." This statement reveals the status of each family of instruments at the time. The German composer Reichardt, who was staying in Paris during the Consulate and frequently heard the Conservatoire orchestra and the Rue de Cléry orchestra performing Haydn symphonies, was surprised by the quality of the brass and woodwinds and how much they had improved since the last years of the Monarchy.

As for singing, Sarrette declared that "this discipline of music was always poorly taught in France." Sarrette was always glad to criticize the choir schools, where pupils were systematically taught always to sing with full voice so that they could be heard through the vast spaces of the cathedrals. Consequently, theaters were "obliged to recruit their singers from the chapter schools and were forced to submit to the ecclesiastical style." Between this excess and that of servile imitation of the "sweet and expressive Italian" singing mode, the Conservatoire intended to create an original French school of singing. Unfortunately, the results did not match their expectations.

Curiously, from the very start of official education in France, voice teaching has been the most controversial discipline. The first masters to be appointed at the Conservatoire were Lays, Adrien, Persuis, and later, Garat. Were their methods at fault, or were the students responsible for the poor results? At the dawn of the nineteenth century, every contemporary—French or German—agreed in declaring the French national school of singing mediocre. They sounded just like the eighteenth-century critics of *urlo francese* (French howling); nothing had changed. They denounced the tired voices that were pushed too far and often went out of tune as a result, the raucous sounds, and the "ridiculous, dreadful outbursts." In 1801 at the Grand Opera, only Lays was spared by a critic who thought that "every singer, male or female, had retained a barbaric style of shouting and vocal contortions unworthy of Polyhymnia's Temple." Even Madame Branchu, one of Garat's students who had received all her training at the Conservatoire and had obtained First Prize in 1797, was not spared. After she had sung in concert a scene from Cherubini's *Médée*, she was accused of already showing the faults that made opera singers unfit for the concert stage. "The charm in her voice has already been ruined by her habit of throwing out the sounds and yelling in order to be heard and applauded."[6]

In an article dated 23 August 1809, the *Allgemeine musikalische Zeitung* delineated the weaknesses of the French singing school and did not hesitate to write that the Conservatoire had completely failed in this area, that the students were poorly guided, that each teacher "yelled" in his own fashion. In short, the problems associated with vocal art teaching in France ever since the opening of the Conservatoire have yet to be fully resolved even in our own day.

In other areas, however, the founders of the Conservatoire came up with some brand new ideas that would soon have a remarkable effect on musical pedagogy. For instance, they systematically taught music theory and history side by side, along with mathematics, literature, and aesthetics. They proposed to teach the theory of art in relation to "mathematics, poetics, and history." Through the laws of acoustics, physics would explain "the devices used by the Ancients to augment the sounds and enable them to be heard unaltered and uninterrupted by every member of a large audience." The study of the basic laws of physics would also encourage progress in the making of instruments by providing wind instruments with "low-register volume required for outdoor performance." Finally, they stressed that "drama, the science of the soul, the only one that can bring life to the chords and expression to melody, should not be forgotten" in this new, complete music curriculum.[7]

In addition, a library would be created in order to facilitate the students' practical and theoretical studies of music. It would place at their disposal "the writings by the masters of all times and of all nations." This idea was absolutely original, though it may seem common today; at the end of the eighteenth century, music students did not have access to a specialized music library. The Conservatoire planned to acquire one copy of every new musical score and to collect all available original manuscripts or copies of manuscripts. Such decisions were bound to give a remarkable boost to music education by at last making accessible to students a large number of masterpieces of the past which had been out of their reach. What could possibly have been the repertoire of the average provincial choir school before 1789? Today, when every music student has access to most of the literature of the past, not to mention all the recordings, it would be astonishing to determine exactly what scores were heard and performed by young people during their years in the choir schools. In many cases their collection was probably limited to only a few pieces of religious music that offered little in the way of representing different time periods and styles.

Before it officially became the Conservatoire (in 1795), the National Music Institute (the decree pertaining to its status was signed on 29 August 1794) had to establish its own teaching principles and implement them throughout France, so it decided to publish some elementary manuals "for the study of music, singing, harmony, composition, and all the instruments." For the first time in the history of French music education, a standardized curricula that would apply to the nation as a whole would be set down in writing in a great centralizing effort to affirm the superiority of Paris and her Conservatoire over all of France.

The courage shown by the pioneers of this project commands our admiration. There had been exalted discussions among musicians who envisioned a better future for their art and from their art and, in an outburst of messianic generosity, wanted to change the world order. After the commitment was made, musicians ran the risk of being ignored, but such was not the case. Promises were kept, and beginning in 1800, a series of treatises and methods was issued by the Conservatoire's own music publisher, created back in 1794 as the "Music Store for National Celebrations and the Conservatoire."[8]

Mention should be made of the tireless activity of Sarrette and his team as they engaged in a variety of enterprises. In addition to teaching, all of them performed in national celebrations, and many of them were composers as well. Composers may have wished to publish their own music, not only for personal and financial gain, but also for the public good: They wanted their music sent out into the provinces "to enable citizens of all the départements to take part in civic celebrations" and to supply the troops with song sheets that would inspire patriotism.

Such an association of artists was the first of its kind, but it unfortunately did not meet with much success. During the first two or three years, initial editions were sold without difficulty to the army all over France and even overseas. Then the interest in revolutionary music began to wane, and the Conservatoire Music Store had to publish other types of works, including romances and chamber music. It also published a series of fifteen methods and treatises that became an immense learning tool. For the first time, France adopted an official state music education system. The first volume, *Principes élémentaires de musique* (Elementary Principles of Music), was prepared by Gossec and published in 1800; the last volume, *Méthode de plainchant à l'usage des églises de France* (Plain-Chant Method for Use in the Churches of France), was the work of Abbé Roze and came out in 1814. Between these two dates, a special volume was devoted to each principal instrument, voice, and harmony and was written by a full professor of the Conservatoire considered to be a virtuoso on his or her instrument: Louis Adam for the piano, Frédéric Duvernoy for the French horn, Pierre Baillot for the violin, Étienne Ozy for the bassoon, and so on.

In determining an official teaching system, the Conservatoire certainly helped many young people who had been tossed from one teacher to the next and one method to another. On the other hand, the establishment of a single doctrine ran the risk of immobilizing an education that by definition could be dynamic only if it remained flexible. It is quite obvious that a new order was needed to put an end to the anarchic succession of eighteenth-century vocal and instrumental treatises. J.-B. Pujoulx shared this opinion in 1801 when he commented on the creation of the Conservatoire in his study entitled *Paris à la fin du XVIIIe siècle* (Paris at the End of the Eighteenth Century):

> Among the improvements needed for the benefit of art, the adoption of methods is, in my opinion, the most urgent one. Without them, teachers will continue to impose their different methods on their students. Besides, elementary methods will set the basic rules of everyday teaching and save the students from having to begin their instruction anew when entering a new teacher's class.

On 6 September 1800, the *Journal de Paris* announced the first of this series of treatises, praising a promising enterprise that would bring "the most desirable uniformity" to education. Today, many educators would doubtless be shocked by such a program, especially in music. But the Paris Conservatoire gave itself high marks:

> In this matter the French Conservatoire is far ahead of those of Italy, where every school takes on the color of its master, and where the form and spirit of the lessons are as varied as the teachers' names.

The debate over methods of teaching music continues today, but such an authoritarian and centralized view of education certainly was intentional on part of the government in the early part of the nineteenth century. The emperor himself, although totally ignorant of musical technique, was nonetheless interested in this project and followed its implementation personally.

The extent to which this series of methods helped education is at present hard to determine. Even a detailed study of each individual volume would not reveal its real influence outside the Conservatoire. As far as the theory of harmony was concerned, Catel's *Traité* undeniably showed an effort to retain at least some of Rameau's ideas. Just like Rameau, Catel took the sound body as a starting point and drew from it all those primary chords that can be used unprepared, either in root position or in inversion. But then he thought it sufficient to divide harmony into two groups of chords: a simple or natural group and a compound or artificial group. Simple harmony included every chord needing no preparation, and compound harmony was formed from a simple chord with one or two notes held over to the next chord. Catel obviously attempted to simplify in the interest of teaching. He deemed it necessary

> to spare the students the almost insurmountable difficulty of having to classify by memory a long series of isolated chords all presented as being different, making harmony very difficult to conceive and even more difficult to write well.

The principles defined by Catel in his *Traité* still serve as the basis for the modern approach to teaching harmony.

Leafing through each volume, one really gets the impression of a clear teaching method that always aims at smoothing over the difficulties without ever losing the main objective, which is to form musical taste. When Louis Adam's pianoforte method came out in 1805, his contemporaries were struck by the fact that a whole chapter was devoted to "the art of touch itself—separate from fingerings—and to everything relative to the beauty of sounds."

From the first years of the Conservatoire's existence during the Directoire and the Consulate, it often became the target of violent attacks, although its status was never really threatened. Its fiercest opponent was one of its own five inspectors, composer Le Sueur himself, who was also personally at odds with Sarrette. Le Sueur did not agree with the principle of treating vocal and instrumental instruction equally. As an operatic composer trying to preserve a great French vocal tradition, he blamed the Conservatoire for its inability, over several years, to produce a single student—except for Madame Branchu—capable of singing Rameau, Gluck, and Sacchini.

I shall not relate here the details of this quarrel, although it had a dramatic outcome: Le Sueur, one of the leading composers of his time, was simply fired from the Conservatoire in 1802. Among other important questions, voice pedagogy was at the center of the debate. Le Sueur had received all of his training from the provincial choir schools and wanted them reinstated on the grounds that Europe was overrun with instrumentalists, but most opera houses were short of actors and singers. This was an accurate assessment, but since when did choir schools ever supply opera singers? Le Sueur's point of view was that of a composer who always preferred vocal music and completely neglected instrumental music.

And so, at the very beginning of the nineteenth century when the signing of the Concordat was going to make possible the reopening of the choir schools, a movement against the Conservatoire sprang up in France, and Le Sueur himself was often leading the opposition. In Prairial year IX (May–June 1801), an anonymous booklet that could not formally be attributed to Le Sueur appeared in Paris. A single copy of this very rare text has been found and is kept in the Brussels Royal Library. It is entitled

> Project for a general outline of music education in France, with an emphasis on vocal and compositional instruction, establishing the need to reinstate the former primary musical studies (the so-called choir schools) and to create in Paris a *collège de musique pour le perfectionnement du chant et de la composition* (a Music School for the Advanced Study of Singing and Composition).

The intention behind this project was to reopen all of France's choir schools in the form of "primary schools" for music and to create in Paris an advanced vocal school—a sort of graduate music program—where girls would be admitted along with sixteen- or seventeen-year-old boys graduating from the choir schools. In addition to composition and voice, this advanced school would teach acting and stage direction, as well as piano, violin, and cello. In making this project public, its author, who may or may not have been Le Sueur, could not hope to do serious damage to the Conservatoire. This great revolutionary institution may indeed have had an undeniable weakness in its voice teaching, but it was nonetheless solidly based on wider objectives: the training of composers, virtuoso performers, and orchestra players, as well as singers. However, the nostalgic movement in favor of the former monarchy kept on demanding the reopening of the choir schools until the time of the Restoration, and the Conservatoire continued to be denigrated by many, more or less because of its revolutionary origin. The Count Fortia de Piles, a composer and former officer of the king, wrote in 1812:

> Has the Conservatoire taken the place of nearly one hundred schools in all parts of France, that is to say, in most of our cathedrals? These schools used to provide the training for young musicians who wanted nothing else but to make music from their youngest age and who, by the age of fifteen, knew it as well as their mother tongue. Today, out of the Conservatoire come a few virtuosos who will show off in our theaters and orchestras, and that means that three quarters of France will never hear of them.[9]

In my own research I have found an anonymous pamphlet that dates from that time (Revolutionary year X, or 1801–1802) entitled *Le Russe à l'Opéra ou Réflexions sur les institutions musicales de la France* (A Russian at the Opera, or Thoughts on France's Musical Institutions). It levels the same criticism—the Conservatoire's alleged inefficiency in the training of truly operatic voices—and suggests that the former choir schools "could have competed" with the Italian conservatories.

In the absence of systematic research into the various church chapters of France, it is impossible to tell exactly what became of the former choir schools after the Concordat was signed in 1801. According to the information in the entry *Conservatoire* in Choron's *Dictionnaire historique* of 1810, the choir schools were reinstated in 1802 thanks to the efforts of the teachers who had been excluded from the Conservatoire. "There was even an attempt to persuade the government that the choir schools alone would suffice to fulfill the needs of the art of music in France." Choron believed this to be a mistake, since the choir schools had never trained opera singers nor musicians for the army, but a compromise seems to have been reached soon after:

> As things have now calmed down, it can finally be admitted that choir schools and conservatories can all be useful in their own way.

The formers' chief objective should be to supply the seminaries and church choirs, while the latter should mostly serve the needs of the operatic stage, military bands, and public celebrations.

The circumstances under which certain choir schools reopened during the Empire and the Restoration require better documentation. The information that is available is contradictory. On the one hand, Castil-Blaze asked for their reinstatement in 1820, since only they "can stop the decadence of music by populating our provinces with excellent musicians."[10] On the other hand, in the preface of his *Dictionnaire*, Choron announced their reopening as early as 1810, although under poor conditions:

> At least the former *maîtres de chapelle* were composers. But lately, the shortage of candidates has required, with a few exceptions, that anybody be hired. Here a parish chorister, there a violin teacher or even a trumpeter is in charge of training the singers. These days, one would have great difficulty in finding among the total of two or three hundred pupils a single one who is capable of singing a seven-note scale without missing four or five.

The Conservatoire was favored by the Imperial government and received its protection. Until 1815, however, it was under fire from the opposition. In 1807, Portalis, the minister in charge of the churches, wrote a report that was addressed to Napoleon and quoted by Bigot de Préamneu: "I know from past and present experience that only the choir schools can give to our men the very best training in vocal music."[11] The little research that I could do in the Paris diocesan archives quickly convinced me that the reopening of the choir schools—when it did occur—took place under such conditions that prevented these small music schools from ever competing with the Conservatoire. At Saint-Roch, for example, the choir school was reinstated around 1810 under Father Aubert. As its *maître de musique*, he earned "eight hundred francs a year to take care of all twelve children of the parish, as well as providing for his lodging, heat, music supplies, paper, and so on." At that time, a professor at the Conservatoire received a salary of approximately 2500 francs. Except for two serpent players and Antoine Lefébure-Wély, an organist and quite a good composer, I found no mention of any other instrumental performers listed in the Saint-Roch archives, raising many doubts as to the musical training of these young children.

Despite the controversy, the existence of the Conservatoire was never questioned during the Empire. Budget restrictions in March 1800 and September 1802 caused only a reduction in the number of teachers and students. For instance, in 1806, there were only three inspectors and thirty-five teachers for a little over three hundred students. At that time, the library contained about eight thousand volumes "chosen among the best works in every style." No other musical collection of such importance existed in France at that time. This unique library was further enriched under the Empire by rare books and manuscripts "collected" from Italian conservatories. In 1815, the Austrian ambassador demanded that they be returned.

On the other hand, the return to power of the Bourbon dynasty in 1814 was to bring gloomy times for the Conservatoire, which the new regime intended to penalize for its revolutionary origin. Sarrette was immediately suspended at the time of the first Restoration (17 November 1814). He was reinstated by the emperor in the spring of 1815 only to be dismissed again on 18 December of that same year. The Conservatoire was abolished and replaced in March 1816 by the Royal School for Voice and Drama: the name of the former music school founded in 1784 by Louis XVI.[12] In spite of a reduction in the number of teachers—about thirty were discharged—many of them stayed in the new school. The most important administrative change was the placement of the Royal School for Voice and Drama under the authority of the Ministry of the Royal House instead of the Ministry of the Interior, where it had been during the Empire. The direction of the school was entrusted to composer and historian François Perne, named general inspector of classes. He remained at this post until 1822, when he was replaced by Cherubini. Cherubini was given the old title of director, but the name *Conservatoire* does not reappear until 1831. For as long as they occupied the throne, the Bourbon kings never forgave the first French music school its revolutionary background.

Besides the Conservatoire, there were still very few official music schools in Paris during the Empire and the Restoration.

The Opéra maintained for a long time within its walls a small singing school for about twenty students of both sexes under the watchful eye of a singer named Lays. Naturally, this small school was jealous of the Conservatoire and was still operating at the beginning of the Restoration. In 1818, the conflict between the two rivals appeared to escalate. The schools did not teach the same vocal techniques, and since several students attended both institutions, some unfortunate wavering resulted. Garat taught in both schools and seemed to enjoy making matters worse. A report about him mentions that he had taught only a dozen lessons in two years at the Royal School (the Conservatoire) and did not spare his colleagues his sarcastic and scornful comments. Meanwhile, at the Opera School, he continued to "disapprove of the studies of the Royal School and to regard them as merely preparatory if not worthless." Such an attitude on the part of one of the most important masters of French singing did not contribute to the happiness of the students, already suspicious of the reliability of the teaching methods.[13]

In contrast, the various attempts, starting in 1812, made by Choron in the field of music education are much more interesting. Choron had meditated for a long time about the methods of music education. He published a considerable number of volumes devoted to *solfège*; to vocal, piano, and organ techniques; and so forth. He had studied the *solfège* methods used in his time, including the *Solfèges d'Italie* and those by Rodolphe, which were often reissued, as well as the Conservatoire's own *Principes élémentaires*. He was convinced that they all failed to distinguish, at the learning stage, *tone* from *duration*, "both of which present specific difficulties." He refused to integrate these elements systematically, insisting that they be taught successively.[14]

Choron was also the first in France to attempt to teach music collectively using what he called his *méthode concertante* (concerted method). He was in favor of a mass music education system that he modeled after the Naples and Venice conservatories, making a single teacher responsible for one or two hundred students, the better ones taking turns tutoring the weaker. Choron was in charge of several music schools during the last years of the Empire, and so he was able to apply this concerted method, especially in the *École normale de musique* created in 1812. There he taught *solfège* to groups of children. During the Restoration in 1817, he started a class called *Pensionnat royal* (the Royal Boarding School), which had a rather undefined objective. The government supported it and considered it to be preparatory to entering the Conservatoire. In fact, Choron's ambitions reached even further: He hoped to improve education in order to make music progress in France, in theaters and orchestras, and in the cathedrals of the provinces. He himself traveled in the départements to recruit top students and to convince every local authority to follow his example by opening a free school.

In 1820, this true apostle of music education at last obtained from the government full recognition for his music school under the title *École royale et spéciale du chant* (the Royal School Specializing in Voice). Once admitted, all twenty-four students of both sexes were completely taken care of by the *Maison du Roi* (the Royal House) during their four years of study. The goal of Choron's school was to "train singers capable of filling the front ranks of our best operatic institutions." In this role, it rivaled the Conservatoire, but after 1825, it quickly changed its direction, becoming the Royal school for religious music in France. Its main function then was to prepare future church musicians—choir boys, choristers, organists, and music teachers—to replenish cathedrals and parishes. The school was very prosperous until 1830, when Louis-Philippe dealt it a fatal blow by cutting its budget. One hundred and fifty students were attending at the time.

Choron used very personal teaching methods. Not only did he, as we have seen, teach the basics and *solfège* to groups according to his concerted method, he also had a very different concept of vocal pedagogy from that of the Conservatoire. He did not like to have his students sing the great solo arias of the modern repertoire, teaching them sixteenth- and seventeenth-century pieces for small vocal ensembles instead. In so doing, he avoided wearing out students' voices too soon and paid more attention to forming good musicianship and taste. For the first time in France, he introduced the students of his school to the great vocal works of Palestrina, Handel, and Bach. Fétis was right in considering Choron

> responsible for introducing in France the German way of training vocal ensembles, training without which the faithful performances of the great masterpieces would be impossible.[15]

This was an absolutely new field in France, and it remained out of the Conservatoire's reach, despite all its possibilities.

As for teaching composition, Choron also had his own original ideas. To start from Rameau's theories and "fundamental bass" was, in his view, disastrous. According to him, there were still far too many teachers who "introduced their students to composition by first displaying principles of physics and geometry far above their understanding and with no relation to the music." Boredom and aversion would quickly result from this approach that consists of memorizing catalogues of chords "that even the best mind could not assimilate in less than a year."

Instead of using a method that he found dull, Choron encouraged teachers to expose their students as soon as possible to an extremely simple bass line and then show them how to harmonize it in the most suitable way. He claimed that this was the approach used in Germany and Italy:

> They go straight to the point. First, the student is presented with very simple but well-designed and correctly modulating basses. Then, all the possible implications of a bass line are examined, the most suitable chords are learned for each case, and the accompaniment of figured bass from the harpsichord is practiced at length. After this initial study, he is given a melody and taught how to place the best bass lines underneath.[16]

This method also had the tremendous advantage of introducing the composition student to counterpoint, which was no longer being taught at a time when all that was necessary was a "chordal harmonization." No serious composition study is conceivable without the mastery of counterpoint, the study of the different styles, and the knowledge of musical literature of the past. In Choron's opinion, the Conservatoire was not yet completely rid of these flaws that were inherent to French education because its faculty was "restrained by the fear of running against local prejudices and had not yet achieved all that they wished to achieve."

Apart from these official schools in Paris, most of the music education in France was provided through private instruction from master to pupil. This practice naturally left almost no trace of documentation, so its influence or its quality is difficult to evaluate. Anybody could pretend, then as now, to be a music teacher. In 1799, for example, a Paris music teacher placed an announcement in the press proposing "violin or voice lessons" for one franc at his home or 1.25 francs at the student's home—a concert seat then cost between two and five francs. A private instrumental lesson cost more than a voice lesson, and when several students were taken as a group, the prices were naturally lower. "Citizeness Hardy, a vocal artist at the Feydeau theater" advertised a new studio in her home at a price of six francs for twelve vocal lessons and nine francs for twelve instrumental lessons. A private lesson apparently lasted two hours then.[17] The *Journal de Paris* dated 14 December 1801 announced that a certain Regny was opening an "elementary music course" in the *Lycée pour les langues étrangères* (the Secondary School for Foreign Languages) on the rue Vivienne. During twenty-four one-hour sessions, "the principles of practice, theory, and harmony would be demonstrated, first at the blackboard as a science, then in performance on a keyboard instrument." The notice does not specify whether the instruction was private or collective, but it indicates that an "elementary course" included the simultaneous theoretical study of *solfège* and harmony and the practice of an instrument.

After the choir schools were shut down during the Revolution, many music teachers were forced to make their living by providing private instruction. Such was the case for Jumentier in Saint-Quentin. In 1810, a certain M. Lender, an unknown figure who claimed to have "directed for twenty-five years one of the best-known choir schools in France," opened a vocal and instrumental music school on the rue des Saints-Pères in Paris. It was advertised as "following the model of the Italian conservatories," probably to cash in on the vogue of the Italian theater of Paris.[18]

As far as music education in the provinces is concerned, there is not nearly enough information to evaluate the situation, and we are often forced to admit our ignorance. In Revolutionary years V and VII, the government received proposals, from Daunou in particular, to reduce enrollment in the Paris Conservatoire in order to allow for the creation of twelve special schools in the provinces. This number later grew to sixty. The project to open branches of the Conservatoire in the départements was temporarily dropped and then revived in May 1801. The plan was very carefully prepared and included the creation of

1. Thirty so-called first-degree music schools with fifteen pupils in cities of the fourth order.
2. Fifteen so-called second-degree music schools with forty pupils in cities of the third order.
3. Ten so-called third-degree music schools with one hundred and twenty pupils in cities of the second order.[19]

It thoroughly covered all France and was supposed to enable the most gifted provincial students to reach the fourth-degree school, namely the Paris Conservatoire. This project, however, failed, just as the previous ones had. Were the successive failures due only to financial reasons, or were ideological differences to blame? It was the latter, according to Bruno Brévan, a specialist in the sociology of music and the author of the most recent study of this period: "In the Revolutionary society which claimed to be a model for equality, the newly created Conservatoire was an elitist institution with a field of action voluntarily limited to the capital."[20] Very early on, the provinces had felt the need for new official schools capable of spreading musical instruction throughout the country. J.-B. Pujoulx, in his book *Paris à la fin du XVIIIe siècle* (Paris at the End of the Eighteenth Century), which was published in 1801, posed the problem in the following way: "Since this national instruction is intended for the well-to-do, it must be made available more widely, for those who cannot afford this instruction [in Paris] can even less afford to leave their home to travel twenty-five miles for it."[21]

In the absence of any official policy, the few institutions laboriously established in the French provinces lacked sufficient financial and musical solidity. Many were short-lived, and the départements could never compete with Paris.

The Concert Society of Lille, providing free musical training to twelve young ladies and twelve young men, applied in November 1802 for the status of conservatory after the Paris model. Needless to say, it was turned down. On 12 June 1812, the same society made a direct appeal to the emperor and reminded him of his long-past promise for a "special music school." In spite of the flattering tone of the epistle, the appeal was in vain. It was not until 1827 that a royal decree converted the 1816 music school into a branch of the Paris Conservatoire.[22]

The history of the music schools in the provinces in the beginning of the nineteenth century is littered with miscarried projects. In Arras, for example, city officials received from composer Antoine Glachant a proposal for "a Music Academy or Institute to be established in Arras under the auspices of the Lord Mayor," along with a letter including the following terms:

> It is my opinion that by favoring this enterprise with your own authority, you will anticipate the intentions of our government whose Supreme Ruler relentlessly attends to the rescue of the art of music. This institution is made necessary by the closing of the choir schools, which gave our state its greatest masters.

The project included, in addition to a vocal music program as a foundation, courses for various instruments and co-educational teaching, modeled after the Paris Conservatoire.[23]

Official music education outside of private schools did not take shape in the provinces until the Restoration. Some information on the city of Lyon can be found in the Rhône Departmental Archives.[24] In 1818, a man named Laflèche opened an elementary school at 12 Rue Mulet, where he set out to "teach the elements and the complete theory of vocal music"—no mention is made of instrumental music. As he intended to enlarge the school, the number of his students grew to twenty-four in 1821: twelve young men and twelve young ladies. The school was co-educational in name only, since the former attended evening classes from seven to nine o'clock, and the latter attended morning classes from eleven to one o'clock. On 27 June 1821, Laflèche applied for a city subsidy and an authorization to name his school *École royale élémentaire du Midi* (the Royal Elementary School of the South). He was turned down on very specific administrative grounds. It would be "contrary to existing territorial divisions. Prosperous music schools already exist in Toulouse, Nîmes, and Marseille. There are city schools and *écoles de département* (regional schools), and the latter extension is the only one that is officially recognized." The Prefect of the département seemed to hesitate to authorize the change but finally granted the school the more modest title of *École royale élémentaire de musique du département du Rhône* (the Royal Elementary Music School of the Rhône département).

In 1822, one year later and again in Lyon, a certain Constant wrote to the Prefect of the Rhône asking for permission to open a music school "modeled after the Paris Conservatoire." It would take a century and a half for this wish to be fulfilled, although the government did authorize several local schools to become, if not true conservatories of the provinces, branches of the Paris Conservatoire. In his request, Constant argued the following points:

> I am not going to enumerate all the advantages for Lyon society and the neighboring départements. How useful this school would be to the theaters, and especially their choruses, which always perform poorly! Other cities of lesser importance than Lyon, having realized the need, are already deriving considerable advantage. Let me mention Lille, Rouen, Marseille, Nantes . . . . The city of Lyon has an excellent school for painting, a veterinary school, and many more institutions. It seems to be begging for a music school that will raise this art to the level of all the others.[25]

It is not known if this request was finally granted, but the government became aware of the need to give an official structure to the artistic and cultural life in the provinces. A number of orders were issued to change progressively several local music schools into branches of the Conservatoire, such as Toulouse in 1826. The great Paris institution remained the model: it was the reference and the goal of young provincial musicians' aspirations.

The Paris Conservatoire established in 1795 served as the exemplar. Although the new national school did not altogether stop the anarchic profusion of more or less serious small local schools, it established for the first time in France an official music education system, thus setting a standard to be followed by future generations to the present day.

Chapter 2

Revolutionary Hymns and Songs

A definitive anthology of hymns and songs from the French Revolution was collected by Constant Pierre almost a century ago and represents a unique archive in the history of music. Although it is limited to France and covers only a ten-year period (1789 to 1800), it draws from a variety of styles and does not invent any new musical forms.

Constant Pierre documented approximately 160 works—from simple band marches of only a few bars to large musical frescoes for several orchestras and choruses, with solo recitatives and arias—though there must have been many more. The German newspaper *Frankreich*, which appeared in Altona starting in 1795, published the lyrics and music for a great number of works. Constant Pierre overlooked several of these—all the hymns composed by Trahcier (which may have been a pseudonym for Reichardt) and the works of the Theophilanthropists' cult—and nothing is known about the fairly large number of works by regional composers. Recent research conducted in Saint-Quentin by André Vacherand for the Academic Society indicates that on 27 November 1794, the municipal government called on amateur artists for the ten-year celebrations and asked Jumentier in particular "to devote his talents to the performance of odes and canticles sent by the Committee of Public Welfare, as well as his own compositions." Jumentier was a former *maître de chapelle* and, no doubt like many of his colleagues in the provinces, occasionally acted as composer of revolutionary music.[1] On 30 November 1793, the church of Saint-Quentin was converted into a *temple de la Raison* (Temple of Reason). This event is commemorated by Jumentier's hymn for large chorus and orchestra, beginning with the words *Vous gentilles fillettes* (You, Gentle Maidens). On 21 January 1799, two more works by Jumentier were performed at a ceremony marking the anniversary of Louis XVI's death, with lyrics written by local poets especially for the occasion. Saint-Quentin is certainly not the only example. Following the Paris model of that time, hymns and songs were heard all over France, but most were forgotten by the next generation.

Works commissioned for special occasions were usually short-lived, even those written by the most illustrious composers of the time and performed during the big Paris celebrations. Two of them, however, have been passed down from one generation to another with remarkable success: "Le Chant du Départ" ("The Song of Departure") by Chénier and Méhul and, of course, "La Marseillaise" by Rouget de Lisle.

All of the works composed for specific celebrations were given titles such as *hymn, ode, stanza, air, cantata, patriotic scene,* and so forth, and the titles alone do not reveal much about their content or form, not that it mattered. Indeed, ever since the beginning of the nineteenth century, the revolutionary repertoire has often been viewed with a degree of contempt. Regardless of the ideological bias that may be reflected in the criticism, when the criteria and methods used to analyze other types of music are applied, the results are disappointing: the structure, harmonic language, and melody in many of these songs and hymns are unspeakably ordinary.

The significance of these works can instead be found by focusing on the role of music itself, as conceived by committee members charged with organizing the revolutionary celebrations. Fortunately, the recent studies by Mona Ozouf[2] and the Clermont-Ferrand Symposium on *Les Fêtes de la Révolution*[3] have cast a new light on these celebrations in general and the music of the Revolution in particular.

In the hands of the organizing committees, the revolutionary celebrations became an instrument of propaganda and political education. They played an important part in educating citizens because they had the power to evoke strong feelings. "Man, a sensitive being, is moved by striking images, grand-scale scenes, and deep emotions," Mirabeau declared in 1791. For the revolutionary leaders, a celebration was simply a propaganda device.

The end of the eighteenth century saw the emergence of a new sensitivity that might even be called pre-romantic, and the governing powers used the revolutionary celebrations to capture people's hearts through the use of sensitive imagery and symbols. Much has been said about the important role played by tableaux in the revolutionary celebrations—Mirabeau's "striking images"—such as the Trees of Liberty, the effigy of the Bastille or the guillotine, the staging of the king's execution. The celebrations took on a theatrical quality in that they revolved around a few objects or a few images. Like a play, the celebrations were scripted and structured. Instead of being a spontaneous gathering of people rejoicing and improvising the day's events as they went along, celebrations became institutionalized, and impulsive invention had no place. In 1794, Barère declared that popular education was useful only "if public institutions were surrounded with ceremonies and celebrations, or if the institutions themselves turned into ceremonies and celebrations."

In this context, the government considered music to be just one more propaganda instrument, but a particularly effective one, since it could generate deep emotions and make people all the more impressionable. Revolutionary music must therefore be considered with its purpose in mind rather than simply as a traditional work of art. A piece of music was prized not because it was deemed beautiful or scholarly according to traditional standards but because it most successfully conveyed the message.

The main difference between traditional music and Revolutionary music was where it was performed. Most hymns and songs were intended for outdoor performances, which put certain technical demands on the composers. Outdoor performances were a completely new phenomenon. Up until 1789, common townspeople and country folk in particular had never had an opportunity to hear a large musical ensemble, though they may have heard folk songs played by traveling musicians and jugglers or fanfares by military bands. They did not go to concerts, and church services offered only plain-chant with organ or serpent accompaniment. Imagine the emotion and surprise felt by simple and sensitive souls hearing large-scale sounds for the first time and perhaps even being asked to participate in a musical celebration! Music was a simple and potent means to indoctrinate individuals susceptible to this form of emotional propaganda.

For the first time, music was taken out of the churches and concert halls. The significance of this move is confirmed by Sarrette, founder of the Conservatoire, in a speech inspired by revolutionary ideology and delivered to the *Convention nationale*: "The spirit of the French has recovered its original grandeur. It will no longer be weakened in effeminate salons or temples consecrated by traitors."[4] As a result, it immediately became necessary to compose accompaniments only for wind instruments, since stringed instruments could not withstand bad weather. Dating back to its days as the National Music Institute, the Conservatoire was especially devoted to the training of wind players, and the *Journal de Paris* from 27 November 1793 mentions some interesting details on this matter:

> Since the national celebrations cannot and do not have other boundaries but the celestial vault, and since the sovereign people is their audience as well as their greatest ornament, they should never be enclosed in a limited or covered space; therefore stringed instruments cannot be employed. Harsh weather absolutely prevents their use, and besides, the quality of their sound does not allow them to be heard from a distance. Therefore, we recommend the exclusive use of wind instruments, for they are not influenced by air in the same way, and their volume when carrying a tune is eight times louder than that of stringed instruments.

As a consequence, revolutionary music frequently called for woodwind and brass ensembles, most often supported by percussion. For example, I found a 1791 description of a ten-piece National Guard wind ensemble in Caen that included four clarinets, one serpent, one French horn, one quinte (alto), two cymbals, and one bass drum.[5]

The preference for wind instruments may have reflected the influence of the Masonic Harmonic Column (two clarinets, two French horns, two bassoons). Contrary to what has been said, the relationship between revolutionary music and freemasonry is far from obvious, and it is well known that a number of Masonic lodges were opposed to the new ideas. Nevertheless, it is true that in a fragment of the *Hymne à l'Être Suprême* (Hymn to the Supreme Being), the great themes of human fraternity, virtue, and eternal wisdom were developed with all the phraseology of the Monarchy's freemasonry. According to Masonic music specialist Roger Cotte, another example is found in the *Hymne à la Victoire* (Hymn to Victory) by Cherubini, which contains "the simple and obvious formula of three broadly played chords, also found in many of Giroust's ritual works." Roger Cotte offers proof that when the Conservatoire first opened in 1795, three out of five music inspectors—Cherubini, Gossec, and Méhul—and most of the professors were initiated freemasons. None of this, however, demonstrates that freemasonry had a major influence on the music of the Revolution. In order to communicate the new ideology, poets and composers were submitted to imperatives of a different nature.[6]

When the celebrations were moved outdoors, several hundred thousand people might attend, and it became difficult for the human voice to carry the message to such large crowds. For purely practical reasons, music in the form of singing came to replace speaking. Since the democratic concept sought the unity of all citizens, following the model of the ancient Athenian assembly, the limited reach of the spoken voice remained an obstacle. This applied especially to languages that were "muffled and not propitious to freedom," as Rousseau, who never missed a chance to denigrate the French language, said. Constant Pierre tells the story of a notary in Liège who found it intolerable that speeches given at public celebrations could not be heard by the majority of the audience and decided to teach a group of people who had no music background "parts of patriotic choruses." He intended to have these neophytes then go into other groups to teach the people what they had just learned. Unfortunately, according to this well-meaning notary, his students knew only three pieces, and when the warm season came, they grew tired of repeating the same thing over and over and *"ils préférèrent la promenade à la musique"* ("they preferred taking walks to making music").

In a sense, one could consider some of the theorists of revolutionary hymns to be direct disciples of Gluck, who claimed that his music was intended only for "the reinforcement of poetical declamation." Frequently the sole purpose of music was to support and reinforce the accents of the language in order to make the political message heard: hence the extremely simple, syllabic melodies that are almost completely devoid of ornaments or melismas. Melodies had to be elementary for the common people to be able to sing them. For instance, on the occasion of the *Fête de l'Être Suprême* (the Celebration of the Supreme Being) on 8 June 1794, the people and all the school children were invited to sing outdoors *l'hymne consacré par le Comité de Salut public* (the Hymn Consecrated by the Committee of Public Welfare), which was composed by Gossec. It exists in two versions: There is a scholarly version in E-flat major that is intended to be sung by professionals in 2/2 meter with some contrapuntal imitation, and there is a version in C major composed for the people in 6/8 meter, reminiscent of the familiar rhythm of some romances, in a completely syllabic setting of all four voices of the choir. "This melody," says Constant Pierre, "is extremely simple and resembles a brotherhood canticle. Without its *tempo larghetto*, it would lapse into the vulgarity of a quadrille or country dance tune."

There is no shortage of examples such as these in the history of revolutionary music. Méhul also wrote two versions of his *Hymne du IX Thermidor* (the 9th day of the Thermidor month in the revolutionary calendar) using the same lyrics by Chénier. The first version was performed in 1795 and 1796 without popular participation. The second version was written for the collection of *Époques*, published by the Conservatoire Music Store to make hymns "easier to be sung by all citizens, especially those in the country towns." In his thesis entitled *Poésie et musique des fêtes révolutionnaires* (Poetry and Music of the Revolutionary Celebrations), Jean-Louis Jam painstakingly gathered statistics that speak for themselves: The musical accentuation in the second version of Méhul's hymn respects 100 per cent of the accents of the text, versus only 83 per cent in the first version; each note of the popular version corresponds to one syllable, whereas in the original concert version, there are 10 per cent more notes than syllables. Obviously, a perfectly syllabic melody was the key to the easier version. As far as Chénier and Méhul's joint composition is concerned, Jam concluded that the musician respected 91 per cent of the poet's accentuation in the verses and 100 per cent in the refrains. Although this is undeniably a peculiar form of musical analysis, it reveals the structural significance of these works much more profoundly than the traditional aesthetic approach.[7]

For several years, poets were specially commissioned to help composers write revolutionary hymns. They took great care in adapting the words so that they could be heard from all four corners of the Champ-de-Mars and easily memorized. As some contemporary commentaries prove, there was even an attempt systematically to lower the quality of the work in order to make it more accessible and therefore more efficient. Here is an excerpt from a brochure entitled *Avis aux poètes lyriques* (Notice to Poets Writing Lyrics) by poet and composer Framery, published in 1796:

> Poet of the People, is it not your first duty to be popular and to sacrifice to this sacred objective if necessary some of your beautiful poetry when it soars too high? Musician of the Revolution, do you not wish to transcend the coming centuries? How can you do so, if your melody is not simple and easy and within reach of those without a trained voice and a knowledge of art? Are your songs not supposed to resound in the hard-working craftsman's shop and soften his labor? And ease the respectable farmer's chores? . . . Should they

not comfort his virtuous wife and young family left at home with the worries caused by his long absence? What songs are best suited to them? Surely those with an elegant simplicity that seems to be the work of nature alone, those with refrains that are interesting and pleasantly repeated, thus most easily memorized.

We have here a remarkable attempt to define popular art. It would be a grave mistake to overlook such strongly asserted principles in evaluating the repertoire of revolutionary hymns.

Also in 1796, a former member of the Convention named Jean-Baptiste Leclerc defended similar ideas in his *Essay on the Propagation of Music in France and its Relations with the Government*. He was opposed to any kind of musical innovation and even threatened to banish anyone intent on diverting the music of the nation too far from "its social and political mission, even if the same innovations proved favorable to art."

In 1797, La Réveillière-Lépeaux—President of the Directoire, member of the Institute, and a former deputy of the Convention—took his turn at surveying every possible way to communicate the revolutionary message through sung lyrics. He published *An Essay on the Means of a Universal Participation by the Spectators in Every Event in the National Celebrations*. He imagined two or three hundred thousand spectators gathered on the Champ-de-Mars, envisioning that "for a few moments everyone would be an actor." In his words, nothing would surpass "a chorus of two or three hundred thousand voices singing while moved by the same feeling." In this dialectic scheme, music was considered to be a universal language that could surpass all boundaries and could for a moment realize the dream of the great human fraternity—the symbol of this end-of-century sensitivity. The object was to strike an emotional chord in these immense crowds that would make the people vibrate in unison and therefore make them even more receptive to revolutionary ideals. There was no better way to do this, La Réveillière-Lépeaux believed, than to "make an entire people assemble and sing in four parts" according to Méhul's own suggestion: "the first part would sing the tonic, and the second, third, and fourth parts would sing the third, fifth, and octave, respectively. Following this, all four parts would produce simultaneously the four notes." Rameau had certainly never imagined this application for the natural laws of acoustics.

It is useful to take the aforementioned sources into consideration in order to gain an understanding of the spirit in which the revolutionary repertoire was conceived and in so doing, avoid errors in judgment. Not only was this repertoire in no way a scholarly one, but the music was generally considered to be only a tool, reducing it to a simple mass propaganda device created and controlled by public authorities. Not since the beginning of modern times—with the possible exception of Antiquity's patriotic and war songs of which we know nothing—had Terpsichore's art been systematically imposed on such a grand scale purely for practical purposes.

Before studying the repertoire itself, let us first consider songs that were heard on every street corner in Paris and in provincial cities over a ten-year period. Constant Pierre identified over two thousand of them, and many more probably escaped him. There is no other time period for which the history of France was so easily written in songs. Most of the songs were inspired by specific historical events. There were songs of the revolutionaries and songs of the counter-revolutionaries, and a song about the same event could inspire either hatred and pity, depending on the listener. For instance, the *Dialogue de la tigresse Antoinette avec la guillotine le jour de son exécution* (Dialogue between the Tigress Antoinette and the Guillotine on the Day of Her Execution) and the *Complainte de Marie-Antoinette dans sa tour* (Complaint of Marie-Antoinette from Her Tower) were alternately heard, the former to the tune of *Jeunesse trop coquette* (Youth is Too Coquettish) and the latter to the tune of Malborough. It was an ancient custom and a frequent habit for authors to take a famous tune and adapt it to new lyrics that more or less fit the meter. For example, *Complainte de Mme Élisabeth, envoyée par elle aux sans-culottes pour l'engager à la tirer de sa tour* (Complaint of Mrs. Élisabeth, Which She Sent to the Sansculottists to Obtain Her Release from the Tower) was sung to the tune of *Jeanneton prend sa faucille* (Jeanneton Takes Her Sickle)!

Understandably, few of these songs outlived the circumstances that gave rise to their composition. The two most famous songs, *La Carmagnole* and "Ça ira" ("We Shall Overcome"), remained popular for several years and must be considered separately. Their immense success makes it difficult to pass a strictly historical judgment on them, since they existed in many different versions and were frequently taken out of context. The origins of *La Carmagnole* have not been firmly established. It probably first appeared during 1792, after the royal family was imprisoned. It is of unknown authorship but is probably based on a folk song from Provence or Piedmont—Carmagnole is a Piedmont town. Its easy dance-like character invited parody and adaptations, and there were no less than fifty different songs written to the tune and expressing varying degrees of violence. Some of them exalted patriotic feelings and celebrated military victories. Others served as peaceful refrains on the stages of the Feydeau or Vaudeville theaters from 1792. While it is true that *La Carmagnole* was sung and danced around the guillotine, the fate of this revolutionary song was less morbid than is usually thought.

"Ça ira" is somewhat older, first appearing in 1790. It began as a simple country dance for violin entitled *Le Carillon national* (The National Chimes) that was created by an unknown composer at the end of the Monarchy. In 1790, a singer named Ladré borrowed the tune for some lyrics that originally were not the least bit rebellious and did not even mention "hanging aristocrats." Oddly enough, the expression *ça ira* itself came from Benjamin Franklin, who had a habit of repeating it during the War of Independence. The song soon took on variations and additions that gave it a violent and bloody character, turning it into a song of hatred and death, and the Directoire ordered its daily performance in every theater. At one point, it almost became the ideal revolutionary anthem but was superseded by the *Hymne des Marseillais* (the Hymn of the Marseillais), which was, according to a contemporary newspaper, "in perfect tune with the nature of republican values."

The *Hymne des Marseillais* has been the subject of extensive writings. How can its amazing popularity be explained? An answer was given by Framery as early as the end of the eighteenth century: "Which hymn made the deepest imprint on the minds of the people? The one with lyrics and music composed by a man who was neither a poet nor a musician by profession."[8] Despite the apparent paradox, this could well be one of the reasons for its astounding success. It was not the work of a trained musician, and it was written using simple language. The melody of this "revolutionary Te Deum," as Goethe called it, possessed a naïve and elemental strength capable of capturing a very large audience.

This hymn was composed in Strasbourg by Rouget de Lisle, who had been a young officer of the Monarchy and a musical dilettante. It was composed under very unusual circumstances. In April of 1792, the news of the declaration of war caused a great commotion in that frontier city. The mayor declared a state of emergency, and army volunteers began pouring in. During a night of patriotic fever and zealous anticipation, Rouget de Lisle composed what was first called the *Chant de guerre pour l'armée du Rhin* (War Song for the Army of the Rhine). The hymn was sung for the first time in Mayor Dietrich's apartments, with Madame de Dietrich herself accompanying on the harpsichord! Soon after, it spread throughout Strasbourg and was first published there one month later. It was indeed a war song, the cry of a people defending its freedom and independence from foreign powers. It spread extremely quickly throughout France and soon became the war song of the entire French army, not just the army of the Rhine.

While traveling across the country to join ranks in Paris, a battalion of volunteers from Marseilles sang Rouget de Lisle's hymn all along the road. Everywhere the song was greeted with enthusiasm. On 30 July, the *Chronique de Paris* gave the following description of the soldiers' arrival in the capital:

> The Marseillais sing it with great togetherness. At the moment when they wave their hats and sabers, shouting together *Aux armes citoyens* (To Arms, Citizens), everyone shudders. These new bards sing this song of war in every village and inspire civic and martial feelings in the whole country. They often sing it at the Palais-Royal, even during performances, between two plays.

From that moment, the song became known as the *Hymne des Marseillais* and was rehearsed throughout Paris on 10 August. It became the song of the national emergency as well as of the Revolution. On the day of the Proclamation of the Republic, 21 September 1792, baritone Chéron sang it on the stage of the Opéra. In October, the newspaper *La Feuille villageoise* (the Village Leaf) baptized it *Hymne national* (National Anthem), and "La Marseillaise" entered history. After the victory of Valmy, General Kellermann asked the Minister of War to order the Te Deum to be performed, but the latter replied:

> The Te Deum is out of date. We must replace it with something more useful and more consistent with the public spirit. Since you have requested my authorization, I therefore authorize you, General, to have the people solemnly sing—with the same pomp as for a Te Deum—the *Hymne des Marseillais*, which you will find attached herewith.

Moreover, on 2 October 1792, "La Marseillaise" was sung on stage for the first time at the Paris Opéra under the title *Offrande à la liberté* (Offering to Liberty). The choreography was by ballet master Gardel and the musical arrangement by Gossec. Three years later, in October 1795, this "lyric scene" was given its 120th performance. Here is an excerpt from a contemporary account:

> When the curtain opened there were three hundred people on stage. At the verse beginning with *Amour sacré de la patrie* (Sacred Love for Our Homeland), the people and warriors went on their knees, lowering their spears, and an adagio gave the sublime and martial anthem a religious character. Suddenly, when the choir shouted the terrible call for war *Aux armes citoyens* all three hundred actors—men, women, and children—stood up spontaneously to the sound of the tocsin and the drums calling to arms. Everyone rushed to battle waving their weapons, their caps, or their flags, creating an unparalleled, magical effect. This disarray was most skillfully timed. The enthusiasm simulated on stage was truly felt in the audience.[9]

I shall now leave "La Marseillaise" and its rich history, which continues to this day. Some of the other hymns are less famous but are worth mentioning for their musical interest. At the beginning of the present chapter I recommended that this music composed for special occasions and propaganda purposes not be analyzed according to the usual criteria. Some of the better composers of the time, however, were attracted by the new opportunities, and a few examples from this vast repertoire deserve a closer look using a more traditional point of view.

Taking into account the sheer number of pieces composed during this ten-year period, the five top composers of the time are also the best: Gossec (twenty-five), Catel (fourteen), Méhul (eleven), Le Sueur (nine), and Cherubini (nine).

The *Marche lugubre* (March of Mourning) is the most interesting piece by Gossec, but unfortunately it is not performed very often nowadays. It was composed for a funeral ceremony that took place on 20 September 1790 "to honor the memory of the citizens lost in the Nancy incident." It was performed again several times at official ceremonies until 1797—a rare privilege for this type of music—including 11 July 1791, when Voltaire's remains were transferred to the Panthéon, and 1 October 1797, General Hoche's funeral. Every aspect of this very short instrumental piece is unusual for its time. First consider Gossec's instrumentation: two piccolo flutes, two clarinets, two trumpets, two French horns, three trombones, two bassoons, one serpent, a tam-tam, a bass drum, a muted military drum, and in the last performances, a *tuba corva*. It was the first time that the tam-tam was heard in Paris, and it was soon incorporated into other revolutionary pieces, as well as the operas of Le Sueur. Second, Gossec managed to achieve a very fine balance of effects. The brass and percussion were opposed to the woodwinds, and the music was frequently interrupted by expressive rests, a device that was still unusual in eighteenth-century music. All his contemporaries were struck by the use of rests for dramatic purposes, as "an expressive device and perhaps the only way to bring out the emotion in a phrase," according to Debussy's later definition. Finally, Gossec made frequent use of chromaticism and dissonance. These three elements explain why the *Marche lugubre* consistently attracted critics' attention. The symphonic composer's talent was revealed at its best, despite the revolutionary propagandists' mistrust of all instrumental music because of its imprecise and potentially dangerous significance. They did not tolerate marches being played in the army or dances being played in celebrations "if their tunes had not originally been composed on lyrics with a moral or political content."

The interest that the press showed in the *Marche lugubre* is clear evidence that a change of sensitivity was in progress. In the words on one critic, "The agonizing sounds of the funeral instruments filled souls with religious terror."[10] Another wrote: "The notes, detached one from another, broke our hearts and tore at our insides."[11] When Madame de Genlis heard a performance of the piece, it made an unforgettable impression: "This music was extraordinary. The pauses caused shivers—they were truly the silence of the grave."[12] The words chosen by the critics are significant: *souls, religious terror, hearts, the silence of the grave*. It may be the first time that a purely instrumental piece of music inspired such comments. The use of unusual orchestral colors and the exotic effect of the tam-tam conveyed something new and thrilling to the audience. The meaning of the music was in its emotion, vague and imprecise. For some people it opened the way to new dreams. Imperceptibly, the aesthetics of the Enlightenment made room for those of pre-romanticism.

Two novel works by Méhul and Le Sueur, performed at the very end of the revolutionary period, should also be mentioned. This was precisely the time when the better composers grew tired of hearing or composing dull pieces and began to experiment with new ideas. They had at their disposal the enormous choral and orchestral masses that had become customary at the time and were fully aware of this new musical potential, which they tried to exploit in an original way. The two large musical frescoes worth mentioning here are *Le Chant national du 14 juillet 1800* (The National Hymn of 14 July 1800) composed by Méhul with lyrics by Fontanes, and *Le Chant du 1ᵉʳ Vendémiaire* (The Hymn of the 1st of Vendémiaire) composed by Le Sueur with lyrics by Esmenard. They were performed at the church of Les Invalides. Méhul placed three orchestras, each accompanying a separate choir, in separate locations in the church. The orchestras would either play together or answer each other from different parts of the church. The first two orchestras were complete with timpani, trombones, *tuba corva, buccin,* a large drum, and a tam-tam. The third one accompanied an all-female choir and consisted only of a solo French horn and several harps. According to the press, the result was extraordinary, and the public had the distinct impression that something quite new was taking place. "Music lovers could verify that this art still can make progress." It was the first time that anyone dared to create a dialogue between orchestras placed at such a distance from one another. "This daring device can bring useful results for the art," wrote a critic. In short, they had discovered how to reinforce the expressive power of music using spatial effects.

Méhul's *Chant* was immediately printed at the state's expense. Le Sueur's, however, was not, even after its performance on 23 September 1800, and the surviving manuscript has many incomplete parts. This is unfortunate, since Le Sueur went even further than Méhul and scored his hymn for four orchestras and four choirs. One large orchestra was placed in the choir of the church and directed by Cherubini, another was situated next to the organ and directed by Kreutzer. Two smaller instrumental ensembles were located in the side galleries, so that the audience in the nave was truly surrounded by music. Each of the four ensembles had its own separate choir. Le Sueur probably attempted to produce stereophonic effects. The press commented:

> The double trio on the prayer *Dieu, protège la France, conserve ses héros* (May God Protect France and Save Its Heroes), which came from the galleries, had a suave melody and celestial harmony. The religious song on the words *conserve ses héros* was first heard in a dialogue between the two galleries and was then sung by both. It was later repeated as an echo by the voices under the dome and by those near the organ. The song was preceded by a recitative of four solo voices, one coming from the dome, one from each of the two galleries, and one from near the organ.

Méhul and Le Sueur reverted back to an enclosed space for musical performance and understood that the source of sounds, tone color, and harmony are equally important factors. They were one-and-a-half centuries ahead of their time in realizing exactly what Stockhausen did with *Gruppen* (1956) or *Carré* (1957). Admittedly, their own precursor was Gabrieli, who had two orchestras perform in Saint Mark's in Venice, but no other composer had gone further than they did in researching the properties of sound.

Obviously, this wild experimentation completely modified revolutionary music. Long musical frescoes with recitatives, solo arias, and choruses were not suitable for popular performance. On the contrary, spacing the various performers required experienced artists. These attempts are, however, fascinating for musicologists. Méhul and Le Sueur were already convinced that space was an essential element of music. They produced some grandiose effects of musical spatialization in Les Invalides, the very church where one generation later, in 1837, the four fanfares of Berlioz's Requiem would be heard. These were exceptional pieces of music, and though they may have signaled a new artistic genre, they certainly were not in line with the efforts made by the propagandists of the French Revolution. Even so, these performances marked the end of outdoor concerts. In this first year of the nineteenth century, music was brought back into the imposing setting of the Invalides Church, a symbolic choice.

Chapter 3

Musical Theater

When it first appeared in France in the seventeenth century, opera met considerable success with Paris audiences, although not always for entirely musical reasons. Tragédie lyrique left much to the visual elements of the performance: staging and ballet. For most spectators, the dramatic substance—the quality of the libretto, the plot, and the literary style—was the main thing. The story came first, and the music was incidental.

In the eighteenth century, the French public became infatuated with opera. Besides tragédie lyrique, other new genres appeared: opéra-comique and opera buffa, the latter performed by Italian theater companies newly established in Paris. Every important musical quarrel of the eighteenth century was sparked off in the opera house. Some philosophers and literary experts, writing profusely about the arts and artistic techniques that they often knew little about, came up with theories on aesthetics that almost always found their origins in opera. Instrumental music was not necessarily held in disdain by true connoisseurs, but still, it was a secondary concern. In the minds of many well-educated people of the time, the only true music was vocal music. In Chapter 6, I point out the disproportionate attention given to all forms of vocal music by the theorist Lacépède in his *Poétique de la Musique* (Poetics of Music), which was published at the start of the Revolution. His attitude perfectly reflects his contemporaries' musical taste. During the Consulate and later the Empire, the situation changed: Instrumental music in France made such considerable progress in the early part of the nineteenth century that it worried some of the older generation, who defended a declining classicism. However, musical theater remained fashionable and continued to attract an ever-increasing audience. Surpassing the Enlightenment, the nineteenth century was to become the great century of French opera.

Great masterpieces of the French repertoire were not created during the period from 1789 to 1830, but many composers had their works performed in one of the three full-time opera houses in Paris: the Opéra and two opéra-comique theaters, known as Opéra-Comique and Théâtre italien after 1801. The number of performances given during these forty years is impressive, far exceeding the number of productions in our own time; premieres followed revival performances in rapid succession. On the whole, there were many failures and few perfect works, but there was also a large number of original attempts, anticipating the major transformations yet to come. Here and there a new sensitivity began tentatively to emerge, first becoming evident in the choice of plots: Reference to Celtic and Scandinavian mythology, the use of Old Testament episodes, and as well as a hint of the Middle and Far East combined to bring a sense of excitement to the main French operatic stages that was previously unknown. Also, classical harmonic language began imperceptibly to wear out. This was no sudden mutation brought about by a single earth-shattering masterpiece. On the contrary, it was brought on by a collection of diverse talents. No national school was able to emerge, and there was no single figure to take the lead of a radical movement. It was as if each composer were following a solitary path, without hesitating or retreating, but always ready, in case of error, to choose a new direction.

With such an abundance of new growth, it is the historian's duty to do some careful pruning in order to gain some perspective. Changes in taste and sensibility are often undetectable: their symptoms can be seen only with great attention and probing. There existed a continuous link between a certain form of neo-classicism, a component of the Louis XVI style, and romanticism. Moreover, some pivotal works (Spontini's *La Vestale*, for example) seem to have been intentionally created at the crossroads of two centuries and two aesthetics. Contrary to other times in the history of music and the visual arts, artists during this period did not systematically strive for radical change. Paradoxically, at the time of the most drastic political and social changes perhaps ever encountered in the history of France, musicians were scarcely revolutionaries in their art. They were never seen to oppose tradition and often seemed to want to perpetuate it. In short, operatic composers did not try to single themselves out in order to impose a personal or original concept of art. In their writings, composers of this period (including in this instance Berlioz) showed their admiration for the great masters who preceded them: Gluck and Sacchini for opera, Grétry and many others for comic opera. The literary scandal around *Hernani* had no counterpart in the history of French opera, which may in part have been due to the absence of a strong personality to lead the movement. And yet, even though there was no revolution proper or even a rejection process in French opera at the turn of the eighteenth century, the public never failed to recognize and celebrate the new important works. In 1810, Napoleon created prizes to be awarded every ten years to acknowledge the best operatic works of his time. Spontini's opera *La Vestale* and Méhul's opéra-comique *Joseph* were among those chosen by the French National Institute to receive the prize.

In spite of unprecedented management difficulties experienced by most opera house directors both in Paris and in the provinces, the French public continued in the early part of the nineteenth century to support this art form in increasing numbers from increasingly widespread social circles. At that time, the gap separating the composers from the audience was not very wide. There were, of course, cases of undeserved overnight success as well as regrettable failures, but such has been the case in any period of art history. In the following pages, I shall attempt to give an objective reporting of the facts.

Opera in the Service of Political Power

One would expect that opera, a traditionally aristocratic genre, should have been decimated by the opening salvo of the French Revolution. Indeed, when asked to write a report on *L'Établissement de l'Opéra*, M.-J. Chénier did not hesitate to conclude his study in such terms: "a free country needs highly moral behavior: should we turn to opera for a model? Will little airs and pas de deux contribute to educate our citizens?"[1] Actually, opera houses were never closed down, and since opera had to serve the various regimes that were to come to power between 1789 and 1830, there were a few attempts to use it to "educate the citizens." The use of opera for propaganda purposes goes back to its early days: In 1745, Voltaire and Rameau collaborated on *Le Temple de la gloire* (The Temple of Glory) to celebrate the victory of Fontenoy.

Most attempts made by the various regimes to control opera for their own purposes were ineffective; as was often the case, special performances staged at great expense did not survive the circumstances that had inspired them. There were rare exceptions, such as *Le Triomphe de Trajan* (The Triumph of Trajan), written by a mediocre composer named Persuis at Emperor Napoleon's "invitation"; it was consistently performed from 1807 until 1827.

Soon after the fall of the Monarchy, France's earliest opera theater became a stage not for operas, but for patriotic or allegorical operatic scenes. These were melting pots of fashionable airs and patriotic songs performed either by soloists or by choruses. Perhaps the first and most typical of these was *Offrande à la Liberté* (The Offering to Liberty), dated September 1792, with music arranged by Gossec as best he could. It was in fact a grand staging of "La Marseillaise" and "Veillons au Salut de l'Empire" ("We Must Preserve Our Empire") and can be considered as a sort of archetype for a whole series of performances in the same vein that took place at the Paris Opéra over the next twenty years. Nearly all the Consulate's and the Empire's military victories were celebrated in a similar fashion at the *Académie de musique*. In most instances, the manuscript scores were saved and the librettos printed, as was customary for true operas. These performances, however, did not feature characters or intrigue, but were purely static situations with allegorical representations, choruses of heroes, choruses of the people, and so on. With the help of sophisticated machinery, sets, and costumes, the stage was supposed to exemplify precisely that which should remain intangible in a sound concept of choral music. But at no time while reading these scores and the—falsely?—naive accounts in the press is one given the impression that a new musical genre has evolved: these allegorical scenes were not true operas.

Such was not the case for a number of works of republican or revolutionary inspiration, about fifty of which were performed at the Paris Opéra and the Opéra-Comique between 1790 and 1800. These compositions have been forgotten today, even though they were written by the best composers of the time. Most of them did not survive more than a few performances. In February of 1794, no less than twelve composers that included Grétry, Méhul, Cherubini, Dalayrac, Kreutzer, and Berton worked together to present in Salle Favart a piece entitled *Le Congrès des rois* (The Congress of Kings). The opera ends with the kings and queens, in revolutionary dress, fleeing and shouting: *"Vive la République!"* It was performed only twice before the revolutionary government censored it under the pretext that "aristocrats were portrayed as good patriots." Most of the occasions for such performances were contemporary events: the death of heroes such as Viala and Bara, the siege of Thionville, or the battle of the bridge at Lodi. This last was commemorated with music composed by Méhul. There were cannons firing throughout, which was unheard of "and which frightened a great many spectators. The explosions caused such smoke that one could no longer see anything on stage or in the hall."[2]

When librettists ran out of contemporary themes to use for a new opera, they usually turned to Greek or Roman Antiquity, where they were certain to find examples of the republican virtues: Lemoyne's *Miltiade à Marathon* (1793) and *Toute la Grèce ou ce que peut la Liberté* (All of Greece, or What Can Liberty Achieve, 1794) or Méhul's *Horatius Coclès* (1794). Bonaparte, later emperor, would simply use these ancient themes for rather similar productions.

It would be a mistake to think that all these pieces overshadowed the traditional repertoire. They were performed in addition to the opera productions, not in competition. A review of the comic operas of Grétry, Berton, and Dalayrac in *Le Moniteur* of 12 February 1794 stated that "these discolored miniatures must be replaced by viril and vigorous tableaux representing their true duties to all republicans," but none of the composers' names were crossed off the billboard. It was merely decided to censor the famous line: "Ô Richard, ô mon Roi" ("Oh Richard, oh my King"), just as the word *Seigneur* had been replaced by *Monsieur* in contemporary performances of classical drama at the Comédie-Française. It did not imply a great upheaval in the repertoire. In 1793, *L'Almanach des spectacles* (The Guide of Theatrical Performances) announced that some works—*Roland, Iphigénie en Aulide, Chimène, Œdipe à Colone*—were going to be cut from the programs "since they portrayed kings and could hurt the eyes or ears of the delicate republicans who now attend the theater." But it did not happen. Gluck and Sacchini were never banished from the Paris Opéra. In *Les Changements de la vie musicale parisienne de 1774 à 1799*, Bruno Brévan rightly mentions that at the time of Louis XVI's death sentence, the Paris Opéra presented Gluck's *Iphigénie en Tauride,* which contains the following verses:

Et quel monstre exécrable
A, sur un roi si grand, osé lever le bras?

And what abominable monster
Hath dared to lay hands on such a great king?

Mr. Brévan also points out that on 16 October 1793, the day of Marie-Antoinette's execution, the Opéra-Comique billed Grétry's *Le Tableau parlant* (The Speaking Tableau) from 1769, which contains some commedia dell'arte characters "in an entirely joyous atmosphere."

A specific musical genre that could be called revolutionary opera never really existed. There were a great number of operas inspired by contemporary topics or revolutionary ideals, but the music, sets, and machinery were no different from those of any other opera of the time. I would like to quote a phrase by Henri Focillon that perfectly describes this situation: "Revolutions do not necessarily create their own art. They act upon institutions, they modify life styles, they lead the way, but they use forms that preceded them."

In any case, most of these productions did not run for very long. The works were of rather poor musical quality, since they were written in a hurry. They so depended on the events of the day that they were doomed to be forgotten, in spite of attempts to stuff them with episodes from famous operas in an effort to try and heighten their interest. For instance, the one-act opera *La Nouvelle au camp de l'assassinat des ministres français à Rastadt* (The Announcement of the French Ministers' Assassination to the Camp in Rastadt) was produced on 14 June 1799. Its composer, Henri Berton, inserted in it a chorus from Sacchini's *Dardanus* "which naturally applies to this horrible disaster and to the call for revenge on the part of every nation."[3] It was a vain precaution: like so many others, this operatic scene was short lived.

A short while later, during the Consulate and the Directoire, Bonaparte's victories were also celebrated by special productions on various operatic stages in Paris and in the provinces. For example, I found evidence that *La Fête de la Paix* (The Celebration of Peace) was presented on 7 January 1798 in Nantes to mark the signing of the Campo-Formio Treaty. It was the work of composer Saint-Amans, who is now forgotten although he was for a while a professor at the Conservatoire, and it was probably conceived in the style of Paris productions.[4] One can imagine that productions praising successive regimes found their way onto the operatic stages of the main provincial cities after 1789.

Bonaparte was personally interested in theater, particularly opera. He insisted on having his say in the choice of productions and used the Paris Opéra to disseminate his personal propaganda. In May 1802, a register like those placed in other public forums was set up at the Paris Opéra, and citizens were asked to record in it their response to the following question: "Will Napoleon Bonaparte be Consul for life?" A letter in the Paris Opéra archives from Céllerier, the director at the time, to the State Counselor in charge of public education states: "The day before yesterday I opened a register at the secretary's office of the Theater of the Arts, and already the majority of the artists and employees have put down their names." In less than two days, three hundred names were collected, and all of the responses were affirmative![5]

Beginning with the Consulate, every production at the Paris Opéra was submitted to censorship. Even if the works appeared completely foreign to the day's events, they were altered to include references to the emperor and his policies that had won the public's warm acclaim. In 1803, when Paisiello brought *Proserpine*, a kind of French opera seria to the Paris stage, the authorization for its performance was transmitted to the Prefect of the Palace by a secret report that now resides in the National Archives: "I have read *Proserpine*. Not only did I not find in it anything contrary to the government's wishes, but the First Consul is portrayed as Jupiter, a god who is victorious over the seditious Titans and is also conciliatory and a pacifist." [6] During the Empire, control was further tightened in matters of censorship. When Mozart's *Don Giovanni* was about to premiere at the Paris Opéra, the director received a letter from the Prefect of the Palace reminding him of the prerequisite examination of the libretto (9 May 1805): "It is the wish of his Majesty the Emperor that every play, new or revived, should be submitted for police examination before its performance. You will be kind enough to send a copy of the opera *Don Giovanni* to the ministry of this department and scrupulously do the same for works to be performed in the future."[7] The Opéra-Comique was also subjected to a censorship committee representing the Ministry of Police. The minutes of their deliberations are kept in series F^{21} of the National Archives. Méhul's innocent *Joseph* (1807), whose theme had already been used in Baour-Lormian's Biblical tragedy, received the following comment: "The substance of this work did not prompt any reaction on the French stage, and there is no reason why it should prompt any in another theater." The censorship committee's review of Dalayrac's *Sargines* (also 1807), which features the character of Philippe-Auguste, included the following assessment of the king: "As remarkable as he may have been in the last dynasty, he did not leave a very profound or powerful memory, removing the kind of danger that the person and the court of a former King of France could represent."

Soon, every great imperial victory echoed on the stages of the Paris Opéra and theaters in every main provincial city. Several musical devices were used to immortalize these feats of arms. First, a new scene or a new chorus could simply be inserted into a well-known work, as was the case for a March 1806 performance of *Castor et Pollux* by the German composer Winter. He wrote new verses that "were naturally understood as being references to the warriors of Austerlitz."[8] In most other cases, imperial victories inspired allegorical representations that were hastily composed for the occasion. Generally, the librettos were printed the following day, or their manuscripts were kept in archival collections. A detailed study might reveal every official propaganda theme in all of its guises, even the most subtle, but is unlikely to unearth any previously undiscovered masterpieces—the texts were painfully commonplace. For example, the return from Austerlitz was heralded by a *Fête de la Victoire* (Victory Celebration) that featured a choir of the nations in national costumes singing to the heroes' glory:

> *Un nouveau siècle est né des débris du vieux âge*
> *Une Europe nouvelle et plus libre et plus sage*
> *Lui devra des jours plus sereins!*[9]

A new century is born from the remains of the old age
A new, freer, and wiser Europe,
Thanks to it, will know more peaceful days!

When Napoleon visited Nantes in 1808, great festivities were held in his honor. The Chapeau Rouge theater staged an "operatic scene with a large orchestra and a production to fit the circumstances." The lyrics were written by a local celebrity, the poet Blanchard de la Musse, and the music was composed by a certain Schleyermann, credited as being "one of the best piano teachers in town." The scene took place in a public square where a crowd is gathered to greet Iris, the messenger of the gods, who comes to announce the emperor's arrival. Following this, a peasant sang

> *Ah! qu'il sache que le Breton,*
> *Tout en changeant de nom,*
> *N'a point changé son caractère,*
> *Que fier, loyal et sincère,*
> *Il met sa gloire la plus chère,*
> *À chérir, à servir, le grand Napoléon.*

> Ah! let him know that Bretons,
> While they have changed their name,
> Have retained their character,
> Proud, loyal, and sincere,
> And will stake their dearest honor
> To cherish and serve the great Napoleon.

I quote this simple doggerel so that it may be compared to another text by the same poet. When the Duke of Bourbon visited Nantes in 1815, Blanchard de la Musse eagerly wrote the following poem, to be sung to the tune of "Richard Cœur de Lion":

> *Et zig et zog*
> *Et fric et froc*
> *Oui, jurons,*
> *Foi de Breton,*
> *D'aimer toujours les Bourbons.*[10]

> And zig and zog
> And fric and froc
> Let us swear,
> On our word as Bretons,
> To always love the Bourbons.

It is true that such poetic turnabout can also be found in the twentieth century from the pens of contemporary poets!

On the stage of the Paris Opéra, ballet also could be used to spread the Empire's propaganda. In the archives I found a censorship report dated 11 August 1809 concerning the ballet *La Fête de Mars*, which celebrated in a vast retrospective every imperial triumph "from 18 Brumaire to the Austrian campaign." The author uses the most mundane allegory imaginable: "Discord has disturbed the happiness of a nation. Priests, political leaders, merchants, and farmers are fighting each other. Mars comes and appeases them . . . . He triumphs successively over all people and they celebrate his victory. Olympus opens up, and Mars returns to his place among the gods." The two censors who wrote this report, the poet Esmenard and the historian Lacretelle, concluded with feigned naïveté: "So many things in one ballet!" [11]

In March 1811, the birth of the King of Rome—Their Imperial Majesties' newborn son—was the occasion for poets and musicians to try and outdo each other's flattery. A newspaper wrote: "For the past three weeks, every theater has given birth to one or two children, and the public rushed to be their godparents."[12] The Paris Opéra's contribution was the presentation of an opera-ballet by Kreutzer called *Le Triomphe du mois de Mars ou le Berceau d'Achille* (The Triumph of the Month of March or Achilles's Cradle). In this work, the year, the seasons, and the months are personified. March obtained the crown "by lowering Achilles's cradle from the sky. This cradle was a replica of the one offered to Their Majesties by the City of Paris." Every newspaper praised this opera: "A succession of delightful tableaux charmed the audience. Nothing in art could be more pleasing or attractive."[13]

The privilege of celebrating the imperial birth was not only reserved for the Paris Opéra. Although the Feydeau theater, now known as Opéra-Comique, customarily presented far more modest productions than the Opéra, considerable efforts were made for this occasion, and the company featured a piece on a libretto by Pixérécourt with music by an unidentified composer. For this allegorical scene, the theater displayed extraordinary pomp: "Through Mercury's mediation a heavenly beehive flies down from Olympus, under the supervision of Minerva and Cupid. It opens up and reveals the cherished child, granting everyone's wishes in Europe."[14] Vaudeville was a very fashionable genre during the Empire, and in it, verses and short arias set to music played an important role. In its own way, vaudeville acts also found ways to flatter the emperor, but instead of representing allegories of Olympian gods, it made rather crude references alluding to the marriage with Marie-Louise and to English hostility. The press of the time summarized the plot of a vaudeville sketch presented in the Spring of 1811 at the theater of *l'Ambigu-Comique* (The Ambiguous Comedy) entitled *L'Espoir réalisé ou la Suite du mariage de la Valeur* (Hopes Realized, or the Follow-up to Valor's Marriage):

Valor has married the daughter of Monsieur Lallemand (Mr. _____ the German). Nine months have already gone by, and the precious fruit of this union is impatiently awaited. An Englishman, Mr. Beefsteak, who is relegated to the Island of Swans, is the only one who does not take part in the general rejoicing. The happy news comes, and he is left in further dismay. Everyone rejoices at his expense with clever verses seasoned with sharp spice, and it turns into a general celebration, since the public shares the same rapture.[15]

The Théâtre italien was more independent in its choice of repertory in spite of also being subjected to censorship. Although infrequently, it continued to display its devotion to the regime and its prince. In 1806, Spontini, not yet known as the great composer of *La Vestale*, was in favor of Empress Josephine and presented a form of cantata sung in Italian, *L'Eccelsa gara* (The Illustrious Competition). The performance was filled with such blatant flattery that it must have caused more than a few discreet smiles. In it, Apollo and Minerva come down to the Champs-Élysées (the Elysian Fields) and request that all of the most famous poets of Greece and Italy celebrate "the hero who presides over the destinies of France." Homer, Virgil, and Tasso respond and compete for the honor. Apollo puts an end to the competition by declaring that it would take all the gods of Parnassus to praise the hero's merits. The opera ends with the crowning of the emperor's bust.

On some occasions, circumstances caused gestures of praise and adulation to backfire. In 1809, for example, the emperor wanted to attract attention to the war against Spain. He commissioned Spontini and his librettist, Jouy, to write an opera about Fernand Cortez and the conquest of Mexico. In the meantime, the expedition against Spain more or less failed, and allowing the choir of soldiers to sing the following words was an affront to Napoleon:

Cortez va nous conduire à des succès nouveaux;
À son génie il n'est rien d'impossible
Et l'Univers appartient au héros.

Cortez will lead us to new victories.
His genius stops at nothing
And the Universe belongs to the hero.

Confusion erupted at the Paris Opéra, and the police had to stop the performances for a while.

On the other hand, Napoleon commissioned one of the official poets of the regime—the one whom Stendhal called "Esmenard the spy"—to create an opera, and it was met with unprecedented success. It is, in fact, the longest-running Pans Opéra production since 1789. It celebrates an episode from the Prussian campaign following the battle of Jena (1806). Napoleon, a modern Augustus, shows his clemency by destroying a document that could incriminate the Prussian lieutenant general. The opera was to immortalize this generous gesture, and so it transposed the events into Roman Antiquity and cast Napoleon as Trajan. The score was entrusted to a very mediocre composer, Loiseau-Persuis, one of the stage masters of the Paris Opéra. He was accustomed to this type of commission, since he had already composed an operatic scene celebrating the victory of Jena and although the full-length version was based on a rather commonplace argument, it was certainly not any worse than that of many works of the time. Moreover, it was staged with an unprecedented wealth of scenery, props, and costumes: trophies, triumphal arches, ancient altars, lictors, and vestals filled the stage. *Le Triomphe de Trajan* (The Triumph of Trajan), as it was entitled, was a triumph of neo-classical staging. No less than 432 costumes were made, and the total cost of the production amounted to the exorbitant sum of 72,000 francs. The Franconi brothers supplied a dozen horses to pull the imperial chariot during the scene of the emperor's triumph. The opera premiered in October 1807 with extraordinary success and went on to become one of the most remarkable productions of the imperial period, making its 100th performance in 1814. The greatest singers of the Imperial Academy of Music sang at the premiere, including Madame Branchu and the bass Derivis.[16]

Despite its musical insignificance, *Le Triomphe de Trajan* preceded *La Vestale* by only two months and drew at least as many accolades. Aside from political considerations, its triumph can now be seen as a sign that public tastes were evolving. For many in the Paris Opéra audience, the visual element was becoming the most important. It is surprising to read a description of the performance by renowned musicologist Fayolle, whose account scarcely mentions the music: "Nothing could be more flattering to one's senses, which is what is intended at the Opéra. . . . All their efforts are for the senses, and it should not be surprising that the intellectuals are getting bored here."[17]

Le Triomphe de Trajan was so successful that during the *Cent Jours* (One Hundred Days) many foreigners back in Paris wanted to see it. Surprisingly enough, the new government of Louis XVIII authorized the revival of this panegyric of the Usurper. However, archival documents reveal that

> some changes were made, the most important of which was the cutting out of a scene where Trajan burned the evidence of a conspiracy. This action was a reference to our times and was not deemed appropriate. Anyway, this piece is so well known and so boring that it can be considered a beautiful presentation and nothing more.[18]

This last evaluation is most distressing: The music was inferior and the tableau was so poor that it was not even worth looking at, but the dazzling staging was enough to attract attention. Works designed to spread imperial propaganda can be appreciated only for reasons that have nothing to do with the music, and it must be pointed out that they mainly served to distort the taste of the opera audiences at the beginning of the nineteenth century. From a certain point of view, they either followed the trend of revolutionary productions or were even worse. The quality of music did not improve at all, but the staging became increasingly flashy. For theater specialists interested in the history of staging, costumes, sets, and machinery, this repertoire represents a most interesting showcase of French neo-classical fashion in the early nineteenth century even as the musical quality continued to erode. Opera became a feast for the eyes and nothing more. In a police report found in the National Archives, the following phrase aptly describes the producers' intentions: "An occasional production at the Grand Opéra Theater is indeed a kind of public celebration."[19] Indeed, the Empire directly took over after the Revolution, but whereas the Republic had dramatized events of the day or borrowed episodes from Greek or Roman history, the new regime preferred to use allegory and mythology for its propaganda. Everything was conceived around one central figure, that of the emperor. It was almost as if a process of deification had been put into play.

For the more gifted librettists, the extremely restrictive working conditions were often an obstacle to the blossoming of their talent. The following letter, dated 13 December 1812, was written by Jouy, Spontini's brilliant librettist. It expresses his fears as the Censorship Commission examined his libretto for Cherubini's *Abencérages*:[20]

It is impossible that even after the most careful scrutiny one could find in this work the slightest intention or a single word that could cause worry. In *Fernand Cortez*, I staged the Spaniards at the most glorious time of their history. Here in *Abencérages*, they appear only in the festivities of the first act and are mentioned again only when the Moors' victory over them is announced. Also, I cannot imagine what comparisons could possibly be made with the quarrels between the Zégris and the Abencérages. Anyway, if grounds for political censorship can be found in this work, then it will be hopeless ever to write a single innocent line.

And yet Jouy changed hats depending on who was in power. The return of the Bourbons in 1814 did not end the well-established practice of using opera to spread political views. The Paris Opéra continued to sing the praises of the government, but in a much less flashy way. For one thing, the new king had more economical tastes. The time of great feats of arms had passed, and there were no more military triumphs to celebrate or heroic gestures to immortalize. The Bourbons were more discreet and stopped spending enormous sums of money for sumptuous but short-lived opera productions. Still, during the *Cent Jours*, the new Royal Academy of Music staged *Pélage ou le Roi de la Paix* (Pélage, or the King of Peace), and it premiered on 23 August 1814. It was composed by none other than Spontini, Josephine's former protégé, who must have been writing furiously, unless he had started the score in previous years! Jouy's text featured the good king Pélage who, after being driven away by the Moors, finds refuge in the Asturias. His only consolation is the devotion of his niece, princess Favila. The scene takes place in the eighth century, but the end of the Opéra includes the appearance of heavenly spirits who represent Saint-Louis, Louis XII, and Henri IV. A police report dated 12 May 1814 naively acknowledged that

> the dramatic action in this piece is almost worthless but can suffice as an interlude. The references to the situation of France are so striking that it really is nothing but an allegory. The tender scenes between the uncle and the niece are handled with feeling and will certainly be very well received.[21]

And indeed, the work was well received, at least according to a review that appeared in *Le Moniteur universel* on 25 August: "The public was deeply moved by the sight of a king sent into long exile away from his land and called back, after many setbacks, by his own people."

In 1821, two historical interludes at the Paris Opéra celebrated the birth of the Duke of Bordeaux, "the miraculous child." The first one was *Blanche de Provence* (Blanche of Provence), a three-act opera, written by a team of five composers: Berton, Boïeldieu, Cherubini, Kreutzer, and Paër. The second one was *Le Berceau d'Henri IV* (The Cradle of Henri IV), which portrayed Jeanne and Henri d'Albret. In 1823, Blangini produced a one-act opera, *Le Duc d'Aquitaine* (The Duke of Aquitaine), at the Feydeau theater. A review appearing in *Les Débats* on 14 December obviously alludes to the Spanish campaign of the Duke of Angoulême: "That this is an allegory is easy to conceive. The public had no difficulty restoring mentally the real name of a Son of France, an intrepid warrior, and a generous and human conqueror." In that same year, these princely feats were celebrated in *Vendôme en Espagne* (Vendôme in Spain), an opera by Auber and Hérold. Under the Restoration, librettists no longer chose subjects from Antiquity. The new monarchs had no need for mythical ancestors, drawing instead on their own past. This may be one reason, among many others, for the romantics' renewed interest in the Middle Ages and the Renaissance. The choice of mythology changed, but the musical quality of the commissioned operas showed no improvement. The censorship report for *Le Berceau d'Henri IV* expresses the following cynical conclusion:

> This work is but a succession of conversations without any action or movement, but since nothing could be found in it that was contrary to good principles, the royal censors are pleased to submit to Monsieur le Directeur General that the performance of this opera should be authorized.[22]

The censorship committee of the Paris Opéra and the Opéra-Comique continued its vigilance during the Empire. Literary men like historian J.-C. de Lacretelle managed to stay in office in spite of the change of regime. Lacretelle was named imperial censor in April 1811 and royal censor in October 1814. He must have learned to read librettos from different points of view! In fact, when one of Rossini's French operas, *Le Siège de Corinthe* (The Siege of Corinth), debuted at the Paris Opéra in 1826, Lacretelle wrote the following comment: "This work contains multiple references to the present cause of the Greeks and especially Missolonghi's Greeks. These comparisons seem to guarantee its acclaim."[23] Later, when the libretto of

La Muette de Portici (The Mute Girl of Portici) was submitted to the censorship committee, Lacretelle concluded that the subject was skillfully presented but that "its serious drawback was to set a revolution on stage." The comment sounds ominous when one thinks of the reception of Auber's opera in Brussels in 1830.

The Paris Opéra

The Paris Opéra occupied at least five different theaters in succession since it was created in 1672. Between 1789 and 1830, it was forced to move several times in accordance with different regimes and different designations.

When the Revolution broke out, the Opéra was located in the Theater of the Porte Saint-Martin, where it had been since 1781 and was known as the *Académie royale de musique* (the Royal Academy of Music). The theater had been built by architect Nicolas Lenoir especially for opera and was large enough to seat at least 1800. During the Terror of 1794, the Committee for Public Welfare decided to reserve the Theater of the Porte Saint-Martin for popular and political meetings and move the Opéra to the National Theater of Rue de la Loi, which had been built by architect Victor Louis in 1791. The Rue de Richelieu had been renamed the Rue de la Loi in 1793; it was located on the site of the present square Louvois. By settling in this new district of Paris in 1794, the Opéra moved closer to the heart of the theater district in the capital. The *Comédie-Française* and the two opéra-comique theaters—Favart and Feydeau—were located nearby.

Ever since the final years of the Monarchy, the theater district of Paris had undergone important architectural renovations. Compared to construction in this century, the number of theaters that were newly built in Paris in less than half-a-century is astonishing, to say nothing of the fact that most were completed in less than one year. A decree put forth by the National Assembly and approved by Louis XVI on 19 January 1791 recognized "every citizen's right to erect a theater and present plays of all kinds, submitted to preliminary review by the local municipal authorities." This *liberté des théâtres* (freedom of the theater) was ended by the imperial decrees of 1806 and 1807, but until then, Paris theaters proliferated during the Revolution: at one time there were fourteen in Paris, thirteen on the Right Bank alone. According to Daniel Rabreau, the Rue de Richelieu, between the Boulevards and Rue Saint-Honoré, was the greatest beneficiary of this inflation of theater and speculation, before the fever was caught, during the Restoration, on the Grands Boulevards, Faubourg Montmartre, and Faubourg Poissonnière.[24]

With the nearby Palais-Royal gardens recently opened to the public, the Rue de Richelieu became, for a while, the center of Paris business and pleasure.

In 1794, the Opéra was officially renamed Theater of the Arts; from 1797 on, it was known as the Theater of the Republic before becoming the Imperial Academy of Music in 1804. When the Opéra was moved to the National Theater of Rue de la Loi in 1794, its directors did not suspect that this would be its permanent home for more than a quarter century. In 1820, the Duke de Berry was assassinated in the Opéra foyer, and the theater was immediately closed down and subsequently destroyed. The Opéra, which had in the meantime been given back its eighteenth-century designation as the Royal Academy of Music, moved several times in the following year until it was finally assigned temporary quarters in a theater built especially for it at no. 10 Rue le Peletier, the location of the hotel of Choiseul. It remained here until the theater was destroyed by a fire in 1873. In 1875, the Opéra finally took possession of the new Palais Garnier.

The eighteen hundred-seat hall of Rue Le Peletier was somewhat smaller that the Rue de la Loi theater, but its proscenium was wider, its stage was deeper, and its balconies were roomier. The Rue de la Loi theater, which had staged every important opera during the Directoire, the Consulate, and the Empire, was hampered by small exits being too small. An anonymous report entitled *De l'Opéra en l'An XII* (On the Opéra during the Revolutionary Year XII), dated 1803–1804, stated that the hall was insufficient and lacked side rooms. The audience suffocated and had to "fight against the accumulation of breathing, odors, and candle-burning, all of which deprive the air of the elasticity necessary for the good transmission of sounds . . . . One can see little and hear even less." Rue de la Loi had one advantage over the Opéra's previous locations, however: the *parterre* (the ground floor reserved for standing room only) was eliminated, and the whole audience was seated. An article in *La Décade philosophique* offered the following explanation: "This change was demanded by good sense and by the respect owed to the people. One cannot understand how some theaters could still, after the Revolution, have the impudence to crowd French citizens in and let them stand."

At the beginning of the nineteenth century, the Opéra orchestra was composed of seventy-five musicians: twelve first violins, twelve second violins, six violas, twelve cellos, six double basses, four oboes, two flutes, three clarinets, five bassoons, five French horns, five trombones or trumpets, one timpani, and two cymbal players.[25] During the Restoration, the size increased to seventy-nine, the violas, for example, increasing from six to eight.[26] A decree dated 23 September 1805 provided for the addition of two harp players who had been needed since the creation of Le Sueur's *Les Bardes* the preceding year. By 1800, the different sections were led by the best soloists in Paris, who could also be heard in the concerts of Rue de Cléry and elsewhere in the capital: violinist Rode, clarinettist Lefèvre, flutist Devienne, French hornist Duvernoy, bassoonist Ozy, cellists Levasseur and Janson. These excellent performers were also composers and, as such, they provided their instruments with a much-needed solo repertoire. I am willing to suggest that this elite group was the best in Paris if not the whole of Europe. In 1817, a German journalist found the orchestra's interpretation of classical operatic masterpieces to be remarkable, but thought that its style was not appropriate for the more romantic—or more modern—works. This critic[27] chose as his example *Les Mystères d'Isis* (The Mysteries of Isis)—nothing less than Mozart's *The Magic Flute*—which he claims he had a hard time recognizing because of the stiff interpretation that left no room for dynamics and nuances of light and shadow. During that time, the orchestra was conducted by J.-B. Rey, who had already been director of the Concert spirituel orchestra just before the Revolution. Himself a composer, he occasionally arranged the works that he conducted. For example, in 1800, he gave a performance of Gluck's *Armide* with added trumpets and timpani. This sacrilegious change was criticized, and the excessive noise at the Opéra was denounced.[28] For a time, Rey was the only conductor, but in 1800, it became apparent that a second conductor was needed to help direct rehearsals. Devisme, the theater director, announced an audition for "the position of second time-beater." The notice specified that it should be someone who is "an excellent composer and has a particularly thorough knowledge of the score."[29] Double bass player J.-B. Rochefort, who had composed mostly ballets and opéras-comiques, was chosen and kept the position until 1815.

Singers posed a serious problem for the Paris Opéra between 1789 and the Restoration. French as well as foreign critics were consistently unanimous in denouncing the mediocrity or at least the considerable short-comings of the company's soloists. Until 1800, there were very few singers to begin with: seven men and four women, and a few understudies, according to the 1800 edition of the *Almanach des spectacles de Paris*. The small number required them to appear in many productions, and they were often scheduled to sing several times a week. In 1815, the ensemble had grown to twelve men and seven women, which was still small considering the variety of the repertoire and the number of performances. The Opéra chorus, however, was stable at around fifty-five members. In 1815, the voices were still divided according to the traditional classification of the vocal quartet at the end of the eighteenth century: dessus or treble part, which included first and second sopranos (the terms *alto* and *contralto* were not yet used in official documents); *hautes-contre* (counter-tenors); *tailles* (tenors); and basses. Most of the great male voices that gained acclaim during the Revolution and the Empire were in fact trained during the Monarchy and had become known shortly before 1789 at the Concert spirituel. The most famous of them all was F. Lays, who finally retired in 1823. For over forty years, he was heard hundreds of times at the Opéra, taking every classical role from Gluck to Sacchini and Piccini and also appearing in contemporary operas. Because of his enormous success, he made considerable financial demands on the company. A review of all the roles he sang makes it difficult to determine what his vocal range and style really were. He appears to have sung many different types of roles from Gluck to Grétry and including certain roles that would be now called baritone parts. For example, he sang Mozart's "Figaro" in 1793 and "Papageno" in 1801. He probably had a low tenor voice with a well-developed falsetto register. Fétis heard him often and wrote that "his vocalization was heavy." He did not know how "to even out the different registers in his voice, so that he went from his chest voice to his mixed voice with a sudden change from a formidable organ to a fluted voice, which made an effect more ludicrous than pleasant." Fétis's parting statement about Lays, who was chosen to be professor at the Conservatoire as early as 1795, seems very significant to me: "His shortcomings were those of his time, since there did not exist any vocal school in France when he debuted."

Lays's colleague Étienne Lainez also had a very long career. He was assigned first tenor (high tenor) roles, which were called haute-contre, and he also created many roles during the Empire, especially in Spontini's operas (*La Vestale* and *Fernand Cortez*). He apparently never enjoyed the same popularity as Lays and retired in 1810 to become director of the Lyon

Opera. Lays had adopted revolutionary ideas, but Lainez was a royalist and a conservative. During the Empire, he was consistently defended by the ultra-conservative critic Géoffroy, whose opinions, according to one of his colleagues, "were received with fanatical submission."

During the Restoration, a very young tenor named Adolphe Nourrit debuted with the Paris Opéra in *Iphigénie en Tauride* (1821). The son of Louis Nourrit, the understudy and then successor to tenor Lainez at the Opéra, Adolphe was destined for a brilliant but short and dramatic career. He was a student of Garcia, the father of Maria Malibran and Pauline Viardot. After some intensive study, he had acquired an extraordinary voice with which he could tackle the works of Rossini as well as Meyerbeer and created Meyerbeer's main roles after 1830. Only a few years older than Gilbert Duprez, he was the first great French tenor of the romantic period.

As for bass voices, the best member of the company at the end of the eighteenth century was A. Chéron, who began with the Paris Opéra under the reign of Louis XVI and went into retirement in 1802. In the roles of noble fathers he was replaced by H. Derivis, who made his 1803 debut as Sarastro and was one of the first Opéra recruits to come out of the Conservatoire. One of his greatest successes was the role of Oedipus in Sacchini's *Œdipe à Colone*. He also created the role of Mohammed in Rossini's *Le Siège de Corinthe*. Unfortunately, his heavy voice was always forced, and in these vocalizing bass roles, he could not compete with L. Lablache, one of the rising stars of international *bel canto*, nor with F. Galli. Both of these singers were Italian and had been trained using a radically different technique.

Among the women soloists of the Opéra company, two singers stood out: Mademoiselle Maillard and Mademoiselle Armand. They both started their careers at the Opéra-Comique at the end of the Monarchy and gained their fame in all the important roles of the French repertoire (Gluck and Sacchini). However, they had to relinquish the starring roles as soon as Caroline Branchu came on the scene in 1801. She was only twenty years old, and just out of the Conservatoire, where she had been a student of Garat. Over the next twenty-five years, she was the most brilliant representative of the French school tradition, a tradition that was to a certain degree without her. She possessed a big, dramatic soprano voice—what would be called Wagnerian today—and was particularly successful in the great roles of Gluck, Sacchini, Salieri, and especially Spontini. She was the first Vestale and premiered the first female roles of *Fernand Cortez* and *Olympie* (Olympia). Her retirement in 1826 coincided with the introduction of

Rossini's masterpieces and the new stars of *bel canto* at the Théâtre italien. Because of her training, her technique, and her own taste, Branchu had remained outside this Italian tradition. Berlioz still had the privilege of hearing her upon his arrival in Paris, and he was struck not only by her voice but also by the dramatic quality of her interpretation. He devoted some very enthusiastic pages to her in his writings. For instance, he thought that she had "a rare soprano voice, full and resonant, sweet and strong, able to dominate the choir and the orchestra or to descend into the softest whisper of shy passion or fear or dream."

The list of great voices at the Paris Opéra from 1789 to 1830 would not be complete without mentioning Laure Damoreau-Cinti, who made her debut in 1826, at the end of the Restoration and the year Madame Branchu retired. She was the great interpreter of Rossini's French operas. Fétis wrote, "Never has anyone been heard to sing with such perfection in the old temple of vocal drama." Although she was a native of Paris, Damoreau-Cinti first sang at the Théâtre italien, where she attracted Rossini's attention. She soon equalled Henriette Sontag and Maria Malibran. In 1829 and again in 1830, these three opera stars joined together on the stage of the Paris Opéra in performances of separate acts from different operas. In the first act of Cimarosa's *Il Matrimonio segreto* (The Secret Marriage), their charm was matched only by their talent. According to Castil-Blaze, it was "the best singing you could imagine."

Between 1789 and 1825, with the exception of Madame Branchu, the most famous singers of the time did not come together on the Paris Opéra stage. It is well-known that Garat always refused to sing there. During the Consulate and the Empire, Paris welcomed and acclaimed Madame Grassini and Madame Crescentini, although their nationality and their Italian repertoire denied them access to the Paris Opéra stage. On the other hand, the opening of the Théâtre italien in 1801 brought to Paris, one by one, the best virtuosos from the Italian Peninsula. Many of them had won international acclaim and introduced the Paris audience to an entirely different vocal technique. French singers rarely ventured outside the country, though the training that they received from the Conservatoire was criticized from the start. The criticism most often expressed in the press was that they were being taught to force their voices, to shout rather than sing. Nothing seemed to have changed since Rousseau and Grimm's diatribes against *urlo francese* (French shouting). Speaking of Mademoiselle Maillard, a foreign visitor in Paris wrote: "The more excited she becomes, the more she shrieks, and the louder the bravos and the stamping in the audience." In 1818,

Sévelinges, although a very nationalistic journalist and fervent defender of French opera, wrote in *Le Rideau levé* (The Raised Curtain): "Only one discipline still leaves much to be desired in our country: singing. I would not hesitate to blame the decadence and the corruption of our singing on the childish desire for achieving effects by excessive, heavy accentuation marking of accents." This desire was not even concealed by an actor's vanity in the following specious statement:"My first objective must be to render the meaning of the words." Good French singers were in such short supply during the Empire that in March 1805, the government circumvented the Conservatoire and advertised in the press to recruit "young people from the départements with a well-established counter-tenor, tenor, or bass voice," on the condition "that they present a noble appearance." The Opéra administration even promised to pay "the expenses of army replacements for those who were subject to conscription."[30]

Salary records from the Paris Opéra archives reveal the social status of composers, librettists, stage artists, and orchestra musicians. Star worshipping, which developed at the beginning of the nineteenth century, caused a marked increase in celebrities' salary that in some cases became quite exorbitant.[31]

Records from September 1798 indicate that annual salaries of Opéra singers started at 1800 francs for small roles and understudies and went up to 12,000 francs, whereas instrumentalists were paid more modest sums that ranged from 1100 francs to 2400 francs (for the concertmaster). The conductor earned 6000 francs.[32] Some stars were demanding "special considerations" in a thinly veiled attempt to blackmail the administration as was the case with the tenor Lays. A confidential report dated November 1802 from the Opéra director asserts that Lays's annual salary of 20,000 francs was no longer enough: he demanded a "supplementary fee of 100 francs for each performance, so that if he sang sixty times in one year, he could earn 26,000 francs." If one compares this salary with that of the other artists, "one will find it exorbitant, but it must be observed that citizen Lays, once his name is mentioned on the bill, increases the receipts by one half or one third at least." For a director, this argument is decisive but this extraordinary bonus "has to be paid on the side, without the other artists' knowledge."[33] These fabulous salaries continued to increase for the great stars of the Restoration. In 1821, the Intendant of the Royal Theaters hired Giuditta Pasta for eighteen months, beginning in April 1822, for a salary of 30,000 francs per year and two evening benefits.[34]

It appears that the payment of royalties was improvised during the Revolution, subject to a decree of 23 September 1805. Interestingly enough, librettists and composers received a comparable amount, which shows that at the time the music and words were of equal importance. In any case, royalty amounts decreased with each repeat performance: both received 300 francs for each of the first twenty performances, 200 francs for the next ten, and 150 francs for the last ten. If the number of performances reached forty—which happened only rarely—though Grétry's *La Caravane* was presented three hundred times during his lifetime—the composer and the librettist each received a five hundred franc bonus and one hundred francs for each additional performance. These figures applied to grand operas, the five-act works that filled a whole evening. A program of one- or two-act operas required the addition of another presentation, usually a ballet, so the above figures were reduced by one third or one fourth.[35] Authors often received extraordinary bonuses for successful runs, especially if they were in the government's good graces. For example, in 1819 Count De Pradel promised Spontini 1500 francs for each new act (not each new work) that he composed for the Royal Academy of Music.[36] In the first years of the nineteenth century, ticket sales on a very good night at the Opéra might reach 10,000 francs and, during the Empire, the price of the best seats was twelve livres (balcony) and eight livres (first-tier box). In spite of these high prices, the Paris Opéra, like its provincial counterparts, operated at a loss. The budget showed an annual deficit of around 200,000 francs. Expenses amounted to 1,500,000 francs, but receipts did not exceed 1,300,000 francs (including an annual subsidy of 600,000 francs).[37] In 1821, an article in *Le Miroir des spectacles* alleged that the annual deficit was 900,000 francs: "The receipts of the Royal Academy of Music are nothing compared to its enormous expenses. The Academy barely attracts enough spectators to bribe employees." The successive directors of this institution met with considerable management difficulties and, during the Empire, were placed first under the authority of the prefect of the Luçay Palace and later that of Monsieur de Rémusat, the first chamberlain. Under the Restoration, the Paris Opéra was directly incorporated into the Household of the King. Regardless of which agency they reported to, the directors had no power and were merely puppets subject to the government's command.

Clear conclusions can be drawn from studying the list of works presented at the Paris Opéra at the end of the eighteenth century. First, there were relatively few productions: no more than two or three each year and few of any

significance. In the year 1798, for example, the only new productions were
two uninteresting, short-lived operas: *Olympie* (Olympia) by Kalkbrenner
and *Apelle et Campaspe* by Alsatian composer André Ehler, who was better
known for his instrumental music. Second, the Opéra presented about
twenty different productions each year, including two or three ballets. Not
one foreign work was presented, even in a French translation. The main
part of the season consisted of revivals of Gluck's five operas, along with
works by Sacchini, Piccini, Salieri, and two or three titles by Grétry, including *La Caravane du Caire* (The Caravan of Cairo) and *Anacréon chez Polycrate* (Anacreon Visits Polycrates). Clearly, the programming was extremely
monotonous and reserved the top billing for Gluck's *tragédies lyriques* and
those of his followers. Rameau and his predecessors had disappeared from
the bill and entered a long-lasting purgatory. It was as though French opera
had begun with Gluck in the 1780s. Third, subjects borrowed from Greek
and Roman Antiquity were still very much enjoyed. More than ever, neo-
classicism was in fashion, both in the arts and in everyday life. For example,
the two new works presented in 1800 were Granges de Fontenelle's *Hécube*
(Hecuba) and Porta's *Les Horaces* (The Horatii), two composers who are
forgotten today, as well they should be. The most gifted young masters of
the new generation—Le Sueur, Catel, and Cherubini—desperately attempted to reach the Holiest of Holies. Prior to 1800, only Méhul succeeded with his work *Adrien* (Hadrian), a production that caused him no
end of trouble. The work was ready as early as 1791 and rehearsals began,
but the content was soon forbidden by the revolutionary government,
which demanded "cuts and changes" in the libretto. Méhul and his librettist
Hoffmann changed a few details in the action, but the work was given a
lukewarm reception. It was acclaimed only after its revival in 1801, which
inspired the following review in *La Gazette nationale*: "Hadrian's chariot is
pulled by white horses, harnessed in the ancient style and led by slaves. This
novelty adds to the truth as much as to the effect of this opera, which is one
of the most pompous of all those seen at the Theater of the Arts." This was
one of the earliest comments of its kind, but dozens more would follow
during the Consulate and the Empire. The end-of-century neo-classic fashion gradually changed. Sumptuous productions replaced the austere ancient
stage sets, and music became secondary. The Franconi Brothers' team began
to work for the Paris Opéra, which in turn was working for the government. The imperial triumphs that were to come can be predicted. Around
1800, the press was full of long articles denouncing this situation. One
from *Le Journal des spectacles* dated 25 October 1801 gives the following de-

piction of the leading French operatic stage: "The public has been satiated with Gluck's sublime productions for the past twenty-five years, and has not yet heard anything to equal them." The following remark reflects something of the musical life of the time: "In recent times there has been such a new frenzy for instrumental music that this has become the only fashionable genre." This was the time when the Rue de Cléry concerts began. For some, the traditional supremacy of vocal music over instrumental music seemed temporarily to be in question.

The result of this situation was that everyone yawned at the opera but developed a passion for ballet:

> Now high society arrives at the Opéra only for the ballet. A fly could be heard when Vestris, Mademoiselle Clotilde, or Madame Gardel dance, but the patrons cough, spit, chat, or smirk when Alcestis or Iphigenia sing.[38]

Every contemporary account raved about the extraordinary quality of Paris ballet, with its sumptuous productions. Its popularity was in large part due to the operatic audience's growing weariness with the same old repertoire with no renewal or innovation. From this standpoint, the decade between 1789 and the end of the century was appalling. After 1800, the situation began changing, but only gradually and with no bold moves. France did not have C. M. von Weber or his *Der Freischütz*. Musicologists can easily detect in several new operas, however, the first signs of the great revolution in taste and sensitivity that was about to take place and in which the operatic genre took part. The year 1801 saw the beginning of a quarrel over Mozart, which will be dealt with in detail in another chapter.[39] Mozart's name became a symbol for a group of people claiming to be modernists and showing their deep contempt for contemporary French opera. They became known in the press as *mozartomanes*, foreshadowing the *dilettanti* who regrouped fifteen years later around Rossini and Stendhal and fervently defended Italian music. On 20 August 1801, these young Mozart avant-guardists gave a triumphal ovation to *Les Mystères d'Isis* (The Mysteries of Isis) when it was performed at the Theater of the Republic and the Arts. It was, of course, an adaptation of Mozart's *The Magic Flute*. The libretto was modified by Morel de Chefdeville and the score "arranged" by the Czech composer Lachnith, residing in Paris. The result of this adaptation, or "parody," as it was then customarily called, was probably less disastrous than has been declared by others. Despite undeniable mutilations, long fragments of Mozart's masterpiece in their original form, including the overture, were revealed to the Paris audience. In any case, it was a real triumph and, for many, an amazing experience. It is striking to find in the French press of that time commentaries showing that part of the public was deeply moved: "This music contains energy and strength, and heavenly melody as well." It is not surprising that when Napoleon decided to award decennial prizes by the French National Institute in 1810, *Les Mystères d'Isis* outstripped all other operas on the basis of the number of performances, sixty-eight to be precise. It remained one of the very rare foreign masterpieces presented in translation at the Paris Opéra.

Indeed, the reform movement of the early part of the nineteenth century had its roots in French opera itself. Two names appeared on the bills for the first time: Catel and Le Sueur. As if they had planned it together— in reality they were known to dislike each other—they turned away from Greek and Roman subjects and chose to try their luck with new subject matter. With *Sémiramis* (Semiramide, 1802) and *Les Bayadères* (The Bayadere Dancers, 1810), Catel moved the action to the Middle East and the Far East, while Le Sueur—*Ossian* (1804) and *La Mort d'Adam* (The Death of Adam, 1809) evoked Celtic and Scandinavian civilizations and Biblical antiquity. These operas did not all have the same success nor the same influence. But at the dawn of the nineteenth century, each and all of them showed a deliberate intention to explore new possibilities.

In 1802, Catel was a young professor at the Conservatoire preparing for his writing debut in the theater. Up until then, he had only composed revolutionary and instrumental music. His *Sémiramis* failed, but more because of plots directed against him than because of his score, which was not uninteresting. Catel may not have been a counterpoint scholar, but he was a brilliant tone painter in his evocation of the Orient. In the history of opera, *Sémiramis* marked a turning point. Weber admired its overture, which later on was often played in concert: its novel instrumental effects and use of original tunes, such as the passage in which trombones and strings carry on a dialogue, were much admired. The librettist had the brilliant idea to use Voltaire's tragedy—soon to be used by Rossini as well—as his inspiration. In *Sémiramis*, Catel abandoned the bogus Orient staged by eighteenth-century French opera. Exoticism, with its mixed fragrance of sensuality and cruelty, was slowly beginning to appear on the Paris Opéra stage, foreshadowing its destiny in the arts and literature of the entire nineteenth century and the first part of the twentieth.

In a sense, *Les Bayadères* confirmed this first attempt. The action takes place in a far-off oriental place, the city of Benares, in a curious blend of the themes of love and death. In order to have access to the House of the Gods, the prince, fatally wounded by a poisoned arrow, needs to be wed. The bayadere Laméa agrees to sacrifice herself for love, and they end up together on a nuptial pyre. This theme of the leper's kiss and salvation through love was completely new. With stage sets worthy of *Lakmé*, this opera hinted at the great themes of Wagnerian romantic opera. In 1810, it must have sent a strange shiver through the audience of the Imperial Academy of Music.

The same audience had already been surprised and delighted as early as 1804, when Le Sueur presented *Ossian*, which turned out to be one of the greatest successes of the Paris Opéra during the Empire. Unlike Catel, Le Sueur had struggled for years and was no beginner when he finally reached the leading Paris operatic stage. Made famous at the dawn of the Revolution by his nomination to the head of the choir school of Notre-Dame during 1786 and 1787, Le Sueur had also attracted public attention with his successes at the Feydeau theater between 1793 and 1796, as well as with his revolutionary music. When *Ossian* was presented to the Paris audience in July 1804, Le Sueur had just been named *maître de chapelle* at the Tuileries by Napoleon. He became the official composer of the new regime that had just been proclaimed in May 1804. *Ossian* was the first new work produced by the brand-new Imperial Academy of Music.

The period bordering the two centuries witnessed a craze for poems that the Scottish writer MacPherson attributed to the bard Ossian and claimed to have translated from the Gaelic. This literary fraud was rewarded with a phenomenal success. The whole pre-romantic generation adored these epic songs, in which they found whatever they were seeking, in addition to what was really there: the suggestion of an ancient, mysterious, and storm-eroded Scotland, supernatural manifestations through the clouds, the cult of heroes, the call of infinity. For sensitive and melancholy souls, this new folklore was the gateway to a world of dreams.

Le Sueur had the brilliant idea of composing an opera about Ossian. It was the first attempt, at least in France, to stage Ossian, which is surprising, considering the success of the literature at that time. Napoleon himself had a passion for it, but it is not true that he commissioned this opera from Le Sueur, though that is the claim to this day. Le Sueur had in fact begun sketching his work before 1800, when he did not yet know the future emperor.

Unfortunately, Le Sueur was poorly assisted by his librettist, an obscure pen-pusher named Dercy, who invented a relatively simple storyline tracing the rivalry between a Scottish clan and a Scandinavian band but devoid of truly strong or poetic situations. The bard Ossian was portrayed by a young and brave warrior who fought and triumphed in order to recover his fiancée. In the fourth act, Dercy and Le Sueur decided to add a scene for which they found no model in the epic poem, and so they invented it: the famous episode of "Ossian's dream." In his prison, the hero is struck by a supernatural vision, and his soul rises in a sort of mystic ascent to the heavenly kingdom of his ancestors. This is the scene that later inspired Berlioz for Faust's sleep in his *Damnation de Faust* and Ingres for his famous painting of *Le Songe d'Ossian* (Ossian's Dream). It marked an important step in the change of taste and sensitivity. Sleep scenes had always been common in French opera ever since its origin, but here sleep had become dream, and the object of the dream was depicted on stage. The world of fantasy inside the sleeping conscience was given shape and an objective, human form. It now became possible to represent the subconscious in the theater.

The audience of that time gave the opera a triumphal reception, but we cannot be sure that they truly appreciated this change. In any case, the dream scene was an occasion for sumptuous staging effects that had a lot to do with its success. Long after the event, the Duchess of Abrantes still remembered it with amazement:

> The immensity unfolding before the spectators plunged us into one of those fantastic dreams so strongly suggested by Ossian's poetry—quite in fashion at the time. We were transported into a misty environment, surrounded with vapors enveloping golden palaces suspended in mid-air. These shiny columns served as supports for groups of young maidens whose white veils and long, wavy hair entwined the hazy clouds . . . .[40]

Unfortunately, the composer was not quite on a level with his subject. How effective these fantastic visions could have been in the hands of a true romantic! Le Sueur had many original ideas but little experience, and while this score contains some brilliant flashes, it is spoiled by conspicuous weaknesses. I believe a revival of *Ossian* is unthinkable today, but at least some of the better excerpts should have been revived long ago through recordings or concert performances. They would surprise us with their occasional harmonic innovation and originality. The few bars of the recitative introducing the dream scene are a good example of a technique that to my knowledge was unique at that time in all of French opera. In order to depict the heavenly vision that fills Ossian's soul, the composer changed keys in each new measure, a typically romantic device. This tonal instability gave the impression of progressing deeper and deeper into a mysterious and unknown world:

Vous vous ouvrez pour moi, séjour heureux et pur,
Plaines de l'air, brillants palais d'azur,
Où le guerrier retrouve et ses goûts et ses armes,
Le Barde sa couronne et la beauté ses charmes . . .

Let me in, o pure and felicitous places,
Aerial plains, shiny blue palaces,
You restore to the warrior his taste and his arms,
To the bard his crown, and to beauty its charms . . .

The original orchestration also contributes to the modern character of the work. Besides the use of twelve harps, the combination of the tam-tam and the harp at the moment when the bards, singing in seven parts, strike the sacred shield is the same gesture used on Irminsul's shield by the priestess Norma in Bellini's opera. We can discover in *Ossian* a great number of the dramatic situations and compositional devices typical of romantic opera. The costumes—designed by the painter Berthélemy, whose drawings have been preserved—seem to be right out of a Wagner opera: fierce warriors carrying spear and shield, and a double-vaned helmet like those worn by the mortals in the Gibishungen kingdom or the Valhalla gods. In *Ossian*, Celtic and Scandinavian mythologies were introduced to the Paris Opéra for the first time. Later they would be found again in some of the nineteenth-century masterpieces, but for the time being, audiences had to be content with only a glimpse at an unknown world.

Although the opera certainly had a strong impact on the audience of the time, the presence of the emperor and the empress, who came to applaud Le Sueur at the second performance, probably had something to do with the triumph of *Ossian*. Its success lasted for a few years until weaknesses became more noticeable: its novelty eroding, *Ossian* did not survive the Empire. The last performance—the seventy-seventh in all—took place in September 1817. It was the only success at the Opéra for the emperor's official composer. In 1809, Le Sueur miserably failed in his attempt to present another opera, *La Mort d'Adam* (Adam's Death), which was scoffed at and called a *capucinade* (a dull, affected sermon, like that of a Capuchin friar) in the press. This drama was adapted from the German poet Klopstock and took as its subject the death of the father of the human race. It was half opera and half oratorio, with action that was much too static to be pleasing on the stage. However, for the musicologist studying French opera, *La Mort d'Adam*, like *Ossian*, is of great interest because of its musical originality. I shall only take as an example here the epilogue, a pure invention by Le Sueur, in which Satan's struggle against God for Adam's soul was represented by a truly Dantesque vision—inspired, in fact, by reading Milton's *Paradise Lost*. There were all the ingredients to make this scene into an important moment in French pre-romantic opera: far-off voices of the spirits rising from hell, heavenly voices from above; the appearance of Satan coming to claim his prey; and tremendous orchestral effects with trombones, timpani, and trumpets. It represented a sort of musical counterpart to the vast frescoes by Lamartine, Vigny, or Hugo from the Old Testament, but for once, the musician preceded the poets. In 1992 the epilogue of *La Mort d'Adam* was given its world premier at the festival of *La Chaise-Dieu (France)*, where it met with great success. A CD has been recorded, thus providing an opportunity for the present generation to discover that music of the Empire could be very different from what is commonly thought.

In 1803, while the French composers were carefully exploring in new directions, a young, ambitious Italian arrived and settled in Paris. Prepared for anything and full of self-confidence, Spontini was determined to repeat the feats of his fellow countrymen of the previous generation–Piccini, Sacchini, and Salieri. He was still a young man—twenty-nine in 1803—and choosing Paris as the first stop on his European career path is very significant. For a foreign composer who had already authored several opere buffe successfully produced in his native country, Paris was one of the operatic capitals that had to be conquered. Despite the Paris Opéra's very poor situation at the end of the eighteenth century, it was operative to gain recognition there. In this regard, Paris was living off her past reputation. Like his predecessors, Spontini came to Paris to look for success, which he eventually obtained, by composing works in French for the Opéra. Paradoxically, from Gluck to Meyerbeer, most of the French opera masters were foreigners.

Like his fellow countrymen, Spontini had to be very talented and work very hard to assimilate so intimately the nuances of French language and culture and to understand the demands of the French operatic stage and its audience. After getting mixed results in a few attempts at the Paris Théâtre italien and at the Opéra-Comique, the young composer, personally protected by the empress, was given access to the Imperial Academy of Music as early as 1807. There he presented to the Paris public *La Vestale* on a libretto by Étienne de Jouy.

To reach this goal, Spontini had to overcome many obstacles, including a coterie that had been active since Mozart's success in Paris and the opening of the Théâtre italien in 1801 and was definitely hostile toward foreign composers. This nationalistic current of opinion was led by the critic of *Le Journal de l'Empire*, Géoffroy, whose views were often biased and petty. Still, *La Vestale* was an enormous success. Very soon, it was performed in the provinces and in most foreign countries, which was not the case with the operas of Catel or Le Sueur. No other French opera between 1789 and 1825 was as successful. This was the fullest and the most significant work in the repertoire of that time. Historically, it falls precisely between two worlds or two aesthetics.

La Vestale retained many characteristics of the French tragédie lyrique in the style of Gluck. Antiquity was the source for its subject, though it was Roman history rather than greek mythology. The vestal, unfaithful to her chastity vow, is condemned to being walled-up alive, but the last-minute intervention of Zeus brings a happy ending with dances of rejoicing. This storyline was well suited to the eighteenth-century demand for light, amusing opera. Librettists of grand opera still avoided tragic endings. In this sense, tragédie lyrique did not always live up to its name; Cherubini's *Médée*, produced at the Feydeau theater in 1797, is one of the few exceptions. In later productions, Norma and Pollio would be burned at the stake, and no gods would intervene by removing the stone that sealed the tomb where Aïda and Ramses were left agonizing. But for now, the spectators could recognize in *La Vestale* the familiar settings of Roman altars, temples, and columns and appearance of their favorite characters of lictors and pontiffs that they appreciated. They did not get the impression of a break from the well-established Paris Opéra tradition. In addition, the action was reduced to the bare minimum, there were no sub-plots,[41] and emotions were of a touching simplicity reminiscent of the purity of the great masterpieces of classical theater and Gluck and a far cry from the complicated intrigues and melodramatic new developments that characterize romantic opera.

Spontini succeeded beautifully in assimilating the traditional elements of French grand opera of the time, yet he was able to express in his score his own artistic nature. He was a disciple of dramatic truth as it had been defined by Gluck, but he knew how to soften it with melodic charm and sensuality. The Italian character is emerging and in many pages of this great French opera, and in it floats a new lyrical fragrance still foreign to the French masters of the time. Bellini's suave cantilenas are foreshadowed in *La Vestale*. A very convincing example is Julia's exquisite prayer, *Ô des infortunés* (O Latona, Patroness of the Unfortunate Ones), with its unchanging and intentionally insignificant triplet accompaniment that leaves the voice exposed in the forefront, alone and sublime, as if desperately in search of support:

La Vestale

Prayer sung by Madame Branchu

Words by M. Jouy

Music by M. Spontini, personal composer of the Queen-Empress's Chamber

and *maître de chapelle* at the Naples Conservatory

Arranged for piano or harp by the composer

Price: F 1.10

Published in Paris by the Êrard Sisters, Rue du Mail N°21

(Property of the Publishers)

All the magic of *bel canto* already permeates these pages. It did not matter that the new score was attacked from a technical point of view by purists and bitter critics for its compositional errors: awkward modulations, unresolved dissonances, and so forth.[42] The audience gave it triumphant and long-lasting acclaim. By 1830 this masterpiece had been heard more than two hundred times in Paris. In recent history, Maria Callas revived the great tragic role, which was well suited to her. A later, Italian version of *La Vestale* has been produced in a great number of opera houses worldwide. The original French version, which in 1810 was proclaimed to be the best opera produced in Paris since 1800 by the jury of the decadal prizes, was performed for the gala opening of Milan's La Scala in December 1993 under the direction of Riccardo Muti. It was well received.

Spontini's Paris career did not end with *La Vestale*. He remained in the capital until 1820, at which time he left for Berlin, where new success awaited him at the court of the King of Prussia. After his "French period" the Italian composer began his "German period." Before leaving Paris, however, he produced two grand operas, *Fernand Cortez* during the Empire (1809) and *Olympie* during the Restoration (1819).

Fernand Cortez was less original than *La Vestale* and was not as successful, at least in the beginning. Spontini, who was by then better acquainted with Parisian taste and had been away from his native country for several years, attempted this time to display great pomp in his opera: There were exotic costumes, Mexican ballet, and even a parade by Cortez's Spanish cavalry, with a cavalry charge on stage that caused panic among the Mexican women. A German journalist who attended the premiere in Paris wrote that "the leading opera house in France had turned into a riding rink" and that the success of a new production "was proportional to the number of horses on stage." *Fernand Cortez* certainly lacked the dramatic restraint and the Italian charm of the melodies of *La Vestale*. On the other hand, it was the first French "grand opera," a forerunner, in many ways, of Rossini's *Guillaume Tell* (William Tell) and Meyerbeer's masterpieces. Spontini resolutely turned his back on eighteenth-century aesthetics. He demonstrated an extraordinary flair for orchestrating—the large, romantic orchestra of the 1830s was already formed, with bass drum, cymbals, and triangle—handling large choral masses and seeking large-scale scenic effects. This does not mean that the solo parts were neglected, and after *La Vestale*, Madame Branchu was again chosen as the ideal female lead—and was unanimously acclaimed. What was missing in *Cortez* was passion, or at least this was a somewhat cold depiction of love compared to the story in *La Vestale*.

Princess Amazily and Cortez sing two duets, but their love is not in the forefront. They are Corneille-type heroes, thinking first about their glory and seeking to fight to defend the freedom of their people.

Fernand Cortez did not begin to be really successful until 1817. Spontini made a few changes, and the new version traveled throughout Europe. It has recently been rediscovered and recorded, much to everyone's surprise. Grand opera lovers now consider it to be an outstanding example of the genre, and rightly so. The main drawback of Spontini's last French opera, Olympie, was that its subject was taken from Greek history, and by 1819, neo-classicism was no longer in fashion. The action takes place in Ancient Greece, and the setting of the first act is Diana's temple in Ephesus. As in La Vestale, there are two female roles; that of Statira is for mezzo-soprano. In the middle of the second act, Spontini wrote for his two heroines a duet that could be the forerunner of every great female duet in romantic opera, from Rossini to Bellini and Meyerbeer. From the dramatic point of view, the history of opera at certain moments shows sudden changes and innovations that turn into new models and can be traced through several generations. During the period from 1775 to 1830, for instance, the dramatic exploitation of Gluck's and Piccini's couple Orestes and Pylades can easily be followed: the hero has a secret friend who is ready to sacrifice himself for him. This scenario can be found again in Ossian, La Vestale, Norma, and probably in a number of operas forgotten today.

Spontini's stay in Paris during the Empire and the first years of the Restoration was decisive for the evolution of French opera. His works were quickly known and appreciated and made a strong impression on his contemporaries. No one can ignore Berlioz' passionate admiration and enthusiastic analyses of La Vestale, Cortez, and to a lesser degree, Olympie. Every romantic figure, including Weber and Wagner, referred to these works and often used them as examples. It is most likely that without Spontini, the French grand operas by Rossini, Meyerbeer, Halévy, and many others would not have been exactly the same. The real originality of the Italian master was not to start a revolution—actually, there never was any interruption—but rather to assimilate, upon his arrival in Paris at the start of the nineteenth century, the Gluckist-French tradition and then redirect it in a way that he instinctively knew would generate future masterpieces.

It is really too bad that one of the strongest musical figures of that period, Cherubini, stayed away from Paris operatic life during the Consulate and the Empire. It has been rightly said that Napoleon did not like the man or his music, although his successes at the Feydeau theater until 1800 had made him famous throughout Europe. In 1803, the Paris Opéra produced his new work, *Anacréon ou l'Amour fugitif* (Anacreon, or Love Fleeting). Except for the overture, which continued to be famous for a long time, the production was a failure because of a stupid plot by the adversaries of German music at a time when Mozart began to be recognized in Paris. Cherubini was believed to be a scholar and therefore considered German. The critic of the *Allgemeine musikalische Zeitung* reviewed the premiere performance of *Anacréon* in the following terms:

> Before the beginning of the overture, I was surprised to hear people talk about this opera as if it had already been played at least ten times: noise, instrumental music, cleverness, German music. Not one spark of grace, softness, kindness, or sweetness.[43]

His hopes dashed, Cherubini left for Vienna in 1805. There he met Beethoven, attended the premiere of *Fidelio*, and successfully produced his own opera, *Faniska*, in 1806. Back in Paris in 1813, he made a new attempt at the Paris Opéra with *Les Abencérages* on a libretto by Jouy; the same theme would become the subject of a 1826 short story by Chateaubriand. The result was not convincing. Only the critic of the *Allgemeine musikalische Zeitung* was again on his side and accused the French press, Géoffroy in particular, of musical incompetence and gossip.[44] At that point, Cherubini gave up on conquering the Paris Opéra. He would return to theater again only for occasional compositions and, after 1830, for the production of his surprising *Ali Baba*, the swan song of this spirited and melancholy seventy-year-old man. Meanwhile, beginning in 1815, most of his activity was with the Tuileries Chapel, where he was recognized as the master of French religious music. It is important to mention here that Cherubini, perhaps the most gifted dramatic composer of the period, never really succeeded on the leading operatic stage of Paris.

Following the end of the Empire, the Paris Opéra again went into a lethargic period in spite of a few promising important works. The French composers had come of age and were "dozing"; no young talent was yet on the rise. Until about 1825, the repertoire was not updated, but was still made up of revivals of operas by Gluck, Sacchini—his *Œdipe à Colone* remained one of the more successful—and, of course, Spontini. Whenever the receipts went down, a revival of *La Vestale* would temporarily replenish the Opéra coffers. For a decade, no notable new work was created. With the beginning of the Restoration, however, the Théâtre italien grew tremendously and became more fashionable every day. A whole faction of the young Paris avant-garde attended it and regrouped around Rossini. On 23 February 1821, the *Miroir des spectacles* published this laconic notice:

> The sad state of our Grand Opéra and of the Feydeau theater— where a true bass voice has not been heard in a long time—the little success gained by our composers' latest scores, the new popularity of Rossini—more brilliant than solid—all contribute to the public infatuation for Théâtre italien.

Two days earlier, the same newspaper was already denouncing the negative influence of Italian opera on French opera: "As amateurs familiarize themselves with Italian melodies—so original, so suave, so varied—they have become more demanding of French opera." This conflicting situation caused a pen battle between Stendhal, Rossini's defender, and French composer Henri Montan Berton, a member of the Académie des Beaux-Arts and professor of composition at the Conservatoire. I recounted elsewhere the details of this exchange,[45] which began in 1821. Each of the adversaries expressed his ideas through a newspaper devoted to his cause: Stendhal and the *dilettanti* in *Le Miroir des spectacles* and the traditionalists in the academic journal *L'Abeille*. In *Vie de Rossini* (Life of Rossini) published in 1823, Stendhal perfidiously compared Rossini's *Otello* and *The Barber of Seville* to Berton's *Virginie*, "a quite decent grand opera that is getting a tremendous success right now at the Royal Academy of Music and will be known around the world." It is true that Berton and Desaugiers' *Virginie* premiered at the Opéra in 1823. Based on an ancient subject, it could offer only conventional situations and well-crafted but ice-cold music, and it did not succeed in warming up the audience of the Paris Opéra. With difficulty it remained in the repertoire until 1825 and then disappeared from the programs for ever. A follower of Gluck whom he still considered to be an ideal model, Berton was defending the classical principles of unity and truth of action that he feared were threatened by the school of Rossini. This dispute was but an episode in the struggle of the classical rear-guard action against the young romantic generation that occurred around 1820. Soon Stendhal's *Racine et Shakespeare* and Hugo's preface to *Cromwell* would sweep away the last resistance. At the Paris Opéra, Berton was at the center of one of these small groups. He once compared the taste of the "modern Orpheus"—the Rossini advocates—to the contemporary taste for gothic architecture, that "shapeless peculiarity" that eliminated ancient beauty and order. He went on to say: "The reasons why one prefers the bizarre to the true today are the same that led Seneca's flashiness to replace Cicero's sound eloquence in Ancient Rome."

When one cannot bring an enemy down, one should try and make him an ally. This principle was adopted by Baron de La Ferté, the administrator of the royal theaters. The Archives of Foreign Affairs contain a letter addressed to a French diplomat at the Embassy in Rome dated 17 January 1821, asking him to contact Rossini and beg him to agree that his works be performed in French at the Paris Opéra: "the sooner certainly the better, for our Grand Opéra is threatened by total eclipse. Rossini is the only one who could bring glamour and warmth back to it."[46] It seems that the government finally satisfied the request of Rossini's follwers that their idol be given access to the Paris Opéra with one of his works translated in French. In 1821, there was a project to present *Tancredi*, and Castil-Blaze prepared a translation, but it was abandoned and replaced by *Moïse* (Moses).[47] It was not until 9 October 1826 that an opera by Rossini was finally performed in French in Paris: It was *Le Siège de Corinthe* (The Siege of Corinth), adapted from *Maometto secondo*, which had been performed in Naples in 1820. By then, Rossini had been successful for ten years at the Théâtre italien. When his contract as *Directeur de la musique et de la scène* (director of music and stage) of the Théâtre italien expired, the government of King Charles X appointed him *Inspecteur général du chant en France* (General Inspector of Singing in France).

By switching from the Théâtre italien to the Royal Academy of Music, Rossini did not disappoint his fans; far from it, his fame only increased. *Le Siège de Corinthe* was a triumph. The composer had gone back to one of his earlier scores and accomplished the enormous task of adapting it to the new French libretto. The Paris critics appreciated the quality of this libretto. In *La Gazette de France*,[48] the critic A. Delaforêt wrote:

> Whatever we think of Italian music, it used to apply itself to such stupid or ludicrous, purely ultramontanist canvases that our enjoyment of its melody was often distracted, shaken, sometimes even spoiled.

To inaugurate this new manner and to be certain of his public success at the Grand Opéra, Rossini developed effects, scenic as well as vocal and orchestral. According to Berlioz, this score struck the hour "of the instrumental revolution in theater orchestras." The author of the *Traité d'instrumentation*

(Treatise on Orchestration) was extremely sensitive to this aspect of the new opera:

> Rossini scored the bass drum everywhere, and the cymbals and the triangle, and the trombones and the ophicleide in whole bundles of chords! He struck out madly with precipitous rhythms and produced from the orchestra such sparks of sound—if not harmony—and such thunder that the audience was awakened to enjoy this new kind of emotion, more vivid—if not more musical—than that experienced up till then.[49]

This opinion seems to me to express very well the novelty of this French opera by Rossini. The musical substance itself may not have been any richer than that of many preceding works, but it was skillfully presented. The audience of the Royal Academy of Music got the kind of flashy production (sets, stage effects, ballet) that it loved so well. The following year, Rossini's *Moïse* was equally well received (26 March 1827). It was also an adaptation for the French stage of a previous Italian score, *Mose in Egitto* (Moses in Egypt), which premiered in Naples in 1818. For this new French version, Rossini changed the original orchestration and rewrote several numbers, including the finale of the third act, where he made abundant use of the percussion (cymbals, bass drum, and triangle), even on every beat of the measure in certain passages. Again, Berlioz wrote:

> In this piece, the orchestra and the choir are arranged in such a manner and the sound of the voices and instruments is so striking that the music floats on top of these thundering noises. This time, the musical substance gushes out and fills every corner of the hall, in spite of its vast dimensions, grabbing, shaking and stirring the audience, producing one of the most impressive effects ever experienced in the Opéra since it was built.[50]

This new triumph made the Italian composer the master of French grand opera. In the final years of the Restoration, what French composer other than, perhaps, Auber, could possibly have competed with him? Auber had been highly acclaimed at the Opéra-Comique for a decade and won a well-deserved success at the Paris Opéra in 1828 with *La Muette de Portici*, a subject borrowed by Scribe from the seventeenth-century Neapolitan story of the orator Masaniello. In Auber, Richard Wagner saw one of the fathers of European romantic opera: "*La Muette de Portici* surprised everybody as something radically new. Never had anyone seen such a lively opera. Auber succeeded in keeping his score burning hot like a lava flow. For the first time, a crowd really took part in the action." This extraordinary quality of expression was as much the result of Auber's music as Scribe's libretto.

As a matter of fact, it is to Scribe, an ingenious dramatist in his own right, that Rossini turned for the subject of his next French opera, *Le Comte Ory* (April 1828), lighter and less tragic than his two preceding works. It was a kind of opéra-comique with recitative, using the spirited and vivacious music of *Il Viaggio a Reims* (The Voyage to Rheims), composed in 1825 for the crowning of King Charles X. It was one of the first productions in which the set designer Cicéri introduced gothic decor in the style of the troubadours, which would become extremely fashionable in the romantic years.

Following the success won by *Le Comte Ory*, Rossini felt very secure and went on to produce a French opera no longer related to his previous Italian works, but entirely conceived for Paris. It was *Guillaume Tell* (August 1829) from a libretto by Spontini's former librettist, E. de Jouy. Following the premiere performance, the critic of *Le Globe* wrote: "For three years Rossini has been practicing with our language and preparing his singers, his public, and his genius for the extraordinary work that has just been born. A conqueror as prudent as he is daring, he did not venture on foreign grounds." Curiously though, after becoming the unchallenged, absolute master of the leading French stage before 1830, this conqueror could not, or did not wish to, take advantage of his victory. *Guillaume Tell*—for which the artist's genius "had undergone a last and complete transformation," in Fétis's estimation—was the last opera written by this prolific composer. Rossini went into almost complete retirement at the age of thirty-seven. In a bitter debate with the Viscount de la Rochefoucault, the general manager of the Beaux-Arts administration, over the material conditions of his engagement in Paris, Rossini promised in writing (27 February 1829)[51] to compose five more operas over the next ten years for a fee of 15,000 francs each, with "the guarantee that his 6000 franc regular salary become a life pension, independent of the new operas promised." Two months later, Rossini had not been granted his financial request. On 10 April 1830, he took time out from rehearsing for *Guillaume Tell* to write to the minister of the King: "My musical career has been quite full from all points of view. I do not have the need to further it, and nothing would prevent me from going back to my homeland to enjoy a sweet retirement."

Whatever the true reasons of Rossini's decision to stop composing after *Guillaume Tell*, his last score opens a new era in the history of French opera. Some of the dilettanti who had been praising the maestro since his debut at the Théâtre italien in 1817 were probably surprised or even disappointed by their idol's new style. It did not matter. Rossini's French operas captured another audience, those who had remained faithful to the tradition of the French grand opera and suddenly found it again embellished and adorned with new marvels in *Guillaume Tell*. In a letter dated 11 August 1869, Gounod, a fervent admirer of Rossini, stated that "*Guillaume Tell* and the French version of *Moïse* belong, at their best, to Gluck's operatic tradition, especially in the recitative and declamatory parts." It is indeed obvious that the choruses, the tutti, the orchestration were more substantial and more powerful than his preceding works without once losing their *bel canto* charm or brilliant vocal virtuosity. This harmonious synthesis of elements from the French and Italian operatic traditions was never used for its own sake, but had a dramatic purpose that was a sensation for the Paris public between 1825 and 1830, as unlikely as that seems today. In his thesis on *L'idée et l'influence de la musique chez quelques romantiques* (The Idea and the Influence of Music on Some Romantic Authors), Francis Claudon appropriately wrote that instead of "simple decorative devices, a new theatrical language was being inaugurated," the new language of romanticism. This time, Rossini's ultimate metamorphosis directly opened the way to the great masters of nineteenth-century French opera. In turn, this metamorphosis had been prepared for a long time before Rossini by other composers whose works define the history of opera since 1800. Such a revolution in sensitivity and taste could not have taken place one day; it took much trial and error to achieve.

The Opéra-Comique Theaters

The fact that the operatic repertoire was broken down into specific genres exclusively assigned to certain theaters caused a great deal of confusion after 1789. As a genre, comic opera emerged during the eighteenth century and had become well-defined at the start of the Revolution as a form of musical theater in which singing alternated with spoken episodes. Most often, the subjects were inspired by simple daily life, the intrigues were straightforward, and the outcomes were happy, even after occasional dramatic scenes. Toward the end of the century, the plots turned toward sentimentality or moralizing. With the music of Monsigny, Philidor, and Grétry and the librettos of Sedaine, comic opera displayed all the characteristics of pre-romantic sensibility. The orchestra was light and remained in the background to yield to the melody. The melody had to stay simple and sincere; it alone expressively translated the different emotions moving the characters. The Da capo, multiversed aria, related to the romance, was one of the favorite vocal forms of comic opera composers.

From 1789, the profile of this genre began to evolve in an unexpected way, short of completely disappearing. Grétry, the master of pre-1789 comic opera, continued to produce a few works; *Lisbeth* in 1797 was based on a novel by Florian; *Elisca ou l'Amour conjugal* (Elisca, Or Marital Love) in 1799 brought the composer an on-stage ovation and was revived in 1812 during the Empire with extraordinary success. After Grétry's death in 1813, many of his works continued to be performed in spite of frequent and severe attacks from the critics. Public taste was changing, and some of the audience no longer appreciated this kind of moving simplicity, then considered out of fashion. Romanticism was calling for stronger emotion. Grétry's *Guillaume Tell* was an occasional work of 1791, filled with praise for revolutionary virtues. It was again revived in 1828 at a time when Rossini's *Guillaume Tell* at the Opéra was much talked about. The anti-Rossinists, led by Berton, had decided to oppose the Italian composer with a nationalistic work. The government press questioned the validity of this revival in the following terms: "Do we really want again to have a National Assembly, national theaters, and national works?"

Although some operatic works did pursue *mutatis mutandis* the comic opera tradition in the style of Grétry, until 1830 and beyond, this genre underwent some deep transformation, beginning as early as 1790. The composers responsible for this were of the new 1790 generation: Cherubini, Le Sueur, Méhul, and Berton. These young composers were unsuccessfully trying to gain access to the Paris Opéra, offering works that were not selected. So in order to have them performed, they fell back on the only other operatic theaters accessible in Paris at that time: Favart and Feydeau. From this point of view, the decade between 1790 and 1800 was decisive for the evolution of comic opera. At a time when the Theater of the Republic and the Arts was dormant and refused to renew its repertoire, all Paris operatic activity was concentrated in these two so-called secondary theaters. All the masters from the younger generation reaped their first laurels on these two stages, although comic opera did not remain as homogeneous a genre as it had been prior to 1789. Before studying this new repertoire, I shall first describe the story of the two theaters that enabled these young composers to be recognized and also gave, outside the Paris Opéra, a remarkable impetus to French opera.

From the Old Monarchy the Revolution inherited Salle Favart, an opéra-comique theater built in 1781 at the corner of Rue Favart, Rue Marivaux, and the future Boulevard des Italiens. The theater, designed by architect Heurtier, could seat around 1200. It was built especially for the Opéra-Comique company, itself the result of the fusion in 1762 of the Opéra-Comique de la Foire (Comic Opera of the Fair) and the Comédie-Italienne. Although the title of Opéra-Comique had officially replaced that of Comédie-Italienne in 1780, the old name often remained and is a source of confusion for historians. For a long time, even after 1789, the name of Opéra-Comique, Salle Favart, or simply *Les Italiens*—even though it was anything but an Italian company—were used interchangeably in the press.

The Théâtre italien, which will be examined in detail, was created in 1789 and placed under the protection of the Count of Provence, Louis XVI's brother. It was named Théâtre de Monsieur and was authorized to present different genres: vaudeville, comedy, Italian opera buffa, and French opéra-comique. After it had been in two or three theaters that proved unsuitable, it was moved in 1791 to a new theater by architects Legrand and Molinos especially built on Rue Feydeau, very close to the Grand Opéra as well as to Salle Favart. This modern theater was larger than Salle Favart and could seat around 1800. With its rich Pompeian architecture and its outside porch giving shelter to the spectators as they got out of their carriages on rainy days, the Feydeau theater quickly became one of the most fashionable places in this Right-Bank district known for its theaters, promenades, gardens, and attractions of all sorts and crossed by one of the most lively Paris streets, the Rue de la Loi (formerly Rue de Richelieu).

Italian singers were part of the cast of Feydeau to provide opera buffa. When foreigners had to leave Paris from 1792 to 1801, the theater management rapidly had to build up a more substantial French repertoire. Naturally, it could not present grand opera productions and had to limit itself to comic opera, so for about a decade the Feydeau company competed with the neighboring Favart company. This was a productive, lively, and loyal rivalry, as in the days of the Molière company and that of the Hôtel de Bourgogne. The companies borrowed subjects from each other so that two *Lodoïska*, two *Paul et Virginie*, two *Roméo et Juliette*, and two *Télémaque* were heard. When Feydeau had considerable success with Le Sueur's *La Caverne* in 1793, Favart soon replied with *La Caverne* by Méhul, and one of its characters, Gil Blas, singing the following final vaudeville:

> *Sur la scène avec avantage*
> *Un Gil Blas déjà s'est montré.*
> *Moi, comme lui, fils de Lesage*
> *Un peu plus tard j'y suis entré.*
>
> *Il a recueilli l'héritage:*
> *Sera-t-il le seul fortuné?*
> *Je respecte fort mon aîné,*
> *Mais je réclame le partage.*
>
> *Messieurs ne me refusez pas:*
> *Tout doit être égal ici-bas!*

> Gil Blas already came on stage
> In a previous successful theater.
> I, too, a son of Lesage,
> Came on a little later.
>
> This most fortunate brother
> Earned his legacy of acclaim.
> With due respect to my elder,
> My fair share I come to claim.
>
> I beg you, Messieurs, to treat me
> In universal equality!

Except for a few cases of desertion, each theater had its own company that was thought to be excellent according to some accounts by foreign visitors. In 1790 the Favart company included about thirty singers—more than the Grand Opéra at the time.[52] At the forefront were two female stars, Madame Dugazon and Madame Saint-Aubin, two of the most famous interpreters of

French comic opera. Madame Dugazon sang maiden's roles at first, then turned to mothers' roles. According to Madame Vigée-Lebrun, she had "one of those natural talents that seem to owe nothing to studying." She was the ideal interpreter for Grétry but also for Méhul in *Stratonice* and Boïeldieu in *Le Calife de Bagdad* (The Caliph of Bagdad). As for male voices, the young star of the company was the famous Elleviou, who had begun as a baritone and later became a tenor.[53] A young man with an elegant demeanor, he was particularly brilliant in roles of young officers. Among his more than ninety roles, his greatest successes were Dalayrac's *La Maison à vendre* (The House for Sale), Della Maria's *Le Prisonnier* (The Prisoner), Boïeldieu's *Le Calife de Bagdad*, and especially Méhul's *Joseph*, a role he created in 1807. In 1795, the baritone Martin left the Feydeau company for Favart. Famous for his improvisations, he had adopted the Italian style of adding ornamentation to solo arias. Grétry, upon hearing an opera of his sung by Martin, is said to have declared: "I have just attended Monsieur Martin's opera."[54] Elleviou and he were friends and, like him, he sang dozens of roles and had a very long career. He still appeared on stage after 1830, when he was over sixty years of age.

The Feydeau company had fewer stars than Favart, especially after the loss of Martin. Among the men there still remained Juliet, Gavaudan, who came from a family of singers; and Gaveaux. Gaveaux himself was a composer who supplied the theater with a large number of opéras-comiques, including in 1798 *Léonore ou l'Amour conjugal* (Leonore, or Marital Love), a work that gave Beethoven the idea for *Fidelio*. For a female star Feydeau had only Madame Scio, who created Cherubini's *Lodoïska* and *Médée* and who sang the works of Le Sueur and Steibelt. According to contemporary accounts, she had a splendid voice but was not very musical and learned her roles by ear with the help of a violinist playing her parts!

During the Revolution, each of the two theaters had a different political orientation. Favart accumulated patriotic productions and carefully avoided "anything that could have shocked republican ears."[55] A newspaper article of 1793 found that its artists had "captured the meaning of the Revolution." On the contrary, Feydeau was hostile to the new ideas. Aristocrats liked to gather there. Conforming to its royalist origins—formerly théâtre de Monsieur—this theater was increasingly considered by the authorities as a counter-revolutionary meeting place. It was closely supervised by the police. I have found several reports from Revolutionary year IV (1795–1796) proving that the Chouans, Royalist insurgents from the western provinces, disturbed the performances at times. The audience refused to sing along with the revolutionary songs imposed on every theater production by the Directoire.[56]

In spite of many and often long-lasting successes, the two theaters, like most French theaters of the time, operated at a loss. Beginning in 1795, they were forced to close several times for weeks on end. In 1801, the return of Italian singers to Paris to sing opera buffa meant an additional difficulty: there was no place in the capital for three established opéra-comique companies. The artists understood this situation and, after another closedown and an ultimate attempt to compete with the newcomers by presenting Italian works themselves, the two companies decided to merge. The reopening took place at Feydeau on 16 September 1801. On that day, they symbolically presented Méhul's *Stratonice* from Favart's repertoire and Cherubini's *Les Deux journées* (The Two Days) from Feydeau's repertoire. The orchestra, led at Feydeau by La Houssaye and at Favart by Blasius, was turned over to Lefèvre, the brother of Madame Dugazon. The names of these three musicians were frequently encountered since they conducted most of the important concerts in the capital. The new orchestra was reduced to forty members by a new set of regulations on 8 July 1802. The company, which combined the principal singers of the two former theaters, though understandably not without resentment and jealousy, was incorporated as the Comédie-Française. Each actor owned a share,[57] and beginning in 1801, there was only one opéra-comique company in Paris. It took the name Opéra-Comique and settled in the Feydeau theater, although it occasionally went back to Salle Favart in times of renovation, and eventually moved into the Salle Ventadour (1829).

The statutory repertoire of the two theaters was that of opéra-comique, which could only be defined in relation to opera as the combination of singing and spoken text. To define it more precisely would be imposing a musical style through a set of regulations. The only obligation facing composers was to replace the mandatory recitative of the grand opera by spoken dialogue. According to Castil-Blaze, the genre was not identical in both theaters despite common characteristics.

> The Opéra-Comique theater had a reputation to maintain. With its many actors excelling in the art of making their audience laugh, it presented its own repertoire with only a few serious subjects. The

Feydeau company, on the other hand, did not have a previous repertoire and tried to establish its own style. In order to bring forth Madame Scio's enchanting talent, it gave reference to heroic dramas.

This account is absolutely true and faithfully reflects the situation.[58]

The Favart theater had long been devoted to the traditional opéra-comique repertoire: Duni, Philidor, Monsigny, and Grétry. It continued to draw from this older stock for its programs but also took on creations by contemporary composers. The following young masters, among others, made their debut on its stage: Dalayrac, who had begun his theater career just before the Revolution; Solié, who, like Gaveaux, was a singer in the Favart company; Jadin; Della Maria, an Italian composer from Marseille who died prematurely but whose comic opera *Le Prisonnier* (The Prisoner) was premiered at Favart in 1798 by Elleviou and won extraordinary acclaim for half-a-century; Boïeldieu, whose first important work, *Zoraïme et Zulnare,* was premiered the same year; Berton, whose *Montano et Stéphanie* was premiered on 15 April 1799, one of the important dates in the history of Salle Favart and the first big success for a composer who was soon to become one of the masters of the French school. To these more or less known names one must add that of Méhul, of course, the most prestigious of all. It was on the stage of Favart and not at the Opéra, that he made his mark.

When one looks closely at the repertoire performed in Salle Favart between 1789 and 1801, one is astonished by its intense activity, demonstrated by the very large number of productions, while the Opéra did not produce more than two or three new works each year, as has been previously seen. In 1789, for instance, there were no less than sixteen productions at Favart, twenty-three the following year, seventeen in 1793, and so on. Some of these were vaudevilles, of course, as well as short-lived productions of the revolutionary type, but there were also many small, one-act opéras-comiques. Only the provincial theaters matched such feverish activity during that period. While reading Elleviou's biography, one is amazed at the sheer number of new roles learned by singers in a very short time, and for only one or two performances. True, many of these short opéras-comiques contained only one aria, one duet, and one ensemble for each of the actors. As for the spoken texts, they most often described stereotyped situations. Certainly these stars of comic opera were experienced enough to cover up occasional memory lapses and land on their feet.

Compared to the number of actors and the astonishing pace of the performances at the Favart, the Feydeau theater was probably more peaceful but certainly no less satisfying musically. For example, beginning in 1795, a season of annual concerts, among the most brilliant in the capital, were organized there, but the short opéras-comiques were not as frequent as at Favart. The chief "little master" during the decade was Devienne. Also known for his instrumental music, he had several of his opéras-comiques performed at Feydeau. The most famous of these, *Les Visitandines* (about a religious order known as the Visitation) was produced in 1792 and owed its success, at least at first, to political circumstances. The play drew its comic effects from ludicrous situations relating to life in the convents. For instance, a servant would mistake a convent for an inn, and so on. *Les Visitandines* included one of the most famous arias of the time, *Enfant chéri des dames* (The Ladies' Darling Child); after 1800, Devienne was accused—wrongly, in my opinion—of having plagiarized the theme from a Papageno aria in Mozart's *The Magic Flute*, a fact that did not prevent different versions of *Les Visitandines* from being played on Paris stages until the middle of the nineteenth century. But with the exception of Steibelt's one-time Feydeau success with *Roméo et Juliette* in 1793, the theater's greatest claim to fame were the works of Méhul and the operas of Le Sueur and Cherubini, the three most important names in French opera between 1789 and 1800.

At a time when the Opéra survived almost exclusively on the repertoire of Gluck and his followers, it was at Favart and Feydeau that changes began to be felt and future transformations foreshadowed. In fact, if these three young composers worked for both Opéra-Comique theaters, it was probably more by necessity than by personal choice, since, as has been said, the Opéra had closed its doors to them. Although their artistic preference was for the grand opera style rather than for traditional comic opera, they had to conform to the only rule of the genre, namely, to replace recitative with spoken dialogue. This led to the creation of some mixed works, a unique result in the history of musical theater up until then. These were grand operas in the dramatic quality of their librettos and in musical style, but the traditional recitative had disappeared, and the action progressed through spoken dialogue. For the first time, the usual distinctions between different genres were abandoned, and even a certain confusion arose because the titles given to many of the new productions no longer indicated their character. Méhul's *Stratonice* (1792) was called a comédie héroïque, as was Cherubini's *Lodoïska* (1791), although from a dramatic point of view the two works had little in common. Le Sueur's *La Caverne* (1793) was a drame héroïque; Cherubini's *Médée* (Medea, 1797) was simply called opéra, as was Méhul's *Ariodant* (1798) despite the essential differences between them. Le Sueur's *Paul et Virginie* (1794) was the one most closely related to traditional comic opera. It was first produced without mention of any genre and, in its second edition, as drame lyrique. One should notice the absence of the words opéra-comique in the titles of all these important scores. None of this had much significance anymore; after 1789, composers wrote what they wished without concern for traditional classification. A spirit of freedom was undoubtedly appearing in the world of creativity. The sacrosanct respect for genres was abandoned, showing a crack in the old classical form. Artists learned how to free themselves from traditions without a clear break or a systematic rejection of the past and began to express themselves more naturally. As has already been stated, this end-of-century evolution took place smoothly and without any iconoclastic frenzy.

From the major works produced at Favart and Feydeau between 1790 and 1800, it is just about impossible to draw any general, common tendencies because their extreme diversity prevents any classification. Indeed, Méhul, Cherubini, and Le Sueur worked separately. There was no school, no leader. Each composer searched and innovated, turning around without hesitation to start anew if he felt it necessary. Librettists were free to choose their themes. Cherubini's *Médée* was probably the richest work of the decade. For its libretto, Hoffmann, faithful to Gluck's tradition, borrowed directly from Euripides. Méhul's *Ariodant* and Berton's *Montano et Stéphanie* were inspired by Arioste. Le Sueur's *La Caverne* was drawn from an episode of Lesage's *Gil Blas* and told the story of an eighteenth-century couple of Spanish nobility imprisoned by thieves. It is an extremely violent, modern drama, at times full of realism. A pitched battle takes place right on stage, and gunshots can be heard everywhere. But this violence is tempered by a happy ending—unlike *Médée,* which refused the academic apotheosis of a final ballet and was probably one of the first operas to end tragically— and by a few light ariettas with often ambiguous lyrics, in the purest tradition of comic opera before 1789. Following the same lines, Méhul's *Ariodant* shows the juxtaposition of great, dramatic, highly developed arias,

with heavy orchestration including trombones, trumpets, and timpani—
such as Ina's aria in the second act

with pleasant romances with verses, limited harmonically to the opposition
of the major and minor modes. The highly heterogeneous character of
some of the large works produced at Favart and Feydeau foreshadowed the
mixed genres later conceived by romantic operatic composers. On the contrary, the two *Lodoïska*—one by Cherubini produced at Feydeau in July of
1791 and the other by Kreutzer produced at Favart in August of 1791—are
true dramas from beginning to end. The action takes place in a sinister
region in of Poland exposed to invasion by the Tartars. This somber melodrama abounds in tragic and violent situations, such as the destruction by
fire of the castle in the final act. But it has a happy ending: the fair

Lodoïska, kept prisoner in a tower, is finally freed by her beloved. As for Cherubini's *Les Deux Journées, ou Le Porteur d'eau* (Two Days, or The Water Carrier), one of the major French opera successes in Europe in 1800, it was also very dramatic and filled with episodes bordering on melodrama. The action is supposedly taking place during the rule of Cardinal Mazarin, but the libretto was really inspired by the humanitarian philosophy inherited from the Revolution and focused on the theme of the brotherhood of mankind that was so common in literature and the arts.

On the contrary, Méhul's *Stratonice* and *Ariodant* are based on plots with little substance. These are dramas of love and jealousy, devoid of exterior or secondary episodes. From this point of view, *Stratonice* resembled *Mithridate*, but in a more bourgeois character. In this work, the influence of Diderot's aesthetic theories can be felt. The drama became humanized: father and son are rivals, but when the father learns the truth, he generously makes way for his son. Unlike some librettos of the time, which already included melodramatic action and marked the nineteenth-century debut of romantic opera, those of *Stratonice* and *Ariodant* were in a wholly classical vein and focused almost exclusively on the passions of the characters. Added evidence of this tendency can be seen in the intentional simplicity of the sets: a bedroom with an old-fashioned bed in *Stratonice*; a palace, a gallery, and a garden in *Ariodant*.

The librettos showed a great variety of inspiration during that period, and there was increased musical unity insofar as every composer, following Gluck's model, was primarily seeking to express psychological truth. This was probably the common feature of all these operas. In Méhul's words, "never will taste demand that truth be sacrificed to the graces."[59] This important concept of the graces represented the visual aspect of the production, as well as the seductive quality of the *bel canto* phrase, regardless of the words associated with it. It was from that period, indeed, that French critics began to compare *musique savante* to *musique chantante* (learned music and singing music). Some of the audience could never really accept that pleasant and easy musical phrases would no longer be heard at Favart or Feydeau; they considered this repertoire as learned, although it was anything but *musique savante* in the usual sense of the word. The defenders of melody and the chantant gathered at the Théâtre italien around Paisiello and, after the Revolution, Cimarosa and Mozart. It is well known that Stendhal himself was always comparing the chantant and savant styles and regarded Méhul as the perfect representative of the latter. As Fétis rightly pointed out in 1791, "Méhul and Cherubini had just produced a musical genre filled with the kind of energy to which, perhaps, grace was a little too much sacrificed."[60]

This characteristic was already apparent in Cherubini's *Lodoïska* (1791), which opened new perspectives for French musical drama. While pursuing his search for true expression, Gluck could not have foreseen that his admirers—if not his disciples—one generation later would literally take up his aesthetic principles by aiming primarily at the free representation of human feelings before addressing problems or finding solutions regarding form. In this desire to place human concerns systematically in the forefront, one can see a kind of expressionistic sentimentality that already foreshadowed, though still faintly, some aspects of romantic aesthetics. From this point of view, works like Cherubini's *Lodoïska* or Le Sueur's *La Caverne* undoubtedly revealed above all a search for expressive intensity. In *La Caverne*, one has only to observe the syllabic and vigorous choral writing or the so-called incorrect or incoherent harmonic progressions to underscore the importance of a word or an idea. Classical forms clearly began to be dismantled, but this transformation took place, at least at first, in the name of a deeper search for true expression.

Cherubini and Méhul gave the orchestra a leading dramatic role that neither Rameau, despite his complex harmonic theories, nor Gluck, following his ideal of a true drama, had ever assigned to it. On occasion, Méhul developed certain motives, as in *Euphrosine and Coradin* (1790), in a way that is much closer to a symphonist's technique than an operatic composer's. The dimensions that he and Cherubini gave to their overtures are well known. Méhul's Overture to *Le Jeune Henri* (Young Henry, 1797), a sort of *symphonie de chasse* (a hunting symphony), has been performed all over the world. As for Cherubini's overtures, Hans von Bülow wrote that they would be played "at every time and place where instrumental concerts would be presented." Although his prediction may not have been realized, it remains certain that many of the larger works produced at Favart and Feydeau were certainly known and appreciated in their time in Germany, where they were rightly considered to be exemplary of contemporary French opera. In Vienna, Beethoven closely followed the new Paris productions. In 1803, for example, both rival companies of the Austrian capital— *An der Wien* and the *Am Kärntner Thor* theaters—presented a different translation of Le Sueur's *La Caverne*. A critic wrote: "The final scene was truly bloody. About forty gunshots were fired at such close range that one really thought heads were being shattered. Tremendous applause followed."[61]

Of all Feydeau productions with any kind of influence on their time as well as on later developments of opera, the most original was Cherubini's *Médée* (Medea, 1797). It was indeed a full-scale tragédie lyrique, where spoken dialogue necessarily took the place of recitative. However, what was customary and completely accepted as part of light action in a traditional comic opera became a much more delicate matter in the case of a tragédie lyrique. It was perhaps on this point that the attempt to merge different styles proved impossible to realize. *Le Censeur des journaux* (The Censor of the Newspapers) dated 14 March 1797 reflected the surprise of part of the audience:

> We have already noted how ludicrous it is to speak and sing alternately in dramatic situations. We cannot help being surprised and upset by ordinary spoken language following a great aria, and no less surprised to hear an actor suddenly start singing on a high note after a quarter-of-an-hour of familiar conversation. These sudden transitions numb our interest, whereas recitative could have concealed their absurdity.

Hearing *Médée* in the original French version would be a fascinating revival from the historian's point of view. A later Italian version of the work for which Lachner wrote new recitative in 1854 is still interpreted nowadays by a few great female operatic stars.

Ten years prior to Spontini's *La Vestale*, *Médée* was an important landmark. The subject did not scare away the public, for it had the authority of Ancient Greece and Euripides. Yet the excessive passions expressed, the paroxysm of the heroine's fury, the violence of the music—especially in the vocal writing—were unheard of in music drama. It was not without good reason that Wagner considered this score "grandiose" and Brahms saw in it perhaps "the greatest work in the operatic repertoire." As the synthesis of Gluck's theory of true expression and the new ideal of a more ardent, vibrating—in short, more human—type of opera taking shape from 1789, *Médée* was truly a transitional work. In this work, antiquity was not represented exactly as it had been, either in the classical manner or by Gluck. Fate, which weighs heavily on the hero and consumes him, reminds us eerily of the blind Destiny that some romantic outcasts hopelessly confronted. In 1807, *La Vestale*, another great masterpiece of French opera, also exploited an ancient classical subject from a new perspective and with musical originality, although probably with less dramatic substance than *Médée*.

In spite of false appearances, an aesthetic transformation was taking place in the way classical antiquity was interpreted. Gluck could not have imagined that his artistic revolution in the name of truth would bear such consequences and that by the end of his own century some of his followers, bolder than himself, would take his theory so much further. In a way, he was responsible for a transformation that he had neither wanted nor foreseen. Classical aesthetics were toppled at the turn of the new century in the name of principles that he himself had defined, although without always being fully aware of all their potential. Indeed, the romantics made no mistake in consistently referring to him with veneration, Berlioz and Wagner included.

One can see from this what an important role the Favart and Feydeau theaters played in the evolution of French musical theater during the final years of the eighteenth century. Aside from their activities in the field of traditional comic opera, which they continued to carry out, they also served as experimental stages for young, talented composers who wanted to try out new forms. Some of these attempts turned out to be decisive for French opera.

The merging of the two companies in 1801 obviously reduced the opportunities for the performance of new compositions. Besides, it was at this time that the Paris Opéra seemed to awake after several lethargic years. The stage of the Imperial Academy of Music was again made accessible to some of the masters, who for ten years had demonstrated their talents at Favart or Feydeau, and it was there now that the destinies of French grand opera would be decided.

Méhul remained faithful to the Opéra-Comique. Starting in 1801, he produced several different types of works, though they were much closer to the new romantic literary and dramatic themes than those of eighteenth-century French comic opera. An exception was *L'Irato* (1801), dedicated to Bonaparte, a "one-act opéra-bouffon" that was a sort of pastiche using the characters of commedia dell'arte. On the other hand, *Héléna* (1803), for example, exemplified the troubadour style, and the trumpet fanfare interrupting its overture may have given Beethoven the idea for his *Fidelio* overture. *Uthal* (1806) was inspired by the Ossian epic. Produced as an answer to Le Sueur's *Ossian* previously presented at the Opéra in 1804, this drama had nothing to do with comic opera. In order to darken his musical colors, Méhul simply did without violins in the orchestra. According to Gossec, this opera needed "a musical score that would not suggest a so-called opéra-comique."[62] And finally, *Joseph* (1807), to this day the most famous comic opera of the imperial period, had a Biblical theme. The success of this opera is surprising for the time, given the imperial society's preference for pompous evocations of Greek and Roman Antiquity over the patriarchal simplicity of the Old Testament. Le Sueur would learn that lesson two years later when presenting the beautiful score of *La Mort d'Adam* (1809) at the Opéra. Contemporary to Le Sueur's oratorio series—*Ruth et Booz, Ruth et Noémi*, and so on, all intended for the Tuileries Chapel—Méhul's *Joseph* was a kind of Biblical oratorio already foreshadowing Berlioz' *L'Enfance du Christ. Joseph* was totally off the beaten track of comic opera of the time: the very simple action devoid of amorous intrigue; a single character, that of Benjamin, scored for a female voice; the modal writing as a device to give an archaic quality to the music; even the famous romance, which is not as simplistic as it appears. This score, which exudes from beginning to end an atmosphere of great tenderness, was always praised by the romantics, whose poetry relied heavily on Biblical inspiration. Berlioz thought it remarkable, of course, although he felt that "its simplicity carried to such limits as are dangerous when approached so closely." Weber had words of praise, as did Wagner, who had the work performed in Riga in 1838 and claimed that *Joseph* "transported him into a superior world." To Champfleury on 16 March 1870, Wagner wrote further of his admiration for Méhul: "This great artist I include among my mentors. His life and compositions are not known nearly well enough in France." Wagner cited *Joseph* among the operas he wanted to see produced in the first phase of his plan to "build in Paris an international theater where great works from the various nations would be produced in their original language."

Méhul was the most original but not the only composer to supply works to the Opéra-Comique after 1800. His contemporary, Catel, whose name appeared on the bills of the Opéra at that time, presented several works at the Opéra-Comique but never won the public's favor. The most interesting ones were *L'Auberge de Bagnères* (The Inn at Bagnères, 1807) and *Wallace ou le Ménestrel écossais* (Wallace, Or The Scottish Minstrel, 1817). The former was subtitled *Comédie mêlée de chant* (A Comedy Mixed with Singing), and the latter, based on Scottish folklore and taking place at Bothwell Castle, was called opéra-héroïque. In Catel's works, the spoken dialogues were reduced and the music expanded. The harmonic base was richer, the style was more elevated than in traditional comic opera, and the orchestration was often very heavy. For instance, in the first act of *Wallace*, the minstrel sang the traditional comic opera romance but was backed by the full orchestra—with harp, trumpets, and timpani!—which completely altered the usual style of the romance.

Another "scholarly" composer, Henri Montan Berton, the son of the former director of the Paris Opéra, brought to the Opéra-Comique repertoire a large number of works, some of which were successful for a while. Berton was a professor of composition at the Conservatoire and a member of the Institute and was fiercely opposed to Rossini during the time of the latter's successes in Paris. It is unfortunate that no modern study has yet been done of this important but unknown figure of French music between 1789 and 1830. Most of his activity was in the operatic field, at the Opéra as well as the Opéra-Comique. Berton's style, like that of his contemporary Le Sueur, bears a strong individualistic mark. Like Le Sueur, Berton was an academic and an official composer of the Empire and the Restoration. Unlike Le Sueur, Berton left a very large body of works—several dozen operas and comic operas—much of which is of questionable interest. He succeeded at the Opéra-Comique with *Montano et Stéphanie*, which premiered at Salle Favart in 1799, although the audience first booed the piece because a church setting and the character of a bishop were included in the second act. When it was revived in 1801, *Montano et Stéphanie* had a long run in Paris, in the provinces, and in foreign countries. It is a comic opera based on Arioste, like Méhul's *Ariodant*, and a sort of melodrama dealing essentially with jealousy. Also in 1799 Berton produced *Le Délire* (The Frenzy), even closer to a drama than a comic opera; in 1803 he produced *Aline, reine de Golconde* (Aline, Queen of Golconda), a subject already used by Monsigny during the Monarchy, and soon after by Boïeldieu in Saint-Petersburg. In the latter work, Berton opened the door to dream and fairy tale: from one act to the next, the action moves from an imaginary East to the landscape of Provence. There was an obvious search for local color effects in this score, with more poetry and less seriousness than in the previous works, and a heroic pastoral style more commonly associated with comic opera.

This brief survey demonstrates the various directions taken by composers of comic opera after 1800, and confirms that Méhul, Catel, and Berton did not intend to perpetuate the tradition of Grétry and the Old Monarchy. Each of them in his own way gave comic opera a dramatic as well as musical character that it certainly lacked before then. The new generation of composers all turned away from the style of comedy mixed with ariettas and tended to reduce the gap between opera and comic opera.

This does not mean that the eighteenth-century tradition fell into neglect. It was revived by another group of composers, less ambitious yet continually successful until 1830: Dalayrac; Nicolo; and, later, Boïeldieu, who established himself as the leader in this genre until the end of the

Restoration. Dalayrac ended his career soon after 1800. His works were light and graceful, giving priority to melody over orchestration and harmony and still leaving an important part to spoken dialogue, and they remained fashionable well into the early part of the nineteenth century. With good renditions by credible singers and actors, these works won over an imperial audience that usually preferred considerably flashier productions. In 1802 at Feydeau, the German composer Reichardt saw *La Maison à vendre* (The House for Sale), one of Dalayrac's greatest successes (along with *Adolphe et Clara* in 1799) and was entranced by the acting and voices of the lead singers—Madame Dugazon, Elleviou, and Martin. "It is not an exaggeration to say that often and even during the comic scenes, the perfection of this performance moved me to tears." In *Adolphe et Clara* it was Madame Saint-Aubin's turn to star with Elleviou. The same Reichardt, who in his lifetime saw many productions throughout Europe, did not hesitate to write: "They gave me the most refined enjoyment that can be experienced in a theater. Their graceful, distinguished, and natural performances were irresistible, and their vocal technique was perfectly suited to Dalayrac's fine score."[63]

This perfect harmony between a company of singers and actors, a composer, and the audience, can be seen again with Boïeldieu after his return from Russia in 1811. The Maltese composer Nicolo Isouard's quick success in the meantime was short lived and never really threatened Boïeldieu's reputation. Following his return to Paris, the composer of *Le Calife de Bagdad* (1800) and *Ma tante Aurore* (My Aunt Aurora, 1803) went on to write new masterpieces. He never sought to "lead comic opera astray" and never claimed to be a scholarly composer, despite his thorough musical knowledge. His harmonic language was always simple and limited to consonant chord progressions. Nearly the only dramatized sound he allowed himself was the diminished seventh chord. In 1856, Berlioz found this harmony "a bit monotonous" but never tired of praising its grace and "Parisian elegance, well liked and in good taste." Boïeldieu's orchestration was light but always very careful and meant to enhance the vocal line that remained in the forefront. In this sense, Boïeldieu was a disciple of Grétry and Rousseau: a simple song without ornaments was more meaningful and had more dramatic power than a learned and intricate harmonization. What seems quite remarkable to me is that with Boïeldieu, comic opera regained the cheerfulness it had lost at the end of the eighteenth century when it adopted a sentimental and sorrowful character. *Les Voitures versées* (The Overturned Stage Coaches) was composed in Russia in 1808 and presented in Paris in 1820. It was a kind of light comedy with a dialogue that was irresistibly funny in places. Following the premiere in 1812 of *Jean de Paris*, which starred some historical characters in a fantasy medieval setting suggesting the troubadour style, an article in *Le Mercure* stated: "Here is, thank God, a comic opera worthy of the name, at last a lyrical comedy."[64] I think that this sigh of relief is quite revealing of the taste of part of the Paris audience in the early nineteenth century. They came to the Opéra-Comique to be entertained but with the refinement of witty dialogues and light, charming music. In 1825, after the production of *La Dame blanche* (The White Lady), Boïeldieu's ultimate masterpiece, a reviewer in *L'Opinion* made the following excellent comment: "Music and comedy could not be united with more craft and good taste. Monsieur Boïeldieu has solved the problem of their union."

How can the unbelievable success of *La Dame blanche* be explained? It was performed 150 times in one year at Feydeau and 1000 times in Paris by 1864, and it is still performed throughout the world to this day. Upon reading the score, the harmonic simplicity and severe overall unity might seem disappointing, but by setting the action in far-off and misty Scotland, which Walter Scott's novels had recently made popular, Scribe's libretto catered to the public's new taste. Boïeldieu even introduced a Scottish folk song into his score, although it cannot be said that the search for local color worried him much. But the very fine finale to the second act with the auctioning of the castle is really enjoyable. The animated dialogue and well-crafted vocal ensembles in which the characters are affected by conflicting emotions seem to foreshadow some of *Falstaff's* or *Gianni Schicchi's* farcical scenes. Above all, it may be the irresistible grace of certain melodies that has won over generations of audiences that love vocal music. One could almost say that Boïeldieu became the best representative of a certain form of French *bel canto* just as Rossini triumphed at the Théâtre italien.

During the Restoration, some new names besides Boïeldieu's appeared at the Feydeau theater: the Italian Carafa, who made his debut in 1821 with his historic drama *Jeanne d'Arc* (Joan of Arc); Auber; and Hérold.

Esprit Auber began by following Grétry's tradition. After 1820, he was for a time influenced by Rossini. He began to meet success only when he teamed up with Scribe, a collaboration that was productive and long lasting. One of the best productions at the Opéra-Comique by these two authors was *Fra Diavolo* (1830), a kind of musical comedy that curiously mixed French comic opera tradition, such as some very simple romances, with the influence of Rossini, detected in the vocal ornaments in some of the solo parts. Auber's career extended far beyond the Restoration. After

1830, this composer, more skillful than profound, acquired an international reputation. He was considered to be the master of French opera and comic opera, although comic opera began to change under his influence. Unlike his predecessors, his aim was first to please his audience, even if it meant giving up true psychological characterization, which had been, from Grétry to Boïeldieu, the first priority of the French masters.

Although a student of Méhul's, Ferdinand Hérold turned out to be Boïeldieu's spiritual successor. After a string of failures at the Opéra-Comique, he finally met with success there with *Marie* (1826). He was thirty-five years old then and would live only another six years. The score of *Marie*, completely forgotten today, is a product of many influences. The action takes place in a Swiss mountain setting in the best tradition of Rousseau. A young orphan girl, Marie, and Count Adolphe are in love. Barcaroles with verses and romances are sung in succession until, suddenly, the tone changes. Marie's great aria at the end of the second act is truly romantic; stylistically it belongs after Rossini and Weber and right before Bellini. The study of both of Hérold's best works, *Zampa* and *Le Pré aux clercs* (The Clerks' Meadow), produced in 1831 and 1832, reveal that this composer has been unjustly neglected and is a real master with many original ideas. Ongoing research into his works should determine his exact place in the history of comic opera; he was its best representative during the very first years of romanticism in France.

In order to complete this summary of the Paris operatic scene during the Restoration, I should mention that a few theaters other than Feydeau occasionally enjoyed the privilege of presenting operatic productions for a limited time. From 1820 until 1824, the *Gymnase dramatique* (located on Boulevard Bonne-Nouvelle) was authorized to hold performances of works from the Opéra-Comique repertoire provided that they be in the public domain and condensed to one act. Thus, several older comic operas were heard, including, in September 1821, Méhul's *Le Trésor supposé* (The Presumed Treasure), which had been written in 1802.

More interestingly, the Odéon theater was active in the operatic field from 1824 to 1828. During that time, it was able to present not only comic operas, but also "works chosen from the German and Italian repertoires." Many of Grétry's and Dalayrac's popular comic operas that were no longer performed at the Feydeau theater were presented clear evidence of their lasting success during the Restoration. Condensed versions of several Mozart and Rossini operas were also billed. It was also at the Odéon theater that Weber's *Der Freischütz* was presented to Parisians for the first time on 7 December 1824, although it had been mutilated by Castil-Blaze's adaptation under the new title of *Robin des bois* (Robin Hood). On 17 November 1825 followed another work of Weber's, *Preciosa*. Finally, in March 1826, a name still nearly unknown in Paris appeared on the Odéon theater bills: that of "Monsieur Mayer-Beer," whose *Marguerite d'Anjou* was presented, arranged for the French stage with sets by Cicéri.

Such was the history of French comic opera during the forty years that ranged from Grétry to Hérold. It was marked by such widely differing endeavors as Cherubini's *Médée* and Boïeldieu's *La Dame blanche*. The fact that these works have been discussed under the same chapter heading is not really significant. It must be restated that this disparity naturally was found not only in individuals but also in the institutions. Indeed, in spite of a profound change of mentality, the distinction between the genres—imposing spoken dialogues at the Opéra-Comique and rejecting them from the Opéra—continued into the nineteenth century well beyond 1830. This distinction remained artificial, as evidenced by the tragédies lyriques performed at the Opéra-Comique at Feydeau between 1789 and 1801, often under whimsical titles. The repertoire of the Opéra-Comique attracted a very faithful audience until 1830, despite all the mishaps that often altered it almost beyond recognition. In 1827, Fétis noted in his *Revue musicale*: "Comic opera is decidedly the type of entertainment the Parisians are fond of." Thanks to further transformation, its success was to last another century or more.

Surprisingly, French comic opera of the Revolution, the Empire, and the Restoration stirred great interest among romantics throughout Europe. Already at the end of the eighteenth century, Beethoven knew and often admired a repertoire that quickly spread to Vienna. There are countless testimonials—many of them superlative—to French comic opera from Weber, Schumann, Liszt, and Wagner. Often the German romantics went so far as to equate the spirit of comic opera with the spirit of France. This is precisely what Schumann meant when commenting on Boïeldieu's "masterpiece" *Jean de Paris* in 1847: "*Jean de Paris*, [The Marriage of] *Figaro*, and the *Barber*, are the primary comic operas in the world if for no other reason than they mirror the nationalities of their composers." As for Wagner, he found in Boïeldieu "the vivaciousness and natural grace of French *esprit*."[65]

The names mentioned in this chapter represent only a small number of all the composers who contributed to the repertoire of comic opera between 1789 and 1830, and only a few of them are still universally recognized today. As I wrote before, the role of the music historian cannot be limited to the analysis and study of universal masterpieces. It is at once more modest and more ambitious in its effort to capture in contemporary writings the changes in taste and the various steps in the evolution of sensitivity. With this in mind, the history of comic opera from the Enlightenment to romanticism is exceptionally rich.

Italian Opera

The Théâtre italien and the Théâtre de la Cour

From the time of the Renaissance, the continued presence of Italian artists in France has contributed richly to French culture. An obvious example is the decisive role played by Italian singers who came to France during the seventeenth century at Mazarin's invitation. It was then that Parisians, to their delight, discovered opera and were quick to establish it at home. French opera, newly created in the seventeenth century as a national art, did not necessarily cause a break with or a rejection of Italian opera. On the contrary, a productive rivalry developed between the two countries throughout the eighteenth century. The famous *querelle des Bouffons* (the Buffoons' Quarrel) and, later in the century, the war between Gluckists and Piccinists represent only two of the most important episodes of the long debate on aesthetics that occurred between musicians, philosophers, and encyclopedists. In spite of unavoidable pettiness, there is no question that this debate really did encourage a meaningful search into the function and essence of music.

Without going into too much detail of these fascinating quarrels, I should like to point out that Italian artists sang their opera buffa repertoire in Paris and in most European capitals throughout the eighteenth century. The presence of foreign companies could only be beneficial for French composers, whether they were imitated or rejected, insofar as it generated some fruitful comparisons. Until the nineteenth century, the bulk of German musical theater was completely unknown by the French, who tend to believe that nothing produced outside their borders is of any worth. By the turn of the eighteenth century, contacts with the Italians had become more and more frequent and close. Italian composers even established themselves in France just before the Revolution (Sacchini, Piccini, Salieri, and Cherubini, for instance) and composed French operas as Gluck had done previously. During the Consulate and the Empire, Paris welcomed Paisiello and then Spontini, and during the Restoration, Rossini, was the idol of the *modernes* and the *dilettanti*. Eventually he composed French operas in Paris and finished his career there.

Toward the end of the Monarchy, several companies of Italian singers performed in Paris. During the summers of 1787 and 1788, Parisians could hear many opera buffe by Cimarosa, Paisiello, Sarti, and Anfossi presented in the most authentic Italian tradition of singing and staging. The success of these performers convinced Léonard-Alexis Autié, Queen Marie-Antoinette's hairdresser, to request a royal privilege in order to open and manage an Italian opera buffa theater in Paris. Thanks to his important patroness, his request was granted on the condition that he pay an annual royalty of 30,000 livres to the Royal Academy of Music, which had expressed concern over this new competition.

The new theater was placed under the joint direction of Léonard and violinist and composer Viotti, an Italian who had settled in Paris in 1782. Pending the construction of a new hall, the theater was established at the Tuileries under the patronage of the Count of Provence, brother of Louis XVI, hence its name *Théâtre de Monsieur*.

The theater was inaugurated on 26 January 1789, with *Le Avventure amorose* (Amorous Intrigues), an opera by the contemporary Italian composer Giacomo Tritto. It was performed in the Salle des Machines of the Tuileries until December of that year. The following year, the theater used the former Salle des Variétés at the Saint-Germain Fair. Then, beginning on 6 January 1791, it moved to the newly built Feydeau theater. The Italian company shared the Feydeau theater with the French opera company, as well as with comic theater and vaudeville companies. In the previous discussion of French opera I have already described the changing fortunes of the Feydeau theater. Léonard prudently left for England in 1791 and was no longer part of this association; Viotti alone remained as head of the company. Under his direction, the Italian company stayed at Feydeau until August 1792. After that date, political events forced it to leave France. During its three-year residency in Paris, it had counted among its members some of the best singers of the time, including two prima donnas, Madame Morichelli and Madame Bandi. The former had already had a long career in Italy prior to making her debut in Paris in 1789. She had been an unchallenged star in most theaters of Italy and later Vienna, especially in opera buffa roles. After 1792, she triumphed anew in London. Da Ponte, while he recognized her exceptional talent, drew a cruel portrait of her in his memoirs: "She was a woman of the theater. She was devoted to the same gods as all of her colleagues. These gods were Greed, Arrogance, and Envy."

As for Giorgi-Brigida Bandi, just as famous as her rival, she had appeared at most European theaters in contemporary Italian roles, and especially at La Scala, where her partner was Crescentini. She was not unknown to the public in Paris, since she had already sung on the stage of the Royal Academy of Music before the Revolution.

The management of the new theater could claim to have hired the best Italian male voices of the time, tenors Viganoni and Mandini. The former was a good friend and interpreter of Paisiello, and the latter was universally recognized for his Cimarosa roles. There was also the basso buffo Luigi Raffanelli, nicknamed the Italian Préville by the Parisians because of his excellent acting.

Thanks to Viotti's efforts to form a company for his theater, for three years Paris audiences were able to hear and appreciate the best Italian interpreters of opera buffa in the works of Paisiello, Anfossi, Cimarosa, Bruni, Sarti, Piccini, and Bianchi to name only those most famous at the time.

Many of them are forgotten today, but their reputations at the time had spread well into Italy. For instance, Mozart himself occasionally composed pieces to be inserted in the opere buffe of some of these composers whose works he knew extremely well. In 1783 he composed several arias for Anfossi's *Il Curioso indiscreto*; in 1789 he wrote one aria for Cimarosa's *I due baroni* (The Two Barons) and another for the German adaptation of Paisiello's *The Barber of Seville*. Interestingly enough, this enabled the Paris public to hear for the very first time, although they probably did not know it, a piece written by Mozart for the theater. On 15 June 1789, the Théâtre italien of Paris presented Bianchi's *La Villanella rapita*, composed in 1785, for which Mozart had written a quartet and a trio. The trio, "Mandina amabile," with its A major key and its charming melodic line, curiously foreshadowed "La ci darem la mano" of *Don Giovanni*. During the performance in Paris, did anyone in the audience notice the change from Bianchi to Mozart? Perhaps the conductor. . . .

To conduct his orchestra, Viotti had originally chosen a composer named Nicolas Mestrino, a native of Milan who had traveled throughout Europe and had even stayed in Hungary for a few years at the court of the Esterházy princes. When Mestrino died in 1790, he was replaced by Giuseppe Puppo, a violinist from Lucca who had been for years a professional musician in Spain and in London. These important details are not simply anecdotal. They confirm that from the start the Théâtre italien attracted artists of Italian origin who in the last quarter of the eighteenth century had traveled extensively to all the important music centers of Europe and had thus been exposed to music different from their own and had experienced different traditions and styles. From this point of view, they brought a breath of fresh air to the Paris of 1789. Paris had been much too inward looking; with its natural tendency toward dissatisfaction, there was a temptation to consider itself as the one and only music center of Europe. Parisians were stifled by quarrels that often had nothing to do with music and seemed totally unaware of what was happening elsewhere at the time. One cannot overemphasize the importance of the creation of a permanent foreign opera company in Paris in 1789. A certain form of musical cosmopolitanism began to emerge late in the eighteenth century, and the term certainly applies to these Italian artists.

When peace returned after the Revolution, the Italian artists were called back to Paris. The situation was favorable. The campaigns in Italy had brought the two nations closer together, and the First Consul was a passionate lover of Italian opera buffa. In 1801, a Neapolitan poet living in exile in Paris, Alessandro d'Azzia, published a pamphlet entitled *Sur le rétablissement d'un théâtre bouffon italien à Paris* (On the Reinstatement of Italian opera buffa in Paris), from which the following excerpt is taken:

> With the reinstatement of peace and the lasting tranquillity which it seems to promise, Italian musicians are again encouraged to return to the capital to reap the acclaim which they deservedly received time after time in the past. The alliance formed between the two nations and the long stay in Italy by the French—where they got to know the Italian language and music—lead us to suppose that the new opera buffa will be at least as successful as its predecessors.

In fact, the idea of reopening an Italian theater in Paris seems to have come from the famous Italian diva Giuseppina Grassini, whom Bonaparte often heard and applauded in Italy and even made his mistress for a time in Milan. When she came to join her protector in Paris, this magnificent, unanimously praised Italian contralto remained there for a few years and played an important part in Paris musical life during the Empire. We shall meet her again later on in the book.

Soon after she arrived in Paris, Grassini thought about opening an Italian theater that would present opera buffa as well as opera seria, since the latter was still completely unknown to Paris audience. She detested French opera and kept repeating the same litany about the Théâtre des Arts (the Grand Opéra): "I never go there! I fear too much that it would finally get to me." On 23 August 1800, she wrote to Bonaparte to ask for permission to run the Theater of the Olympic Society at 15 Rue de la Victoire. She never received an answer, and that same request was granted to Mademoiselle Montansier a few months later. The latter set to work with much determination and assigned Italian poet d'Azzia the task of recruiting the best Italian singers of the time.[66]

The only member of the original company of 1789 to return was the basso buffo Raffanelli. The tenor was Lazzarini, then at the end of his career and replaced as early as 1803 by Andrea Nozzari, who was only twenty-five then. He became famous in Paris in the role of Paolino in *Il Matrimonio segreto* (The Secret Marriage). Fétis heard him there and wrote: "From him I first got to know beautiful Italian singing, although according to Garat, he was inferior to Mandini and Viganoni. Few Italian singers suffered more from the unfortunate influence of the Paris Opéra: within one year his voice had lost some of its loveliest high notes and grew progressively weaker."[67] Back in Italy in 1804, he continued singing for twenty more years and created the first tenor roles of several of Rossini's operas, including *Otello* and *Mosè*.

The new prima donna was Teresa Strinasacchi, who was born in Rome in 1768. She was to become one of the music stars in Paris during the Consulate. She won over the Parisians in her favorite role of Carolina in *Il Matrimonio segreto*, which she sang with Nozzari as her partner. However, the composer Reichardt heard her in 1802 in Paisiello's *La Molinara* and found her disappointing in the same role in which she had excelled fifteen years earlier in Prague and Leipzig: "Her heavier figure rules out the title of prima donna that she claims for herself, and no matter how pleasing her voice can be at times, it no longer has the bite and the rich accents that are necessary to bring this music to life."[68] An anonymous journalist in *Le Coup de fouet* (The Whip Lash) wrote another very severe comment about her in 1803: "During her last appearance on stage, even her most devoted friends had a very difficult time recognizing her." In 1805 she left the company of the Théâtre italien, but returned for a time in 1816, in the same role of Carolina. The dilettanti, who gave their acclaim to other Italian stars and particularly the famous Catalani, did not appreciate her. On 20 March 1816, she sang Vitellia in the Paris premiere of Mozart's *La Clemenza di Tito*, and the critics were particularly ferocious toward her. She then had to leave France permanently. As the ideal interpreter of Paisiello, she was the soloist in his grand Te Deum with tenor Lazzarini when the work was performed at Notre-Dame on Easter Sunday on 18 April 1802, celebrating the peace of Amiens.

These were the main stars in the company, which also included about fifteen singers, male and female, all of whom were Italian except for Mademoiselle Rolandeau, a former singer at the Opéra-Comique.

The orchestra was conducted by the Italian composer Bruni, who had settled in Paris in 1780. He was for a while the music director of the Italian company at the Théâtre de Monsieur and, according to a contemporary account, "never had this orchestra better accompanied the voices as under his direction." However, Bruni had to retire in his first year and was immediately replaced by the French composer and violinist Jean-Jacques Grasset, who kept the post for the next twenty-five years. According to a German critic, Grasset recruited the players with a great deal of attention to the wind instruments, thus forming an ensemble "that was the first in the capital."[69] At the same time, we find him also conducting the orchestra performing the concerts of the Rue de Cléry. Much later, in 1830, it is he who was chosen to conduct Berlioz's cantata *Sardanapale*, which won its composer the Rome Prize. Berlioz recounted in his memoirs how a clumsy gesture by Grasset "caused the grand finale with fireworks to fail" and triggered one of his most terrible angry fits.

The conditions were ideal for making this Italian company one of the centers of attention of the Paris musical life. The Olympic theater, which seated over a thousand, was one of the most elegant in Paris. It was decorated in light blue and, according to a newspaper account, "lit like a dancing hall." Built in 1795 by the architect Damesme, it had the unusual feature of a stage that opened onto the outside, allowing for very original stagings with wonderful theatrical effects. According to another contemporary,

> there were vast corridors leading to a very pleasant garden behind the stage, so that the latter could be extended far in the distance in a combination of nature and art. The decor thus represented the far reaches of an immense garden which, once illuminated, offered an enchanting point of view.[70]

Very soon, ticket prices had to be cut in half. They had been fixed at the outrageous amount of fifteen livres when the theater was first opened in 1801, and the company attempted to perform two opere buffe in succession. The evening began at eight o'clock and ended at midnight. The critics reported the audience's weariness, and thereafter it became customary to perform only one opera at the time.[71] For those in the audience who did not understand Italian, the writer Alessandro d'Azzia had a French translation distributed before the beginning of each performance. He claimed that "by knowing the play in translation ahead of time, one can then fully enjoy the charm of the music without paying attention to the words, which are often lost in Italian singing."[72]

The repertoire had not changed much since 1789. Paisiello and Cimarosa remained the two opera buffa composers whose works were most often performed, and Paisiello's arrival in Paris in 1802 as the new director of the Consul's Chapel reinforced his reputation in the French capital. The single work most frequently performed and most liked in the first years of the nineteenth century was certainly Cimarosa's *Il Matrimonio segreto*. It was in fact the work chosen to be performed at the opening ceremony of the new theater on 31 May 1801. Stendhal had a passion for Italian opera and attended the theater's performances regularly when he visited Paris. The following comment is from his journal: "I attended *Il Matrimonio segreto*, which Madame Strinasacchi and Nozzari sang divinely. Both were in voice. The latter repeated the aria "Prima che spunti l'aurora." This was one of the loveliest performances of the work that I have heard. I was most satisfied." Several of Paisiello's operas were also acclaimed at that time, namely *La Molinara* (The Miller's Wife), *The Barber of Seville*, and *La Nina*.

These were a few of the best examples of the opera buffa genre, which has recently been rediscovered. One has only to leaf through a catalog of recent recordings to see that. The plots often appear to be simplistic. They do not contain any surprises, but they always move along briskly. Some of the devilish spirit and the joie de vivre found in the commedia dell'arte was transmitted to many opera buffa librettos. In this sense, opera buffa differs widely from French opéra-comique and very seldom bears the latter's sentimental and moralizing characteristics. A work that illustrated this tendency was Piccini's *La buona figliuola* (The Gentle Maiden), inspired by Richardson's *Pamela*. Most often the librettos were full of life and gaiety—many of them were written by Goldoni—and their first purpose was to please and entertain. Characters were few and, as opposed to those found in opera seria, borrowed from daily life: a maid, a miller's wife, a graybeard. Occasionally, the librettist used professional types—a soldier, a physician—to create caricatures who spoke the Neapolitan or Piedmontese dialect. Arias, duets, and less frequently, vocal ensembles were sung in rapid succession, separated by secco recitatives accompanied by keyboard and cello. The da capo aria was used to slow down the action and gradually disappeared after the mid-eighteenth century. As for the recitative, an article from *Le Journal de Paris* dated 30 October 1801 confirms that what was done in Paris was in the purest Italian tradition: "The Italian recitative is supported only by the bass instrument and the harpsichord. The recitativi obligati are the only ones to be accompanied by the whole orchestra." Spoken dialogues did not exist in opera buffa. All the interest of this music resided in the vocal line, which was often exquisitely charming and best served by a light orchestral accompaniment—strings alone in many cases. The aria "Il mio ben quando verrà" from Paisiello's *La Nina* is one the best models of this type: languid without being sentimental, with its unchanging string triplet accompaniment and its sensual dialogue between voice, flute, and oboe, it is an ideal expression of amorous anticipation:

Of this famous excerpt, everything including the key of F major recalls Susanna's aria "Deh vieni, non tardar" by Mozart. By comparing the two arias, which are, give or take a few years, contemporary, it is easy to see all that Mozart borrowed from the opera buffa tradition of his time and also what he added to it. By the end of the eighteenth century, the opera buffa fashion had spread throughout Europe, from Saint-Petersburg to Madrid. Arias from *Il Matrimonio segreto* or *La Molinara* were being sung everywhere. Beethoven himself found it appropriate to use the theme from the aria "Nel cor più non mi sento" from *La Molinara* and compose a charming set of variations for piano. In the field of opera buffa, Cimarosa and Paisiello were often compared to Mozart—see Stendhal's own critical evaluations—and on occasion found to be superior.

From its new beginnings in Paris in 1801, Italian opera appeared to seek the goodwill of the government. According to the press, in November 1801, Italian artists sang three times in a row a sort of lyric scene called *La Paix* (The Peace), a composition based on an Italian poem by Alessandro d'Azzia. It was obviously intended to celebrate the reconciliation with England during the preparation of the Treaty of Amiens. Under the auspices of the Master of the Gods, Peace united Mars, the protector of French valor, to Neptune, defending Albion with his trident. Such a heroic subject would have been perfect for the Grand Opéra, where such mythological scenes glorifying the regime would frequently occur during the Empire, as has been discussed. It is surprising to find it set to musical themes by Paisiello, Cimarosa, Guglielmi, Mozart, and Winter. Decidedly, the Italian singers did not want to venture outside their usual repertoire, even for this special occasion.[73]

The first years of the Théâtre italien in the early nineteenth century were rough. Administrative and financial difficulties compelled Mademoiselle Montansier, its director, to move it to another location. In January 1802, the company left the Olympic theater for Salle Favart, left temporarily vacant by the Opéra-Comique. Two years later, in July 1804, it ended up at the Louvois theater, located at the present number 8 of Rue de Louvois. This theater was the work of architect Brongniart and, from its inauguration in 1791 until its closure and destruction in 1827, served as the perfect transitional theater. Several of the most important opera and drama companies of the time, several made their temporary home there.

At the Louvois theater, the Italian buffa company worked under a new director, Picard, the future director of the Grand Opéra. They had to share the stage with the Comédie-Française from the Odéon company—which had been working in that theater since 1801—under a new contract that granted them only two nights a week. As soon as the Empire was proclaimed, the Louvois Theater was renamed *Théâtre de l'Impératrice* (the Empress theater, 9 July 1804). This explains why the Italian singers were often referred to as the Empress Theater Buffoons in the contemporary press. They remained there from 1804 until 1808, when they followed their French comrades of the Odéon to the new theater that architect Jean-François Chalgrin had just completed on the location of the present Odéon Theater. (It was destroyed in a fire on 20 March 1818.) There they stayed until 1815, performing three nights a week. For anyone who wishes to trace the Italian singers through the periodicals of the time it is helpful to know that they could be found under three different names: *Théâtre italien*, *Théâtre de l'Odéon*, or *Théâtre de l'Impératrice*.

During the decade from 1804 to 1815, the Italians won wide acclaim despite a few disappointments. This was the time when they added Mozart's masterpieces to their repertoire. Indeed, they were the ones to present successively *The Marriage of Figaro* (1807), *Così fan tutte* (1809), and *Don Giovanni* (1811) for the first time in Paris in the original versions. This achievement itself should suffice to make any theater be remembered by future generations. At the same time, the Italians experienced some difficulty in maintaining in Paris a stable company compromised of the best singers of the time. A German journalist perfidiously stated that if they remained in fashion, it was only because the Imperial family liked their performances![74]

The truth is that Napoleon was wise enough to choose two successive directors who obtained good results: they were the Italian composers Spontini and Paër. Spontini has been discussed at length in relation to the history of French opera. He arrived in Paris in 1803, and immediately had the Italian company present his opera buffa *La Finta filosofa*, which attracted public attention. He became very famous after the Grand Opéra successes of *La Vestale* and *Fernand Cortez* and in 1810 was named Director of the Italian Opera at the Empress theater.

His first concern was to form a first-rate company with the best Italian singers of the time. In April 1812 *Le Moniteur universel* announced: "Monsieur Spontini recruited the most famous names in Italy. He tempted Neapolitan and Roman virtuosi with the prospect of a Paris triumph, and he was successful: the arrival of several new stars has been announced." Around 1812, the opera buffa company included what would today be called an array of "international stars." All of them had sung or were scheduled to sing at the most famous theaters in Europe. Indeed, most of them remained only a few years in Paris. I should point out here that at that time, very few French singers had had the opportunity to establish such an international career. The two leading tenors were Crivelli and Tacchinardi. Crivelli had succeeded Manuel Garcia, father of La Malibran and Pauline Viardot, members of the company of the Théâtre italien from 1808 until 1811. His was a broad and sustained singing technique, with very few ornaments, as opposed to Tacchinardi, who sang all ornaments with wonderful ease. The two basses of the company were Mathieu Porto and Luigi Barilli, one of the few singers to have remained more than fifteen years with the Italian opera of Paris. The two prima donnas were Madame Barilli and Madame Festa. They were rivals and each had their admirers.

A contemporary critic did not hesitate to write: "Madame Barilli far surpasses all her French counterparts." He even added some technical comments, which was very unusual for a critic at that time: "She reaches high D's and high E's without effort. She is able to sing for a quarter of an hour the most difficult passages, not a single note out of tune, or even doubtful or hesitant. She is especially at ease in the bravura arias and goes up and down as accurately as a flute." Unfortunately, it seems that her dramatic temperament, which was unusually rich, was not always served by her perfect technique.[75]

Stendhal, who was at that time the lover of Angelina Bereyter, a singer at the Théâtre italien, was personally acquainted with all the singers of the company. He claimed to have heard Madame Barilli, whom he much admired in *Il Matrimonio segreto*, "sixty to a hundred times." In any case, she is the one who was chosen to sing the role of the Countess in *The Marriage of Figaro*, in its original version, heard in Paris for the first time on 23 December 1807. According to a journalist, she sang "consistently in the spirit of the composer." In November of the following year, all of Paris rushed to the Théâtre italien to hear her again in the role: "Madame Barilli is, in Paris, even more fashionable than Mozart himself. A large audience gathered not only to hear Mozart's music, as divine as it was supposed to be, but especially to hear Madame Barilli's voice, which was even more divine if that is possible. There was a duet (*Sul aria*), which in itself ensured her success."[76] Upon reading the press commentaries of the time about Madame Barilli and her rival Madame Festa, one senses that a new myth was being born, that of the diva. The stories of their whims and successes were told with infinite kindness. Twenty years later, the actresses fighting such a duel would be called Pasta and Malibran.[77]

Nowhere in the voice classifications could one find mention of a baritone, or its French equivalent, such as a basse-taille. In most cases, the opera buffa roles corresponded to a vocal distribution by character types. Every lover is necessarily a tenor, every father and every old man a bass, most often a basso buffo. This rather simplistic classification leaves no place for baritones or noble bass voices, as if men always became comical or ludicrous as they grew older. It was only a few years later that baritones and basses finally acquired their stamp of nobility with the works of Rossini and the romantic operas of Bellini and Donizetti.

From this point of view, it is very significant that when Spontini decided to renew the repertoire of his theater and to present *Don Giovanni*, he gave the role of the seducer to the tenor Tacchinardi. There is no doubt that in 1811 it was he who was granted the honor to sing at the Paris premiere of the original Italian version according to the press. Should we suppose that some of the arias were transposed, or that this tenor had a deep enough lower register to carry the role? There is no mention of this by the critics. In his journal (April 1811) Stendhal wrote about the Italian singer: "Tacchinardi, a beautiful tenor voice with a few notes in basse-taille, but an extremely unfortunate appearance." When, in 1810, the tenor Garcia sang the role of Almaviva in *The Marriage of Figaro*, the press was generally very enthusiastic about Mozart's masterpiece but also mentioned that "of all the actors in the present company, Garcia is probably the best for the role of Almaviva, as actor as well as singer. But no tenor can bring out the full effect of this role, which was conceived in bass clef for a baritone. They are forced to transpose many passages by an octave, which completely alters the harmony."[78] This enables us clearly to understand how it was possible for some artists, such as Lays at the Grand Opéra, to tackle roles in such varied ranges. Scrupulous respect for the written note is a modern concept. Generations of singers considered it normal to adapt the scores to their own vocal abilities.

In 1811, Spontini programmed *Così fan tutte*, which had had its Paris premiere in January 1809. It was magic, and a delight for the connoisseurs, which included the Germans in particular. One of them wrote: "The performance was yet more refined and striking than the one we had formerly heard in Leipzig."[79] Unfortunately, the evening was spoiled in part by the Italians' deplorable habit of inserting pieces foreign to the work being performed. The critic from *Les Tablettes de Polymnie* (Polyhymnia's Tablets) questioned this practice: "The duets "Guarda sorella" and "Prenderò quel brunettino" have an exquisite melody and were very well sung by Madame Barilli and Mademoiselle Néri. Unfortunately, Mademoiselle Néri added to her role a Polacca that paled in comparison to Mozart's music. The fact that most of its passages did not fit her voice only made it worse."[80]

This was not a new practice. On the contrary, it was a tradition well-established in the history of opera buffa. As has been seen, Mozart himself participated by composing arias and scenes to be inserted in works by Bianchi, Cimarosa, and Paisiello. When Cimarosa's *Il Convito* was performed in Paris, some critics were surprised to hear an aria by Guglielmi, another by Marinelli, and a duet by Farinelli, all of which had been inserted in order to give new life to the work. This is clear evidence that within a plot made up of stereotyped psychological situations, the arias were interchangeable. The French, probably seeking stylistic unity and dramatic coherence, were really shocked. Following the performance of Zingarelli's opera seria *La Distruzione di Gerusalemme* (The Destruction of Jerusalem), which included the insertion of an aria by Nasolini, among others, a critic wrote:

> It is well-known that at the Théâtre italien it is customary never to perform a work as it was intended by the composer. They say that it cannot be avoided, and that one might as well get used to it. *La Distruzione* was not spared this strange practice. The overture was by Farinelli, who composed it in Venice for a one-act opera buffa entitled *Il Testamento*. If we are asked why it is that Zingarelli's overture was not played and why a buffa overture was played for a serious opera, we shall answer: it is a mystery.[81]

To remain in the field of opera buffa as it was performed at the Empress theater, I would like to quote yet one more contemporary witness after one of the performances of *The Marriage of Figaro* in November 1810. Mademoiselle Gloria, who sang the role of Susanna, took out the aria "Venite, inginocchiatevi" in the second act but added to her part Cherubino's "Non so più cosa son." A journalist candidly asked why this aria was moved from one role to another, "since it was perfectly well adapted to Madame Garcia, who played the young pageboy with all the required grace and refinement." In addition to being robbed of one of her arias by Susanna, the unfortunate Madame Garcia—who would one day be Malibran's own mother—was also stripped of her second aria by the Countess! Indeed, the latter role was given to Madame Barilli, who simply added for herself the famous "Voi che sapete."

> We must deplore it since in the whole opera this is the aria that she sings the most poorly. She has this thing about adding everywhere and almost in each phrase a sort of grupetto of three little notes, which we must advise her to get rid of. Its effect becomes monotonous, boring, and most tiring. However, she was superb in the two other arias, "Dove sono," and "Sento mancarmi l'anima."

We shall not look for the latter in Mozart's score, since "this is the only foreign aria which they dared introduce in Mozart's work: it is by Mayr. "Fortunately, the conclusion of this report is more reassuring: "This aria certainly does not seem to be at home here."[82] In 1810, *The Marriage of Figaro* was just one opera buffa among a hundred others. There is no reason why it should have received special treatment!

Another custom at the Théâtre italien surprised the French critics. It was the ornamentation practiced by the singers. This was a very deeply rooted tradition in the eighteenth-century Italian vocal schools. The students had to memorize scores of ornaments to be added to their performances. The most gifted and the most musical of them even created their own, different from one aria to another. Some of them, especially castrati, who had incredible breathing powers, had gained international fame with the ingenuity of their ornamentation. The French were not accustomed to these devices, particularly since Gluck's reform, and were surprised by them. About the tenor Nozzari, the press commented that "he placed ornaments with good taste, always varying them and improvising them with self-assurance."[83] This practice, however, could lead to excesses and even completely distort vocal phrases. The tenor Aliprandi, once a member of the company at the Empress theater, had the reputation of embellishing his singing with chromatic scales that were rendered with extraordinary agility. A contemporary critic wrote about him: "His singing remains pure. Although he might occasionally embellish his musical phrases, they are never altered beyond recognition."[84] Coming from a French commentator, this is highly flattering.

I have only dealt with opera buffa so far, since the Théâtre italien had not been authorized to perform any opera seria. Strangely enough, this repertoire had remained foreign to the French in the eighteenth century, whereas it was extremely well received in most of the great European centers during the Enlightenment. Performances of works by composers such as Leo, Hasse, or Jomelli had been banned in Paris by the exclusive privilege granted to the Royal Academy of Music. Only excerpts of their music had been played or sung in the homes of wealthy patrons. It is astonishing to witness French musicians and philosophers of the eighteenth century endlessly quarreling about the respective merits of Italian and French musical styles, when most of them had never attended a stage performance of an opera seria. These quarrels would have been far more valuable if, instead of comparing Rameau's and Gluck's French tragédie lyrique to opera buffa, they had compared it to opera seria, its exact Italian counterpart.

Napoleon knew opera seria, since he had heard it in Italy. It is conceivable that he intended to introduce Paris to this form of Italian opera when he called Paisiello to the post of director of his chapel at the Tuileries in 1802. This is what was implied in the press.

In fact, the buffa company of the Empress theater made a similar attempt in 1805 when they performed an opera seria in Paris for the first time since the seventeenth century. It was *La Ginevra di Scozia* by the Neapolitan Giuseppe Mosca, a mediocre composer who had been established in Paris since 1803, fulfilling the duties of keyboard accompanist and director of music for the buffa company. This attempt was not a success and was not repeated, at least not in this theater.

Napoleon, infatuated with Italian music, hired singers to perform music privately, and appointed the Italian Ferdinand Paër to direct them. Napoleon had met Paër in Germany, where he was working in the service of the King of Saxony. Paër had written numerous operas and, since Cimarosa's death in 1801 and Paisiello's retirement, was considered to be their successor in the field of opera buffa. He moved to Paris in 1807 and remained there until his death during the July Monarchy in 1839. During that period, he played an important role in Paris musical life.

Napoleon hired Paër as director of his private music at a considerable salary of no less than 30,000 francs a year (in 1802, he had offered 10,000 francs a year to Paisiello when he called him to Paris to direct the music of his chapel). Paër's wife was the first singer of the emperor's private music, and she, too, earned an exorbitant salary of 30,000 francs a year. Along with them were gathered some of the most renowned Italian artists of opera buffa: Teresa Strinasacchi, tenors Nozzari and Aliprandi, basses Martinelli and Crucca. To this group Napoleon added the famous Giuseppina Grassini, who had been his mistress in Italy a few years before and had followed him back to France. She was an artist of extraordinary talent, kind but at the same time unscrupulous. She had had immense success on the Italian stages, where she had quickly risen to stardom thanks to her contralto voice and dramatic talent.

She at first appeared in only a few concerts in Paris. After all, she was a foreigner and spoke French poorly, so she had no access to the Grand Opéra. On the other hand, her repertoire was opera seria, so she could not lay claim to a role at the Empress theater, where her colleagues sang opera buffa. She sang in Paris for the first time on 24 July 1800 at the Invalides, which had been converted into the Temple of Mars, on the same day Méhul presented his *Chant de triomphe du 25 Messidor* (Triumphal Hymn of 25 Messidor) for three orchestras. In the presence of her lover the First Consul, she and her colleague Bianchi sang an Italian cantata, *Gloria delle armi, la Cisalpina liberata* (Glory to the army, to the liberated Cisalpine land). Following this concert, *Le Moniteur* wrote:

> It is the first time that Madame Grassini and the citizen Bianchi were heard in Paris. They have come here to contribute their talents to the success of this event and celebrate the glory of the army that reinstated peace in their homeland, ancient Italy, the symbol of a famous past.[85]

When the emperor's private music was organized, Napoleon awarded Madame Grassini the prestigious title of First Singer of His Majesty, The Emperor and King, along with an even more prestigious salary of 36,000 francs a year. No artist had ever received such a sum. For seven years, Madame Grassini kept this title and received her salary, along with other regular compensations.

The emperor's private music included only Italian artists and was at his permanent disposal. They followed him on his campaigns. Ordinarily, they performed at the Tuileries or in Saint-Cloud. The chronicles of the time recount musical evenings where Italian vocal music always held the first place. In 1806 Napoleon also hired for his court the famous castrato Crescentini, one of the last celebrated sopranists in history. He had heard him in 1805 in Vienna, where the internationally renowned singer was the vocal coach of the Austrian Imperial family. What Napoleon had done for Paër and Paisiello he did for Crescentini: he enticed him away from his employer with an offer of a considerable salary. In Paris, Crescentini met again his former partner Madame Grassini, with whom he had frequently sung in Italy. Soon Napoleon grew even more ambitious. Not satisfied to have his private music performed at the Court's concerts, he decided to have a private theater at the Tuileries. He had a room within the castle especially fitted by Fontaine. The stage was placed against the Marsan Pavillion, between the Carousel Court and the Tuileries Gardens. It was from that time, because of the specific disposition of this stage, that theater people began to distinguish *côté cour* (opposite prompter) from *côté jardin* (prompt side), as they still do today.

The *Théâtre de la Cour* (the Royal Court Theater), which was, of course, a private theater, was for a few years the only theater in France where opera seria was performed. All the contemporary commentators agree about the extraordinarily high quality of some of these performances. The most brilliant ones were doubtless those given by Madame Grassini and Crescentini in 1808, when they teamed up at the Tuileries to sing *Romeo e Giulietta* by the Neapolitan composer Zingarelli, whose works they had sung in the old days in Milan. Napoleon and Josephine asked for several repeat performances of this opera. When the Imperial couple traveled to Fontainebleau, they were almost always accompanied by the Court company of Italian singers. Mademoiselle Avrillon, a lady-in-waiting of the empress, left in her memoirs a description of some evenings when excerpts of different works were sung as part of the same performance. According to her,

> The performances at Fontainebleau were more like concerts than operas. Most often, the programs included one act from an opera buffa and one act from an opera seria. This created very unusual contrast for those of us who were not accustomed to these kinds of pastiches, although they were very common in Italy. Since I, as well as many others, did not know Italian, I could only enjoy the quality of the music and the decor. What a bizarre experience it was, after seeing pleasant landscapes at sunrise, garlands of flowers, and shepherdesses, to witness a sudden change of sets and discover Juliet's tomb in the depths of a dark cave.[86]

It was in this last scene of Zingarelli's opera that Crescentini added an aria of his own "Ombra adorata, aspetta," which immediately became famous throughout Europe. Contemporary listeners agreed that this singer's talent was outstanding. Fétis wrote: "There never was more sublime operatic singing and acting." Everyone knows the story—many times told—of Napoleon moved to tears by this altogether extraordinary voice. Not knowing how to express his satisfaction to the castrato, Napoleon decided to award him the title of *chevalier* of the Order of the Iron Cross. The Baroness de Bawr, in her memoirs written much later, also recounted the extraordinary evening performances:

> There are many people still alive today who attended the Court performances in the Emperor's days. They all would have something to say about the opera *Roméo et Juliette* sung by Grassini and Crescentini. Her voice was a magnificent contralto, which she complemented through her hard work with some rather beautiful high notes. Her technique has been completely lost since that grandiose school has ceased to exist and no one now teaches how to place the voice broadly, to pronounce well, and to sing recitatives.

These private court performances had the advantage of attracting the attention of contemporary commentators who were surprised to discover this Italian operatic repertoire. Rémusat and Montesquiou sent a report to the Emperor asking his permission to add opera seria to opera buffa at the Empress theater. Napoleon's reply, dated 4 June 1810, is preserved in the National Archives:

> It is doubtless an excellent project indeed to have an opera seria in Paris, since it would be for the greatest benefit of the public. If at the Odéon, the Empress theater, an opera seria could be established jointly with opera buffa, they would form together a very enjoyable institution. For now I authorize 120,000 francs for such a purpose.[87]

Thus, after having been forgotten for over a century, opera seria was performed in public at the Empress theater in Paris during Spontini's tenure as director. On 30 January 1811, this theater presented Paisiello's *Il Pirro*, created back in 1787 in Naples. Spontini, who conducted the performance himself, had rewritten some of the recitatives for the occasion. It also marked the debut of tenor Crivelli in the title role. He was favorably noticed next to Madame Festa and Guglielmi, son of the composer Pietro Guglielmi and a member of the opera buffa company at that time. It was all very novel to the public of the Théâtre italien: the character of the music as well as the nature of the plot. Mythological heroes took the place of the familiar opera buffa characters. The plot was inspired by Euripides's Greek epic and told of Pyrrhus and Polyxena's unhappy love. In order to complicate the original storyline, the librettist added to it a parallel intrigue between Chimène, a Greek princess, and Daris, a Trojan prince! To cap it all, an aria called "Chi può trovar," from Cimarosa's last opera seria *Artemisia,* which he had composed ten years earlier in Venice, was added to the second act.

Following this great Paris premiere, the reaction of the press was generally very favorable. One could read in *Les Tablettes de Polymnie:*

> The success was complete and well-deserved. The Théâtre italien appeared in all its glory. A great opera by Paisiello, a well-written poem well-fitted to the music, a very talented first tenor, a well-esteemed prima donna, an excellent chorus, magnificent sets and costumes, a beautiful performance with perfect timing: here are the sure means of success in Paris. This new experiment, in spite of one of our colleagues finding it improper, turned out to be very successful. Never did the public seem so fully satisfied.[88]

Spontini's quick temper generated much opposition. Although the company's management was successful during his tenure, he was fired in July 1812, and his post as director of the Italian opera was given to the shrewd Paër, who pursued the double repertoire programming of opera seria and opera buffa. In the very first year of his directorship, he uncovered an aspect of Cimarosa's talent previously unknown in Paris. He presented Cimarosa's opera seria *Gli Orazii e Curiazii* (The Horatii and the Curiatii) in June 1813. Stendhal marveled at some of this opera's arias, especially the famous "Quelle pupille tenere." Madame Grassini sang for the first time the role of Orazia for this Paris production. The cast also included her colleagues Madame Sessi and Tacchinardi, permanent members of the Empress theater company. One month later, on 1 December 1813, Napoleon and Marie-Louise went to hear once more Madame Grassini in a new opera seria, Nasolini's *Cleopatra.* This was the last public performance they attended together in Paris.

The Empire was coming to an end. One could not speak of a true hegemony of Italian opera over the Paris musical scene at that time, as would occur ten years later. Still, thanks to the performances at the Empress theater during these fifteen years, the French public discovered an art form that emphasized the voice and beauty in singing. The human voice became the principal instrument and, more than the words themselves, the true means of expression of the heart over the mind. The voice generated the emotion. Later on, beautiful voices and *bel canto* carried all the prestige for most romantics. Already, this first romantic generation found in pre-Rossini opera buffa what French opera could not provide, namely an emotional refinement that moved their sensitivity. This is what these poets and writers found pleasure in seeking, so they could analyze its most subtle nuances.

Both Chateaubriand and Stendhal were deeply influenced by pre-Rossini Italian opera. Both were fervent admirers of Mozart, Cimarosa, and Paisiello. We have learned that while in America Chateaubriand asked to hear the duets of Paisiello and Cimarosa. In the evening, he listened to his host's daughters sing the duet from Paisiello's *Zingari in fiera*, "with a desert in the background, or against the whisper of a waterfall." According to his host, "this duet was the piece that Monsieur de Chateaubriand asked me to play most often. He would even enjoy singing himself, after I reminded him of the first few notes, 'Il tuo viso m'innamora'." As for Stendhal, in spite of the *dilettanti's* enthusiasm for Rossini, he never disavowed his own initial emotion when he first heard Cimarosa and Paisiello. He wrote the following objective analysis of the feelings evoked by this music:

> Paisiello never moves as deeply as Cimarosa. Never does he generate in the people's souls the images that bring deep, passionate pleasures. His emotions do not rise above grace. But he is excellent at it. His grace resembles that of *Correggio*: it is tender, seldom pungent, but seductive and irresistible.

Already before the end of the eighteenth century La Harpe, a critic with little inclination for romanticism, used the language of Stendhal to express the feelings aroused by a performance of Paisiello's *La Frascatana*, which had followed performances of *Castor et Pollux*, and had been judged cold and boring by comparison:

> Our ears are becoming tired of the *urlo francese* (the French howling), as the Italians call it, and it seems that this revival will be the last breath of French music. This is confirmed by the extraordinary success won the night before by Paisiello's opera entitled *La Frascatana*. It was its fifth performance, yet it was again followed by frantic applause. This work seems to have been composed in one sitting from beginning to end. The music is always active and full of effects. The singing is simply delicious, the finales divine. On

the other hand, the libretto is meaningless, and three-quarters of the spectators did not understand it. It is quite clear that the music triumphed on its own. This art is best understood when carried to such perfection.[89]

This excerpt is important, for it demonstrates the contribution of opera buffa to French pre-romanticism: the spellbinding Italian voices replacing *urlo francese*. It was not important that the plots were often inept and even absurd. The interest resided in the *bel canto*, which could arouse true musical emotion. Music was at last separated from drama. It was moving and pleasing on its own, regardless of the text, which, more often that not, could not even be understood. The Empire witnessed the first signs of the upcoming Rossini revolution and the change in taste. The new generation of dilettanti would focus its attention upon Italian vocal music, the only one using a language directly communicating with the heart, the only one able to move sensitive souls. Even before Rossini's arrival in France, the pre-romantic generation had decided in favor of Italian music.

During the Restoration, the evolution of Italian opera was influenced by the rise of a first-class star who took Paris society by storm. The discovery of Rossini opened a new chapter in the history of French taste and sensibility. His triumph in Paris was not due to simple fashion. During this decade, while the romantic movement was being born, the Rossini phenomenon spread far beyond the music world.

At the beginning of the Restoration, however, the situation was not very favorable to the Théâtre italien. From their exile the Bourbon kings brought home with them a new prima donna almost unknown in Paris, Angelina Catalani, who was originally from the Vatican state. Only thirty-six years old in 1815, she had already performed, like many of her colleagues, in most of the great Italian theaters and in Lisbon, Madrid, and London. In the summer of 1806, she first came to Paris for a few concerts; she then secretly fled to London in order to escape the Emperor's pressing request that she stay in the capital. She remained in London where she was treated like a queen at Drury Lane and Covent Garden. While in England, she made friends among French royalists, and there the future king Louis XVIII heard her sing. It is not surprising that upon her return to France she easily obtained from the new king the privilege to direct the opera buffa company, scheduled to leave the Odéon, formerly the Empress theater. She took the company to Salle Favart which under the name of *Théâtre royal italien* saw her debut in October 1815. Her new administration lasted until April 1818 and was not, overall, a success. Undeniably, it was a time of decline for Italian opera. In her ambition to remain prima donna assoluta, Madame Catalani made poor appointments and soon terminated some of the better members of the company. The only good find that she could be credited for was Joséphine Mainvielle-Fodor. This Paris singer of Hungarian descent had some extraordinary successes for a few years. One of her best roles, as we shall see, was Rosina in *The Barber of Seville.*

Moreover, the new director was unable to maintain quality repertoire in her theater. She programmed many pastiches, parodies, and operas in which the ensemble numbers had been cut and replaced by the famous *concertos de voix* (vocal concerti) that provided an opportunity for her to show off. The only true success won by the theater under her direction was Simon Mayr's *Fanatico per la musica.* This German composer origin wrote dozens of Italian operas. Although he has been forgotten today, he represented for opera buffa the link connecting Cimarosa and Paisiello to Rossini. His reign ended as Rossini's began.

Madame Catalani soon began to appear uninterested in her own theater and left on a foreign tour for several months. She had to resign from the direction of the Royal Italian Theater, which closed down in April 1818 for almost a year. The following statement is from a periodical of the time:

> It has been said that the privilege granted to Madame Catalani for Italian opera has just been withdrawn. For a long time now the celebrated diva has been neglecting her theater and Italian musical masterpieces have been sacrificed to unworthy throats.[90]

The theater reopened only on 20 March of the following year with an opera by Paër, *I Fuorusciti di Firenze.* This time, the Italian company was placed under the auspices of the Royal Academy of Music and moved to the Louvois Theater. It remained there until 1825, at which time it returned to Salle Favart. Paër kept his title of music director, while the general management was handled by the Opéra. From 1 December 1824 until October 1826, he shared the post with Rossini, now settled in Paris. In 1827, the Royal Italian Theater was again granted a separate management. The first director was Émile Laurent, whose tenure lasted from 1827 to 1830. He was not a musician and featured non-musical events and companies in his theater. In October 1827, for instance, he invited an English theater company to the Théâtre italien.

It would be a mistake to think that Rossini met with overnight success at the Théâtre italien. It took him almost three years to win over the French capital.

Born in 1792, Rossini had been an impatient young composer and made his debut in Italy in 1810. By the time he turned twenty in 1812, he was already famous in his homeland. With unusual natural ability as a composer, he composed five operas in the year 1812 alone. His success was established in 1813 with *Tancredi*, an opera seria written for the Fenice in Venice. With it the doors of the great theaters of Italy opened to him. His reputation quickly spread across the border. In 1813, excerpts from some of his operas were published in France by the *Journal d'Euterpe*. In number 9 of this brand-new musical periodical, the composer A. de Garaudé, also a professor of voice at the Paris Conservatoire, presented the cavatina "Quel dirmi, o Dio" from Rossini's *La Pietra del Paragone*, in a voice and piano reduction with the original Italian text. Three months later, another excerpt, the duet "Lasciarmi, non t'ascolto" from *Tancredi*, was published in number 12 of the same periodical. These two excerpts are probably the two very first French editions of Rossini's works. In any case, this music must have been well received, for the famous aria "Di tanti palpiti" from *Tancredi* appeared in 1814 in the same publication and soon became known throughout romantic Europe, along with a duet from *Demetrio e Polibio* that premiered back in 1811 in Rome. In 1816, before the performances at the Théâtre italien, excerpts from *L'Italiana in Algeri* were published in the *Journal d'Euterpe*, which turned out to be an important mouthpiece for the works of Rossini at his debut in France.

From these historical facts we gather that Rossini's name was well known in the French musical circles during the final years of the Empire. Only during the Restoration, however, did the Théâtre italien of Paris agree to produce one of the young maestro's works, and only thanks to its director, Madame Catalani. On 2 February 1817, *L'Italiana in Algeri* opened the series of Paris performances. On the whole, it was received rather coldly by the critics despite a brilliant cast that included four of the most distinguished interpreters of Rossini: Madame Pasta, still unknown in Paris at that time; Morandi; Garcia; and the bass Porto. One might have imagined that this new opera would set all of Paris on fire, but such was not the case. Following the performance, the newspaper *Les Débats* spoke little of the music and denounced a weak libretto: "This opera should be placed in the category of those that cannot possibly be surpassed or even matched in their absurdity." The critic did admit that the finale of act one was "a bit odd in its writing but very cheerful and original." However, he concluded as follows: "One would hope that other works by Monsieur Rossini will make one more appreciative of this modern composer's talent."[91]

It took two more years before the Italians dared to present another Rossini work. Meanwhile, in the same years (1817–1820), the composer obtained brilliant successes in all the great theaters of Italy and kept producing new operas with astonishing ease. We can be sure that Rossini's access to the repertoire of the Italian Opera of Paris was delayed for a while by his compatriot Paër's unwillingness. As we have seen earlier, Paër was the director of the theater at the time and wished to reserve it chiefly for his own works.

At last, on 13 May 1819, a second opera by Rossini, *L'Inganno felice*, was performed in Paris. This opera buffa ran for several weeks in spite of its mixed and generally unfavorable reviews. In the French press just around that time, there appeared the first signs of a nationalistic reaction against the growing Rossini vogue and against this impertinent and irresistible genius's intrusion into French operatic territory. The budding controversy quickly spread beyond the walls of the Théâtre italien of Paris. Here are a few revealing lines from *La Gazette de France* following the premiere of *L'Inganno felice*:

> The music is by Rossini, the famous Rossini who is currently heading a musical revolution in Italy, a decadent one, that is. After many masterpieces have marked, so to speak, the boundaries of an art form and the road leading to perfection, artists who cannot hope to do as well seek to do otherwise. This eagerness to innovate is a confession of their inability. If it is skill and noise that we want, we do not need to import them from Italy."[92]

It all started in the spring of 1819, and the following telling comment seems to announce a new feud between ancients and moderns: "Everything has already been said and they come too late. Mankind has been at it for 7000 years." A few months later, on 26 October 1819, the Théâtre italien produced *The Barber of Seville*, which had had its premiere three years earlier at the Argentina theater of Rome. It was indeed a success but by no means a triumph. The role of Figaro was sung by Pellegrini who had just made his debut at the Théâtre italien singing the role of the father in Paër's *Agnese*, written especially for him. He soon became the idol of the Paris dilettantes. Ironically, the critic of *Les Débats* found his aria from the first act too laborious and tormented." In the Paris première, Manuel Garcia sang Almaviva, the role that Rossini gave him at the world première in Rome in 1816, and Rosina was sung by Madame Ronzi de Begnis, an Italian singer who had been a student of Garat and was making her debut in Paris. She was criticized and did not help make this first performance a success. For the second performance a few weeks later, she was replaced by Joséphine Mainvielle-Fodor. This time, and thanks to her, the success of *The Barber of Seville* and Rossini in Paris was decisive. This singer turned out to be one of the great interpreters of Rossini's music during the Restoration. According to Fétis, she possessed "a faultless intonation, a very pure tone, a perfection of detail, and an irresistible, spell-binding timbre." The second performance of *The Barber* in Paris marked the beginning of the Rossini craze in France. In the first months of 1820, an important segment of the press—all those who defended the moderns and spoke for the dilettanti—began to support him. They wrote of his "fertile inspiration" and his "prodigious talent." Throughout that summer, *The Barber* was a huge success. It was "better and better performed and appreciated, and each time attracted an immense crowd."[93] In May of the same year, *Il Turco in Italia* (The Turk in Italy) was produced at the Théâtre italien and was also very successful. In November, however, an opera semi-seria called *Torvaldo e Dorliska* failed: "The composer of *The Barber* was unrecognizable in this unfortunate work. It caused unanimous boredom that even the most fervent Rossini lover could not have concealed."[94]

The purpose of this volume is not to inventory in detail the premières of every Rossini opera, serious and comic, produced at the Théâtre italien between 1820 and 1830. It would amount to a long list of successes and some smash hits, as reported by the contemporary press. The *Miroir des spectacles* dated 23 February 1821 included the following comment about the Théâtre italien: "The orchestra seats and the balconies are already filled long before the curtain rises. The boxes have not lost a single subscriber, and tickets are still sold on the street for two or three francs above box-office price."

It is true that at the Théâtre italien Rossini was well served by exceptional interpreters, and the famed Giuditta Pasta, who was already part of the 1817 cast for *L'Italiana in Algeri*, naturally belongs at the top of that list. At that time, she was only nineteen and was unnoticed by Parisians. She is the perfect example—more so than all the excellent singers mentioned in this chapter so far—of the modern diva. She was one of the first if not the first of the great mythical figures who have created much turmoil up until the present time. She was from Milan and became famous in Italy at age twenty through a series of successes in Venice and Milan. In 1821, when she was called by the directors of the Théâtre italien and returned to Paris, she rapidly attracted the attention of all opera lovers. Her voice was that of a great soprano, whom we would probably today call lyric-dramatic. She was able to sing not only Rossini roles, such as Tancred and Desdemona, which she created in Paris, but also later roles composed for her by Bellini: *La Sonnambula* and *Norma*. It is difficult for us to imagine the sound of that voice and the dramatic stage presence that so struck her contemporaries. Stendhal was one of her unconditional admirers and devotees and mentioned her talent many times in his works. Fétis, a musician and a lucid observer of the glory day of Italian opera in Paris, left the following portrait of Madame Pasta:

> Surely, her singing was not flawless from the point of view of vocal production, and her vocalization may not have been perfect, but she already knew quite well how to assign to each of her roles its own character. Her interpretations were so profound and penetrating that she could move her audience at will, and dramatic illusion was always the result of her inspiration.

This portrait of one of the first prima donnas of the nineteenth century could have been that of Maria Callas herself.[95]

During the years from 1820 to 1830, a host of wonderful singers appeared along with Giuditta Pasta on the stage of the Théâtre italien, which became one of the operatic shrines of Europe. There were the tenors Garcia and Rubini; the basses Bordogni, Zuchelli, and Pellegrini; and women like Isabelle Colbran, Rossini's wife; and Madame Damoreau-Cinti, one of the very few French artists of the group. Both women were among the greatest interpreters of Rossini, followed by Henriette Sontag in 1826, who made her Paris debut as Rosina in *The Barber of Seville*, and in 1827 by Maria Malibran, Manuel Garcia's daughter. The latter's greatest successes took place after 1830, in the few years between the July Revolution and her death. At the same time, the Théâtre italien produced the new singing stars Grisi, Rubini, and Lablache. Paris had never seen such a collection of outstanding artists in such a short time span. The simultaneous presence of these kings and queens of *bel canto* was an open invitation for composers such as Rossini, Bellini, and a short time later Donizetti to multiply vocal feats in their works, sometimes at the expense of musical quality.

In 1823, Rossini took advantage of this situation and used his success to establish himself in Paris at a time when the failure of his *Semiramide* in Naples made it more difficult for him to remain in his homeland. That same year, he became a member of the Paris Institut, and the following year accepted the post of *Directeur de la musique et de la scène du Théâtre italien* (Music and Stage Director), a post he held until 1826 when he was named *Inspecteur général du chant en France* (General Inspector of Singing). These official positions served as a springboard to gain access to the Paris Grand Opéra, where there was growing concern about the success of the Théâtre italien and an effort was underway to attract the composer who had become the central figure of musical life in Paris. As has been discussed, this prolific genius eventually ended his career at the Paris Opéra, but this did not stop his Italian works from being very successfully performed in Paris after 1825.

The Théâtre italien now entered the most glorious phase of its history. During the Empire, it was considered proper "to be seen" at the Théâtre italien. It became a must during the Restoration, especially if one claimed to belong to the intellectual and social elite. *La loge aux Italiens* (the box at the Théâtre Italien) became a literary theme and continued to be for many years. In *Le Rouge et le Noir*, by Stendhal, one of the chapters is called *L'Opéra bouffe* (The Comic Opera). Mathilde hears a "divinely graceful" Italian cantilena and begins to dream of Julien Sorel, whom she tries in vain to find in the audience. Monsieur de la Môle, in an effort to help the ambitious young man lose his provincial manners, advises him to go to every performance at the Italien and be there at eleven thirty "to observe from the lobby the exit of *beau monde*" (upper class). In another of Stendhal's novels, *Armance*, subtitled *Quelques scènes d'un salon de Paris en 1827* (Scenes of a Paris salon in 1827), Stendhal includes a chapter called *Au Théâtre italien*. It tells the story of young Octave, who escorts Madame d'Aumale "to the final two or three appearances of Madame Pasta, attended by every fashionable Parisian." Rossini's music became the rallying point of the dilettanti, or moderns, who followed Stendhal's lead and intended to dust off the old wigs. Stendhal's *La Vie de Rossini* (Life of Rossini) was published at the end of 1823, at about the same time as his *Racine et Shakespeare* where his ideas on romanticism were abundantly developed. It is true, however, that the author was occasionally very critical of Rossini's music and sometimes appeared to prefer Mozart's:

> I suspect that we shall still hear about Mozart after Rossini's star has faded. He has been an innovator from every point of view and

in all directions. He resembles no other, while Rossini still takes after Cimarosa, Guglielmi, and Haydn.

Even so, like all the modern thinkers in the 1820s Stendhal was a fierce defender of Rossini and was spellbound by him. Throughout the two volumes devoted to the Italian composer, he praised him lavishly. Why would he reject his own pleasure? Had he not defined romanticism as the art of presenting the people with works that "can provide their greatest pleasure, considering the present state of their customs and beliefs"?

It must have been annoying to the elder generation of French composers to read *La Vie de Rossini* and a series of articles written by Stendhal on the performances at the Théâtre Italien that were published by *Le Journal de Paris* beginning 9 September 1824. In them the author showed his enthusiasm for Italian music and occasionally ruffled the French masters with his impertinent pen. In 1825, composers such as Cherubini, Le Sueur, Berton, Catel, and Boïeldieu must have been concerned about the success of this young foreign master named Rossini, who had all of Paris at his feet while their own works began to sink slowly into oblivion. A real paper war followed between Stendhal and the followers of Rossini on one side and, on the other, the French masters whose narrow-minded and nationalistic jealousy kept them in principle quite hostile to the triumphs of their young Italian colleague. Depending on what camp one had chosen, Berton's or Rossini's, one was considered to be a "good" or a "bad" Frenchman! "The enemy is at our borders," declared Berton, who reprimanded Rossini for the "flaws" of his musical language. Stendhal energetically responded to the accusation by developing his favorite theme about the pleasures of the theater:

> The public is too discerning to be looking for anything but pleasure at the theater. Its last concern is to quibble with a composer over so-called infractions of the Conservatoire's principles and the rules of the purists on Rue Bergère. Its applause does not depend on flawless counterpoint.[96]

Pleasure and emotions were the new features found in Rossini's music by the dilettanti during the Restoration. Today we may be somewhat surprised that some of the better authors of the 1820s and 1830s considered Rossini to be one of them, as in the following lines from Lamartine's *Cours familier de littérature* (An Informal Literature Course):

With Mozart's passing, Rossini was being born, as if Fate meant for the voice and its own echo to be separated for only an instant in the century's ears. When I say echo, I do not mean to bring Rossini's original genius down to a simple role of echoing Mozart's genius. They are different, but equal. Mozart incarnates the prime melodies of Tyrol and Germany, while Rossini expresses Neapolitan gaiety and rapture . . . Mozart sings for singing's sake, Rossini sings to move and to please.

Reading the previous excerpt helps explain the importance of the "Rossini phenomenon" in the musical life of early nineteenth-century France. The French romantics were not, for the most part, true musical connoisseurs. All they demanded was that music be pleasing. "What is music if not first and foremost a pleasure to the ear?" asked Stendhal. From this perspective, what composer could better match their expectations than Rossini? The modern dilettantes could not possibly resist the charming quality of his melodic invention and the apparent ease, happiness, and youth that always emanated from his music. This ease at times led to some degree of triteness or dullness, but scarcely anyone among the young avant-garde of that time could really tell. From this viewpoint, the hostility felt towards Rossini by a true French romantic musician such as Berlioz seems to me to be very significant. The old French masters were irritated and criti-cal, but what could they use to oppose this new melodic surge that swept everything on its path? They had been unable to renew themselves or create a national school, and now they were slowly sinking into permanent oblivion while all of France gave a triumphal reception to *l'enfant de Pesaro* (Pesaro was Rossini's birth place).

This infatuation for Rossini during the Restoration was certainly not without cause, nor effect. In the span of only ten years, he alone generated greater changes in Italian opera—in opera seria as well as opera buffa—than Italian composers had during the thirty years of the previous generation. One has only to compare any page by Paisiello or Cimarosa to Rossini's music to immediately see the difference. All of a sudden, the proportions in Rossini were different. Everything, from the structure of arias to the vocal ranges and the roles assigned to instruments, was now much more devel-oped. Under this irresistible pressure, the old molds showed cracks, and the barriers that kept voices and instruments within proper limits were brought down. Although melodic beauty and expression were still the ultimate goals of Italian vocal art, it is obvious that the means Rossini used to achieve them were quite different. Vocal virtuosity (with ornaments now written out and thus imposed on the singers) as well as harmonic and orchestral craftmanship opened a new door on the future. Whereas his predecessors had settled for dull progressions and very discreet orchestration—almost unchanged for the past hundred years—so as to give prominence to melody, Rossini did not hesitate to use frequent modulations, to pepper his phrases with unprepared dissonances, and to assign an important role to the instruments instead of limiting their use to supporting the vocal line. The public was quite surprised by the effect of the famous orchestral crescendos resulting from the successive instrumental entrances until the tutti is finally achieved. All the basic elements of orchestration of romantic opera were already present in Rossini. In this field his influence was fundamental. We owe it to him to have helped French opera come out of its stagnation. Beginning in 1826 with the production of *Le Siège de Corinthe*, Rossini introduced at the Grand Opéra some of the devices he had originally conceived for Italian opera. Without him Meyerbeer would probably not have achieved his goals.

At the beginning of this chapter I mentioned the important role an Italian opera company permanently based in Paris could play in French musical art and in the evolution of French style. With Rossini, one of the most impressive pages of this company's history was turned, but it was not the last one. Indeed, the Italian singers soon had a new mission: to introduce the Parisians to Bellini's and Donizetti's great masterpieces. However, this second musical romanticism belongs to the next historical period, that of the July Monarchy.

Opera in the Provinces

The Example of a Major City: Lyon

One should not think that opera was restricted to Paris and a few main cities in the provinces. In fact, there were during this period a great number of opera productions in mid-size cities throughout France. Up until now, this was suspected to be the case, thanks to the work of local specialists who are few and far between. Today, documents from the archives of the *Société des Auteurs et Compositeurs dramatiques* (the Association of Theatrical Writers and Composers), founded in Paris in 1777 by Beaumarchais, prove it. Indeed, these archives are an important source for the understanding of the artistic life in the provinces at the end of the eighteenth century and in the nineteenth century. Unfortunately, the series of registers kept by this association is incomplete. It is a pity, for in them are recorded, under each member writer or composer, every performance of his works in the provinces, with the locations and the amount of royalties collected.

I sampled a few of these *livres d'auteurs* (Authors' Registers) for the periods spanning from Fructidor year II to Thermidor year III (August–September 1794 to July–August 1795) and from Fructidor year III to Germinal year IV (August–September 1795 to March–April 1796).

In the French provinces, and especially in the smaller cities, the operatic repertoire was naturally comprised primarily of comic operas, since such works were more easily staged and performed than grand operas. However, some works were performed an astounding number of times within a short span, and reached cities of very average size. For instance, Devienne's *Les Visitandines* was performed 267 times outside of Paris between October 1793 and August 1795. Admittedly, the action of this comic opera had to do with life in convents, a subject particularly interesting for the public during the time of the Terror. This could also explain the success of Berton's *Les Rigueurs du cloître* (The Hardships of the Cloister), performed 121 times in the provinces between August 1794 and August 1795. The composer received exactly 334 French livres for the performances given in the following cities: Arras, Bayonne, Béziers, Calais, Carcassonne, Douai, Dunkerque, Grenoble, Le Havre, Lille, Lyon, Mâcon, Metz, Montpellier, Nancy, Nantes, Orléans, Poitiers, Rouen, Saint-Quentin, Strasbourg, Toulon, Toulouse, Tours, and Valenciennes. Around the same time, Méhul received 318 livres for 51 performances in the provinces. Four of his works—*Euphrosine, Timoléon, Stratonice,* and *Le Jeune Sage* (The Young Wise Man)—were given in the following cities: Amiens, Bayonne, Bordeaux, Brest, Dunkerque, Grenoble, Le Havre, Lille, Nancy, Nantes, Rouen, Tours, and Toulouse.

Still, the grand prize goes to the two masters of comic opera at the end of the eighteenth century, Dalayrac and Grétry. Their success in the provinces certainly was far greater than could have been imagined at the time, and I thought that I was dreaming when I read a daily count of their performances. Dalayrac was performed exactly 1643 times between October 1793 and August 1795. I shall take the liberty to include the list of the French cities where the performances took place. This enumeration, although a bit tedious, is a good indication of which provincial centers were able to maintain an opera company, no matter how average it was: Alençon,

Amiens, Arras, Bayonne, Besançon, Béziers, Brest, Caen, Calais, Carcas-sonne, Châlons-sur-Marne, Châlon-sur-Saône, Dunkerque (then Duneli-bre), Grenoble, La Rochelle, Le Havre, Libreville (is it today's Charleville, or Saint-Étienne?), Lille, Lyon, Mâcon, Marseille, Metz, Montpellier, Nancy, Nantes, Orléans, Perpignan, Poitiers, Rennes, Rochefort, Rouen, Saint-Quentin, Strasbourg, Toulon, Toulouse, and Tours.

For all these performances, Dalayrac earned in one year the handsome sum of 5319 livres. Thanks to Beaumarchais who, at the dawn of the Revo-lution, battled to obtain recognition of authors' performance rights, and even advocated going on strike, composers could now receive compensation for performances in the provinces. This proved to be a substantial source of income for the most famous ones. In less than one year, from August 1795 to April 1796, Dalayrac earned exactly 16,439 livres. However, the most impressive figure was reached by Grétry. During the same period, his works were performed a total of 1552 times in the provinces and earned him a total of 16,684 livres.

What operatic work today could possibly be so well distributed throughout the provinces in such a short time? In any case, these figures lead to the conclusion that during that period some composers reached a much larger audience outside Paris than one would have thought possible. Famous arias from these highly popular comic operas were hummed throughout France. They probably were the equivalent of some of our hit tunes of today.

Although it is true that the whole country was involved, I noted that Western France seemed to be visited less often than other regions. Rennes, and especially Brest, remained somewhat excluded. One day it may be pos-sible to establish a map of France that would indicate the number of per-formances, the names of the most frequently performed composers and titles, and the receipts collected for ten-year periods. Up until now, all we had were older data gathered by local scholars, which have nonetheless been the source of important information. For instance, performances of Champein and Grétry were mentioned in Arras[97] in 1793, and perform-ances of Berton were mentioned in Metz[98] in 1798. However, a final account cannot be drawn before completion of the ongoing research into the musical life in the French provinces. Then it will be possible to compare those conclusions with the existing data found in the Paris archives of the *Société des Auteurs et Compositeurs dramatiques.*

In any case, première performances outside of Paris—today referred to as "provincial premières"—were very few in those days, regardless of the genre (opera, comic opera, comedy with ariettas). Rare exceptions were the talented composers who pursued their entire career in the provinces, without seeking success in Paris, such as Franz Beck in Bordeaux or Luce-Varlet. Luce-Varlet produced several of his operas in Douai starting in 1820 and also presented them in nearby Valenciennes and Cambrai. Apart from these isolated examples, one can say that all of France only had eyes for Paris. It is the unique model that everyone tried to imitate more or less successfully. Provincial theaters simply restaged Paris hits, sometimes after a very short interval, in some cases less than a year. This was quite a feat considering how difficult it was to obtain a score—if indeed a score had already been engraved in Paris by then—as well as handwritten parts for the orchestra, the soloists, and the choir. For instance, the Caen opera theater was very fast in producing some of Méhul's works: *Euphrosine* in 1792 (after Paris in 1790), *L'Irato* on 27 October 1802 (after Paris in 1801), and *Joseph* in 1808 (after Paris and Marseille in 1807). Also, Le Sueur's *La Caverne* could be heard in Rouen just a few months after its triumph in Paris in 1793, and Spontini's *La Vestale* was seen in Nantes shortly after its Paris première in 1807.[99]

At times, the provincial custom of copying the Paris programs caused negative reactions from the local critics, especially in the larger cities. In *Le Bulletin de Lyon* of Revolutionary year XI (1802–1803) I found a very critical review of the Opéra *Le Roi et le Pèlerin* (The King and the Pilgrim) performed at the Grand Théâtre in Lyon: "Must the Lyon audience have the leftovers from the Paris Boulevards? Actually, we do not know where this opera was performed, but it should be taken out of the aforementioned theaters, for that is all it deserves." Earlier, the same periodical did not hesitate to comment on the failure of Nicolo's *Michel-Ange* (Michelangelo) in the same theater:

> Although Paris may hold the sole privilege of producing good works, it shares occasionally with the provinces the ill fate of producing some very bad ones. . . . New operas are brought to provincial theaters without any preparation. In Paris, they receive favorable support, but in the départements only the truth is on their side. Without support or recommendations, they are presented to a silent public, like a foreigner to a tribunal.[100]

As far as the number of performances for each work is concerned, there was at that time a basic difference between Paris and the provinces. No opera, no matter how successful, was expected to be scheduled for more than a few performances outside of Paris. Notable exceptions were *Joseph*, performed sixteen times in three months in Nantes from September 1808, and *La Vestale*, which had seventeen performances when it was produced in Marseille during the 1808–1809 season.[101] Most of these works, especially short comic operas and comedies with ariettas, had only two or three performances. Cities with less than a hundred thousand inhabitants could not be expected to provide enough opera lovers to fill the house more than a few times.

To be sure, ticket prices were substantially lower in the provinces than in Paris but also varied from one city to the next. In Metz in 1792, they ranged from twelve to forty-eight sols. In Marseille in 1789, the best seats cost three livres and twelve sols, and the gallery twelve sols. During the 1827–1828 season, prices had gone up only slightly, to 3.3 francs for the highest and 65 centimes for the lowest. In Nantes in 1813, prices ranged from one to three francs. In Lyon during the 1828–1829 season, a box cost 1.5 francs in the last tier and four francs in the first tier. Also, the Grand Théâtre in Lyon sold yearly subscriptions that were less costly and guaranteed a reserved seat for all the season's events. Subscription prices for the 1813–1814 season were 190 francs for men and 120 francs for women! For the 1828–1829 season, prices had risen to 240 francs for men and 120 francs for women.[102] In Marseille, subscription prices for the 1827–1828 season were 200 francs for men, 150 francs for members of the military, and 120 francs for women. As a reminder, prices at the Feydeau theater in 1792 ranged from six livres to one pound sixteen sols. At the Paris Opéra during the Empire, they ranged from twelve francs down to three francs sixty.[103]

This state of affairs led to a contradictory situation. A company could not hope to fill the house night after night with the same work, so they changed works often. In order to do so, a theater had to close for several days a week. The activity of provincial opera and comic opera houses is astounding, especially in larger cities, as shall soon be seen for Lyon. For an average-sized city like Lille, however, there were over 250 performances for the 1815–1816 season; of those, 134 were operas, comic operas, and ballets. Indeed, in most provincial cities there was only one theater for drama, comedy, and opera. These figures seem unbelievable, even for that time. And yet, as early as the Empire, the Lille Opera was able to present ten or twelve new comic operas each year, chosen from among the contemporary Paris repertoire: Catel, Dalayrac, Solié, Gaveaux, Méhul, and Nicolo.[104]

It is difficult to imagine how theater directors managed to sustain such a pace, especially considering the poor quality and small number of their assistants. Local ensembles of singers were often created quickly and haphazardly. However, it was not unusual to find the same name in the same city several years in a row. Payroll lists, when they existed, reveal that singers were classified according to their role types, usually after the model of a famous Paris star. For instance, a female singer might sing the same roles as Madame Dugazon the Elder, and a male singer those of Martin or Elleviou. It is likely that once this arbitrary system of voice classification was established, singers were directly assigned to new roles that corresponded to their type of voice. The typical opera company in the provinces had very few singers. Although there were ten men and ten women for every season in Lille during the Empire, there were only six men and eight women in Nantes in 1791 and seven men and six women in Metz in 1793, and these singers were also asked to play occasional roles in comedy. In Marseille at the end of the Restoration, the opera company had fourteen men and ten women. These numbers compared to those found in Paris at that time, but some of the local celebrities may have had limited talent. At the Graslin Theater in Nantes during the Empire, there was a popular prima donna named Mademoiselle Valeroy. It was said that "she did not know her alphabet any better than her notes, so she had someone help her memorize her roles, as well as a vocal coach for her singing." Along these lines, one could read in the local press in December 1821, at the time of a performance of *The Marriage of Figaro* in Lyon: "Frequently, opera singers travel to Paris in order to study their roles from the first tier of the Louvois Theater." In the absence of personal talent, mimicry can do the trick.[105]

Although Castil-Blaze cannot always be trusted when he assumes the role of historian, he was nevertheless an unsurpassed witness of his time. His recollections on this subject are firsthand information. His translation of *The Barber of Seville* was performed in Marseille in December 1821, and that of *The Marriage of Figaro* was used in different cities, particularly in Nantes in January 1822. He knew the life of provincial opera theaters in every detail and made fun of it on many occasions: "You do not need to have years of experience in the provinces to observe that you never meet three good actors in the same theater, and two only rarely, and then only in theaters located in some main city." In such cities, unfortunately, the author did not give names—performances were never good, and in most cases barely acceptable: "One or two singers support the opera and the rest do their best but never any worse than routine will tolerate." Indeed things do get worse in cities "of second and third categories." Castil-Blaze denounced certain practices that would not have been suspected to exist without his report:

> I have seen the same actors sing roles of both characters who were on stage at the same time, namely Theseus and the High Priest in Sacchini's *Œdipe à Colone*. After finishing his part, the King of Athens turned around as if to spit and sang the part of the Pontiff while a soldier of the garrison, dressed in priestly garment and wearing the sacred headband, opened his mouth, rolled his eyes, spread his arms, and threw incense on the fire.[106]

The situation of opera choruses was apparently even more pitiful. Sometimes there were very few singers, and they were poorly trained, in addition to being mere amateurs. In Nantes during the 1813–1814 season, ten men and women made up the chorus, and they barely made a living wage. Depending on their qualifications or years of service, they earned from 300 to 1100 francs a year, whereas soloists earned from 1500 to 5000 francs. In spite of its special status, the Grand Théâtre of Lyon was not much better off than Nantes. In 1811–1812, its chorus included seven men and nine women whose yearly earnings added up to 17,400 francs.[107] Numbers were much higher in Marseille: during the 1827–1828 season, there were 30 men and women, an exceptionally high number. In some of the smaller cities, choruses ended up being reduced to a quartet of soloists, and it would not be unusual to hear them all sing in unison or in octaves. According to Castil-Blaze,

> Women's choruses produce nothing but cacophony. As long as the lower part always follows at the interval of a third, these two parts go together rather well. But when they begin to move in oblique or contrary motion, there is an immediate state of confusion. The altos try in vain to find their notes, only to be saved by the sopranos whom they attempt to follow in unison.

Moreover, there were cases in which the lack of chorus members meant that a single chorus member was forced to sing all the parts, provided that the writing was not entirely contrapuntal. In connection with this, Castil-Blaze recounted one of those anecdotes that he could not have made up even if he had wanted to:

It is rather surprising to hear a singer cut the words so that he can account for the different vocal parts that he overzealously took on. As an example, the chorus of the Furies who gave way to Orpheus after his victory in the second act of Gluck's opera, with its successive fugato entrances, would have become: "He is vic' he is vic' he is victorious!"[108]

One cannot help but think that most of the opera orchestras were also rather thin and often made up of more or less distinguished non-professionals. On the eve of the Revolution, the orchestra of the Metz theater included sixteen players. In Nantes in 1791, there were eighteen players. Marseille enjoyed a special status all around and was proud of its thirty-two piece orchestra soon after the Revolution. In 1827, thirty-five years later, that figure was raised to thirty-five: six first and six second violins, two violas, eight cellos and basses, two flutes, two oboes, two clarinets, two bassoons, two French horns, one trumpet, one trombone, one timpani player. Obviously, these were the musicians exclusively employed at the theater, and their numbers were probably about the same during the period that followed. Indeed, there is written evidence of much larger orchestral ensembles—sixty or seventy players—for some very important concerts. On those occasions, the non-professional players of the town were probably called to join their colleagues of the opera orchestra. During the regular season of operas and comic operas, most productions were very routine performances. Castil-Blaze remembers: "I saw *Paul et Virginie* being performed without orchestral parts. The conductor and the bass player played from the full score, and a few wind instruments, scattered in the pit, accompanied from memory or doubled the melody in unison."

In spite of these extremely precarious working conditions, singers from Paris did not hesitate to travel—especially during the summer months—and sing on provincial stages, where they brought with them all the prestige of the famous Paris theaters. The press of that time is filled with accounts of these guest engagements that enabled other French cities to acquire a touch of Paris glamour, as the *Allgemeine musikalische Zeitung* reported in 1809.

In 1785, the famous Madame Dugazon was in Toulouse, where she sang in *Les Trois Sultanes*. During the summer of 1793, Lays left for Bordeaux, where he was scheduled to sing in at least twenty opera performances. Because he was well-known for his revolutionary ideals, his presence in the Grand Théâtre caused a scandal, and he was expelled from the city. At about the same time in Marseille, his colleague Lainez had to interrupt a series of performances of Gluck's *Alceste* and *Iphigénie en Aulide*. He did not conceal his royalist preferences and refused to sing the song "Ça ira." He received the same treatment as Lays but for opposite reasons. Also from the Paris Opéra, Chéron and Rousseau were heard in Bordeaux at the end of the eighteenth century. In June 1797, as soon as the Favart theater was closed for renovation, several of the best singers of the company left for the provinces. According to the newspaper *La Quotidienne* dated 27 June, Chénard and Solié "proposed their services for a dozen performances in Lyon" of various works, including Dalayrac's *Raoul, sire de Créqui* (Raoul, Lord of Créqui) and *Philippe et Georgette*, Kreutzer's *Lodoïska*, and Monsigny's *Rose et Colas*. After Lyon, the artists went on to Marseille. One month later, *Le Courrier des spectacles* dated 24 July announced that "the actors of the Favart company took advantage of the closing of their theater to travel to the départements." Madame Crétu went to Bordeaux at the same time as Madame Scio, the female star of the Feydeau theater. As for Elleviou, he was singing in Montpellier at that time and could be heard in Lyon in 1805. One year later, it was Madame Branchu's turn to sing there. The comings and goings of these artists were carefully monitored by the government. In regard to Lyon, for example, I found a voluminous correspondence between the Prefect of the Imperial Palace, de Luçay, and the Prefect of the département of the Rhône.[109] It stipulated that the traveling artists had to be back in Paris by a given date. Beyond this date, they were not allowed to sing "on any stage within the département." The best bass from the Paris Opéra company, Derivis, was in Lille in October 1810 and in Nantes in 1817. Among other roles, he sang in *Œdipe à Colone*, one of his great personal successes in Paris. He had probably expressed his intention to come to Lyon to sing in January 1817 without authorization from King Louis XVIII's Ministry of Police. As a consequence, the Prefect of the Rhône received a very stern letter from Paris requesting that he keep Derivis out if he ever attempted to enter the département: "If he showed even the slightest delay in complying with these orders, he would be severely punished." In 1812, on his way to a tour of Belgium, Elleviou made a stop in Lille and sang *Joseph*, one of his best roles. In January 1828, Nourrit planned four special performances in Lyon and accepted in writing "a fee of 600 francs for each performance, plus a 40 franc allowance for each day he would need to spend in Lyon."[110]

There is no need to bring up additional examples. Rather, we should ask why the best singers in Paris were willing to appear so frequently in the provinces, knowing how poor the rest of the productions were likely to be.

They never seemed to complain about the very precarious conditions of some of the productions. In fact, they must have taken great pride in their own superiority over their local colleagues. Strangely enough, local critics were the ones who at times deplored the appearance of Paris stars on their stages. On occasion, they even found them to be inadequate, as was the case of the famous Lainez, who failed in Lyon in 1802. The newspaper *Les Petites Affiches de Lyon*[111] brought him down in a short commentary:

> The first singer of the Paris Opéra never had much of a voice. Cries and quaverings in the worst taste are all that is left of it today. His manners and his gait are conceited. He overacts to compensate for being weak. He is a waning actor. He should be seen at least once, out of respect for who he was. The public of Lyon bid him farewell.

As a matter of fact, the people of Lyon would encounter Lainez again, but this time as director of their opera theater.

On the other hand, some provincial journalists were fascinated by the talents of the Paris artists on tour and wondered why they visited the local theaters. "It would be easy to approve if one only considered our hopes for progress in the arts," answered the newspaper *Le Bulletin de Lyon* dated 7 December 1803, following a series of performances by Gavaudan and his wife in that city. "Unfortunately, these actors are being acclaimed during the time of their visit, but after they depart, what remains usually is cold and stodgy theater." They probably deserved these great triumphs if only for their personal talents, but at the same time, "the actors from the big city, by temporarily depriving their local colleagues of their roles, deprive them of many small successes. After the former leave, the latter will not venture to appear in the same works." Quite understandably, they feared "an unfavorable and often humiliating comparison."

As I mentioned earlier, these opera houses presented mostly short comic operas, but some provincial cities were more ambitious in their programming and included great works from the Paris Opéra, Favart, or Feydeau. In Caen there were performances of Gluck's *Iphigénie en Aulide* (1792), Le Sueur's *Les Bardes* (1805), and Spontini's *La Vestale* (1809). In Nantes, *La Vestale* was presented several times between 1807 and 1815, with special appearances by Mademoiselle Pelet, formerly heard in the main Paris theaters. She moved permanently to Nantes in 1815. Also, Nantes had its premiere of *Don Giovanni* in 1814, an event that went almost unnoticed by the critics. All that *Le Journal de Nantes* mentioned was that "the lavishness of the sets equalled that of the music."[112] The following year, Nantes produced *Les Mystères d'Isis*, and in 1823, it gave a cool reception to *The Barber of Seville*. *La Dame blanche* and *La Muette de Portici*, however, met with unprecedented success in 1826 and at the end of 1829, respectively. In 1822, Spontini's *Cortez* was performed with great success in Toulouse.[113] In 1827 to 1828, *Cortez* was, along with *Œdipe à Colone* and *La Vestale*, on the program at the Grand Théâtre of Lyon. In 1829, Marseille staged two Paris masterpieces, *Le Siège de Corinthe* and *La Muette de Portici*. These examples, taken at random from theater programs show, that the French provinces had roughly the same opera repertoire as Paris; only the quality and the conditions of the performances were different.

As in Paris at the time of the Revolution, provincial opera theater-goers witnessed fights—often violent ones—between royalist spectators and advocates of the new ideas. I already recounted the troubles experienced by Lays in Bordeaux and Lainez in Marseille. Every director of a provincial theater had received orders from Paris to have "the beloved Republican songs" sung before raising the curtain, as was done in Paris. The public had to hear "Ça ira," "Le Chant du Départ," "Veillons au Salut de l'Empire," and "La Marseillaise," which was often repeated between the two operas on the program. In Prairial year VIII (May–June 1800), *Richard Cœur de Lion* (Richard Lionheart) was canceled in Nantes. Its famous line, "Oh Richard, oh my King" had become the motto of the Royalists and had to be changed to "Oh Richard, my heart is devoted to thee!" Confrontations were frequent in Metz during the Revolution. On 11 July 1795, a performance of Monsigny's comic opera *La Belle Arsène* created a scandal. Yells, whistles, insults, and obscene remarks resounded in the theater. Again in March 1797, municipal authorities had to step in to forbid Dalayrac's comic opera *Sargines*, "considering that the whole opera was filled with worship of kings and could foment trouble and unrest, especially so close to the forthcoming session of the Primary Assemblies." Monvel, the librettist, had to make changes in the parts concerning the monarchy, and two months later, permission was granted to perform the new version.

It is clear that in the provinces the operatic world tried to imitate that of Paris. Theater was an important part of social life; all the regulars knew each other and liked to meet there. They formed a small, fashionable circle that mimicked the Paris high society, but they attended only the theater events of their town, which they considered a familial duty. Castil-Blaze left a description of the atmosphere:

Everyone greeted one another, or paid visits to each other in the boxes or the balconies, for they all had their favorite seats. Most reserved boxes were inherited. They stayed in the families and were named after those who had been occupying them for the past half-century.

It is true that some of the performances in the provinces were bad, and some bordered on the ridiculous. However, for the great majority of the spectators unable to attend the Paris theaters, these productions provided the only chance to satisfy a love of opera or to be entertained by actual voices—even average ones—and to see up close their heroes personified by the actors in all the mysterious glory of the stage. The fact that there existed local, resident opera companies throughout France is evidence of definite if modest musical activity in the provinces.

In most provincial cities there was generally only one performance hall that was used for both opera and theater, though some of the larger French cities had more than one until early in the nineteenth century. For instance, Lyon had four: the *Théâtre des Terreaux*, also known as Grand Théâtre; the *Théâtre des Célestins*; the *Théâtre de la Gaîté*; and the *Théâtre de l'Émulation*. During the Empire, Napoleon decided to limit the number of provincial theaters, as he had done in Paris. The *Règlement pour les théâtres* (Regulations for the Theaters), signed by Interior minister Champagny and dated 25 April 1807, contains a *Tableau des divers théâtres de France* (Table of Various Theaters in France) and stipulates that only five cities could keep two companies from then on: Lyon, Bordeaux, Marseille, Nantes, and Turin (Torino). Everywhere else, there could be only one permanent company.

I shall describe briefly the operatic activity in a typical provincial center at the beginning of the nineteenth century.[114] In Lyon, second only to Paris, I discovered a wealth of information about opera and comic opera in local archives.

The 1807 regulations limited not only the number of authorized theaters in Lyon to two. They also determined how the different genres could be distributed between the two theaters. The Théâtre des Terreaux, or Grand Théâtre, was exclusively devoted to drama, comedies, operas, and ballets; the Théâtre des Célestins, or Théâtre des Variétés, was granted the right to produce small comedies, comic operas, melodramas, and "a few ballets." The looseness of this last category caused frequent conflicts between the two theaters. Very soon, the management of the Grand Théâtre requested the monopoly of all ballet productions, leaving to the Célestins "small numbers incidental to melodramas and other plays of the kind."

Between 1806 and 1830, the Lyon Grand Théâtre had several directors go bankrupt one after the other. There were no profits, and there were always open conflicts between the management and the municipal authorities or the prefect of the département. An earlier director, Prat, had written to the prefect on 6 Thermidor year VIII (24 July 1799) to ask for a reduction of the license and the tax for the poor "considering the state of disrepair that his theater had suffered for the past ten years due to various circumstances." The following paragraph taken from his letter contains interesting information concerning the management of some of the provincial theaters:

> Marseille has two main theaters, and their annual receipts amount to 750,000 to 800,000 livres. Their director, citizen Bonneville, can certify to you that he only pays 16,000 livres a year in taxes for both theaters. We make only 260,000 livres, and we pay 22,000. What a difference between the one's receipts and the other's expense! Presently, Strasbourg makes 150,000 livres and only pays 3000 livres in taxes. Nancy makes 120,000 livres and only pays 12,000 or 15,000 livres.

I do not know if the prefect granted this request, but the Grand Théâtre went bankrupt in the very first years of the Empire, while the Célestins prospered. On 25 May 1808, the Minister of the Interior himself wrote to the prefect of the Rhône to instruct him to re-open the leading theater of Lyon, but with the following changes:

> You will not impose on your shareholders the production of grand opera and ballet, for it would lead them to bankruptcy. That kind of production is far too costly. It seems to me that it should be reserved for the capital city until the three or four main cities of the Empire have regained their past grandeur.

Thus in the following years, the management tended to increase the number of theater productions and decrease that of operas and especially ballets, which were more expensive. Following a well-established tradition, there were many performances in Lyon. In July 1808, when Michel Delisle and Philippe Brulo were hired to be the new directors of the Grand Théâtre starting on the first of October, their contract stipulated that they should give a performance "every day of the week, closing only as required by actors' illnesses."

Despite the new measures, things did not go better for the Grand Théâtre and forced the prefect of the Rhône to request information on the management of other French theaters. He received a report on the situation in Bordeaux. It was not brilliant either, in spite of special conditions that did not exist in Lyon, such as a reduced tax for the poor and a decree of the prefect authorizing the director to "deduct a fourth of the gross receipts of all other public attractions: balls, concerts, jousts. . . ." In addition, the presence of over 200,000 enlisted men in Bordeaux since the conflict with Spain resulted in an unexpected source of income. Before each performance, the authorities distributed "a first tier box ticket to every officer and 300 orchestra tickets to non-commissioned officers and soldiers." The income from these tickets went to the director who "could not have managed otherwise." Thus it seems that just about every theater in the large cities operated at a loss.

In Lyon, the appointment of Paris singer Lainez as director of the Grand Théâtre on 4 June 1812 did not improve the situation. In 1814, he was nearly bankrupt and had to obtain a special 20,000 franc subsidy from the city. On 12 March 1817, Lainez' successor, Charasson, was granted the privilege of running both theaters in Lyon but quickly went bankrupt as well. The Célestins attracted the crowds, but the performances at the Grand Théâtre were deserted. In 1818, the premiere of a new comic opera by Boïeldieu, *Le Petit Chaperon Rouge* (Little Red Riding-Hood), completely failed. "In spite of a careful and brilliant production, no single performance of this opera brought more than 500 francs in receipts." Apparently, the public quickly grew more demanding but also less interested in opera productions, preferring short comic plays with ariettas like those produced at the Célestins. Before Charasson declared bankruptcy in February 1820, he wrote several reports to the municipal authorities. In one of them, dated 12 March 1819, he summarized the situation as follows:

The fact that the productions of the Célestins are sold out and the Grand Théâtre is always deserted can easily be explained by the decadence of the arts and public taste, the political circumstances, the stagnation of trade, and the scarceness of money. Countless examples and irrefutable facts can be quoted in support of the statement about the decadence of the arts. In cities like Marseille,

Toulouse, Strasbourg, Metz, Nîmes, Montpellier, and so on, where different genres are produced on the same stage, crowds of people attend performances of melodramas, dramatic plays, and vaudevilles. For the performances of operas by the classical or modern masters, however, the theaters remain completely empty.

Only a few years later, theater bankruptcy hit Bordeaux, Toulouse, and Marseille. Opera theaters ran into such operating problems that they were forced to close down. An article in *Le Miroir des spectacles* on 26 February 1821 attributes this financial failure not only to the increasing number of productions with machinery and more orchestra musicians, singers, chorus members, but also to the growing population of melodrama.

It is clear that the public was losing interest in French grand opera. During 1815 to 1825 the decline took place in Paris, where the Grand Opéra lost much of its audience to the Théâtre italien. In Lyon, however, there was no second theater with an all-new repertoire, and the Restoration saw a definite decline of operatic activity from the time of the Empire. It is probable that the public grew increasingly tired of the extremely poor productions due to a lack of qualified singers and totally unrealistic programming practices.

For example, in the final years of the Restoration, Singier, the director at the time, found himself in disagreement with the Lyon municipal authorities, just as his predecessors had been for the same reasons. Astonishingly, the administrative correspondence from February to March 1828 reveals one of the city's complaints against the director of the Grand Théâtre:

> Monsieur Singier has failed to live up to his obligations toward the city, so that out of 500 works that he had included in the repertoire as ready for production, only 160 were actually staged in a ten-month span (300 days).

It should be added that the list of the 500 works—which still exists—includes operas as well as tragic and comic plays, vaudevilles, and short comic operas. These productions must have been put together in tremendous haste, which was fatal to their quality. It is conceivable that the Lyon audience of the mid-1820s was no longer satisfied with quasi-improvised performances given by very poor singers. What was still possible in 1800 in a medium-sized town had become unacceptable in a major provincial city in the days of romanticism.

One of the facts the Mayor of Lyon held against director Alexis Singier's management was the poor quality of the company. During the 1827–1828 season, he had been forced him to reduce the number of performances of French grand operas as well as Italian operas translated into French:

> The quality has been so low that only three true French grand operas, *Œdipe à Colone*, *Fernand Cortez*, and *La Vestale* were presented. Besides, the general level of performance was so poor that they would not have been allowed without the participation of the actor Nourrit and the help of the ballet, the only part of the company with a satisfactory staff.

The same fear of presenting poor productions caused the withdrawal from the repertoire of Italian operas such as

> *Othello*, *The Marriage of Figaro*, *The Thieving Magpie*, *Don Giovanni*, and all similar works that are decidedly well liked by the public and have strongly contributed to attract the same public to the old Grand Théâtre.

Italian opera, though as successful in a major city like Lyon as it was in Paris at that time was only performed in French translation. The only record of the presence of a foreign company in Lyon before 1830 was that of the Paris opera buffa in July 1805. A production of Paisiello's *La Serva padrona* at the Célestins Theater starred Madame Strinasacchi and Madame Martinelli.[115] At that time, the public was not familiar with the Italian repertoire, and these performances failed, as reported by *Le Bulletin de Lyon* of 20 July 1805:

> Actors are few, there is little action, the language is unintelligible. The audience is bored and yawns, and is put to sleep by the recitatives. Yet the theater is well attended; it is the meeting place of high society. There can be no harm in good company.

In any case, until at least 1830, the Grand Théâtre operated at a loss. When the City of Lyon decided to replace the director Singier in August 1828, it had to post notices on the walls to invite potential successors to come forward as soon as possible.

Various municipal archives in Lyon also contain information about the staff and the programs of the Grand Théâtre between 1805 and 1830. The number of orchestral musicians decreased slightly from forty in the early years of the Empire—there were twenty-six players at the Célestins—to only twenty-nine for the 1811–1812 season. A trombone is mentioned in this orchestra for the first time in 1812 and a harp in 1813. By the end of the Restoration, the number had increased to thirty-eight for the 1828–1829 season. There were four French horns instead of three, one trumpet, a second trombone, and a cymbal player. During the Empire, the *maître de musique* earned between 2000 and 3000 francs a year depending on the year and who held the post; orchestral musicians earned between 600 and 1600 francs.

Until 1815, the number of singers in the company remained about the same, between eleven and fifteen. Men were always paid a little more than women. In 1811–1812, the two best-paid men in the company were Boucher and Rousseau, each earning 8000 francs a year; the two female stars received only 7600 francs each. During the Restoration, the number of opera singers increased slightly to eighteen and then twenty, but was always insufficient if the company had to perform several times a week, let alone attempt new productions of good quality. Being so few, the singers were under much stress. For instance, on 18 January 1828, a singer named Henri appealed directly to the mayor to inform him that he was too tired to sing the role of Gaveston in *La Dame blanche*. His arguments would convince any modern opera director who cares for the health of his singers and the quality of his productions:

> Since last Saturday, I have been off only once, yesterday. Although I must sing two heavy roles tomorrow and Sunday, I proposed to act tonight—since I am unable to sing—in a comic play of any kind. It would mean appearing in a series of eight different works in nine days. I believe, Mr. Mayor, that this schedule is more than what is reasonable and proves my constant good will.

On occasion, singers remained in Lyon for several seasons in a row and managed to establish a local reputation. During the Consulate, for instance, Madame Sainte-James was an excellent interpreter of several of Grétry's and Boïeldieu's roles and was sorely missed when in May 1803 she finally left Lyon for Montpellier, where she had been engaged. Also at that time, the press of Lyon[116] gave high praise to Mademoiselle Rousselois, a newcomer who made her successful debut in the role of Antigone in Sacchini's *Œdipe à Colone*. In May 1803, she once more displayed her great talent in Steibelt's *Roméo et Juliette* and in Méhul's *Héléna*. Mademoiselle Rousselois's success in Lyon turned out to be such that she was soon engaged by the Paris Opéra, where she pursued a brilliant career.

The number of chorus members on payroll at the Grand Théâtre was about twenty, and their salary in 1812 varied between 600 and 1300 francs a year. I doubt that there were always that many. Indeed, the *Bulletin de Lyon* of 14 November 1804 reported a series of performances by Mademoiselle Clairville, "formerly resident artist of the Theater of the Arts" (The Paris Opéra)." The reporter found the performances excellent, but regretted that the chorus of Pluto's priests in Piccini's *Dido* was poorly executed because it was performed by "four wretched soloists." Such an observation lends credibility to the story about the chorus that was sung by a single singer in Gluck's *Orfeo*.

In brief, all these musicians, orchestra players, and singers , were submitted to overwhelming work schedules that probably did not leave any room for studying their roles in depth or reflecting on subtleties of interpretation. This is easily confirmed by examining the programs of the time.

During the first years of the nineteenth century, before the 1807 decree assigning a specific repertoire to each of the theaters of Lyon, the rivalry between the companies of the Grand Théâtre and Célestins created added pressure that was also detrimental to the quality of performances. In *Les Petites Affiches de Lyon* of 21 August 1802, I found a long report on Méhul's comic opera *Une Folie* (An Act of Folly) just after its premiere at the Grand Théâtre. The critic praised the play and the music, and then he added:

> It is too bad that this work was staged in such a hurry that it did not receive the attention to ensemble and the purity of expression it deserved. Obviously, the company had to compete with the Célestins, and even get even with them, all at the expense of the public.

After the 1807 decree theoretically determined the productions genres authorized in each of the two theaters, this kind of conflict stopped for the most part, but the sheer number of performances on both stages continued to work against high quality productions. The Archives of Lyon contain several listings of works produced within precise time frames. Here are some examples. Between 28 April and 20 October 1811, not quite six months, The Grand Théâtre of Lyon presented seventy-seven operas, divided among the following genres: eleven grand operas, including Gluck's *Alceste* and *Iphigénie en Aulide*, Piccini's *Dido*, Sacchini's *Œdipe à Colone*, and Spontini's *La Vestale*. Also classified in the category of grand operas were Lemoyne's *Les Prétendus* (The Engaged Couple), Cherubini's *Anacréon*, Grétry's *La Caravane du Caire* (The Caravan from Cairo), Kreutzer's *Aristippe*, Grétry's *Colinette à la cour* (Colinette at the Court), and Rousseau's *Le Devin du village* (The Fortuneteller of the Village); twenty-one three or four-act operas; thirteen two-act operas; and thirty-two one-act operas. For the entire 1823–1824 season, the Grand Théâtre presented 132 different operas, indicating an average pace of one new production every two or three days, whether it be a revival or a premiere, a grand opera or a short one-act opera. It is possible to establish annual statistics through 1830 from the original records. Except in the case of grand operas, most performances included two or even three separate works: a comedy, a short opera, and a ballet. The total duration of a typical performance must have been considerably longer than it is today. For instance, on 23 November 1828, the Grand Théâtre presented in one evening *Tartuffe* and *La Dame blanche*.

Up until 1830, the programs presented at the Grand Théâtre followed closely the Paris premieres. Weber's *Der Freischütz*, in its new French adaptation by Castil-Blaze under the title *Robin des bois*, had its Paris premiere at the Odéon Theater on 7 December 1824. On 17 October 1825, it was presented at the Grand Théâtre in Lyon. In spite of some ludicrous sets and machinery, it was a success. On 20 October, a review in the newspaper *L'Eclaireur du Rhône* stated:

> For a moment, the waterfall ceased to flow, as if a sudden drop of temperature had caused it to freeze. Luckily, they managed to make it go again. Dragons and winged fish flew through the air, sideways, backwards, even upside down. Among the bats, some flapped only one wing.

What was needed was obvious: fewer effects, better executed. The critic concluded:

> In Paris, they do not use all this gear. Curiously, the provinces seek to surpass the capital with complicated effects, while they do not have the means to do it with the accuracy needed to create the illusion.

In spite of the poor staging, Weber's music was enthusiastically received in Lyon. One month later, however, the same *L'Eclaireur du Rhône* declared:

> The zeal shown by the gentlemen of the orchestra has already cooled off. Several instruments have vanished. At this rate, *Robin des bois* will soon be accompanied by only four or five violins, one clarinet, and the indispensable double bass.

These comments reveal the lack of discipline and cohesion of the orchestra at the Grand Théâtre. Well-balanced productions, with equal quality in the pit and on stage, were difficult to come by in the provinces.

This picture of a grand opera theater in the provinces at the beginning of the nineteenth century would not be complete without mentioning its allegiance to the successive political regimes. Just as in Paris, opera in the provinces was a tool of those in political power. Several original documents certainly prove this to be the case in Lyon, and the same probably holds true in most large French cities at that time.

I found a letter from the director of the Grand Théâtre to the mayor, dated 15 January 1806, informing him that "an occasional work celebrating the success of our army and their imperial commander would be presented very soon." Unfortunately I was not able to find the title or the nature of this work. Could it have been a one-act, occasional opera, like those produced at the same time at the Imperial Academy of Music in Paris? Or is it possible that the regime had its devotees in every town, so that for once the provinces presented original productions that had not yet been seen in Paris?[117]

Reading between the lines of certain reports of the time, one can guess that successive changes of regime probably led to purges, probably more often of chorus members, orchestra musicians, and dancers than of opera singers. On 17 April 1816, the police chief of Lyon sent a report to the mayor to inquire why some names had been crossed off the list of artists to be hired for the following season:

> The Director is requested to give the reasons for such exclusions, since all these individuals are known to have a good reputation, and it seems that a choice was made to fire only royalists.

Another report, unfortunately not dated, deplores that "generally speaking, the actors and actresses of the Grand Théâtre have a very poor reputation."

A list of the seven "most dangerous ones" including Boucher, first singer, and Rocher, *second maître de musique* (second orchestra conductor). The report explains:

> All of them hold opinions quite contrary to the government and appear incorrigible in this matter. If the management did not require the employment of these actors, it would be essential to weed out a few, such as Boucher, Bruillion, and Dugrenet, who could easily be replaced.

Since this document bears no date, I cannot tell if the government that it refers to is that of the emperor or the king, but it makes little difference. This text still proves that part of the staff of the Grand Théâtre was opposed to the government, and for that reason, was under strict police surveillance. There again, opera theaters in the provinces followed the Paris example!

Chapter 4

Sacred Music

The break caused by the Revolution was probably deepest and most permanent in the field of sacred music. The Enlightenment had brought about many changes that were the result of the *Philosophes'* constant attacks against religion, and especially against the Church, and indicated an evolution—some called it a degradation—of the expression of religious faith.

The *concert spirituel* created by Philidor in 1725 had accustomed Parisians to hearing sacred music outside its original church setting. The role played by this institution was essential up until the very first years of the Revolution. The *concert spirituel* greatly contributed to the development of a typically French genre of sacred music, the grand motet, which had spread over the whole country from Versailles. Recent research accounts for over one thousand grand motets composed in France between 1683 and 1789. These motets *avec choeurs et symphonie* (with chorus and orchestra) were originally conceived for chapel services but gradually turned into a sort of fashionable sacred music. They were perfectly suited to the needs and tastes of a society that was refined but not very austere in expressing its faith. Grand motets were almost always based on psalm texts and called for full orchestral accompaniment, including, in many cases, brass and percussion instruments. Soloists and choruses alternated in a succession of recitatives, arias, duets, trios, and larger ensembles, each illustrating a verse of the same psalm. The unsurpassed master in this genre was Michel-Richard de Lalande, whose genius is being discovered today. At first, the grand motet had its natural setting at the royal chapel service in Versailles. There remain many unanswered questions that I will not address here; for example, when was the twenty-five minute grand motet heard during office and mass?

As it moved from the church to the concert hall, the grand motet quickly lost its sacred character and became a simple decorative piece. Some psalms were especially popular because their verses allowed imitative musical effects, which was what the audience of the *concert spirituel* wanted. For instance, the psalm *Super flumina Babilonis* (By the Rivers of Babylon) called for an illustration of the running waters of the Euphrates. During the second half of the eighteenth century, the masters of this genre were Mondonville and Giroust. Around 1750, the public apparently grew tired of the grand motet because of its standard effects and stereotyped texts. Audience and composers alike aspired to the renewal of sacred music forms. In his *Spectacle des Beaux-Arts* published in 1763, Lacombe wrote: "We must diversify the materials of our sacred music." In 1783, the *Mercure de France* concluded: "The grand motets no longer excite the people's interest."

The tree, having born its best fruit, was exhausted. Just before the Revolution, there was a lack of interest in sacred music as it had been practiced traditionally for a century. As a matter of fact, French composers knew little else but the mass and the motet. The Latin oratorio was completely unknown. Some composers, like Mondonville, Gossec, and Giroust, made repeated attempts with *hiérodrames* (sacred dramas), but these works were based on French librettos, usually adapted from the Old Testament and intended to be performed in the concert hall, not in the church.

As the Monarchy agonized, French sacred music was also looking for a new direction. In his book on French music in the baroque era, James R. Anthony rightly noted that up until the Revolution, the repertoire of the royal chapel was dominated by grand motets of composers of the first half of the eighteenth century. The last volume of the *Livre des Motets pour la Chapelle du Roi* (*Book of Motets for the King's Chapel*) listed the titles of motets performed in the Chapel of Versailles from 1787 to 1789 and in the Tuileries Chapel until August 1792. From January to June 1792, for example, there were twenty-five motets by Madin, fourteen by De Lalande, thirteen by Campra, five by Gervais, and four by Bernier.

An exception was the attempt made by a young *maître de chapelle* with bold and original ideas named Jean-François Le Sueur. Head of the choir of the Notre-Dame Cathedral for one year (1786–1787), the second church choir in France after Versailles, he caused a tremendous scandal and became the center of attention of the whole city. In a previous book[1] I recounted in detail the various episodes of this little drama, the real cause of which seems obvious to me. By accusing Le Sueur of introducing soloists and a full orchestra into Notre-Dame, thereby transforming the service into a "beggars' opera," his contemporaries chose up sides against him. During the eighteenth century, instruments were no more exceptional in the church than opera singers when performing high masses. The truth of the matter was that the clergy and the ecclesiastical hierarchy were offended by the young composer's ideas about sacred music. He had declared that he would no longer compose grand motets or masses on the usual texts, which were always the same and seemed to obstruct his free invention. He turned instead to a new dramatization of sacred music. To do so, he altered the meaning of some of the texts, introduced additional Latin texts from other sources when he felt the need, and distributed the words among the different actors to form a small dramatic scene. The mass itself was conceived as a sort of sacred drama in Latin. What was heard on the occasion of Easter of 1787 in Notre-Dame actually was an oratorio recounting in Latin the resurrection of Christ. Easter 1787 marks an important date in the history of French sacred music: the birth of the oratorio in Latin that went on to prevail in the nineteenth century, and the death of the grand motet, which had been slowly on its way out since the middle of the eighteenth century.

Le Sueur's 1787 attempt failed, since the canons of the chapter decided to dismiss him from the chapel, but it had important consequences later. After the revolutionary turmoil, Le Sueur returned as director of the Tuileries Chapel, a post that made him head of French sacred music. He stayed there for over a quarter of a century and was always faithful to the principles established before 1789.

Such quarrels, interrupted by the Revolution, show that spiritual life in France was going through a deep transformation at the end of the Enlightenment. The civil constitution of the clergy abolished the choir schools, dealing sacred music a death blow. The revolutionaries never succeeded in completely preventing secret worship, but for over a decade, composers of sacred music were obviously silenced. When peaceful times returned, attitudes had changed, and the conditions under which free worship was reestablished point to the new direction taken by sacred music in France in the early nineteenth century.

The Concordat signed in July 1801 and the official legalization of worship triggered the renewal of musical activity in French churches. The people of France had stopped going to church, but for many of them this ten-year interruption had been a painful experience. Although information about the musical life of some of the main provincial chapters is now coming to light, details about music-making in the country parishes at the beginning of the nineteenth century—a period neglected by scholars—are sketchy. A complete analysis of available archives—registers kept by local chapters or manuscript memoirs of the time—will need to be made to reveal what musical life in French churches was like at the beginning of romanticism. Without these resources, historians are limited to the city of Paris. Information concerning even the main chapters such as Notre-Dame, Saint-Gervais, or Saint-Eustache is extremely scarce. Although some of them, including Notre-Dame-des-Champs, or Notre-Dame-de-Lorette, have preserved their own archives, most of the surviving documents concern the Tuileries Chapel, which served a consular, imperial, and royal chapel in turn. During the twenty-five years of the rise of romanticism in France, the Tuileries Chapel was the real center of sacred musical life in the country. The best composers of the time had their works performed there, and many foreign personalities visiting Paris commented on and praised its activity. A closer look at the repertoire performed in the chapel will help to cast a better light on some little-known aspects of French taste in the early nineteenth century, but first, I shall describe the institution itself.

Immediately after the signing of the Concordat, Bonaparte decided to create a chapel in the Tuileries, his usual palace of residence, thus resuming the centuries-old tradition of the French kings in Versailles. His taste in music is well known. He was not very knowledgeable, but he was very sensitive to the quality of a pretty voice or a pleasant and simple melody. He loved Italian vocal music. Cimarosa and Paisiello were his favorite composers. Their music was being played everywhere in Europe at that time, and the First Consul had attended many of their opera performances. Exhausted after his political imprisonment in Naples, Cimarosa had died at the beginning of 1801 in Venice, so Bonaparte called on Paisiello to direct the new consular chapel. By then, the composer had already travelled through most of Europe, including an eight-year stay at the court of Catherine the Great in

Saint Petersburg. He accepted the First Consul's offer and, on 25 April 1802, he arrived in Paris to a prince's welcome.

It was a generous offer indeed. The Italian composer would receive an annual salary of 10,000 francs and a housing compensation of 4800 francs. In addition, a state coach was placed at his disposal.

The service of the new chapel began on 20 July 1802. At first, there was no comparison to the former Royal Chapel of Versailles, which at the end of the Monarchy included thirty-nine singers and forty-five musicians. According to Castil-Blaze, the mass was celebrated in the room of the State Council; no more appropriate space existed in the Tuileries, for the old chapel had been destroyed. Behind the singers, two rows of violins played in a small gallery facing the altar. Singers and players could hardly move because of the lack of space. The German composer Reichardt, then visiting in Paris, affirms that this did not prevent Paisiello from conducting with the same fire and energy as on a Naples public square, "in the midst of fishermen's wives and *lazzaroni* (beggars)." At that time, the chapel did not yet have its own choir, but students from the Paris Conservatoire came to the Tuileries to sing on Sunday mornings. Beginning in 1802, famous singers such as Mademoiselle Armand and Madame Branchu were schedule to appear.

French composers must have been deeply disappointed when Bonaparte chose a foreign musician for the official post of director of the chapel, and Paisiello soon felt the jealousy of his French colleagues, particularly Méhul. The failure of Paisiello's French opera *Proserpine* at the Grand Opéra in 1803 did not help his position in Paris. The First Consul had commissioned *Proserpine*, hoping to see the creation of a French grand opera after the model of Italian opera seria. Paisiello made the following cynical comment to Reichardt: "The First Consul pays me so generously and covers me with so many presents that I cannot refuse to compose a French opera for him."[2] Bonaparte was probably outraged by the failure of his protégé. Bonet, director of the Opéra, wrote a secret report to the Prefect of the Palace: "Part of the merit of Mr. Paisiello's work comes from the position of its composer. To program it from time to time is a duty governed by powerful considerations."[3]

In spite of these so-called "powerful considerations," Paisiello was disappointed and in the Spring of 1804 decided to return to Italy. Nonetheless, he had composed twenty-five masses and sacred pieces for the repertoire of the Tuileries Chapel. A few years ago, I discovered these unpublished works in a collection of chapel manuscripts at the Paris Con-

servatoire. No study has yet been made of them. For these masses performed in the Tuileries, the Neapolitan composer probably followed the
customary practice of the time and recast some of his numerous earlier
works. It is even possible that he made new use of fragments of his countless operas by substituting sacred texts.

In any case, the first great religious celebration since the reinstatement
of free worship was Easter Sunday in Notre-Dame on 18 April 1802 with
music by Paisiello. During the papal mass celebrating the proclamation of
the Concordat as well as the ratification of the Peace of Amiens, the First
Consul chose to hear a Te Deum by his favorite composer, performed by
two orchestras under the direction of Cherubini and Méhul.

Although Méhul was also a candidate, Bonaparte decided on Le Sueur
to take over Paisiello's post. On 11 April 1804, Le Sueur became "Director
of the First Consul's Music"; the title changed three months later to "Director of the Emperor's Music."

One of the first important tasks for Le Sueur was to organize the musical part of the new emperor's coronation ceremony, scheduled on 2 December 1804 in Notre-Dame, but contrary to a long-held belief, Le Sueur did
not compose the two major works performed on that day. The great mass
and the Te Deum for double choir were Paisiello's, commissioned by
Napoleon before the composer left France. I have studied these two unpublished scores in detail.[4] I have also studied other short pieces that were performed at some specific moments of the ceremony, all by Le Sueur: *Tu es
Petrus*, for the Pope's processional, *Unxerunt Salomonem* for the unctions,
Accingere gladio for the remittal of the imperial sword, and the March for
the entrance and exit of the emperor and the empress. The *Vivat* by Abbé
Roze was also performed that day and was probably performed often in official imperial ceremonies.

These works were scored for very large numbers, far larger than had
been used on occasions in the past, such as the coronation of the French
kings in Reims, but comparable to those demanded by some revolutionary
pieces. For their performance, Le Sueur must have recruited every known
instrumentalist and singer in Paris. His own allegations are probably exaggerated, but the total number of performers was about 400: 133 singers, including soloists; 190 orchestra players; and 77 musicians of the guard for
the brass fanfares.

To appreciate fully this very elaborate music, it would have to be heard
under the same conditions as the original performance. For Le Sueur's *Le
Chant du 1ᵉʳ Vendémiaire* or Méhul's *Le Chant national*, both performed in

1800 at the Invalides, the composers obtained stereophonic effects by placing the performers in different areas of the building. Similarly, an orchestra and choir were located at each end of the transept of Notre-Dame. To the right, the first orchestra was conducted by Rey and the first choir by Candeille. To the left, the second orchestra was led by Persuis and the second choir by Le Brun. Le Sueur probably coordinated the whole ensemble from a spot visible to the four other conductors. The two separate groups sometimes played alternately, sometimes together. The impact of such sound combinations must have been striking, although a perfect synchronization of groups so far apart must have been quite a challenge without the help of a video monitor!

Napoleon wanted a more grandiose chapel, so he decided to have a new one built in the northern wing of the Tuileries Palace, between the Marsan and the Rohan Pavilions, along the Rue de Rivoli. The new project was entrusted to Percier and Fontaine in January 1805, and the construction was promptly completed; the new chapel was inaugurated on 2 February 1806. Several detailed descriptions and engravings of the Tuileries Chapel remain, adorned with the cold neo-classical decoration of Doric pillars. A description of the inaugural ceremony[5] appeared in the *Journal de l'Empire*:

> Last Sunday, the mass was celebrated in this chapel where the public was invited to witness, with customary admiration, the Imperial Restorer of Religion preside over the opening of the temple that he has just consecrated within his palace.

The total cost came to the handsome figure of 800,000 francs.

In 1804, the chapel[6] included about forty instrumentalists and singers, among whom were violinists Kreutzer and Baillot and singers Lays, Nourrit, Derivis, Madame Branchu, and Mademoiselle Armand, all members of the Paris Opéra company. The numbers steadily increased over the years, which can be verified by monthly payroll reports kept through 1830. The numbers reached fifty-three in 1810 and almost a hundred in 1814. I have in my collection the payroll report of June 1814, signed by Le Sueur, who wisely used the title "Director and Composer of Music"—it was advisable at that time not to specify whether it was the music of the emperor or the music of the king! The report for the month of June specifies total wages of 12,560 francs, and Le Sueur's annual salary of 10,000 francs. The most famous singers and instrumentalists in Paris belonged to this musical institution. Among the fifty-three instrumentalists listed in the report, for instance, I found the names of violinists Kreutzer, Grasset, Baillot, and Urhan; flutist Schneitzhoeffer, oboist Vogt; French hornist Duvernoy; and bassoonist Gebauer. The players' annual salaries ranged from 1000 francs to 4000 francs in the case of Kreutzer, and varied according to reputation. The singers' salaries were between 1000 and 3000 francs a year.

The Bourbons' rise to power in 1814 brought no profound changes to the organization of the Tuileries Chapel. Le Sueur easily joined in with the new regime, although he continued to be secretly devoted to Napoleon. However, a new difficulty soon arose. Martini, now seventy-three years old, made claim to the post of superintendent as the former reversioner of the chapel of King Louis XVI. After several months of dispute, a compromise was found, and in January 1814, Martini and Le Sueur were named joint superintendents. Each received six thousand francs per year, reducing Le Sueur's salary almost by half. Cherubini received Martini's reversion (*survivance*), and Persuis received Le Sueur's. In reviving the practice of the reversion, Louis XVIII renewed an old tradition of the Monarchy that had been abolished under the Empire.

Martini did not have much time to enjoy his new position; he died on 14 February 1816 in Paris and was automatically replaced by Cherubini. Le Sueur and Cherubini agreeably managed the Royal Chapel of the Tuileries together until 1830. Cherubini was in charge for the first and third quarters of the year and Le Sueur for the second and fourth quarters, when most religious festivals occurred (Easter, Pentecost, Corpus Christi, and Christmas).

The management of the chapel was first entrusted entirely to Baron de La Ferté, who was in charge of the king's entertainment (*Menus-Plaisirs*). In 1821, the powers were split, and the Duke of Châtre, first lord of the king's chamber, became personnel director, while Ferté was left with only the equipment to oversee. Several reform projects were submitted in a fifteen-year period, all of them attempting to reduce the chapel's budget and thus the number of personnel and their salaries, but none of them went through. Personnel increased in 1815 to around one hundred twenty and remained stable until 1830.

During the Restoration, musicians of the chapel fulfilled the same duties as they had during the Empire. The chapel followed the Court wherever it went and took part in Sunday services at the Tuileries, in Saint-Cloud, or in Fontainebleau. They also participated in some of the secular concerts performed at the Tuileries. When this happened, their service coincided with that of the emperor's or king's private music directed by Paër, which explains why a few secular pieces were found in the collection of manuscripts of the Tuileries Chapel. The chapel was also expected to take part in all official ceremonies marking important royal events, such as the baptism of the Duke of Bordeaux in Notre-Dame (1 May 1821) or the coronation of Charles X in Reims (29 May 1825). The latter ceremony[7] was grandiose and marked the last days of glory of the chapel of the kings of France. As for the coronation of Napoleon in Notre-Dame in 1804, Le Sueur organized and directed the entire musical part of the ceremony. The coronation lasted several days, since the religious services began the day before, with motets by Le Sueur and Plantade's Te Deum, and went on for two days afterward. For the coronation itself, Le Sueur programmed a Te Deum of his own and excerpts from three great Coronation Oratorios he had composed for the occasion. The mass was by Cherubini. It became well known and is still performed occasionally. It includes the famous March for the King's Communion, about which Berlioz made the following surprising comment, considering how much he disliked Cherubini: "If the word *sublime* was ever used truly and appropriately, it was in reference to Cherubini's March for the King's Communion."

The decree of 13 March 1830 by Charles X reorganized the chapel and placed it under the direction of only one directeur-compositeur with an annual salary of 8000 francs. The 1830 Revolution blocked this reform, but another one, more radical, came soon after. Since the *Roi-bourgeois* had no use for music in his chapel, the two music superintendents were notified on 9 September 1830 that their posts no longer existed. Thus Cherubini and Le Sueur were the last two men to hold a position that had for several centuries enabled many great musicians to win fame in the history of French music. Protests came from several sources after the suppression of the Royal chapel by the new regime. Fétis wrote against it in his *Revue musicale* but his effort was in vain. Louis-Philippe was not disposed to burden his finances with such a costly institution, and all the artists were forced to retire.

After reviewing the history of the Tuileries Chapel as an institution, I shall analyze its repertoire to try and identify French taste in sacred music at the beginning of the nineteenth century.

During previous research, as I have mentioned, I was very fortunate to discover the complete collection of unpublished manuscript from the Tuileries Chapel, scrupulously kept since 1830. This makes it possible to draw up a list of all the composers whose works were performed at the

Tuileries Chapel between 1802 and 1830 and to establish a summary count
of each work:

Paisiello	Twenty-four masses and various sacred works, the great Te Deum for the coronation of Napoleon, and ten miscellaneous pieces (including one *Judicabit* for a solemn occasion and six *Domine salvum*).
Le Sueur	Twenty-nine masses and thirty-two miscellaneous pieces.
Martini	Nine masses, one Te Deum, and fourteen miscellaneous pieces.
Cherubini	Twenty-three masses and forty miscellaneous pieces.
Plantade	Ten masses and thirty-six miscellaneous pieces.
Persuis	Five miscellaneous pieces.
Roze	One miscellaneous piece.
Zingarelli	One mass and fragments of a Stabat Mater.
Pergolesi	One Stabat Mater.
Giroust	*Le Passage de la mer Rouge* (The Crossing of the Red Sea).
Gossec	One *O Salutaris*.
Lefebvre[8]	One funeral march and one triumphal march.
Desvignes[9]	One *Pie Jesu*.
Jomelli	One mass, one Requiem, and one Miserere (with Italian words).
Naderman[10]	Three miscellaneous pieces.
Durante	*Litanies de la Vierge* (Litanies of the Virgin).
Homet[11]	Requiem.
Mozart	One mass (K. 192), the Requiem, and the Ave Verum.
Haydn	Six masses, one Stabat Mater, one miscellaneous piece.
Paër	One mass.
Rossini	Ave Maria.

Naturally, this list calls for some comment. First of all, the composers
most represented are the contemporaries who held official posts with the
chapel: Paisiello, Le Sueur, Cherubini, and Martini. Second, the earliest
composers on the list are Italian: Durante, Pergolesi, and Jomelli. Thus no
work dating before Pergolesi and Durante was heard at the Tuileries; the
great masters of the Renaissance and the seventeenth century were com-

pletely unknown. Finally, none of the great sacred works of French music of the seventeenth and eighteenth centuries remained in the repertoire.

This is evidence that there was a total and systematic break with the French tradition of the eighteenth century: none of the great motets was ever heard at the Tuileries. The only reason for a performance of Giroust's *Le Passage de la mer Rouge* was Louis XVIII's special request to hear this composer of the old Monarchy to renew a link with the past and hear again a kind of music that he had admired in his youth at Versailles. One can see that the repertoire was essentially limited to the works of three or four contemporaries. Almost all of these works, with the exception of Cherubini's masses, have remained unknown to this day.

One obvious explanation is that most sacred works by composers such as Paisiello, Martini, and Plantade were never engraved. Although most of Cherubini's sacred music was indeed published, the manuscript collection of the chapel contains several of his unpublished works. As for Le Sueur, he did not publish his sacred music until 1826, at the end of his life, and the task was completed by his widow after his death in 1837. Very often, before the engraving of his masses, oratorios, and miscellaneous pieces, Le Sueur revised them to conform to works performed at the Tuileries. So it was only by studying the manuscripts of the chapel collection—now in the process of being deposited in the *Bibliothèque nationale*—that I was able to draw some general conclusions about this body of sacred music. For the reasons just given, this music never reached beyond its original setting and was not known in the French provinces nor, obviously, in foreign countries.

In order to avoid any misunderstanding, I must clarify one important point: While I was studying these manuscripts, I observed that in the vocabulary of the time, the title "mass" was commonly used as a generic term that could be applied indiscriminate to any piece of sacred music, not just a mass in the proper sense, but also to an oratorio or a religious cantata freely adapted to Latin words of the Vulgate. Only in the event of major official ceremonies, such as the coronation of Napoleon or Charles X, did composers set all five parts of the Ordinary and the *Domine salvum fac Imperatorem* (or *Regem*) to conclude the service. For the usual Sunday services at the Tuileries, only one or two of the parts were performed, either alone or interspersed with settings of texts not taken from the Ordinary; with "petites scènes bibliques," short oratorios in Latin using a compilation of texts most often borrowed from the Old Testament; or with a succession of arias for soloists and chorus using Latin words borrowed from a great variety of sources.

Comments made by contemporaries corroborate the study of these scores. Fétis, a witness of the time, made this definitive comment:

> The ordinary service of the chapel of Kings Louis XVIII and Charles X consisted of a low mass, with musicians singing various pieces not exceeding in length the mass said by the priest. It was rare that an entire mass be sung in the Royal chapel. Often, the time of the service was taken up by a Kyrie followed by a motet.[12]

Berlioz agreed completely with this: "The works performed during the ordinary services of the Royal chapel—at least during Le Sueur's tenure—were rarely masses in the proper sense."[13]

Thus, while the priest celebrated the mass at the altar, the music was heard with a text that differed completely or partially from that of the service. This custom had been introduced by Paisiello during the early days of the chapel in 1802. The following example shows the composition of his Mass No. 4 with full orchestral accompaniment. It lasted twenty-three minutes, with an additional five minutes for the *Domine salvum fac* (the timings are indicated on the manuscripts):

Kyrie eleison, chorus
Gloria in excelsis, chorus
Credo, chorus
Dominus a dextris tuis, soprano aria (text taken from Psalm 110)
Si respirando in pace, tenor aria (text not yet identified)
Domine salvum fac, soprano aria

Similar examples can be found in Plantade's music. His Mass No. 5 does not contain any of the Ordinary parts. It is a sacred piece entirely composed on some of the verses of the Psalm *Super flumina.* His Mass No. 6 included a Kyrie sung by the choir followed by a trio for three female voices, *Ecce advenit dominator* (on an unidentified text), and finally, a succession of choruses interspersed by recitatives on the following texts:

Credidi (unidentified text)
Quid retribuam Domino (Psalm 116)
Calicem salutarem accipiam (Psalm 116)

The Sanctus and the Agnus Dei, at least, are obviously missing in all of these mass settings. None of Le Sueur's masses performed at the Tuileries included an Agnus Dei. He certainly was the composer who took the greatest liberty with liturgical texts, and I suspect that he sometimes invented new Latin texts that were not in the Bible. His *Cantate religieuse*, composed for the marriage of Napoleon and Marie-Louise, used a succession of texts borrowed from different psalms as well as from the book of Ecclesiastes. It included one introductory phrase—the only one in the whole work that pertained to the celebration of marriage—with the words *Veni sponsa mansueta, coronaberis*, an extremely free setting of some of the verses of the Song of Songs. In Mass No. 5 of the chapel repertoire, moreover, he dared to introduce into the opening Kyrie words totally foreign to this prayer: *Deus, Agnus dei, Deus bonus pastor, miserere nobis, exaudi nos*. Then, with a mention in the margin of his score that "the prayer becomes a song of praise," he followed with a setting of one verse from the *Gloria, quoniam tu solus sanctus*.

Such aberrations were foreign to German music of the time and call for an explanation. It is given by Berlioz, Le Sueur's pupil, who commented on this Kyrie:

> In order to avoid excessive repetition of the words Kyrie eleison, Le Sueur added words of liturgical origin that allowed him to use many different rhythmic forms and to vary the accents of the prayer while making the best of the principal idea.[14]

This comment made by a great romantic composer brings us to the heart of the problem. Foreign texts are added to the Ordinary in order to "vary the accents of the prayer." It is as if by the beginning of the nineteenth century the three words that make up the entire Kyrie—*Kyrie eleison, Christe eleison*—were far too limiting to the composers' fantasy and to their taste for an imitative and dramatic style of sacred music. It seems as though the strict and traditional liturgy was too tight a fit for the spiritual expression of these musicians. Their vivid imagination was in need of detailed pictures. Here is clear evidence that religious feelings had changed since the high classical period. We have only to think of the monumental dimensions that Bach had achieved at the beginning of his Mass in B minor on the simple words of the Kyrie.

In fact, a comparison with one of the giants of German sacred music of the previous century should help us understand the musical reason for this difference and this evolution. Bach saw no need to "vary the accents of the prayer" since he used as a means of expression the endless possibilities of counterpoint and fugue. The composers who worked at the Tuileries

Chapel since Paisiello were not, except perhaps Cherubini, experts of counterpoint. One of the primary characteristics of French sacred music of the
early nineteenth century—including that of Paisiello, Martini, and Cherubini—is that, for reason of taste as well as ignorance, composers did not
make use of the richness of counterpoint and refused the *style savant* (the
learned style), which had been traditional in church music. Instead, they
introduced into the church many effects that came from the operatic style
of their time.

From this point of view, all the German visitors to the Tuileries at that
time were quite amazed. The German musical critic of the *Allgemeine
musikalische Zeitung*[15] expressed a very unfavorable opinion of the many
masses and thanksgiving Te Deums performed all around Paris after the
proclamation of the Empire in 1804. On a mass by Desvignes sung in
Notre-Dame, he added the following comment: "I wish that Parisians could
hear the wonderful music of our churches!" Composer Reichardt was surprised to find, in a mass by Paisiello, "a charming little duet for harp and
French horn," obviously added there to please Madame Bonaparte, who
was very fond of these two fashionable instruments. The harp and French
horn duets were performed at the Tuileries Chapel, as was customary, by
two well-known virtuoso players, Dalvimare and Frédéric Duvernoy. Such
pieces were in demand and were frequently included in the concerts and
opera productions of the time. The two instruments moved from the concert stage and the opera pit into the church. They were called for by
Paisiello in his Great Mass for the Coronation of Napoleon, still unpublished: in the Credo, a harp and French horn obligato accompanied Mademoiselle Manent in the verse *Et incarnatus est*, and both Mademoiselle
Armand and Madame Branchu in the *Et resurrexit*. On Pentecost Sunday of
1804, another mass by Desvignes was performed in Notre-Dame. The *O
salutaris* and several other prayers were "accompanied by four harps, French
horn and violin obligato, which produced the most delightful effect."[16]

Paisiello, the founder of the chapel, gave his church music a fashionable
and secular character, which corresponded to the taste of contemporary
French society and influenced French sacred music for a long time. This
was already obvious to the most discerning observers of his day. In 1811,
after hearing a Te Deum with large chorus and orchestra, a critic wrote:
"Nowadays, the House of the Lord resounds with songs that would be better suited to the Feydeau theater than to Notre-Dame."[17] In 1810, a mass
by Plantade was performed in Saint-Eustache in Paris to celebrate Saint
Cecilia's Day. The newspaper *Les Tablettes de Polymnie* published a severer

comment. Plantade's music may have been well received and his songs pleasing and easy to listen to, but "their melody was not appropriate to their subject. The color of the Agnus Dei belonged to the pastoral genre. Although *Agnus* means lamb in Latin, it is not sufficient reason to introduce shepherds into the House of the Lord."[18]

The tendency to merge the operatic with the sacred style arose in Paris as soon as the Tuileries Chapel was inaugurated in 1802 with the Masses of Paisiello and persisted until 1830. The German composer Spohr stayed in Paris in 1820 and heard several services at the Tuileries. In his autobiography, he recorded his amazement at having heard this French sacred music. First he criticized Plantade's style, which reminded him of comic opera. Then, about Le Sueur's midnight mass on Christmas Eve, he wrote:

> At midnight on 24 December, we heard the *messe de minuit*, composed by Le Sueur. First, we had to endure a long test of our patience. For two whole hours, from ten to midnight, nothing but psalms sung in the most monotonous manner, interrupted at times by primitive organ interludes. At midnight, finally, the mass began. It was again in the same frivolous theatrical style as Plantade's, but at this solemn time of night, it sounded even more unpleasant. What surprised me most coming from Le Sueur, who enjoys here a reputation as an excellent harmonist and, if I am not mistaken, teaches harmony at the Conservatoire, was that not once did I hear true four-part singing. There are times in opera when simple two-part writing can produce an effect, with the sopranos doubling the tenors and the altos doubling the basses, which is easier to perform by the often mediocre opera choruses. However, it seems to me quite primitive to introduce this device into the church. I would be curious to know what Mr. Le Sueur's intentions were in doing so, since he is doubtless an intelligent artist. In the place of the Offertory, I heard variations by Naderman for harp, French horn, and cello played by the composer, Mr. Dauprat, and Mr. Baudiot. As you know, back in Germany, a symphonic movement heard at this moment of the service already seems to me far too secular. You can easily imagine what an unpleasant feeling I had upon hearing these variations for harp in the French style galant. Still, I saw the congregation pray with fervor. How could they have a single pious thought when hearing such trivial music? Either this music has no meaning to them, or they have mastered the art of shutting their

ears tightly. Otherwise, this music should inevitably remind them, as it does me, of ballet scenes at the Grand Opéra, where the same three instruments are used in the same manner in the most sensual of dances.[19]

From a German point of view, this criticism is quite justified, since German sacred music was associated with the *style sévère* (strict style), and fugue and counterpoint were the foundation of the musical language of the church. It is interesting to compare two different viewpoints on the subject of Cherubini's great Mass in F major which premiered in a private performance by some of the best Paris artists at the *Hotel de Chimay* in 1809. Here is what Fétis wrote:

> I shall never forget the effect produced by this beautiful work performed by such great artists. Every Parisian celebrity from all walks of life was present for this occasion, which resulted in an unprecedented success for the composer. During the pause between the Gloria and the Credo, the audience gathered in groups in the salons and everyone expressed unqualified admiration for this new style of composition, with which Cherubini surpassed every previous attempt in the sacred concertante style. The combination of the severe beauty of the fugue and counterpoint with the dramatic character and the rich instrumental effects showed us Cherubini's genius at its best.[20]

Without a doubt, of all the composers who worked at the Tuileries Chapel during that period, Cherubini was the most advanced contrapuntist. Yet an anonymous German journalist criticized him in the *Allgemeine musikalische Zeitung* for the predominance in his mass of the dramatic and theatrical style over the *style sévère* and concluded with the following comments:

> In order to compose perfect works in this genre, one must have practiced counterpoint and fugal style all one's life. This was true for Mozart. All his great works bear the seal of a man who had mastered this style so well that he was able to use it without constraint in the freest expression of his genius. The German nation has the merit of being the only one to have produced great geniuses whose *style sévère* will always serve as an example for all other nations: Bach, Handel, Haydn, and Mozart.

Two years later, in October 1811, the same German periodical published an article by its Paris correspondent that stigmatized French interpretation of sacred music as too superficial and theatrical: "If my opinion contradicts that expressed in most local newspapers, please keep in mind that I know German sacred music and that I judge from a quite different point of view."[21]

There are probably several reasons why, at the beginning of the nineteenth century, French religious music tended to use less scholarly forms and was under the constant influence of opera—even comic opera.

The first reason is a fundamental one. Except for Cherubini, none of the great composers of that time—neither Le Sueur nor Plantade nor even Paisiello—was an accomplished contrapuntist, and the teaching in the choir schools should be blamed for that. Le Sueur's teacher, for example, was Roze, whose masses were still performed during the Empire in certain Paris parishes. I have studied the manuscripts of several compositions by this *maître de chapelle* of the old Monarchy who ended his career in 1819 as the Conservatoire librarian. His music is harmonically weak, with the same commonplace accompaniment figures endlessly repeated, unison doublings of voices and orchestra, and shows a regrettable lack of skill. Significantly, on one of Roze's manuscript motets, I found the following alarming comment, written in his own hand in 1770: "The author had just graduated from the seminary when he composed this motet, having not had a teacher since the age of ten and having not heard any music other than his own."[22]

Music education provided during the Monarchy by the choir schools was invaluable because there was no other. No institution in France could teach music students the strict principles of the *style sévère*. Since France had no such tradition at the end of the eighteenth century, composers could teach themselves only by hearing music. Occasions to hear good music were scarce, especially in the provinces where sheet music of foreign origin hardly circulated at all, except in a few places.

Another reason was the influence of the Enlightenment theorists on the change of taste in religious music at the beginning of the nineteenth century. Unexpectedly, they reinforced some of the early romantic aspirations. I shall not discuss here in detail the radical positions taken by most eighteenth-century philosophers in the field of aesthetics. Suffice to say that they considered music as an imitative art form, along with poetry and painting. As a consequence, they had a preference for vocal music over instrumental music, for simple melody over harmony. Diderot, d'Alembert, Lacépède, and Rousseau, among the most famous of these philosophers, always reaffirmed the supremacy of melody as solely capable of achieving a perfect imitation of nature, which for them was the essence and function of music. Rousseau considered melody as a language carrying precise meaning and thought that producing several melodies simultaneously was absurd. It was as if several individuals spoke at the same time on different subjects, producing unbearable cacophony. "If each part is given its own melody, Rousseau wrote, all the melodies heard at once destroy one another and produce no melody."

In this eighteenth century, before Gothic art had been rediscovered, such a concept lead directly to a condemnation of fugue and counterpoint as "barbaric remnants of bad taste that stand, like the portals of our gothic churches, only to disgrace those patient enough to create them."[23]

The influence of Rousseau in particular and the encyclopedists in general was considerable. Composers like Grétry and Le Sueur repeatedly claimed these doubtful theories for their own. After hearing Handel's great fugues, Grétry complained that they had no meaning and in them he searched for melody "with the impatience of a lover searching for his mistress in a thick forest." Le Sueur was, like Cherubini, considered an authority on church music until 1830. He read Rousseau's works when he was young, embraced his ideas, and never changed his mind: "Fugues that depict nothing and have no other purpose than showing off composers' vain skills in overcoming difficulties must be completely banished from our churches."[24] Berlioz's tirades against the fugue are common knowledge. After his teacher Le Sueur, who undeniably influenced him on this particular point, he declared, with the excess so typical of a young romantic:

> I defy anyone with the slightest musical sense who listens to a fugue on *Amen* without warning, not to take the choir for legions of veritable devils making fun of the sacred place, instead of a congregation gathered to praise the Lord.[25]

Romanticism can be seen here as a direct inheritance of the Enlightenment, beyond the break of the Revolution. It believed that the human soul reaches out to God with music that comes from the heart and is not constructed according to abstract rules.

It may now be clearer why most French composers of the early nineteenth century turned out a very different kind of church music from their German contemporaries, who had inherited quite a different tradition. Most important was the search for expression at all costs, for pleasing vocal lines, and for beautiful phrases. Counterpoint was almost always absent, and octave doublings of the voices were extremely frequent. In fact, Plantade or Le Sueur's masses were never written in four real voices. The harmonic fabric was loose, like that of some of those comic operas upon which Suzanne Clercx commented facetiously that one could fit "a six-horse carriage between the bass and the treble lines."

The very simple—easy, I should say—quality of the sacred music of the early romantic period suited the religious feelings of many souls in the aftermath of Revolutionary turmoil. After years of terror for many and mourning for some, life began again. The carefree younger generation went in for eccentricities and excesses that are typical of post-crisis periods. French society's appetite for life under the Directoire is legendary. Religious service had been outlawed, so people had forgotten how to go to church, and the new generation of *Merveilleuses* and *Incroyables* was too young ever to have gone there. Some, more level-headed than others, worried that this atmosphere of entertainment and pleasure would be short-lived and would leave many lonely souls faced with a void. Under these conditions it could be expected that sacred music would take on a theatrical and worldly character, apt to satisfy the taste of the new French society of the early nineteenth century. In *Le Citoyen français*, right at the time of the proclamation of the Empire, I found this revealing comment:[26]

Well-thinking people, even pious people, cannot help but groan and laugh at the most dramatic formulas used to announce religious ceremonies of the Catholic church. The following is an example of one of these announcements: "On such a day, in such church, a Te Deum, or a Salute to so and so will be celebrated. Mr. So and so will officiate as pontiff. The sermon will be pronounced by Mr. So and so, and the famous Mr. So and so will play the organ. The music of this mass or this Te Deum or this Salute will be the composition of the illustrious *maître de chapelle* So and so, and so on, and will be performed by the Opéra orchestra or the student orchestra of the Conservatoire or the orchestra of such and such a theater." And it goes on and on. Would you not think that this is going to be a theater performance? At the risk of being accused of philosophy or philosophism or philosophomania, we will simply declare that these petty secular reasons for calling the congregation into a house of God are not worthy of the religious grandeur that should attract them there. Solemnity deserves eloquent speakers and skillful musicians, but the desire to attend should not be derived from motives having nothing to do with the divine. This manner of requesting their presence seems to mean: "If you simply come to pray, you will be bored, but we have arranged things so that this nuisance will not fall upon you."

At the beginning of the Empire, a full-scale press campaign was undertaken to re-Christianize the people. It was not a very easy task, and one of the means used by the Church was music. In a periodical of the time, *La Correspondance des Professeurs et des Amateurs de Musique*, a series of articles dated December 1804 exemplified some of the concerns:

> For the past twelve years, bad taste has caused an unrelenting search for the refined and the futile. As a result, it has destroyed nearly all profound feelings, making people insensitive to anything religious. Now any attempt to bring these feelings back apparently inspires disgust. . . . Yet some people are beginning to say out loud that in this way we are sinking into an ever-growing vortex, without being able to hold onto anything, that we are poor amid abundance and pleasureless amid happiness itself. Since we are now at the point of realizing this, the moment has come to rediscover sacred music, even if only from a cosmopolitan or political point of view.

To bring souls back to God did not necessarily mean to shake up consciences. The tendency of composers of the time was to give people what they wanted to hear. The younger generation was not in need of theologians or counterpoint specialists, it wanted to be touched and moved. People felt an ardent need for poetry in their souls. As an example, *Le Génie du christianisme* (The Genius of Christianity), an apologia proving the existence of the Creator through harmony and the marvels of Creation, owed much of its success at the time to these particular circumstances. Subtle quibbles were no longer convincing; it was time to please, to open the imagination to the picturesque world of dreams.

Hence the masses of that time give the impression of being written in the spirit of the old oratorio or the cantata. Liturgical texts, to be fully understood, need to be interpreted by actors. A very typical example is Le Sueur's third *Messe solennelle*. Its Offertory takes on unusual importance by being placed between the Credo and Sanctus. At that point in the mass, it was common in those days to use words not belonging to the Ordinary. Le Sueur's poetic imagination went further than that of his contemporaries. He composed a long scene for solo tenor and chorus, a sort of little drama integrated into the middle of the mass. The composer arranged the text from various verses of different psalms. Of particular interest for us today are the indications or stage directions, found in his hand at the beginning of this Offertory:

> David awakes in the middle of the night to praise the Lord in the Tabernacle. The Levites, the priests, the holy women keep vigil with the psalmist to honor God. Later, they add their prayers to the prophet king's melancholy hymn, its religious strains heard alone through the silent night.

This is a true operatic scene, complete with actors and a backdrop. The above text is typical of its time: the silent night, the melancholy hymn, the religious strains seem right out of Lamartine's *Méditations* or *Harmonies*. Overlooking the fact that this was a mass and not a musical drama, Le Sueur wrote the name of David, the singing role, at the beginning of the piece, above the staff, as if this was an opera or oratorio score. When David was through and the night watch ended, the mass resumed, and the choir began the Sanctus.

Generally speaking, the return to religious practice and the renewed interest in sacred music were tempered, at least during the Empire, by a good deal of indifference coming from the ruler himself, setting a very poor example for his courtiers, who imitated him in everything. Several anecdotes support this. One critic complained that during the Mass of Saint Cecilia in 1803 in Saint-Roch, the music could hardly be heard, so noisy were the people "like for a concert at the Rue de Cléry." Also in 1803, during the service at the Tuileries, Reichardt noted how indifferent the First Consul appeared, to the music as well as to the mass itself. It was clear, he added, that "all this had only political significance for him."

In Saint-Gervais on 22 November 1802, Saint Cecilia's Day, the same Reichardt had a stranger experience yet. The music for the mass was by Roze. First, he was surprised to see the grenadiers of the guard standing around the altar and watching the public closely, obviously under very strict orders. At the moment of the elevation, upon a single military command, they fell to their knees in a perfect ensemble. During this mass, another incident surprised the German composer. He saw a policeman enter the

church, walk through the rows of pews, stop in front of a young man, and
after showing him a piece of paper, take him away.

> I seemed to be the only one to take notice of this little game,
> Reichardt added innocently, and when I asked my neighbors what
> it meant, they coldly replied: "The young man was arrested."

Finally, I shall quote one more eyewitness account illustrating the atmosphere in the Tuileries Chapel during the Empire. This one is unknown in
France, since it appears in the memoirs of the German composer Wilhelm
Speyer, who spent two of his early years in France (1811–1813) studying the
violin with Baillot, a musician of the chapel. He attended one of the masses
sung in the emperor's presence and gave a full account of the ceremony,
which I shall quote here, since its interest is not simply anecdotal. It shows
what a small role music plays in this somewhat ludicrous ceremonial. Although music was a sine qua non of this frozen homage that Imperial society
paid to itself, it was in fact only a pretext for it, not an inherent part of it. The
emperor and the court were obviously bored but obliged themselves to listen
almost like a punishment. The crowd showed no true religious feelings, but
was only stirred by the fanfares of the guard outside the palace. It was as if the
whole Imperial Court had only one wish, to leave the confined space where it
was forced to respect a ceremony that it disliked even though it was required,
so it could, at last, watch the real spectacle taking place outside, the brilliant
military parade to the sound of drums. I wonder how Le Sueur felt about
this, as he remained behind in the dark chapel, alone with his musicians.

Here is Wilhelm Speyer's text, the most detailed contemporary chroni-
cle of the Tuileries Chapel during the Empire known to this day. I think
that it speaks for itself and requires no additional comment:[27]

> Le Sueur had previously composed a mass upon Napoleon's orders.
> The Imperial couple had just returned from Holland and Antwerp,
> and Le Sueur received orders to prepare the performance of his
> mass for the following Sunday, 8 December 1811. He called on
> Paër to inform the artists of the Chamber and ask them to be there
> but declared that they should not have too high expectations from
> his music because the emperor's will had put some limits on his
> invention. Napoleon is known to have had a preference for sweet
> and calm music. Le Sueur's reservation won him many a teasing
> joke from the artists present.

The entire Imperial society decided to attend the chapel service on the following Sunday. The Tuileries Chapel is located in the right wing of the castle (seen from the gardens) and is connected to the main residence by a passage.

At noon, the two side galleries began to fill up. The most important figures of the capital—even of the Empire—were gathered in this small space (Talleyrand, Fouché, Ney, and so on).

The entire household of the empress and those of the princesses filled the Ladies' gallery. Wives of ministers, generals, and ambassadors were also present, wearing the most dazzling dresses and the richest jewelry and diamonds. In the nave, under the Imperial gallery stood two halberdiers in Spanish uniforms of the high period. Behind them, a squad of grenadiers and two drummers occupied the whole width of the church. The whole display was at once imposing and picturesque, even though it had a somewhat theatrical aspect.

Around one o'clock, two page-boys walked to the Imperial gallery and placed prayer stools in front of the two Imperial seats. A half dozen officers in light blue uniforms lined with silver then appeared, each holding a cane. The household of the empress followed: first, the Count of Beauharnais, knight-banneret, and after him Prince Aldobrandini, Master of the Horse.

After all the empress's courtiers had taken their places on the right side of the gallery, the empress herself, a youthful blonde woman, walked in, preceded by six page-boys, and sat down on the left seat. The entire company rose upon her entrance. A complete silence followed, indicating that the emperor was about to enter.

That day I saw Napoleon for the first time. All this preparation had made me extremely impatient. I became feverish and excited. As I was going to see the hero of the century in the flesh for the first time, I reflected upon the remarkable exploits of his career. I thought about Egypt, the Battle of the Pyramids, and the Italian and German campaigns, as well as the assassination of the Duke of Enghien.

The halberdiers knocked on the ground with their spears and shouted: *"L'Empereur!"* The officer on duty ordered them to present arms, the drums played a march, the empress rose. At that moment Napoleon entered, wearing the simple uniform of a cavalry grenadier, surrounded by his followers who, wearing brilliant uniforms lined with gold and silver, advanced with measured steps. The effect of contrast was striking and well calculated.

As soon as the emperor had taken his place in the seat on the right, the empress sat down and Le Sueur's mass began. The work was written in a very simple sacred style, lacking spirit and very monotonous. At the Sanctus, the Imperial couple stood. Napoleon seemed agitated and did nothing to conceal it. He snorted several times, leaned his whole body from left to right and bit his nails. At the Agnus Dei, the scene changed. The music was in D-flat major, dolce and *pianissimo*, with muted strings.

All of a sudden, a fanfare began. The loud music of the guard could be heard, and the horse-drawn cannons outside: the troops were taking their places for the parade in the Tuileries courtyard, on the Carousel square, and in the nearby streets. Immediately, the whole assembly seemed electrified. Napoleon himself appeared the most affected of all. His body motions accelerated, and he tapped his leg and his boot with his short riding-whip.

Another no less interesting event now took place. The best troops of the time and the powerful Imperial Guard in close ranks were being inspected by the emperor, their general: the cavalry on the Carousel square, and the infantry in the Tuileries courtyard. One of the windows of the Gallery of Paintings provided a marvelous vantage point on the whole scene. Gone was the theatrical impression left by the previous ceremony in the chapel. Everything now seemed natural and real. The grandeur and the sheer power of the period were symbolized by this impressive military show.

Soon Napoleon appeared, riding his white horse.

Things probably changed some during the Restoration. Louis XVIII and Charles X attempted to restore some of the old Versailles ceremonial,

and attending the church service meant much more to them than a simple
official duty. The constant presence at their side of the Duchess of
Angoulême, First Princess of the Court, whose piety was well known, was a
strong indication that the mass was by no means a masquerade. From 1815
on, the Tuileries Chapel seems to have played an important role in official
musical life in Paris, favored by the simultaneous decline of the Opéra. According to Berlioz, who was Le Sueur's private student beginning in 1823,
the final years of the chapel were those of "its greatest splendor." Several accounts from the Paris correspondent of the *Allgemeine musikalische Zeitung*,
G. Sievers, give a foreigner's objective point of view on Parisian musical life
at the time. He very much deplored the fact that access to the chapel was
not permitted to the public, since the best artists in Paris performed there,
beginning with Kreutzer and Baillot who lead the first and second violins
and whose virtuosity deserved the highest praise. "The effect produced by
this chapel is imposing, grandiose, and majestic, and I often found the precision of its performances astonishing."

To confirm the opinion of the German music press, Dr. Véron, who
was an eager observer of all aspects of Parisian life and the future director of
the Opéra, also stated that during the Restoration, the Tuileries Chapel was
a most important musical center. "Under the direction of Cherubini and
Le Sueur, the king's chapel included a large number of performers. The very
best instrumentalists, the greatest talents, and the most beautiful voices had
been recalled to serve there. New works by Cherubini, full of sentiment and
unction, were premiered at every Sunday service and on certain anniver-
saries. The performances were excellent. Chapel tickets were in very high
demand."[28]

A historical survey of the Tuileries Chapel from 1802 to 1830 would not be
complete without an evaluation of its repertoire as a whole.

I have already mentioned the break that occurred in 1802 from the end
of the eighteenth century. No grand motet was performed at the chapel after
that date. As far as masses go, I have already described the great liberties taken
by composers with the text of the Ordinary and their constant tendency to
make free arrangements of the Latin words to emphasize the dramatic and
theatrical character of sacred music. A closer look at the many masses written
by Paisiello, founder of the chapel in 1802, would certainly document his
influence in this domain on composers such as Plantade and Le Sueur.

Charles-Henri Plantade's output of sacred music (1764–1839) is rather
limited. A writer of pleasant romances, he was, for a time, *maître de chapelle*

under King Louis Bonaparte of Holland. He did not leave a very strong personal imprint on the repertoire of his time. I have read most of the manuscript scores of his masses and was left with a painful impression of blandness. Charming melodies do not succeed in covering up weak harmony and counterpoint.

On the other hand, works composed by Le Sueur for the Tuileries Chapel deserve closer examination. The fact that most of his sacred music is dramatic and descriptive is not sufficient reason to condemn his style as being secular. What criteria can determine if one form of sacred music is more authentic than another? There are many different ways to reach out to the divine in music. In spite of some obvious weaknesses, Le Sueur's music is, on the whole, a witness of religious faith. In its own way it is inspired. It reflects the aspirations of the new century and is perfectly in harmony with its time. Le Sueur had a poetic outlook on the Bible. In writing for the service, he also refused anything too abstract. His tendency was to treat faith poetically and to speak to the heart instead of the mind.

Very revealing was Le Sueur's choice of certain female figures of the Old Testament (Ruth, Naomi, Deborah, and Rachel), around whom he invented librettos for short oratorios in Latin. He was the first to have the idea and, with the works he composed during the Empire, he was the founder of the nineteenth-century Latin oratorio in France. Later, as César Franck's works became better known—his oratorio *Ruth* in particular—Le Sueur's influence became even more obvious. Berlioz also remembered his former teacher when he composed his *Enfance du Christ*. Another famous name should be added, Gounod, also a student of Le Sueur for a time. In his own manner, Gounod used some of his teacher's ideas in his own Latin oratorios.

It was in the genre of the oratorio that Le Sueur composed the most original and forward-looking works. He wrote an *Oratorio de Noël* (Christmas Oratorio), which was performed very often in his lifetime. For this work, he had the ingenious idea of inserting into the musical fabric several popular Christmas carols.

Most representative are Le Sueur's three *Oratorios du couronnement* (Coronation Oratorios). They were composed in 1825 for the coronation of Charles X and not, as the composer himself claimed later, for that of Napoleon in 1804. Together they represent over three hundred pages of music.

These works were put together, according to the coronation ceremony, in a more or less coherent manner using texts of quite different origins.

Their dramatic concept and some original details in the musical writing still make them attractive today.

The visual element was very important in these religious compositions. Le Sueur wrote many stage directions in the margin of his scores and assigned roles as if for an actual stage performance. His works should be understood in the same way as the coronation scene in Musorgsky's *Boris Godunov*.

When he composed this music, Le Sueur had in mind the magnificent site of the nave in the Reims Cathedral. He did not score for solo voices, but set a full choir against small solo choirs, for example "soli de dix basses tailles récitantes" (solo recitative for ten low tenor voices). In order to avoid interference from echo effects from the cathedral vault, he purposely wrote few modulations. Straight-forward harmonies, which elsewhere could have been a weakness, here were a strength. The great number of triads, their many repetitions and the frequent use of weaker degrees in each key gave the music a natural, specific coloration and remarkable strength. Choron called this music "cut in stone." Today, merely reading the scores is very deceptive. The works need to be heard in their original environment, performed by the very large numbers called for. Some fragments may be irretrievable, but I am certain that passages such as the fourth and fifth scenes from the third Coronation Oratorio, *Ora pro nobis*, and *Unxerunt Salomonem*, would produce great effect and show that Le Sueur's sacred style was that of an epic poet. Recording excerpts of this music today would give it the recognition it deserves.

Unlike his colleague Le Sueur, Cherubini did not write any oratorios. He was only fully active as a composer at the Tuileries from 1816, when he began sharing the direction of the chapel with Le Sueur. He wrote little for the church before that time. With the exception of some youthful works composed in Italy, the first work worth mentioning is the large Credo in four voices a capella, begun in Italy and completed in Paris in 1806. This masterpiece of counterpoint, showing the influence of the Italian masters of the sixteenth century, remained practically unknown in France during its time, which explains why it is not found among the manuscript collection of the Tuileries Chapel. Here I should like to recall Spohr's ironic phrase about Cherubini's genius: "If only the man had composed for the Germans instead of the French, what might he have achieved?" During the Empire, Cherubini composed two complete solemn masses—one in F major, the other in D minor—that were not premiered at the chapel. With their exceptionally large proportions, more developed even than Beethoven's *Missa*

Solemnis, these works have always won critical acclaim, particularly from the Germans.

The first one, the Mass in F, was premiered in 1809 in a private performance at Prince de Chimay's residence in Paris. Its large orchestral score was published in 1810 by the *Magasin de musique* of the Conservatoire. It was not performed again in its full, original version until 1833 at the Société des Concerts, but before 1815, it was also sung in Berlin, Leipzig, Vienna, and London. After 1816, in order to build up his repertoire for the Tuileries, Cherubini chose some excerpts from this mass and had them performed alone with reduced orchestration.

After 1816, he concentrated on composing for the Tuileries and his style changed. The masses he composed for the Sunday service were scrupulously timed to match its length. Occasionally, he did away with certain sections of the Ordinary. For example, in his Mass No. 5 in the chapel collection, the verse *Gratias agimus tibi* in the Gloria immediately follows the opening Kyrie, and the Credo is replaced by a setting of *Laudate Dominum omnes gentes* preceding the Sanctus and the Agnus Dei. Cherubini often followed the French practice that originated shortly before the Revolution: He introduced an Offertory and an *O salutaris* at the moment of the elevation. The concept of the mass as a whole changed. The text of the Ordinary became fragmented in a succession of orations, giving way to short, separate musical numbers that were almost interchangeable from one mass to another. The chapel catalog shows, under Cherubini, around ten *O salutaris,* four isolated Kyrie settings, and so on. It was also around that time that the Tuileries Chapel rediscovered such prayers as the Ave Maria, *Tantum ergo,* and *Regina Coeli,* which were set to music hundreds of times throughout the nineteenth century.

This is not to say that Cherubini had lost the sense of large-scale musical form. He showed it by composing his two Coronation Masses, the first for Louis XVIII, the second for Charles X. Since the coronation ceremony of Louis XVIII never took place, the Mass in G major was not performed in Reims and has remained unjustly unknown to this day. The Mass in A major, however, was heard in 1825 during Charles X's coronation ceremony, and is still performed occasionally. It was scored for three-part choir and the largest orchestra ever called for by Cherubini for a sacred work—it included an ophicleide and four French horns. The presence of a fanfare in the Gloria may be surprising, but the Credo has undeniable power. This mass included the famous Communion March that was often played later on; Berlioz never ceased to admire it.

This summary of Cherubini's sacred works would not be complete without mentioning his two Requiem masses, which were composed in France. The first one was commissioned by the Bourbon family in memory of Louis XVI and premiered in Saint-Denis on 21 January 1816. This immense work has often been compared to Mozart's Requiem. It resembles it in proportions, but also shows notable differences. For instance, Cherubini did not call for soloists, probably for fear that solo effects would hurt the overall concept. In addition, orchestration technique had evolved since the time of Mozart, and Cherubini wrote some grandiose brass and percussion effects. At the beginning of the Dies irae, a tam-tam stroke announces the end of the world. Berlioz really admired these new timbre effects, as his own later sacred works show. Overall, Cherubini's Requiem in C minor was received as one of the greatest musical achievements by musicians, such as Beethoven and, later, Schumann and Brahms. As early as 1819, it was performed in Vienna and then in Leipzig (1820), Copenhagen (1821), Berlin (1824), and Munich (1828). Performances have been frequent to this day, especially in Germany, where it has always been very popular.

Written twenty years later, the second Requiem was composed after the Tuileries Chapel was closed. Its main characteristic is that it is written for male choir. It was not a commissioned work, but the swan song of a composer who had reached the end of his life and was thinking of his own funeral. This accounts for its gloomy color and stark character. In any case, it is certain that these two masterpieces made a strong impression on Berlioz, whose own Requiem (1837) follows closely, at least chronologically, Cherubini's Requiem in D minor for male voices.

Naturally, the Tuileries Chapel was not the only center for French sacred music during the Empire and the Restoration. The activity of other Parisian and provincial parishes will be discussed, but I would first like to mention that at the very beginning of the nineteenth century, Parisians were privileged to hear for the first time two of the greatest works of contemporary sacred music: Haydn's *The Creation* and Mozart's Requiem.

Since the Old Monarchy, Haydn's symphonic works had been relatively well known in France, but this was not the case for his great choral works. The pianist Steibelt brought the score for Haydn's oratorio back from a trip to Germany and adapted the work to a French translation by Ségur. In doing so, he made important changes in the original score, including assigning Adam's role to a tenor so that Garat, the star of the day, could sing it. The Paris premiere[29] took place at the Grand Opéra on 24 December 1800 in the presence of the First Consul; that same night, he escaped an attempt on his life in the Rue Saint-Nicaise. The orchestra was directed by J.-B. Rey. Because of its two-hundred-and-fifty member chorus and Garat's enormous fee of 3600 livres, the Paris production of *The Creation* was expensive, so only two performances were held. The ticket prices were raised, and it turned into a social event. Shortly after, a parody entitled *La Récréation* (Playtime) was presented at the Vaudeville Theater. It ended with these lines:

> *Si notre Récréation*
> *Ne vaut pas La Création,*
> *Du moins, dans cette occasion,*
> *Nous n'avons pas doublé les places.*

> If our Recreation
> Does not equal *The Creation*,
> At least, on this occasion,
> We have not doubled our prices.

The piano-vocal score of *The Creation* with French and Italian translations was immediately published by Pleyel. Steibelt's sacrilegious adaptation was considered unsatisfactory from the start and was criticized. From a dramatic point of view, *The Creation* was for French audiences a return to the character of the old Monarchy's *hiérodrame* or *drame sacré* (sacred drama), a dramatic Old Testament plot set to music using non-Latin words. The musical setting and the choral and recitative styles of this oratorio were bound to sound strange to French ears. In the aftermath of this important premiere, a newspaper published the following lines, which tell a lot about French taste in sacred music at that time:

> Those who claim to have a deep understanding of music criticize this highly praised work for being no more than a scholarly symphony, rich in details but without character or poetry as a whole. Its vocal writing seems quite opposed to the spirit and the predominant taste of the French, who almost always want to find in music a theatrical declamation and the accents of passion.[30]

As far as French oratorio goes, the Parisian public especially loved works based on biblical subjects and staged at the Opéra in sumptuous productions. *Saül* was presented in April 1803 and *La Prise de Jéricho* (The Taking of Jericho) during Easter week in April 1805. Morel, then director of the Opéra, explained in a letter addressed to the Prefect of the Palace:

> A concert is a solemn event by nature. If presented on a stage usually reserved for grand spectacles, it will seem colder still. In Italy, where theaters close down during Lent, the traditional opere buffe are replaced by oratorios with speakers.[31]

Thus, under the hypocritical pretext of bringing an oratorio to the theater, the Paris Opéra refused to do away with stage displays during Holy Week. Music did not count for much. *Saül* and *La Prise de Jéricho* were both adapted by the same two partners, Lachnith and Kalkbrenner, on famous arias by Paisiello, Cimarosa, Haydn, Mozart, Piccini, Gossec, Philidor, and others. It seemed the surest way to put into this so-called religious music these "theatrical declamations and accents of passion."

Another important event in the history of French sacred music at the dawn of the nineteenth century was the French premiere of Mozart's Requiem, which took place on 21 December 1804 in Saint-Germain l'Auxerrois under Cherubini's direction. All the great musicians and singers of Paris participated in the performance, as they had at the coronation ceremony a few weeks earlier, and it left a profound and lasting impression. The score of the Requiem was published as early as 1805 by the press of the Conservatoire, and from that time on, the work (or excerpts from it) has (have) frequently been performed in France. The German critic of the *Allgemeine musikalische Zeitung*, who declared that he had heard the work many times in his country and knew it completely by heart, wrote an important account of the premiere performance. He noted the inadequacy of the tenors and altos and the weakness of the choir in some difficult passages, especially *Oro supplex et acclinis*. However, he also claimed that the violins, led by Kreutzer and Baillot, and some of the wind instruments were unsurpassed in "precision, purity, strength, and softness," and that the soloists—Madame Branchu, Madame Pelet, Messieurs Richer, Guichard, and Bertin—were excellent. He ended the article with a final shot of venom: "The fugue of all fugues, Kyrie eleison, was well and strongly rendered, but the French are still far too unfamiliar with this stylistic genre."[32]

On the same subject, the editor of the *Journal de l'Empire* was particularly struck by the Benedictus and wrote the following comment:

Italy itself comes to life in this wonderful quartet, with its suave color, its truly divine melody, its sustained simplicity, and its vocal parts either heard in succession and most happily linked to one another, or blended together in the most melodious ensemble.[33]

This difference in tastes from one nation to another is illustrated by a caustic remark made by a German lady that was repeated throughout Paris. A few weeks after the Paris premiere of Mozart's Requiem, Passion Oratorio, previously composed by Paisiello in Warsaw for King Poniatowski, was performed. The lady is reported to have declared: "In this oratorio I found every existing passion except that of the Redeemer."[34]

Apart from the records about the Tuileries Chapel, information on the musical life of important Parisian parishes during the Empire and the Restoration is distressingly scarce. Several of them, however, kept archives, and an analysis of these records would greatly enhance our understanding of musical life in France at the beginning of the nineteenth century. It is extraordinary, for instance, that there is as yet no existing study on Pierre Desvignes, who was *maître de chapelle* at Notre-Dame of Paris for about twenty years. There is no mention of him in Fétis's *Biographie universelle des musiciens*, and the most recent musical encyclopedias do not even mention his name.

I was able to verify that he had been *maître de chapelle* at the Chartres cathedral before taking up the post at Notre-Dame. The register of deliberations of the Notre-Dame chapter indicate that he was named *maître de chapelle* there on 3 November 1807, with a certain Cornu acting as his *sous-maître* (assistant). The latter also had his own works performed in Notre-Dame during the Empire, particularly a great Requiem mass on 3 April 1811. Desvignes died in Paris on 21 January 1827. All the documents concerning him, his masses and motets, and his unpublished manuscripts are kept at the Bibliothèque Nationale and in the archives of the Notre-Dame museum. Whatever their musical quality might be, a detailed study of his scores is imperative. Unlike Le Sueur, who was his teacher for a time, Desvignes apparently tried for a while to perpetuate the eighteenth-century tradition, through grand motets based on Psalm texts. His works were performed at Notre-Dame for many official ceremonies during the Empire and the Restoration. At Whitsuntide 1804, one of his masses with large choir and orchestra was played. The press announced that the orchestra would be conducted by Don Alexandre Boucher, member of the Royal Academy of Madrid, and the elevation "sung with harp accompaniment." In 1805, a mass by Desvignes was also performed on Napoléon's Day, 15 August, and at Christmas. On 8 November 1824, another of his masses was sung at Notre-Dame in celebration of the coronation of Charles X.[35]

In June 1808, the burial of Cardinal Du Belloy, archbishop of Paris and senator and count of the Empire, was the occasion for an imposing funeral ceremony. The registers of the chapter contain the following record:

> The inside of the church was completely draped in black, the skylights of the choir were covered up from the outside, and replaced by hundreds of lights. The church was filled with music that was simple and full of emotion, accompanied by a large orchestra.

The music was a mass by Mozart and a *Pie Jesu* by Desvignes. I was not able to identify the Mozart mass with certainty: it may have been the Requiem. The only other mass by Mozart published around that time was the Mass in F major in four parts, K.192, which bears the number one in the 1807 catalog of publisher Pierre Porro. Desvignes' *Pie Jesu* is well known since the author took care to have it engraved after the ceremony. This piece is in a very rhythmical, vertical style, with systematic parallel voice-leading. Its distinctive feature is the large orchestra: three trombones, timpani, and even a tam-tam. The tam-tam was first used in France in Gossec's *Marche lugubre* of 1790, and then in various revolutionary pieces and at the Opéra. This was, as far as I can tell, its first use in church.

The name of Jean-Honoré Bertin frequently appeared with that of Desvignes' in the reports of great Parisian religious ceremonies during the Empire. Bertin was an even more mysterious composer than Desvignes and, apart from an Adoremus for vocal quartet and choir published at the end of the Empire, only a few sacred pieces dated 1812 have been found. The press of the time often mentions performances of his masses during the Empire, both at Notre-Dame and at Saint-Roch. Before being a singer with the Paris Opéra company, Bertin was *maître de chapelle* at the cathedrals of Poitiers and Évreux and had probably been trained in one of the provincial cathedral schools, just about the only place for a young talented man to receive a proper musical education during the Old Monarchy.

During the Empire, the canons of Notre-Dame made an obvious attempt to bring some splendor into Parisian religious celebrations. *Le Courrier des spectacles* wrote that "they did not neglect anything that could contribute to the majesty of the religious service. In recent times, various distinguished composers gladly supported them with performances of several masses on high feast days."[36] On Ascension Day 1804, the mass was by J. Doche, former *maître de chapelle* at the cathedral of Coutances. He received a favorable press review, as did the performers, including the choir boys who were praised for their "good technique and comprehension."

The registers of the chapter of Notre-Dame that exist for the period from 1802 to 1830 give valuable information on the activity of the choir school at the leading French cathedral, the succession of Te Deums, and other religious ceremonies of thanksgiving following Napoleon's military successes. These archives also reveal that the Minister of Religious Services during the Empire was closely involved in the organization of the choir school. A decree dated 31 March 1807 grants an annual amount of 3000 francs "to the maintenance of the boys' choir school." Portalis, the Minister of Worship, in a letter to the cardinal archbishop, wrote:

> I have no doubt that the chapter will recognize, in the favors bestowed by His Majesty on the choir school, the interest he bears for this institution and the importance he attributes to its success. I have no doubt that the chapter will contribute with all its powers to the results His Majesty expects.

During that time, the Notre-Dame choir school included twelve choir boys accepted after audition. Only seven- or eight-year-old children were admitted. They remained with the school until the age of eighteen. Their instruction was provided by the music master and the assistant music master, the master of Latin and religious instruction, the master of writing and drawing, and "when the school's income will allow," a master of fortepiano. The latter two were outside instructors.

From a strictly musical point of view, the Paris parishes did not seem very active during the Consulate and the Empire. For instance, during the papal mass celebrated at Saint-Roch on 31 December 1804, the verse Tu es Petrus had to be sung by the clergy: the church organ, which had suffered some damage during the Revolution, had not yet been repaired. A review in *La Gazette de France* expressed regret about the absence of true sacred music on this occasion.[37] In some cases, to be content with works that were quite mediocre shocked true music lovers. In 1808, for example, Momigny pleaded for religious music that would be "majestic and full of reverence, instead of dry, insignificant, and poorly performed, such as I heard some time ago at Notre-Dame de Paris. This is an insult to religion and to God Himself. Plain-chant should only be replaced with music composed by a true genius."[38]

Caricature of composer Gaspare Spontini by Horace Vernet. (Paris, Bibliothèque Nationale, Department of Music)

Portrait of composer Jean-François Le Sueur (1760–1837) by painter Henri-François Riesener (1767–1828). (Nouveau Drouot, sale of 6 April 1981, No. 108)

An oriental setting at the Opéra during the Empire. Set by Isabey for the production of *La Cleopatra* by Sebastiano Nasolini at the Théâtre italien in 1813. (Bibliothèque Nationale, Department of Music)

Exoticism at the Opéra at the beginning of the nineteenth century. Set by Percier and Fontaine for Kreutzer's *Paul et Virginie* (1806 revival as a ballet at the Opéra). (Bibliothèque Nationale, Department of Music)

Two pages from the full score of the final scene of J.-F. Le Sueur's *La Mort d'Adam*. In this vast romantic fresco, the composer created a musical painting of the struggle between God and Satan for Adam's soul.

Madame Barilli. On 23 December 1807 she had the privilege of creating the role of the Countess in *Le Nozze di Figaro* for the French premiere at the Théâtre de l'Impératrice in Paris. This engraving confirms what was already learned through the press of the time: against the most basic laws of operatic truthfulness, this singer incorporated Cherubini's romance *Voi che sapete* to her role. (*Petite Galerie dramatique ou recueil de différents costumes d'acteurs des théâtres de la capitale*, Paris, no date, Volume 3, No. 223)

Façade de l'Orchestre élevé dans le Jardin des Thuilleries, pour le Concert donné le 2 Avril 1810,
à l'occasion du Mariage de sa Majesté Napoléon le Grand, avec Marie Louise d'Autriche. Déposé à la Bibliothèque.

A Paris rue St Anne, N°34.

An example of Imperial decoration from the *Collection des Maisons de Commerce de Paris les mieux décorées* (Collection of the Best Decorated Houses of Trade in Paris). (Bibliothèque Historique of the City of Paris, Rés. Fo 10353)

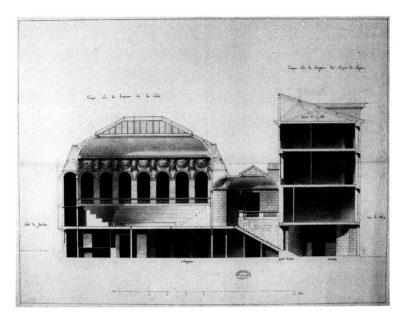

Side view of the Art Exhibit Hall of painter Jean-Baptiste Lebrun (Madame Vigée-Lebrun's husband), where the famous Rue de Cléry concerts took place at the beginning of the nineteenth century. The building was crowned by a skylight that can clearly be seen here. (Paris, National Archives, Department of Maps and Blue Prints)

Magazin de Musique de Mr Boïeldieu, rue de la Loi, N.° 76.

Window of a famous music store in Paris during the Empire: that of Louis-Armand Boïeldieu, the composer's younger brother. Rue de la Loi is now Rue de Richelieu. (Bibliothèque Historique of the City of Paris, Collection of the Best Decorated Trade Houses, Rés. Fo 10353)

Title page of a set of orchestral parts for the Overture to Mozart's *Don Giovanni*. It probably dates back to the last years of the eighteenth century. No other copy of this score has been found to date. (from the Author's personal collection)

The oldest known mention of Beethoven's name in the French press: *Journal de Paris* of 22 Fructidor year VIII (9 September 1800).

At the turn of the nineteenth century, however, a number of new private societies occasionally sponsored magnificent religious celebrations. For instance, according to the *Journal des Débats* dated 23 November 1801, members of the Saint-Cecilia Society celebrated their Saint's Day by organizing a great mass at Saint-Gervais that featured music performed by the Opéra orchestra and chorus. After the mass, written by an unidentified composer, a Haydn motet was performed. The organ was played by Gervais-François Couperin, the last descendant of the famous Couperin family.

Organ recitals were apparently rare. Desperez, the organist of Notre-Dame, played a recital at the end of 1802 that included "older tunes" that evidently disappointed the audience. In 1810, in the preface of his *Dictionnaire*, Choron deplored the decline of the organ during that time: "The organ once found its glory with the great Couperin, Marchand, Calvière, Daquin, but is now decadent. Today only Séjan is following in their footsteps." The Parisian organ school did indeed decline temporarily, and no new repertoire of quality was introduced until 1830. The leading Parisian organist of that time was Nicolas Séjan, already famous prior the Revolution. He died in 1819, having held both the Saint-Sulpice and Invalides organ positions. His son Louis succeeded him. Paradoxically, Nicolas Séjan's legacy as a composer is more significant for the forte-piano than for the organ. The other great organist of the time was a much younger man, Alexandre Boëly (1785–1858), almost unknown during his lifetime. Most of his organ works were published after 1830. A friend of some of the best contemporary musicians, he was among the first to perform Bach's organ works at a time when they were still completely unknown in France. His career took him from Saint-Gervais to Saint-Germain l'Auxerrois and continued long after 1830.

Not much is known about the activity of the provincial choir schools in the early nineteenth century. It will take a detailed analysis of the available registers kept by the main provincial chapters, of local press clippings, and the chronicles of the period to evaluate the musical activity of the various provinces during that quarter-century. For now, no complete picture can be drawn from the scattered information available.

The decline of sacred music that occurred in Paris also took place in the provinces, although perhaps a little later in time: the abolition of worship with the Revolution caused church musicians to disperse. At Nantes cathedral, for instance, the last solemn celebration took place on 25 August 1790, on Saint Louis's Day. On 22 April 1792, to celebrate the adoption of the Phrygian cap as the emblem of liberty, the municipal officials walked in

a procession to the cathedral in order to hear a "military mass."[39] In Caen,
the Saint-Pierre church, an important parish of that city, was converted into
a *Temple de la Raison.* Although many organs were being destroyed, the
organ of Saint-Pierre was saved thanks to the local organist, who agreed to
play "La Marseillaise." In the town of Saint-Quentin, Jumentier lost his position as *maître de chapelle* in 1789 because of the Revolution. Like many of
his colleagues in other parishes, he had to turn to giving private instruction
in town in order to make a living. He regained his post in 1802 and
instructed choir boys until 1825. The Saint-Quentin municipal archives
contain a large collection of manuscript scores of Jumentier's sacred works,
which ought to be better known. While I was glancing at these scores dating from the Empire or the Restoration, I was struck by the large scope of
some of the masses, considering the rather average size of the city. Jumentier wrote for large choral forces and his works required considerable orchestral support, including piccolo flute, brass, and percussion.

Les Petites Affiches de Lyon gives a detailed account of the solemn ceremony to reopen the Saint-Jean Cathedral on 6 June 1802. It tells us that a
Te Deum was sung but does not mention the composer's name. Considering the event's importance, there was probably a great number of performers in the cathedral:

> This new and imposing ceremony attracted a large crowd to the
> cathedral and the nearby squares and touched their souls by evok-
> ing many great and lofty thoughts.

Until 1830, such large celebrations were frequently held in the provincial
cathedrals, sometimes attempting to imitate the pomp of the Parisian pro-
tocol. In Lyon, for the mass of 6 June 1802, the press reported that "some
of the arrangements made previously in Paris for a similar occasion were
adapted here, inasmuch as the local setting could accommodate it."

In Bordeaux, a high mass was celebrated on 23 January 1810 in the
Saint-Séverin basilica in memory of composer Franz Beck,[40] who had been
the center of musical life there. The chorus and instrumentalists of the
Grand Théâtre were invited to participate in the religious ceremony. The
performers reached impressive numbers: no less than twenty-five violins, six
violas, ten cellos, and three double basses, not to mention the woodwinds,
brass, and percussion. The program included Jomelli's Requiem, Gluck's *De
Profundis*, and the overture to *La Mort d'Orphée*, a heroic ballet by Beck
himself.

Until 1815, however, most of the sacred music heard in the French provinces was written by local composers. In Nantes, for example, performances of masses by Haydn, Cherubini, and Mozart are not mentioned until 1817, 1818, and 1822, respectively. In the Saint-Étienne church at Caen, a certain Regnault, former student of the Paris Conservatoire, had his Te Deum performed on 9 June 1811 to celebrate the birth of Napoleon's son, the King of Rome. Three years later, Regnault composed a mass performed on 2 June 1814 to commemorate "the royal victims of 1793." It is a frightening thought that this mass was, reportedly, "sung by a gathering of amateur singers."[41]

Composer Alexandre Guibal du Rivage was born in 1775 and died after 1830. He originally was from the southern town of Béziers and came to Paris to study violin with Kreutzer and composition with Catel and Méhul. He wrote interesting memoirs on the musical life in Béziers during the Empire and the Restoration. He did not fail to make fun of the weaknesses of his provincial contemporaries. Here is an excerpt from his memoirs pertaining to vocal interpretation of chant and sacred music in general in Béziers:

I find provincial composers quite ludicrous when it comes to music for the church. However, they seem to prefer this genre to that of the theater, for they do not have to fear hisses from the audience. Our priests, the directors of our souls, who are far more condoning —or should I say far less demanding—than the directors of our theaters, accept anything given to them at face value. On feast days, they are eager to produce the most pompous religious ceremonies. So they commission music for those occasions without worrying if the works, or their performance, will be good or bad. Most importantly, they want to have as many chairs occupied as possible and attract crowds of curious folks who, unlike the pious souls, need such a display. I happened to hear many times, in the churches of Our Lord, motets, faux-bourdons—indeed, bourdons faux (out of tune!)—Te Deums, even entire masses carelessly concocted by these so-called disciples of Polyhymnia. I nearly died with laughter. The Pange Lingua was a particular target: the color of the first verse was approximately correct, but as soon as they reached the verse containing the words *Laus* and *Jubilatio*, instruments suddenly began to change rhythms and keys to express their jubilation, assisted by the singers, who are belting out the words at the top of their lungs, as if they were in a cabaret rather than a church. One day, as I heard a performance of the Pange Lingua, I thought the composer was depicting the Last Judgment. Obviously, when one hears players blast out of piccolo clarinets, piccolo flutes, French horns, trombones, and trumpets, one is justified to think that God Himself, in His wrath, is about to come down through the vault of His Holy Temple and judge the living, as well as those who are already dead scared.[42]

For many years, there were no printed editions of sacred music. This probably is why works newly discovered in Paris hardly reached the provinces. At the dawn of the Empire, however, two Paris music publishers played a decisive role: they were Pierre Porro and Alexandre Choron.

Pierre-Jean Porro (1759–1830) was a composer of little talent, originally from Provence, who had settled in Paris in 1783 as a guitar instructor. His name should be remembered not for his compositions, but rather for his contribution as a music publisher. He started his own publishing firm as early as 1807. His catalog includes a *Collection de musique sacrée* of forty numbers. This collection, which appeared at the beginning of the nineteenth century, marks a renewed interest in France in some of the great masters of the past, whose sacred works were still inaccessible for lack of publication. Included are works by Durante (*Litanies, Alma Redemptoris Mater*), Leo (*Ave, maris stella* "from the repertoire of the Sistine Chapel of Rome"), Jomelli (*Messe solennelle en ré majeur*, and other numbers), and Pergolesi (*Salve Regina*). There are also several pieces by Haydn (including the first French edition, dated 1811, of his Solemn Mass, the so-called *Imperial Mass*), and Mozart. The piece listed first in this important series is the Mass in F (K. 192), composed in 1774 and first published in Vienna by Hoffmeister in 1802. Thus the first French edition of the work followed the original by only three or four years and bears evidence of accuracy that was unknown until then from the editor's standpoint. At the beginning of the Kyrie, for instance, the French publisher Porro, who published a complete set of parts—strings and woodwinds—added in a footnote: "This score conforms rigorously to the original. The wind parts have been added." Indeed, today it is known that Mozart originally composed this mass with string and organ accompaniment. The woodwinds were added later. Porro's catalog also includes the first French editions of other masterpieces by Mozart: the Ave verum, the *De Profundis*, the trio from *Davidde penitente*, and more. Of particular importance in this collection is the four-part offertory *Misericordia Domini* with string accompaniment, K. 205a. Composed in Munich in 1775, this piece was not published until 1811 in Leipzig. In 1776, Mozart submitted this remarkable piece of counterpoint to Padre Martini for his evaluation. The latter responded that it contained "everything that modern music required." It is the epitome of the so-called strict style that German visitors were surprised not to hear in Parisian sacred music at the beginning of the nineteenth century. It would be most interesting to know what the French composers of the Restoration thought of this music, which they were able to discover through Porro's publications. No commentary of the time gives the slightest clue, and again, I could not find any evidence that the music in this new *Collection de musique sacrée* was performed during that time.

Along with Pierre Porro, Alexandre Choron (1772–1834) published sacred music during the Empire. Not only a composer and a teacher, he was one of the first true music historians in France other than J.-B. de La Borde in the second half of the eighteenth century. Unlike figures like J.-J. Rousseau or composer J.-F. Le Sueur, who far too often merely discoursed endlessly about music that they did not always know, Choron should be credited as being first to try to consult every available edition of older music. For example, he made copies of the hundreds of masses and motets printed by Johannes Donfried in Strasbourg between 1622 and 1628. They included works by Orlando di Lasso and Monteverdi, among other famous composers. Choron also directed his attention to the more recent work of Burney and Hawkins in England and Forkel in Germany. Thanks to these scholars, by the end of the eighteenth century, the two countries already had their own editions of many important sacred and secular works of the older repertoire that were still unknown in France. Choron also had a copy of Padre Martini's *Esemplare o sia saggio fondamentale pratico di contrapunto* (A Sample Book, or Introduction to the Practice of Counterpoint, 1774–1775). Among secular pieces, madrigals, symphonies, and other instrumental pieces, there were many examples taken from the sacred music of Palestrina, Jomelli, and Monteverdi.

Choron was not a scholar in the modern sense of the word. He often published music by simply reproducing scores found in earlier editions without verifying their accuracy. When a printed version existed, he rarely referred to the manuscript. Comparing sources in order to come up with an authentic edition did not occur to him, for the concept of a critical edition did not yet exist. He is not to be blamed for his approach; there had to be intermediary steps. Choron's great contribution was to spend most of his life attempting to know and make known the great masterpieces of the past.

Choron was irritated by the tyrannical stronghold opera had on the contemporary musical scene. He wanted to react against it and return to more austere forms of sacred music. He was quite opposed to the theatrical character of the church music of his time and hoped to instigate important reforms. The manuscript for an essay he wrote in 1825 is kept in the Bibliothèque nationale under the title *Mémoire sur la situation actuelle de la musique religieuse et sur les moyens d'en opérer la restauration* (Memoir on the present situation of church music and the means of restoring it). In it, he dared write that "France is the only European country without its religious music." He thought that the character of the masses he heard in his lifetime was "not religious at all, but quite secular and theatrical." They were performed "by all-around singers working in the theater, about the only musical genre still cultivated in France." For Choron, the a capella style is the perfect form of sacred music. He described it as

> a style of composition usually including every tone of plain-chant, in duple time, for unaccompanied voices. It is found in four different versions: plain-chant, faux-bourdon, counterpoint over plain-chant, and ecclesiastical imitative counterpoint.

With these ideas Choron was obviously going in opposite direction to the religious music of his time, as conceived by the official composers who had been chosen by the different political rulers to direct their chapels. He reacted very early in an effort to make known a certain kind of religious music of the past, then completely forgotten. In 1808 to 1809, he published his *Principes de composition des écoles d'Italie* (Compositional Principles of the Italian Schools), which contained a whole volume of examples where he illustrated each of the four a capella styles with Italian works of past centuries.

In addition, starting around 1805, he projected the publication by subscription, with the Parisian publisher Auguste Le Duc, of a *Collection générale des ouvrages de musique classique* (General Collection of Works of Classical Music), an immense endeavor that would, he thought, take several years and introduce a great number of sacred and secular works still unpublished in France. Under the category of sacred music, he announced works by Durante, Leo, Pergolesi, Perez, Jomelli, Cimarosa, Handel, C. P. E. Bach, and others. The price asked of the subscribers would be nine francs for one hundred sheets. The announcement read:

This collection will not appear periodically. The subscribers will be given advance notice of the next publication of musical works through the musical bulletin of Auguste Le Duc and Company. This collection will be put together with the greatest selective care. Only works universally recognized as classics will be included.[43]

The first volume was probably published in 1809 or 1810. It included seven titles: six sacred pieces, and Mozart's Symphony in G minor. The sacred pieces were Leo's *Miserere*, Josquin des Prés's *Stabat Mater*, Palestrina's *Missa ad fugam in perpetuo canone* and *Stabat Mater*, and Jomelli's *Miserere* and *Missa pro defunctis*. They were the first French editions and appeared in full score with a preface on the historical background of the composers and their time. For instance, in the case of Palestrina, Choron listed the existing foreign editions, such as Burney's, Hawkins's, and Reichardt's *Magasin musical*. He also mentioned several manuscripts owned by Breitkopf in Leipzig. He added:

Several of these pieces will be part of our collection. In France, Palestrina's works are very rare indeed. A handful of scholars own copies of a few pieces, but the Imperial Library or the Library of the Conservatoire does not own a single sheet. The government should be encouraged to have copies made, either in Italy or in Germany, of all that can be found by this great man and have the precious volume placed in one of these two institutions. This would incur only modest expense but would greatly advance the progress of the art of music.

Unfortunately, the first volume of Choron's great collection was also the last. In 1810, he had received less than 400 subscriptions and, for financial reasons, had to give up and part with the publisher Le Duc. This vast undertaking depended on unusual interest in rediscovering the music of the past, but Imperial France was not interested. Such a profound transformation of musical taste could not be brought about by a few scholars.

However, Choron did not give up so soon. With the Restoration, he became director of the *École royale et spéciale de chant* (the Royal School for Advanced Vocal Arts). In 1820, to make repertoire available to his vocal students, he began to publish his *Collection des pièces de musique religieuse qui s'exécutent tous les ans à Rome durant la semaine sainte dans la Chapelle du Souverain Pontife* (Collection of sacred works performed every year in

Rome during Holy Week in the Papal Chapel). Although many of these pieces were taken from Burney, the significance of this publication was that it gave young singers access to all the repertoire of existing Italian sacred music. In a similar effort, Choron published a *Journal de musique religieuse* in 1826 and a *Journal de chant et musique d'église* in 1828. These were series of sacred pieces by German composers from the end of the eighteenth and the beginning of the nineteenth centuries, with piano or organ accompaniment. Until his death, Choron continued to distribute in France a whole repertoire of sacred music completely different from the contemporary repertoire. In 1830, he published yet another collection, his *Manuel de chant classique à l'usage des élèves de l'institution royale de musique religieuse de France* (Handbook of Classical Singing for Study at the French Royal School of Sacred Music). Although it contained secular music, it introduced students to such names as Jannequin, Marcello, Clari, and others.

Unlike Pierre Porro, Choron persisted in spite of his failure during the Empire and ended up having an important impact on French musical life. In 1824, for example, Choron and the Church of the Sorbonne made an agreement that mass in the church would be sung every Sunday by the choir of his school, then called *Institution royale de musique religieuse de France* (the French Royal Institution of Sacred Music). Through these concerts, Choron was counting on attracting Sorbonne students to his choir. He published the following announcement:

> All the student brigades in charge of the service in different churches will gather in the Church of the Sorbonne. That Church will be the central point for the restoration of ecclesiastical music. This new group will form the core of a Sacred Music Society.[44]

It was an ideal occasion for Choron to program some of the older works that he had been publishing for twenty years. These Sorbonne concerts—or rather these masses—were so successful in the final years of the Restoration that Choron decided to organize a number of public student performances at the school, then located in the Rue de Vaugirard. There he continued the sacred music experiment of the Sorbonne and revived for the first time in France a vast number of older sacred works by Josquin des Prés, Palestrina, Jannequin, as well as more recent music by German and Italian composers of the eighteenth and early nineteenth centuries.

Each concert was basically presented in two parts: a first part with several shorter works, such as madrigals, motets, and psalms, then a second part with a large work, such as a mass or oratorio. The first part of the first concert on 22 February 1827 was devoted to Mozart, Vogler, Haydn, Palestrina, and Marcello, followed by large excerpts from Handel's *Messiah*, sung in Latin. Fétis, who thought very highly of this concert, wrote:

> The school directed by Mr. Choron is surely the only place in Europe where one can hear this style of music performed so well. It is unfortunate that most of the masterpieces in this style from the Italian and German schools are unknown in France. What should I say about this *Messiah* by Handel that constituted the second half of the exercise? What words would be adequate to describe this colossal work? One must hear it, admire it, and say nothing. It is commonly believed in France that this severe style, bristling with fugues and imitation, can only appeal to scholars' ears. That is a mistake easily recognized by anyone sensitive to music who hears this work as it was just sung by Mr. Choron's students.[45]

It would be interesting to know whether the French masters of that time, particularly the directors of the Royal Chapel of the Tuileries, attended these concerts. What could they have thought of this style of sacred music, so far removed from their own and revealed to them so suddenly? On the other hand, young Berlioz is known to have eagerly attended these concerts, and the Parisian public had a chance to hear, until 1830, such works as Handel's *Samson* and *Judas Maccabeus*, Beethoven's *Christ on the Mount of Olives*, as well as a large number of works by German and Italian composers of the sixteenth to the eighteenth centuries, even a "motet"—probably a cantata—by J. S. Bach.

These were the first historical performances that took place in France prior to Fétis's own accomplishments in the field after 1830. From Porro's first editions during the early years of the Empire to Choron's concerts during the Restoration, there developed an increasing interest in the master-works of the past, whether by French composers of great foreign masters. An important movement was born that continued to grow during the nine-teenth century, thanks to efforts by such a diverse group of artists as Nie-dermeyer, Vincent d'Indy, or Saint-Saëns. It was prompted by their natural curiosity about their own ancestors, but also by a change in taste. The inter-est in the past grew in other disciplines, too. To take only one example, the work of archaeologist Alexandre Lenoir and his Museum of French Monu-ments did much to bring about a change of mentality. It was in the same

spirit that Choron wanted to create "an actual museum of musical antiqui-
ties." By discovering and learning to understand the art of centuries past
and by accepting the evolutionary process, modern artists became aware of
their potential, as well as their responsibilities and limitations. The heritage
of tradition and history made them reflect on the meaning and value of
their own creation, thus giving a new dimension to their works. The
renewed interest in Renaissance and Baroque music went hand in hand
with the birth of romanticism and the rediscovery of Gothic and sixteenth-
century art. Fétis, when he commented on Handel's *Messiah*, spoke of the
"Gothic sound" of this music. He added: "This Gothic will outlive the new
one that is now being born."[46] The intertwining lines of baroque counterpoint probably made him think of the sinuous lines of the Neo-Gothic style
so loved by Chateaubriand and, after him, the young romantic generation.
After 1825, the sixteenth century became fashionable. Victor Hugo, although not very knowledgeable in music, began to praise Palestrina, whom
he discovered thanks to Choron and Fétis's concerts. In a poem entitled
Que la musique date du XVIe siècle (Music Was Born in the Sixteenth Century), part of the collection *Les Rayons et les Ombres* (Rays and Shadows) of
1837, he attributed—very carelessly—the paternity of all modern music to
"this child of blond Italy." I leave to him the entire responsibility for this
strange statement, as well as for the following definition of the art of
sounds:

> *Ni peintre, ni sculpteur! Il fut musicien.*
> *Il vint, nouvel Orphée après l'Orphée ancien,*
> *Et, comme l'Océan n'apporte que sa vague,*
> *Il n'apporte que l'art du mystère et du vague.*

> No painter nor sculptor he was, but a musician!
> After his old master came New Orpheus,
> But, like the wave brought up from the deep ocean,
> His only art is that of mystery and vagueness.

Such peremptory statements and lack of historical method bring smiles
today, but there they are. The return to the past, as imperfect as it may have
been, was very profitable for the young avant-garde. The wave of musical
archaeology that swept over the reign of Charles X brought about a
renewed interest in sacred music. In 1832, Alfred de Vigny, who attended

one of Fétis's concerts, noted in his *Journal d'un poète*: "There was a five-part madrigal by Palestrina, a delightful piece full of love and sweetness." None of the elderly masters of the Tuileries Chapel of that time could have inspired such enthusiasm from such passionate young romantics, and the closing of the Tuileries Chapel by King Louis-Philippe in 1830 had symbolic significance.

Choron became more and more enthusiastic over Palestrina and decided to publish and perform his complete works but died before realizing this project. In 1834, at his funeral in the Invalides, excerpts from Mozart's and Jomelli's Requiems were performed, along with Palestrina's madrigal *Alla riva del Tebro* (On the banks of the Tiber); it was the least his contemporaries could do for him.

Chapter 5

Public and
Private Concerts

A certain kind of social life that is found only within a stable political context is required in order for private amateur concerts or public professional performances to exist.

The eighteenth century saw the rapid development of public concerts, in Paris as well as in the provinces. There were few cities that did not have their own society of music with its own orchestra of "enlightened amateurs." Paris and even foreign virtuoso performers did not mind making occasional appearances in lesser provincial centers. Many musicians of the time led the life of a touring artist, just as companies of traveling comedians had done for centuries. In Paris, public concerts multiplied during the eighteenth century. The most established institution was obviously the *concert spirituel*, created in 1725 by Philidor; it was one of the few leading musical centers of France during the Enlightenment. This institution still existed in 1789 but was no longer the only one. In his study of *Les Concerts en France sous l'Ancien Régime* (Concerts in France during the Old Monarchy), slightly dated but still unsurpassed, Michel Brenet describes the activities of the various societies that existed during this century. Some of them were short lived; others were very successful, such as the *Concert des Amateurs* founded by Gossec in 1769. It closed in 1781 and was replaced by the *Concert de la Loge olympique* (Concert of the Olympic Lodge), so well thought of throughout Europe that Haydn dedicated six of his symphonies to it.

Unfortunately, there is no research on the period from 1789 to 1830 to parallel Brenet's study of the Monarchy except for a few isolated studies of provincial societies by local scholars. Even the life of leading Paris organizations remains relatively unknown, with the exception of Constant Pierre's detailed history of the *Concerts du Conservatoire*. In order to retrace its development, I consulted a few contemporary chronicles and, mostly, press clippings, which up until 1815 provide the best source of information. Unfortunately, documentation on this subject is still very fragmentary.

Before discussing the history of the concert societies, it might be interesting to look at the public who attended these concerts. Without precise evidence to the contrary, it seems that these concert goers were the same people who attended the opera. Concerts and operas alike were important social events, and to attend a concert provided the dual pleasures of seeing and being seen. The public was not very knowledgeable, so to keep its attention without the advantage of stage effects, anything that might become monotonous had to be avoided. This probably explains why, until 1815, every concert followed the same basic program schedule: alternating symphonic excerpts, solo concertos requiring brilliant virtuoso feats, and vocal excerpts from operas. The modern concept of a vocal or instrumental recital was still completely unknown. A great foreign star visiting Paris was never featured alone in a concert. For instance, the Spanish singer Isabelle Colbran, who was a student of Crescentini and was to be Rossini's wife, made two visits to Paris during the Empire in 1804 and 1808. At each of her concerts, she sang no more than two or three arias and received an ovation, especially with Crescentini's famous song *Ombra adorata* (Adored Shadow). On one of her programs, the public heard the violinist Libon playing one of his own concertos, and the German pianist Wölffl also played a concerto. Another program featured a Haydn symphony and an overture by Cherubini.

Seeking program variety—if not originality—to avoid becoming tiresome or boring was a priority for concert organizations. In 1803, a journalist wrote this very typical comment:

> A concert is a particular kind of show that offers no plot interest like a tragedy, a comedy, or a tableau. [The richness of music] cannot be appreciated if it is not varied. A concert including only

vocal numbers might just be tolerated if there is artful variety, but if only symphonies or concertos are heard, such uniformity would only create total boredom.[1]

A comment dated 1806 from *Le Courrier des Spectacles* also defined a concert as a show: "People attend the concert less to hear than to be seen. What they are looking for are a beautifully lit hall and women exhibiting the most dazzling and luxurious dresses."[2] In his summary of concert events for the 1800–1801 season, another journalist remarked that the two concerts given by Garat at the Feydeau theater were more successful than those by Rode and Kreutzer at Favart. He went on to explain: "In general, the Favart public is less sensitive to this kind of talent and less receptive to women showing off their dresses."

Throughout his career, the critic Géoffroy persisted in writing about music without knowing a single note, a drawback that did not prevent his opinion from being accepted as authority. He is a perfect example of the average French concert goer. After a concert given at the Théâtre italien during Holy Week in 1812, he expressed his feelings to his readers of *Le Journal de l'Empire*:

The fact is all too often forgotten that a concert is a festive occasion, and those who attend it seek to gratify their senses. . . . *Symphonies concertantes* featuring wind instruments are preferable to violin concertos, which invariably bore the audience. All concertos should be short, melodic, and varied. . . . Most listeners judge the beauty of music only by its brilliant ornamentation. . . . Banish, do banish from concerts all that is sad, mournful, or pathetic and all sentimental pieces. Even on Good Friday, the Day of the Passion, no Stabat Mater, no Requiem, no funeral music, no tragic or sepulchral scene. People come to have fun. They have a hard time imagining themselves in Jerusalem, at the foot of Calvary amidst the Holy Women, for they do not know what religious gloom is.[3]

He could not have better expressed his own inability to deal with the subject.

The average listener's musical awareness was still very limited. Until 1815, instrumental music—so-called *musique pure*—was not really appreciated by the main concert-going public. It much preferred vocal music, with the possible exception of Haydn's symphonies. Private societies for symphonic or chamber music appeared only during the Restoration and remained very limited until 1815. In any case, none compared to the salon hosted during the Old Monarchy by La Pouplinière, a wealthy amateur musician and statesman. The Revolution put an end to this type of upper-class patronage, or at least to this type of social activity. Concerts had become purely social events. People were not really interested in the music, and they were bored, although they did not always admit it. "Why are most concerts so cold? Why is the audience so rarely satisfied?" the writer of *Les Tablettes de Polymnie* asked candidly in 1811. The correct answer would have pointed out the musical insensitivity of most concert goers. Instead, the same writer gave the following symptomatic explanation:

> Concerts are comprised of instrumental and vocal music. The former only satisfies the ear without reaching the heart or the spirit and soon becomes tiresome. After two or three pieces, you have your fill. Vocal pieces are composed mostly for the stage, so in a concert they lose half of their effect.

According to Castil-Blaze, audiences gradually became better educated, especially in the provinces, where concert goers at the beginning of the nineteenth century were almost completely indifferent to the music. He maintains that if the good manners of Paris society did ultimately reach the rest of the country, credit was due to the touring musicians, who managed to "give an idea of the truly beautiful, educate public taste, and impose silence during the performance of arias, string quartets, and even [!] piano sonatas." A concert had to be good if the people were to cease their conversations or games. Castil-Blaze added:

> In the past, no one paid any attention to the harmonic noise of a group of amateur musicians. News, politics, quarrels, games of boston, backgammon, or lotto—all went on at the same time as the quartet or symphony.[4]

The year 1789 did not significantly break the rhythm of Paris concerts. The *concert spirituel*, for example, presented twenty-four concerts that year, and ten more in 1790 before closing down permanently. The other leading concert societies, such as the *Concert de la loge olympique* and the *Société académique des enfants d'Apollon* (the Academic Society of Apollo's Children), apparently only gradually stopped their performances as the political situation worsened. On 3 April 1790, *La Chronique de Paris* wrote this comment on Paris major concert events: "The fact that they did not have as good a following as in the preceding years is not to be blamed on their programming, but on the circumstances that forced them away from the center of the capital." In 1792, Reichardt went to the Feydeau theater to hear the first Paris concert of the season and noticed that only a few people attended "compared to the crowds of the old *Concert d'amateurs* or the concerts of the Olympic Lodge." However, in spite of the political situation, a series of major concerts was organized at the Feydeau during Holy Week in April 1792, traditionally a time when theaters were closed. The best singers of the house company took part, as well as violinists Kreutzer, Alday, and Rode. Eighteen-year-old Rode performed five concertos by his teacher, Viotti.[5]

The period of the Revolution gave rise to a few tentative concert series, about which hardly anything is known. Such short-lived societies did not leave any records, and what we know about them is restricted to a few lines in the press. For instance, some concerts took place in 1791 in the National Circus built in the inner courtyard of the Palais-Royal. A notice in *Affiches, annonces et avis divers* (Bills and Various Announcements) dated 2 June announced that there would that evening be "a grand concert with several symphonies" and that a young lady "would perform a pianoforte concerto." No details about the program, the identity of the orchestra, or the frequency of concerts are known. Moreover, the announcement concluded with the phrase: "Ball immediately following, until 11 o'clock." Obviously, the concert was considered to be one form of entertainment among others.

The first important concerts given in the capital during the Revolutionary period were those organized by the Feydeau theater as soon as it opened in 1791. Unfortunately, there is no written document that could help determine exactly how frequent they were. According to Choron and Fayolle, "at the time of the Revolution, all concert activities had ceased, but after the Terror was over, the management of the Feydeau theater began organizing new ones."[6] I was not able to verify this statement, but if it is true that the Feydeau concerts were interrupted for a time, it was probably during the few months preceding the fall of Robespierre. From the first opening of the theater to its merger with the Opéra-Comique in 1801, a year did not go by without the press announcing a concert except when the theater was closed between 1796 and 1801. On 11 February 1800, one more very brilliant concert featuring Madame Scio and Garat took place. The next day, a journalist writing about the event recalled "all the splendor and luxury of past concerts given in this theater."[7]

I researched all press releases for the 1796–1797 concert season at the Feydeau theater. From the fall of 1796 until the final concert of the season on 30 March 1797, there were twelve in all, one every ten or fifteen days. The format of programs did not vary much at all. As an example, here is the program for the fifth concert on 8 January 1797.[8]

A symphony by Haydn
A violin concerto by Viotti
An Italian aria by Mengozzi, sung by Rosine
A pianoforte concerto by Viotti, played by Moreth
An excerpt from Cimarosa's *Le Sacrifice d'Abraham*, sung by Garat
Overture of Gluck's *Iphigenia en Aulide*
Sinfonia Concertante by Devienne
Mengozzi's *Air savoyard* (Air from Savoy), sung by Garat

This is a most eclectic program, featuring vocal, symphonic, and instrumental music by French, German, and Italian composers. It is typical of most Paris concerts between 1789 and 1815, and with very few exceptions, no other concert society in Paris offered their public anything drastically different. The content of programs was of an appalling monotony. There was invariably one symphony—sometimes even two—by Haydn, the symphonist most frequently performed in Paris until 1820. The favor enjoyed by Haydn's music in France in the final years of the Old Monarchy was not affected by the Revolution.

After the mandatory symphony came concertos or sinfonie concertante, which were opportunities for instrumental soloists to display virtuoso feats that the public appreciated. The violin was by far the most frequently featured solo instrument, followed by the flute and the pianoforte; less frequently the cello, the harp, or the French horn; and very occasionally the bassoon or the clarinet. It was common to hear composers perform their own works: Viotti on the violin, Devienne on the flute, Duvernoy on the French horn, and Levasseur on the cello. These composer-soloists were not exclusively employed by the Feydeau theater but appeared in other Paris concert series as well. The orchestra that performed in the Feydeau concerts was the orchestra regularly employed by the theater and was conducted by its own director, violinist Pierre La Houssaye.

A certain number of artists, especially singers, often appeared at the Feydeau and built up quite a reputation for themselves. A leading Italian singer, Madame Morichelli, was the artist most often featured in Feydeau concert programs, particularly during 1791. In August 1792, the Italian opera buffa company left Paris, and two French singers came into favor in Paris: Madame Barbier-Walbonne and the famous Garat. Choron wrote that the duo formed by these two artists "equalled the perfection heard during the reign of the excellent Italian Buffoon Company, disbanded on 10 August 1792."[9] Madame Barbier-Walbonne did not have a long career but was unanimously hailed by the press for her great voice and her musical interpretation. Nicknamed "the female Garat," she sang concert excerpts from the Italian and French repertoires. In February 1797, she sang an excerpt at the Feydeau from Jomelli's *Armida* and was a great success. She also appeared in the Rue de Cléry concerts. After she married the painter Barbier, a student of Gérard, she gave up her career as a concert artist.[10]

Pierre-Jean Garat (1764–1823) became famous during his lifetime, and his name is important in the history of singing. This tenor was everybody's favorite and admired by the most important figures; shortly before the Revolution, Queen Marie-Antoinette herself expressed the wish to hear him privately at Versailles. Yet curiously enough his entire career took place not in the theater, but in concert halls and salons. With his light, flexible tenor voice, Garat could vocalize and enunciate to perfection. It was at the Feydeau theater that he sang for the first time in public in Paris. His repertoire included complete scenes from Gluck's operas, as well as excerpts from fashionable French comic operas or Italian operas. However, his best genre was the romance, of which he was the unsurpassed master for over twenty years. Garat quickly became a star during the Directoire, appearing in every major Paris salon and celebrated by high society, which forgave him his scandalous or impertinent behavior. He worked as a voice teacher at the Paris Conservatoire and trained some of the best French singers of that time, including Madame Branchu, Madame Duret, Nourrit, and Ponchard. He also attracted occasional criticism. For instance, in the early part of 1803, he gave a benefit concert for the Feydeau theater. The theater was sold out, and the women in the audience were dressed up as if for an official ceremony. Among other selections, he had chosen a scene from an opera seria by Nasolini. According to a German critic,[11] Garat made the mistake of trying to force his naturally rather weak voice and to add runs and ornaments in a dramatic scene. In the same program, he sang the "champagne" aria, "Fin ch'han del vino," from Mozart's *Don Giovanni*, which was emphatically not in his range and raised severe criticism, but he recovered all his brilliance in a duet from *Armida*, sung with Madame Scio. Like many singers, Garat probably made the mistake of thinking that he could tackle any repertoire.

Garat's huge successes in the Feydeau theater concerts greatly contributed to their reputation, and they became the fashionable meeting place for dandies and elegant Paris ladies. The Goncourt brothers gave a pleasant description of this enthusiastic Paris crowd preparing for a Feydeau concert: "[The day before the concert,] a host of chamber maids took the fashion shops by storm to pick up the one-hundred franc hat prepaid by their mistress, on the express condition that no other identical hat would be manufactured before the concert."[12]

In fact, the fashion of the Feydeau theater concerts during the Directoire was the subject of at least two short comedies published in 1795. The first was a vaudeville entitled *Le Concert de la Rue Feydeau ou l'agrément d'un jour* (The Concert of Rue Feydeau, or the amusement of one day) created by Hector Chaussier and Martainville for the *Théâtre des Variétés*. The second was a comedy with ariettas, *Le Concert de la Rue Feydeau ou la folie d'un jour* (The Concert of Rue Feydeau, or the one-day extravaganza), the work of René Périn and Cammaille for the theater of *l'Ambigu-Comique*. These two works, otherwise totally insignificant, give some idea of the atmosphere of the Feydeau concerts. They show that Feydeau was the fashionable meeting place of all the Paris beauties, who arrived dressed in Roman fashion, while their husbands had to pay for their new outfits each time and were terrified at the prospect of more concerts.

This amusing little dialogue between a young perfumed dandy and the pretty lady he has come to fetch at her home gives an idea of the kind of people who attended the Feydeau concerts:

Dandy: I don't enjoy myself, or even exist, except at a concert.
Lady: I thought you did not know music?
Dandy: Well, I am not hard of hearing. I admire it, just like everyone else.

The two satirical works described above also reveal that the Revolutionaries strongly criticized the Feydeau concerts. This should come as no surprise, since this theater was attended by a public hostile to revolutionary ideas. As an example, in one of these playlets, the citizen Belval is heard addressing her cousin and asking: "By the way, are those ridiculous criticisms of the Feydeau concerts over at last?" The latter, a good Republican "who fought at the borders" (it is, after all, 1795), answered:

Just knowing who dared to make these allegations is enough to ignore them altogether. The Terrorists finally show their true worth. We know why the concerts of Rue Feydeau do not attract these gentlemen.

This likeable character goes on to sing to the tune of the Montagnards—a Revolutionary anthem—the following stanza against the Terrorists:

L'art affreux d'enfanter les crimes
Pour leur cœur a seul de l'attrait;
Les cris plaintifs de leurs victimes
Voilà le concert qui leur plaît.

The gruesome art of committing crimes
Is their sole way of thriving.
The supplications of their victims
Is the only concert to their liking.

The concerts of the Paris Conservatoire—or the student "public exercises," as they were called in those days—were much more peaceful, at least politically. Even prior to the creation of the Conservatoire, concerts were organized at the old National Institute of Music (1793–1795). On 20 November 1793, a concert was given at the Feydeau theater by the musicians of the National Institute of Music. Members of the Convention were invited in the following terms: "Membership cards of the National Convention can be shown for admission to the first tier of the Feydeau theater."[13] The program included an overture by Catel; a sinfonia concertante for flute, oboe, horn, and bassoon by Devienne, played by the composer, Sallantin, Duvernoy, and Ozy; Gossec's *Marche funèbre* and his sinfonia concertante for eleven wind instruments. It was a great success. Several concerts were presented during the year 1794 by the National Institute of Music. Its director, the clever Sarrette, seized the opportunity to have the Institute transformed into the *Conservatoire national de musique* in 1795.

A decree dated 3 July 1796 stipulated that henceforth there should be six student public exercises each year from then on. The first took place the following year on 24 October 1797 in the hall of the Odéon theater. The program was quite full, with twelve numbers made up of opera overtures, solo concertos, sinfonie concertante, solo arias, vocal duets, and opera choruses. There even was a pianoforte sonata by Cramer.

Serious financial difficulties encountered by the Conservatoire in the early years of its existence compelled the management to consider the cancellation of student public exercises in 1801. However, according to director Sarrette, the students wanted to maintain the exercises, which they deemed "very useful to their studies." For a time, some first-prize winners gathered to perform in concert at the Olympic theater under the title of *Concerts français*. They quickly obtained permission from the Conservatoire's administration and the teaching committee to perform and gave twelve concerts in Paris between November 1802 and 1 May 1803.[14] Thirty-six francs per person was a reasonable price for a subscription to the twelve-concert series. Single admission tickets cost from three to five francs, the normal price for a concert seat in Paris until 1830. After 1803, public exercises took place on Sunday afternoons between one and four o'clock at the Conservatoire itself. The building of a new concert hall soon began under the supervision of architect François Delannois, who was also responsible for the Hôtel d'Abrantès on the Champs-Élysés, as well as the Passage Vivienne. This new hall was officially inaugurated on 7 July 1811. The following description was written at the time: "The hall is in the shape of a parallelogram with a vault lit by a glass roof. The daylight and the green-colored boxes drive ladies to despair by casting yellowish green shadows on their faces, which are not likely to enhance them."[15] And this important detail: "The orchestra is placed at the back, as actors would be on a stage, although in every theater, orchestras are in the middle, between the actors and the public."[16] This hall soon became the site of all student concerts. It turned out to have excellent acoustics, which explains why it still stands today as the so-called Hall of the Old Conservatoire on Rue Bergère.

For the first concert of the new season in the fall of 1802, the German composer Reichardt was sitting in Gossec's box with Cherubini and Monsigny. He wrote his impressions of that evening. The orchestra was made up only of Conservatoire students, without any teacher sitting in, and conducted by one of them. The program included the inevitable Haydn symphony, followed by an overture by Cherubini, which was very difficult and very well performed, according to Reichardt.[17] Following these symphonic selections, there was a tenor aria by Sacchini, a horn concerto, and a violin concerto. This program was not original by any means, following the model of the Feydeau concerts of the time. Reichardt concluded his report by noticing that no member of the grand monde (the high society) was there. This important detail shows that the concerts of the Paris Conservatoire did not, in the early years at least, have the same fashionable character as those given at the Feydeau theater. Among the subscribers, there were probably enough relatives and friends of students to fill the hall, and even if they were not all connoisseurs, at least they did not belong to the fashionable crowd.

The first season of public exercises (1802–1803) was successful, but the Conservatoire administration could not keep up the pace of twelve annual concerts. After the first year, the concerts did not resume until 4 March 1804, with only five concerts between then and the summer. The following year, eight concerts were performed between January and May 1805. However, some of the better students of the Conservatoire took part, along with their teachers this time, in special concerts. For example, on 21 December 1804, they had the privilege of giving the first performance in France of Mozart's Requiem in Saint-Germain-l'Auxerrois Church. In 1807, the number of public exercises was increased again to twelve per season. A complete account of concerts and programs, year by year, would be tedious, but I shall describe some particular aspects of these student public exercises.

Because they took place on Sunday afternoons and, due to the subscription system, had admission prices that were lower than those of other concerts, these public exercises promptly attracted a public of connoisseurs that was very different from the Feydeau audience. Every contemporary commentator—including foreigners who cannot be accused of being partial toward France—praised the quality of the Conservatoire orchestra. While at the time most woodwind players in French orchestras were German, those of the Conservatoire orchestra were naturally French, being students at the Conservatoire, and they were excellent.[18] The only criticism that was occasionally made of the orchestra was that its tempos were too fast.[19] On the other hand, the choir made up of students from the voice classes was at times deemed insufficient. Rehearsals were led by Méhul and Cherubini, but the actual performances were conducted by the best students.[20] Two of them particularly distinguished themselves in the early 1800s. They were Marcel Duret and François-Antoine Habeneck, both violinists, both first-prize winners in 1806 and 1804, respectively. The latter was on the verge of a very brilliant career and already showed exceptional talent. Fétis wrote about him as follows:

> At that time, violinists with a first prize at the Conservatoire shared the direction of the orchestra's concerts for a year. Habeneck was so superior to his colleagues in this difficult task that he kept the position until the Conservatoire closed down in 1815 after the allied armies took Paris.[21]

From 1821 to 1824, before he resumed directing the Conservatoire Society Concerts in 1828, Habeneck was director of the Paris Opéra.

His presence as director of the Conservatoire orchestra probably had a lot to do with attempts to break the monotonous programming. Although a Haydn symphony continued to be mandatory at almost every concert, programs performed at the Conservatoire occasionally included a new work or one rarely performed in those days. For instance, in 1804, one concert featured "Fuggi, crudel,"the duet from *Don Giovanni,* sung in its original Italian version for the first time in Paris, and Durante's *Litanies,* a work little known in Paris during the Empire.[22]

Still, the greatest accomplishment of this orchestra and its young conductor was to have introduced the French to Beethoven's symphonic works. Three of his symphonies were premiered in France by the students' orchestra during the Empire: the First Symphony in C major was performed on 22 February 1807 and again in March 1810, the Fifth Symphony in C minor on 10 April 1808, and the *Eroica* Symphony on 5 May 1811 and again in 1813 and 1814. To complete this initiation of the French public, Habeneck also programmed the Overture to *Prometheus* in 1814. He defended Mozart's music just as actively. Beginning in 1807, he conducted some of the composer's later symphonies, particularly the last three (the G minor, the E-flat major, and the "Jupiter"). I will later discuss how these masterpieces were received by the French press; here I will focus on press reviews of the orchestra's performances.

On 21 June 1809, an interesting account can be found in the *Allgemeine musikalische Zeitung* following a performance of the G minor Symphony by the Conservatoire orchestra. As always, and in contrast to most of the French critics of that time, the German critic seemed to know what he was talking about. To summarize what he wrote, the performance was good in spite of tempos too fast to bring out the countless details that Mozart includes throughout this "masterpiece of all masterpieces." Under such conditions, the best-trained ear could not follow what was intended by the great Mozart, who himself did not conduct at such fast tempos. French orchestras, and especially the Conservatoire orchestra, had a general—and regrettable—fondness for too-fast tempos. Only recently, according to this critic, excerpts from Haydn's "The Seasons," including the marvelous "Spring Chorus" in six-eight time in G major, were performed at the pace of a contradance and thus distorted by the orchestra. What was the origin of this habit? According to the German critic, it was probably the fact that each individual member of this ensemble was a virtuoso, a potential soloist, and each wished to show off. He added this interesting conclusion:

The Mannheim and Munich orchestras, as I recall them from the past, are made up of musicians who individually cannot be compared to the members of today's better Paris orchestras, but they performed German works with a much more authentic spirit.

Two years later, on 30 October 1811, more reviews published in the same German newspaper alluded to the excessively fast tempos chosen by the Conservatoire orchestra. One critic wrote:

> I remember quite well hearing Mozart and Haydn conduct their own symphonies in Vienna. They did not take opening allegros as fast as this orchestra, or as many German orchestras now do. It is true that they took minuets quite quickly. As for the finales, Haydn liked to play them faster than Mozart did.

In spite of criticism, it should be observed that the Conservatoire orchestra's programming was extremely original at a time when every concert in town tended to rehash the same Haydn symphonies. These were far from being mere student exercises. In just a few years, due mostly to Habeneck's exceptional personality, this orchestra acquired a reputation unanimously recognized in the press. I found the following comment in the *Tablettes de Polymnie* dated 20 March 1811:

> Despite their modest title, these exercises are true concert performances, sometimes even better than those heard elsewhere for a higher admission price. Symphonies in particular have reached a level of perfection due to the use of uniform bowing, the very broad style taught in the principal violin classes, and the excellent organization of Mr. Habeneck the elder, the orchestra director.

The latter had just begun his task of introducing German symphonic music, which he carried on after 1828 when he took over the directorship of the new *Société des concerts du Conservatoire*.

Little by little, the success of the students' exercises during the Empire attracted the attention of the fashionable crowd and, by 1812, the atmosphere at these events was quite different from that of ten years earlier. The *Journal de Paris* dated 14 April 1812 gives a pleasant account of this change:

> Humble and timid in the old days, this small music school used to receive few compliments and only the meager applause of a few

friends and relatives. Today, in Paris, it stimulates interest and enthusiasm far beyond that accorded the mighty Academy [the
Grand Opéra].

By noon on concert days, the Faubourg Poissonnière was invaded by a
crowd of horse carriages "taking the little temple by storm." In spite of the
early hour and the previous night's excesses, all the beautiful women were
already dressed up and ready:

> It's time to go. To no avail, husbands curse this new event that robs
> them of their ladies while costing them the purchase of yet another
> outfit. Neglected escorts are dressed again, the theater box has been
> reserved a week in advance. Mozart, Méhul, Cherubini, and Catel
> are the featured composers, and Duret is scheduled to performed a
> violin concerto. How could we miss it?

This new fashion was short lived, and the concerts came to an end with
the fall of the Empire, when the Conservatoire temporarily closed down.
The new regime probably wished to erase the memory of such brilliant and
original musical events organized by an institution that was the product of
the Revolution.

At the time when the Conservatoire concerts began to become regular
events and the Feydeau concerts became scarce due to successive closures, a
new association was formed. Very little is known about it, but it became
one of the important musical centers of Paris during the Directoire: the
concerts of the Rue de Cléry.

An in-depth study of this association has yet to be carried out. Although I systematically searched through the press of the time, I could not
find the exact date for the creation of this new organization, though it must
have been sometime in 1799. An issue of *Annonces, affiches et avis divers*
dated 18 Brumaire year VIII (9 November 1799) reported their eighth
concert, which had taken place on 27 October of that year, bringing to an
end the first season of this new society "formed only a few months ago."

Unlike the Feydeau and Conservatoire concert societies, which had an
orchestra of their own from the beginning, the Rue de Cléry association at
first had to assemble its own orchestra. According to contemporary accounts, this new orchestra was made up of players from the old Olympic
Lodge orchestra that was dissolved at the start of the Revolution, the first
batch of Conservatoire graduates, and capable amateurs. In 1799, the

Gazette nationale praised the musicians who, in the past few months, had performed eight concerts "in which the symphonies were especially admired." They did so "without any resource other than their own dedication and their personal subscriptions—along with that of a few individuals who, like them, missed the unforgettable productions of works by Haydn, Gluck, Sacchini, Piccini, Paisiello, Cimarosa, Mozart, and many other masters."[23]

These concerts were performed in a hall situated at 96 Rue de Cléry and owned by the painter Lebrun (Madame Vigée-Lebrun's husband), who normally used it for art exhibits. The brief description given in the German newspaper *Frankreich* in 1803 offers a wealth of information on Paris life during the Directoire and the Consulate:

> The hall is a square-shaped room of modest size with amphitheater seating and surrounding galleries. It does not measure up to the quality of these concerts. The public is much too near the orchestra, which is often loud, with frequent timpani parts. The whole space is so packed with people from top to bottom and all the way to the doors that you cannot move and can hardly breathe. This has the fortunate effect of sufficiently dampening the sound to save the public from going deaf. I once found myself alone in the hall when it was empty, during a rehearsal of a Haydn symphony, and I received such a shock that I promised myself never to attend a rehearsal there again. The hall is so small that, in order to secure a seat, you must arrive hours before the concert, and exiting to meet your coach at the end is always a very difficult operation.

The map department at the Archives Nationales (French National Archives) still has several drawings of Lebrun's private residence, dating from the end of the eighteenth century. The room where the concerts were held had been remodeled by him to exhibit his paintings and was lit by a large skylight, an unusual and novel feature.

The conductor of this new orchestra was the violinist Jean-Jacques Grasset, who was to become conductor at the new Théâtre italien when it opened in 1801. According to a critic, he conducted "without stamping his foot or striking the desk with his bow,"[24] which tells us a lot about the customary techniques used by the "time beaters"[25] of that time. For these concerts, often referred to in the press as the *Concert des amateurs*, the orchestra included just over fifty players: eighteen violins, led by concertmaster Navoigille; four quintes or violas; eight basses or cellos; three double basses;

two flutes; four oboes; five bassoons; three clarinets; six French horns; one kettle drum; and three accompanists. There were thirteen singers. Only the name of the first soprano, Madame Barbier-Walbonne, is still remembered today. The second year's series (1799–1800) began on 15 Frimaire (6 December) and consisted of twelve concerts. They were scheduled "on the *primidi* (the first day) of each *décade* [of the Revolutionary calendar] at half past seven o'clock in the evening." The price of a subscription to these twelve concerts was low. Men were charged forty-eight francs, women thirty-six francs, and children under the age of fifteen paid half-price "in their gender category." The orchestra was managed and financed by the players themselves and included both music professors and amateurs, the difference being strictly legal and not musical. Amateurs "received no part of the profits."[26] For the first year, there were six hundred subscribers.[27]

The Rue de Cléry concerts were famous for their symphonic performances and specialized in the symphonies of Haydn, according to several accounts. The German journalists staying in Paris prove to be reliable resources, since they were used to the great German orchestras and had no reason to be amazed by the quality of a minor French orchestra without any tradition. In 1801, the Paris correspondent of the *Allgemeine musikalische Zeitung* wrote: "The symphonies of Haydn are performed with unsurpassed precision."[28] Soon it became customary to program two Haydn symphonies at each concert, an early one at the beginning, and one of the later works at the end.[29] At the end of 1801, a German critic who had attended every performance at the Rue de Cléry wrote: "The performances of Haydn symphonies surpass anything I heard in Berlin, Munich, and Vienna."[30] It is difficult to know which of the symphonies were most frequently played. Already in the first years of the nineteenth century, one could choose in the publisher Sieber's catalog from among more than sixty Haydn symphonies, with full sets of parts available. I found mention in the press, at the beginning of 1804, of Symphony no. 103 in E-flat major ("Drum Roll," composed in 1795), and Symphony no. 100 in G major ("Military," composed 1794). These are obviously among the latest works composed by Haydn and were, according to a critic, often requested by the public. In contrast, the symphonies of Mozart were rarely performed at the Rue de Cléry concerts. They were admired but "they did not yet really appeal to the public."[31]

For several years, this very high standard of performance generated enthusiastic commentaries in the press. The Conservatoire orchestra was trying to establish itself at the same time, but the Rue de Cléry orchestra was made up of faculty members or recent graduates rather than students of the Conservatoire's instrumental program.

The makeup of this orchestra was quite different from the great orchestras of the eighteenth century, which had been comprised of players from diverse origins and performing traditions. On the subject of the performance of Haydn symphonies at the concerts of the Rue de Cléry, I found the following commentary in the *Correspondance des Professeurs et Amateurs de musique* (The Column for Teachers and Amateurs of Music), dated 8 January 1803:

> Try and imagine a single instrument performing a piece with all the rhythm and nuances meant for it by its composer. Well, you will think that you hear that single instrument, when in fact you hear sixty of them playing together. Until now, dear readers, we would have thought it impossible to obtain from a whole orchestra the accent intended by the composer for each note of music, which can only be determined or felt by reading the score, or uniform string performance with up-bows and down-bows, expressive and staccato bowings. You must forget all that we said at the time when Lully cranked out accompaniments for his operas. The poor quality of those days compared to today's polish, could justifiably raise fears about the maintenance of art at so high a degree. In any case, it is impossible to attain a higher standard of performance than that achieved in France.

The statement is important because it was written by a critic who obviously knew what he was talking about and did not hesitate to add, a few lines further on, that vocally, the concerts of the Rue de Cléry were very weak. His article leaves the impression that this orchestra represented a major step in the history of symphonic performance in France.

Reichardt's memoirs are an essential source of information on musical life in Paris during the Consulate. Reichardt lived in Berlin at the court of Frederick II, traveled extensively, and was able to hear the best orchestras of Europe. He expressed great admiration for the orchestra of the Rue de Cléry for its performances of Haydn symphonies:

> I must repeat what I already said seventeen years ago [during an earlier trip to Paris] after the excellent performance by the *Concert*

des amateurs. Haydn should come to Paris to hear how perfect his symphonies are. Nowhere else could he hear them in this way.

A few weeks later, after a brilliant performance of Haydn's "Military" symphony, Reichardt wrote that the Rue de Cléry orchestra could play the most violent *fortissimos* and the most delicate *pianissimos* but "lacked some shadings" and was never able to play with the serenity and the grandiose restraint so characteristic of some of the best German orchestras. Conversely, the Germans would never reach "such energy and irresistible strength" nor "this bewitching softness."[32] Perhaps such performances full of contrasts are less emotionally moving (only once was Reichardt, who attended nearly every concert of the season, deeply moved by the performance of a Haydn adagio), but they underline the humor and the astonishing vitality of this music. In the same letter, Reichardt described how the enthusiastic French public, especially the ladies, applauded when the brass and percussion came in on the andante of the "Military" symphony. In order for the enormous drum to be heard in the small hall, it was suspended from the ceiling. Apparently, the effect of this "janissary music" was beyond description.

In 1802, a rumor circulated for a while in Paris that Haydn, having heard of his success there, would attend a Rue de Cléry concert in person. The press announced it, but there was no follow up. However, the old composer's patron, Prince Esterházy himself, did condescend to attend a concert in January 1803, to hear one of Haydn's London symphonies. On behalf of the composer, the prince presented the society with manuscripts of a Haydn Te Deum, Requiem, and Offertory. The society responded by minting a gold coin and sending it to Haydn.[33] On another occasion, it was decided to crown a bust of the composer, which had been engraved with the words "To the Immortal Haydn." There was a very solemn ceremony, and only afterward was it discovered that the bust actually represented Cato![34]

At a time when the concerts of the Feydeau were about to close down and the Conservatoire concerts under Habeneck were not yet fully established, the concerts of the Rue de Cléry were the most successful in the capital for symphonic music. An article in the *Journal général de la littérature de France* (The General Journal of French Literature) stated:

> This concert organization, made up of the top players from the best Paris orchestras and the most distinguished amateurs, will certainly be a milestone in the evolution of music in France. In recent months, it has performed the most beautiful and sublime works

produced in Italy, Germany, and France with the kind of intelligence and orchestral ensemble that would normally only have been inspired by the composers' physical presence.[35]

Despite the participation of singers Garat and Madame Branchu from the Théâtre italien, the level of vocal performances did not compare to that of the orchestra. Nonetheless, the Rue de Cléry had the honor of presenting the Paris premiere of excerpts from *Don Giovanni, Così fan tutte,* and *The Marriage of Figaro* in their original Italian versions a few years prior to the Italian opera buffa performances.

Although the Rue de Cléry concerts were very successful and acquired the reputation of being "the best in the world for instrumental music" and the best "at least in France" for vocal music, the organization experienced great financial difficulties. Concerts had to be canceled at the beginning of 1804 for lack of subscribers. The correspondent of the *Allgemeine musikalische Zeitung* noted:

> In the old days, when wealth was in the hands of those who constituted high society, such entertainment was indispensable. Now that wealth is in the hands of those who call themselves high society, it is done away with without regret in favor of vulgar sensual pleasures sought after by everyone.[36]

But this was an unjust criticism, since it is clear that music held a very important place in Paris life at the beginning of the nineteenth century.

In any case, the planned program of twelve concerts a season at the Rue de Cléry could not be maintained. Eight concerts were held between the fall of 1800 and Easter 1801, and only five were held in 1804. In spite of the erratic performance schedule, these Saturday afternoon concerts quickly became the fashionable meeting place for Paris elegance, as the Feydeau concerts had been before them and the Conservatoire concerts would soon become.

Contemporary accounts agree that the hall was too small to withstand the brilliance of some of Haydn's symphonies, especially his "Military" symphony. But despite its small size, the hall offered a splendid sight on concert days:

> Concerts take place by candlelight. The beauty, elegance, and wealth displayed by the ladies adorning the balconies provide an

enchanting sight to the eye, while our ears are being charmed by music that can be heard nowhere else. Such a perfect combination of pleasures could not be found anywhere else in Europe.[37]

In January 1805, Lebrun, the painter who owned the Rue de Cléry, wanted his property back, and so the concerts had to be moved. For a while, they took place in the Olympic theater, which was located at 15 Rue de la Victoire. It had housed the Théâtre italien from 1801 to 1802 and the Opéra-Comique in 1804. The first concert was scheduled on 6 February 1805, and the hall was remodeled for this event:

> Contrary to customary use, this theater had not been built to accommodate a whole orchestra. Only the front stage has been kept in order to provide space for the basses and double basses. Another lower stage has been added, seating the rest of the orchestra nearly in the midst of the audience, and the sound is contained by a partition placed at the front of the stage and directed toward the hall. Since the third balcony and the central boxes are closed, there has been no loss of sound whatsoever.

Tiers of seats were arranged in a horseshoe shape, the journal goes on, "so that the audience can see into the boxes and insist on silence from anyone who interrupts because he wants to be noticed, instead of listening and letting others listen to the concert." After the first concert, the press was supportive of the new hall: "Instrumental effects did not seem to be reduced, and the orchestra lost some of its excessive strength in this larger hall."[38]

Despite these favorable arrangements, concerts stopped later that same year for reasons that I have not been able to determine. After 1805, there is no further mention of them in the press. Possible explanations include poor management by the directors, among whom were Cherubini, Bréval, and Duvernoy, as well as De Bondy, the former prefect of the Seine Département,[39] or the rivalry with the Conservatoire and its public student exercises, which attracted a growing audience each year. In the absence of any documentation, one cannot be sure. In any case, when this concert society ceased to function, the Consulate lost one of the most brilliant musical institutions in Paris.

The Feydeau, the Conservatoire, and Rue de Cléry, therefore, were the three leading public concert associations in Paris between 1789 and 1814.

There were others, but there is very little information on them: a few concerts here and there can be traced from the program announcements in the press of the time. In most cases, it is not known exactly when these short-lived societies were formed or why they dissolved. I point them out because I feel that their existence proves that society was keenly interested in music during the Consulate and the Empire, whereas it has often been wrongly represented as being consumed by idle and superficial activities.

While going through the press archives, I found mention of an *Académie de musique* created in Paris in July 1803 by "a group of artists from the Opéra, Feydeau, Bouffons theaters, as well as from the Cléry concert." It was originally a school located in the Hanover Pavilion in the Rue Louis-le-Grand, and it was aimed at good amateurs who could take courses there twice a week. The better students, including women, could then appear in concert. Any amateur who would subscribe for twelve francs a month could become a student of this academy and attend classes. The faculty included artists from the leading theaters or from the Rue de Cléry concerts. They formed an orchestra and gave an inaugural concert on 28 August 1803, at a time of the year when other leading Paris orchestras were off. The program included a Haydn symphony, the overture to *Griselda* by Paër, a sinfonia concertante by Wiederkehr, a violin concerto played by Libon, and vocal music by Paër and Nasolini. The orchestra was apparently a great success, since after only four months it had to move to the Salle des Redoutes at 40 Rue de Grenelle-Saint-Honoré, which had a seating capacity of 1200.[40]

The concerts were directed by Kreutzer and violinist Théodore Lefèvre, who was the brother of singer Madame Dugazon, and also led the orchestra of the Feydeau theater. Programs did not differ much from those of the Rue de Cléry concerts. The new association planned to perform at least one Haydn symphony at each concert. The *Allgemeine musikalische Zeitung* judged its performances to be excellent, although not quite so good as those of the Rue de Cléry. On 28 March 1804, for example, the Music Academy presented its third concert of the year and included the "Farewell" symphony, which had not been performed in Paris since the *concert spirituel* at the end of the Monarchy.[41]

The orchestra was made up of good amateurs playing along with their teachers. During its short life, it also presented a large number of opera overtures, sinfonie concertante, and concertos. As was the case with the Rue de Cléry concerts and the public exercises by the Conservatoire students, the quality of the singing left something to be desired. While critics unanimously recognized the high instrumental quality, vocal performance kept getting worse over the years due to inefficient vocal coaching at the Conservatoire. The final concert of the Academy took place on 30 December 1804 under the direction of Mathieu Blasius, the conductor of the Opéra-Comique. The following report on the dying Music Academy can be found in the *Correspondance des Professeurs et Amateurs de musique*: "After the *Concert des amateurs* (Rue de Cléry) and the Conservatoire student concerts, it is difficult to see how yet another concert society could be successful." So the Rue de Grenelle concerts came to an end "because they could not compete."[42]

According to Édouard Fétis, son of the famed musicographer, the Rue de Grenelle concerts survived until the Restoration, at which time the orchestra was divided "between royalists and bonapartists, the former wearing white rosettes, the latter choosing the seditious bouquet of violets for their buttonholes."[43] Various attempts may have been made to revive this society, though there is no evidence in the press of the time to confirm this assertion. I did find the following announcement in the *Journal de Paris* dated 22 February 1818:

> The *dilettanti* will learn with great pleasure that the majority of the teachers who made the success of the Cléry and the Conservatoire concerts have just gathered to form a new group under the modest name of *Concert des amateurs* and will present musical performances in the hall of the Rue de Grenelle-Saint-Honoré.

I do not know how this performance turned out.

A complete list of public concerts held in Paris up until 1815 would probably be longer than is normally imagined. Actually I was surprised to discover the number of orchestras that were formed in Paris between 1795 and 1805. Of course, it may be that the same musicians went from one orchestra to another, or some of these orchestras may have been made up of very mediocre amateurs, but nevertheless a taste for and interest in music was obviously at least as keen as it had been in the last years of the Old Monarchy.

Although the Revolution did not altogether stop concerts from taking place in Paris, it seems that the return to order favored the development of music. From 1795 until the beginning of the Empire, the French stuffed themselves with music to a degree that was never to be matched again. In a letter dated 6 October 1796, Baillot observed with irony:

> The epidemic of musicoragicomania is spreading. . . . Every tiny circle has turned into a concert society, every table into a piano, every woman into a musician, every man into a little Garat. . . . A quarter of an hour is ample time to hear three Gluck operas, a few Italian finales, a few ponts-neufs [popular songs, after the name of the famous Paris bridge], potpourris, romances, and a grand sonata by Steibelt may be thrown in. Nothing mediocre, nothing poor, all perfectly charming, delicious, and sublime. If the voices begin to tire, the quartet takes over.[44]

Admittedly, at that time music was often considered to be a pleasure of the senses like any other and could be compared to a beautiful firework display or even to a good meal.

For lack of documentation on this very eventful period, it is not yet possible to comprise a detailed inventory of the Paris concert societies' performance activities, and there is probably a great deal yet to be discovered on the subject. For example, in 1797, a so-called *Cercle de l'Harmonie* (Circle of Harmony) located in the Orléans wing of the Palais-Royal is mentioned: "The intention of the founders was to gather together in this magnificent setting all the pleasures that talent, games, and art can offer." In this circle, people played billiards, danced, or enjoyed a fine meal. In the refined and epicurean atmosphere of the high society of the Directoire, music still found its place. The famous Chevalier de Saint-Georges, who had just managed to escape the guillotine, conducted some concerts there "that left nothing to be desired as to the choice of pieces and the excellent quality of performance." Although the exact contents of these programs are unknown, Saint-Georges was not an amateur and probably succeeded in forming a first-rate ensemble.[45]

One year later, in a letter dated 21 May 1798, Baillot announced the creation, in the Longueville Hotel, of a new concert society named the *Concert Olympique*. He added: "If I decide to join, it will be to play only in the symphony, as requested of me by my colleagues."[46] This society still existed in 1804, as evidenced by a report in the 31 March issue of *Le Mercure de France* that describes an evening during which both vocal and instrumental music was heard, including a piano concerto by Bontempo and a violin concerto by Viotti.

From 1795, a number of new establishments opened in Paris, sometimes qualified by the press as *lieux de plaisirs* (places for pleasure) and visited by Paris society mostly in the summer months. Several of these places had formerly been privately owned residences that were confiscated during the Revolution. Their gardens were remodeled and illuminated during the summer: Bagatelle, the Élysée Palace, the Biron, and Tivoli Gardens. Admission was charged for dancing, fireworks, and various events, and music was also performed outdoors. These settings were the meeting places of fashionable Directoire society, which included many newly rich, as *La Quotidienne* ironically noted in its 19 July 1797 issue:

> The beauties of the day appear there to be admired, and louts who got rich in the Revolution, all cleaned up in white linen, bring their wives there disguised as real ladies. They stroll past their old masters without the slightest remorse.

For a while, the most popular of these new places was the Hanover Pavilion, famous for the quality of its sherbets and for its newly designed English gardens "with two mountains, three valleys, one bridge, but no river!" What role did music actually play during these fashionable gatherings of a new social class that now had access to pleasures it had not previously known? On 26 July 1797, La Houssaye, conductor of the Feydeau theater, conducted a concert at the Élysée (the Bourbon Hotel, Rue Saint-Honoré). It included "a new Haydn symphony" and a sinfonia concertante for two violins by Viotti played by Vacher and Lafont, two of the best violinists of their time. A fireworks display and a ball concluded the evening, and the following report appeared the next day in *Les Annonces*: "The Élysée is the only place that combines the fine arts and other intellectual enjoyment with the common pleasures found in all the gardens of Paris."[47] In the same setting, a reception with 6000 guests took place one month later to honor the Ottoman ambassador. On that day, La Houssaye, who specialized in outdoor performances, conducted an orchestra of over one hundred musicians. On 6 July 1798, he conducted an important concert of vocal and instrumental music in the Tivoli Gardens.

In addition, there existed many societies whose purpose was not exclusively devoted to music. They were scientific, literary, and artistic circles and held conferences and exhibits as well as concerts. During the Revolution and the Empire, one of the most famous was the *Lycée des Arts* (Lyceum of Arts). Such an important institution of French culture at that time really deserves a study of its own. It published a journal and the *Annuaire du Lycée des Arts* (Bulletin of the Lyceum of Arts). Unfortunately, only incomplete collections of these publications have survived,[48] but based on them, I can give a brief description of this society, focusing especially on its musical activities.

The *Lycée des Arts* was founded in August 1792 by an engineer named Charles Desaudray. A speech made by one of its members in 1804 recalled its history:

> Formed in order to provide a shelter to industry and the arts during times of civil unrest, this institution filled a void in the world of knowledge that was left by the former academies. The University of Paris had succumbed, and the lack of public education saddened and frightened all good citizens. Fortunately, the Lycée then became a free public school of letters, arts, and sciences.

Besides having an educational vocation, the society attracted from the start some of the most brilliant minds of the time and organized public presentations for inventors—our modern researchers—to demonstrate their latest findings. The *Lycée des Arts* played a particularly important role in the development of new techniques. Poets and writers read their works, musicians organized concerts. The events first took place in the vast, indoor amphitheater built in 1790 in the Palais-Royal gardens, which contained several show rooms and "a very attractive concert hall." The whole building was destroyed by fire on 13 December 1798, and the *Lycée des Arts* relocated, first to a room in the Sinking Fund Administration in the *Oratoire* (Oratory) and then to one of the rooms of the Hôtel de Ville (Paris City Hall). The *Lycée des Arts* was renamed the *Athénée des Arts* (Athenaeum of Arts) in May 1802, and in 1804, it moved to Rue de Grenelle Saint-Honoré. In 1805, it included 240 members—plus many associates and honorary members—divided into three categories of 80 members each: one for mathematics and physics, one for letters, and one for the arts.

This society was very definitely hostile to the ideals of the Revolution:

> In the face of the threat to debase the arts and sciences, the *Lycée des Arts* demanded care and respect for them. As the most distinguished talents were felled by the murderous guillotine, this institution honored the memory of these outlawed scholars, the list of which grew by the day.

More detailed research may establish that most of the members of the *Lycée des Arts* were masons and, like the composer Giroust, had been members of the Olympic Lodge before the Revolution. In one issue of the *Annuaire du Lycée des Arts* (year IV of the Revolutionary calendar, page 132), it was deplored that concerts had been temporarily interrupted but mentioned that the administration intended to resume them "by way of gathering together most of the artists belonging to the famous Olympic Concert."

Although no trace of the *Lycée des Arts* can be found after 1805, for fifteen years this society assigned music an important place in its public presentations, which for a while took place every month. In its early years of existence, the administration of the Lycée "had made plans to call on every top artist of every theater to form a large orchestra of 120 or 130 instruments" which was to be conducted by the violinist Blasius, the future permanent conductor of the Opéra-Comique. This early project was doomed from the start by "one of those malevolent and jealous petty tyrants who secretly organized a general network of ignorance and destruction of every art form and all talented artists." In reading such venomous statements, one can imagine the maneuvers of a hostile revolutionary faction against the creation of new concerts, or at least the existence of ferocious ideological rivalries. In any case, the first musical events apparently took place only in May 1794 and were repeated at almost every meeting of the Lycée and, later, of the *Athénée des Arts*. In comparison with the other concerts in Paris at that time, the music performed was predominantly instrumental, particularly concertos and sinfonie concertante, and featured appearances by some of the great masters of the time, such as the violinist Kreutzer, the harp and piano duo of the Naderman brothers, and the clarinettist Dacosta. Symphonies were also performed. For instance, at the fifty-ninth concert on 21 October 1798, Guénin conducted one of his own symphonies. Chamber music was also performed at these programs. On 19 January 1798, a string quartet featured Gebauer on first violin, and on 20 December 1796, a trio for flute, oboe, and clarinet featured three of the best virtuosos of the time: Ozy, Sallantin, and Lefèvre.

The *Lycée des Arts* also tried to give "some new talents wishing to make themselves better known" a chance by featuring many young players and composers"newly arrived from the provinces, so that they receive much-needed publicity in order to advance their reputations." This generous endeavor was in response to the efforts by the Lycée to promote culture in a spirit of human brotherhood, away from "insensitive selfishness and shameless materialism that fears the return to good morals, true principles, and high virtue." Many names of artists mentioned on these programs never made history and are completely unknown to us. On the other hand, young C. Lafont, who would become a great violinist, had his first success at the *Lycée des Arts*. He was applauded by "most of the foreign ministers" attending the concert. A pupil of Kreutzer, he was then only fourteen years old, and the career that he began there took him to all the leading concert stages of Europe during the first third of the nineteenth century.

The most impressive of all musical events organized at the *Lycée des Arts* was the funeral ceremony for Lavoisier. A victim of Robespierre, the celebrated chemist was one of the original founders of the society in 1792 and had presided over several of its meetings in 1793. On 2 August 1797, his colleagues organized a ceremony in his memory. An orchestra of "nearly one hundred players" was put together to perform a funeral piece by Langlé, with the participation of four of the best singers from the Opéra: Lays, Chénard, Dufrêne, and Villotteau. First hidden behind an enormous curtain, the orchestra produced "doleful sounds" surrounded by a choir "evoking dread and sorrow." Three loud strokes were played on the newly discovered tam-tam, and

> the enormous curtain was torn in half and looped up twenty-five feet to the ceiling, revealing Lavoisier's tomb richly decorated with cypress boughs, crowned with the statue of Liberty, and surrounded by twenty young Levites artistically placed and carrying many wreaths of flowers.

The audience was struck both by the grandiose music and by this spectacular scene:

> Amidst the general musical crescendo, accompanied by timpani and trumpets, a pyramid seemed to rise from the earth twenty-five feet up in the air, bearing Lavoisier's effigy girded with the immortal crown that his genius deserves.

This great ceremony honoring one of the most celebrated French scientists with such pathos and sentimentality was enough to awaken some of the nostalgia of the Revolutionary period, for the commentator ended his account of the commemorative event with a scornful remark addressed to all those who feared the return of good morals and virtue:

> Shame on those cold and indifferent souls who either did not see or refused to see, in this great act of justice and recognition, the lofty goals and sentiment of the Lycée's project.

Besides the *Lycée des Arts*, one of the most original cultural institutions of Paris at the end of the eighteenth century, I shall briefly look at a few similar, less important societies, about which there is little information. On 7 November 1801, the *Lycée de Paris* celebrated its sixth anniversary with a literary evening, during which Bernardin de Saint-Pierre read one of his books, followed by a concert "including an excellent choice of works played by amateurs of both genders and of very gratifying talent."[49] In April 1802, this society became the *Athénée de Paris*, located on Rue Hazard. It continued to be active until at least 1812 and for a while presented its concerts at Rue de Cléry. On 18 April 1807, for example, its program included a Mozart symphony, a Viotti concerto, and some vocal music.[50] In the first years of the nineteenth century, newspapers also mentioned a so-called *Athénée des Étrangers* (1803–1804) that also organized public events at which music was performed.[51]

Between 1795 and 1805, a great number of very different events took place. The amount of musical activity of that period, especially the number of different orchestras put together and then disbanded—often too soon for them to have a chance to be known—is astonishing. In 1799, the blind composer Alexandre Fridzeri, of Italian origin, created an instrumental ensemble class entitled *Chambre philharmonique*; it rehearsed in his home on Rue Saint-Nicaise. The class prepared a performance competition that included a Haydn symphony, a Viotti concerto, and some vocal pieces. Admission was charged at three or four francs, a price much lower than that of the leading Paris societies. On 24 December 1800, a dramatic explosion in the Rue Saint-Nicaise put an end to this endeavor.[52]

In November 1808, a new music society was created on Rue Mandar by Théodore Lefèvre, who has previously been mentioned as the 1803 director of the Academy of Music. The press reported on the inaugural concert presented "in a pleasant and well decorated hall, whose only fault was not being large enough to accommodate the crowd of music lovers who had turned out." The musical elite of Paris—Berton, Nicolo, Rode, and others—was there. Apparently, this new society intended to add some variety to its programs, which was extremely rare for that time: "Thanks to the participating artists, we can at last enjoy some wonderful works previously relegated to libraries." For the first concert, the program announced an aria by Handel, who was very seldom performed during that particular period, and a symphony by Méhul "that was very beautiful, even after having heard one of Haydn's most magnificent symphonies." After its second concert, this society announced a new symphony by Mr. Méhul, but left no further trace of its activity.[53]

In the final years of the Empire, a few concerts took place in the Olympic theater on Rue de la Victoire, the same hall that the Rue de Cléry orchestra was using at the beginning of 1805. I have not been able to determine where this orchestra came from, nor the name of its conductor. On 15 January 1810, Théodore Lefèvre appeared again, conducting "an overture by Mozart."[54] All the programs that can still be found show the same monotonous mix of vocal and instrumental music, with the same soloists who had performed ten years earlier: violinist Baillot; pianist Bontempo; cellists Baudiot and Delamare; and oboist Ferlendis, who also played the English horn, an instrument still almost unknown in Paris. In the spring of 1812, the tried-and-true Haydn symphonies were replaced by the symphonies of Jean Schneitzhoeffer, future composer of *La Sylphide*, who early in his career was particularly interested in instrumental music. After this concert (22 March 1812), the *Journal de Paris* found his music to be too scholarly for the ordinary public. The article concludes cynically: "These symphonies make such a noise that our simple amateurs, deafened by such extraordinary beauty, cannot collect themselves properly to enjoy all their qualities."

I should also mention here that all the main opera theaters of Paris, at one time or another, gave their own public concerts.[55] At the Opéra, for instance, such concerts were traditional at Eastertime. Although they were called *concerts spirituels*, they included vocal as well as instrumental secular music, and their programs were often quite similar to those of the other great Paris institutions. The *concert spirituel* of 26 March 1799 announced a Mozart symphony "that has never been performed in Paris."[56] The Opéra-Comique offered a similar program. Even during the Terror, concerts there featured Haydn symphonies and sinfonie concertante by Kreutzer. In addition, the great foreign virtuosos often made their Paris appearances at the Opéra and the Opéra-Comique. In 1800, two Italian singers from Milan sang at an evening organized at the Opéra-Comique. Later, Paul Carillez, the concertmaster of the Great Theater of Madrid, played his own concerto at the Opéra.[57] Even the Louvois theater, which had specialized in presenting various visiting acting or singing companies since 1791, organized concerts. Just before leaving for Saint-Petersburg, Rode played one of his concertos there under Kreutzer's direction.[58]

The Théâtre italien, probably in an effort to achieve some variety in its programs, also gave frequent concert performances, charging the same price as for its regular opera buffa performances. Orchestral music was often included, as on 11 January 1806, when not one, but two Haydn symphonies were on the program![59] In 1810, the concerts of the Théâtre italien appear

to have been increasingly well attended. The *Journal de l'Empire* published
the following lines about a concert given there by the pianist Dussek on 20
March of that year:

> The taste for music has increased extraordinarily, and the country
> has seen the number of its musicians multiply in proportion. Never
> has Paris resounded to so many concerts, and it is flattering to the
> artists that they have so many theaters at their disposal where they
> can present their talent to the public.

The concert was a great success despite the fact that the public of that time
still mistrusted the piano, as shall be seen. The program included, naturally,
a Haydn symphony, as well as the overture to Cherubini's *Lodoïska*, some
vocal pieces, a piano concerto by Dussek, and another for piano and harp
that featured the composer and harpist Naderman as soloists.

A little later, around 1812, the pace of concerts organized by the
Théâtre italien increased. There were at least seven in the month around
Easter, and each featured at least one Haydn symphony. This wave of con-
certs inspired the following commentary in the Journal de Paris of 30 May:

> "O my God, will this Holy Week ever come to an end?" a resident
> of old Paris would probably ask when confronted with the count-
> less musical events that inundate us this year. In the old days, these
> events did not last beyond the religious fortnight. Their chief pur-
> pose was to fill the void left by all other performances. Today, we
> are more musical than devout. Music is what we seek first of all, so
> maybe all is not lost.

As can be seen from the above, in spite of the decrease in concert activity due to political events between 1792 and 1795, there were many concert
societies in Paris at the time of the Directoire. This is a sure sign that there
was a public for them, even if its reasons for attending were not always
strictly musical. Its enthusiasm was often a matter of fashion. Yet we should
not necessarily assume from this that the final years of the Monarchy were a
time of decadence. Haydn's symphonies were well received in Paris by
1789, but they were performed much more frequently during the twenty
years between the Directoire and the fall of the Empire. I am sure that in
this brief period, some of them were heard in Paris hundreds of times,
much more often than at any time before or since. Here is what was written

in the *Journal de Paris* on 24 March 1812 after a performance of Haydn's music at a Conservatoire concert:

> The evening began with a symphony by Haydn, one that is heard every day and everywhere, butchered by the orchestra of the Comédie-Française, and even by the orchestra of the *Café des Étrangers* [the Foreigners' Café] at the Palais-Royal, but it has never been so well played as at the Rue de Cléry or the Conservatoire concerts.

Evidently, the Revolution did not put an end to public concerts in Paris. Quite the contrary, their pace became even more frantic than it was before 1789.

What is certain, however, is that there were practically no public concerts consisting exclusively of chamber music. Chamber music was played in private (by amateurs or professionals), and there must have been very many high-quality concerts that have left no trace. Instead of the press reviews, the historian has to resort to contemporary memoirs and letters that describe the brilliant salon life of the higher social classes. Although it may be true that society during the Directoire and the Consulate was extremely pleasure loving, it was not nearly so frivolous as it has often been made out to be. There was a cultivated élite, possibly even more spoiled than at the end of the eighteenth century yet sufficiently discerning to be able to appreciate good music and to know that it was more than just a passing decoration for fashionable salons.

Bourienne wrote in his memoirs that concerts "afforded the first opportunity to shine in company after Robespierre's death." And it is true that under the Directoire and the Consulate there were few Paris salons that did not give concerts, starting with those of the First Consul at Malmaison. Baillot the violinist wrote in a letter on 27 June 1802: "We have gotten together twice since Rode came back. The first time was at Malmaison for the Pacificator. Rode played two of his quartets, and Paisiello accompanied the singing on the piano."[60] All the important Paris salons were open to music lovers: Barron's salon at the Petit Luxembourg, Talleyrand's, Carnot's, the famous banker Ouvrard's, the poet and minister François de Neufchâteau's, and even the salon of Lucien Bonaparte himself. Lucien Bonaparte had known Boccherini when he was French ambassador at Madrid, and the composer had dedicated six of his quintets to him in 1801

and another six in 1802. He had these quintets played in his Paris salon by
Baillot and his musicians. Baillot was well acquainted with the publishers
Pleyel, Sieber, and Imbault, who had brought out some of Boccherini's
chamber music pieces for the first time in France. He organized concerts at
their houses. In June 1805 Baillot wrote to his friend Montbeillard: "We
played Boccherini's manuscripts at Imbault's house."

During his long stay in Paris under the Consulate, Reichardt, as was his
custom, had visited most of the great Paris salons where chamber music was
played. At the music publisher Sieber's house he found Kreutzer leading a
quartet and a quintet, and he also met André Ehler, an Alsatian composer
who had settled in Paris and who had published a great many chamber music works at the time. The oboist François Garnier also played at this salon.
He had already been a partner of Kreutzer's in Germany. Reichardt was not
slow to praise the quality of these musicians: "One can hardly describe with
what strength, purity and clarity of sound Kreutzer himself triumphs over
the greatest difficulties on his violin."

On another occasion he heard Rode just before he left for Saint-Petersburg at a concert held in one of those "marvelous old French homes that
absolutely breathe music." Rode was leading a quartet that played some of
Mozart's works, and Reichardt says that they performed these difficult quartets "as I have never heard them played." The German composer did have
some reservations and particularly regretted the patronage system of the
Old Monarchy, which had supported many private concerts. Other circumstances also had favored the rebirth of music at the beginning of the nineteenth century. Emigration, for example, had put many of the old French
nobility in touch with German art and culture, and during the revolutionary wars the French had had the chance to see and hear what was being
done outside their own frontiers.

For instance, we know that General Moreau gave chamber music concerts when he was in Frankfurt. Back in Paris, he kept up this tradition at
his private house with the help of his wife, who was herself an excellent
pianist. She played Mozart and Steibelt at a concert in early 1803. During
Holy Week of that year, she organized several private concerts and invited
the German violinist Andreas Romberg, whose brother Bernard was an internationally known cellist and a teacher at the Paris Conservatoire.

Reichardt has left us a detailed account of a musical soirée at General
Moreau's house, attended by "everyone important in Paris" at the time, in-
cluding several nobles from the Old Monarchy, among them the Princess of
Rohan. The program included a piece for two pianos by Jadin, which the

hostess played together with the composer, and some vocal pieces sung by Madame Barbier-Walbonne, the painter's wife, who sang with Garat at the Feydeau concerts. The program ended with a Haydn quartet. Grasset, conductor of the Rue de Cléry concerts, played first violin and Jean-Nicolas Kreutzer, Rodolphe's brother, played second. The composer Louis Jadin played viola and the cellist was the famous Bernard Romberg. Reichardt writes that the public was exceptionally attentive during the recital, but adds: "I wonder how much General Moreau enjoyed himself? Impossible to tell from his expression." A wonderful supper followed the concert. Reichardt was seated next to Madame Moreau and conversed with her about musical life in Paris. We can imagine that the hostess would have asked him all about the latest novelties in German music. This salon life must have encouraged all sorts of exchanges, and French musical life at the beginning of the nineteenth century was enormously enriched by the presence of a great many German artists in Paris.[61]

During the last days of his stay in Paris in the spring of 1803, Reichardt visited several upper bourgeois society homes where he heard some excellent amateurs, both men and women, play the pianoforte. He writes that he found there the same atmosphere as in the great houses of the Old Monarchy that he had known well. The singer Madame Barbier-Walbonne accompanied him to these soirées. Her husband was a painter of portraits and historical scenes who worked in the studio of Gérard at the Louvre. Musical evenings were often organized in Gérard's studio at the Louvre itself, and some of the best soloists in Paris could be heard there.

Eduard Monnais also wrote about these years under the Directoire and the Consulate in his *Souvenirs de la vie d'artiste* (Memoirs of an artist's life), which appeared in 1844. Interest in music was particularly lively in Paris society: "Who could count the thousands of music lovers who were part of this musical world without even leaving their salons or their rooms as they performed, more or less well, Haydn's quartets or Mozart's or even Pleyel's? The remarkable thing is that the Pilnitz coalition in no way interfered with the four quartets that Pleyel dedicated to the King of Prussia!"[62] It is obviously impossible today to evaluate properly the extent and quality of this music that was practiced privately and has hardly left a trace in contemporary writings. There are occasional references, but unfortunately they have never been collected. The composer A.-L. Blondeau, who held a first prize from Rome, makes a frustratingly brief reference in his *Histoire de la Musique* to a "ladies' quartet" that could be heard in the salons at this time. Madame Ladurner, wife of the famous piano teacher, played first violin, and a certain Madame Pain played cello. We will probably never know the names of their two companions. All we know is that these four ladies "made an excellent quartet and performed with all the precision, grace, and energy that this difficult genre requires."[63] Edouard Monnais also reports that in 1802 a quartet was formed by the Count de Grandpierre, a noble who had emigrated during the Revolution.[64]

The Count de Grandpierre had been a violin pupil of Gaviniès and of Jarnowick. He chose a musician from the old Royal Academy of Music, Sébastien Pichard, as second violin for his quartet, along with two good amateurs, Boniface Desaudrais and Emile Buisson, who played the viola and the cello. The first concert by this new ensemble was held on 25 March 1802, with two quartets by Haydn (in E-flat major and D major) on the program. This new group soon left the city of Paris and moved to the country house of one of its members a few leagues north of the capital. For several years, in perfect intimacy, this quartet made up of a noble of the Old Monarchy, a former professional orchestra musician, a rich bourgeois landowner, and the son of a cabinet-maker spent their days playing chamber music together.

Still in 1802, the violinist Pierre Marcou, a former musician from the Versailles Chapel, announced in the Paris press that he was opening a series of students' concerts for "trios, quartets, quintets, sextets, and sinfonie concertante." The pupils' rehearsals would be held once a week and concerts twice a month at the Hotel Le Peletier.[65] This venture must have been short lived because the press does not speak of it again, and in 1804 we find Marcou the violinist established as a music teacher in Bourges. But this announcement does show how much in vogue chamber music was in Paris in the 1800s. Projects like this show how great the demand was, even if they did not always succeed. A great many amateur instrumentalists were looking for groups to join so as to be able to play chamber music together. One has only to think of the unbelievable number of transcriptions for various instruments that were published at the time, especially arrangements of fashionable operas, to imagine the extent to which music was played privately during these years. These were times when, according to one witness, one could hardly imagine "the extraordinary sudden development of music that occurred as we came out of the dark and bloody days of the Terror." In 1804, for example, I find yet another press announcement[66] about the creation of a music society called the *Concert italien*, formed of "true music lovers," whose intention was to perform "all the best quartets of Haydn, Mozart, Boccherini, Pleyel, and other composers." Four sessions a month were planned, first on Rue Verdelet and then on Rue Cerutti. The subscription was to be twenty-four francs for six concerts. This venture does not seem to have prospered any more than the preceding one, but they are both examples of the first attempts in France, before Baillot's concerts in 1814, to set up public concerts exclusively for chamber music.

In a list of private concerts under the Consulate and the Empire, we must of course include the Paris salon of the Italian composer Blangini. He was an opportunist who was excellent at getting along under the successive political systems. He had arrived in Paris in 1799 at the age of eighteen and quickly became famous in the capital as a composer of romances and operas and as a singing teacher. He organized musical events at his house on Rue Basse-du-Rempart in the Madeleine district, where the élite of Paris society could be found. For a while under the Empire he held the post of Music Director for Pauline Bonaparte. The press announced each of his private concerts as they did for the important public concerts. These concerts were usually held in the mornings and seem to have been held every week at certain times of the year, although they stopped for a while when Blangini had to follow King Jérôme of Westphalia, whose music he directed, to Kassel. Although these concerts were private, admission was probably charged. The clever Blangini admits in his *Souvenirs* that "apart from the positive advantage I gained from my concerts, they were also extremely useful to me in that they helped to make me known and increased the number of pupils who came to me for lessons." The press announced these musical matinées, noting that they were less expensive than other concerts, but considering the quality of the public who came to them, one can imagine that the host did not accept just anybody. There was certainly a selection procedure according to social criteria. We are told that Mme. Blangini's concert room was the one "where the best of Paris society likes to come." Vocal music, especially Italian vocal music could be heard there, along with instrumental pieces and symphonies. In March 1811 a violin concerto by Spohr was performed, a composer whose name was not often found on the programs of public concerts at the time.[67] I do not know what the status of Blangini's musicians would have been, but they were probably mostly good amateurs who were glad to find an opportunity there to join a group. Some great artists also performed in this salon, the pianist Dussek, for example, but it is not certain that the members of society who came there would have been able to appreciate the quality of the performances. Witness these lines written the day after a concert of vocal music: "This audience prefers easy tunes to serious works, and half of them know nothing about music, while the others are merely amusing themselves."[68]

There were certainly more Paris salons open to music under the Empire than is usually supposed. At Ingres's house in the Jardin des Capucines (now Rue de la Paix) quartet sessions were held every Friday. Painters, sculptors, and musicians would meet there to listen to the host play first violin. From 1808 to 1810 the most fashionable singers could be heard at the salon of Sophie Gail, wife of the famous Greek scholar. Garat could be found there, as well as Madame Barilli from the Théâtre italien and Garcia, the Spanish singer who had just arrived in Paris with his family. According to Blangini, Madame Gail "preferred the language of music to the language spoken at home with her Greek husband" and was herself a singer and composer of fashionable romances. Extracts from operas and religious works were generally heard in her salon. But the most brilliant of the Paris music salons was incontestably that of the Prince de Chimay, who had a music room large enough to be able to put on real concerts at his town house in the Rue Babylone. He got together an élite orchestra consisting of the best virtuosos in Paris, and he placed himself among the first violins, together with Kreutzer, Rode, and Baillot. The composer Auber, who was still a very young man, played piano accompaniment. A number of remarkable concerts took place in this salon. The most famous was probably in 1809, when Cherubini's great Mass in F was heard for the first time. The first soprano solos were sung by Pauline Duchambge, a composer of romances who was doubly talented as a pianist and as a singer. The Princess de Chimay herself sang the second soprano solos. In summer this whole brilliant gathering would go off to Chimay in the Hainault, where the Prince had a private theater. The host and hostess and their guests were constantly occupied with music, and Cherubini and Auber often joined them.[69] The record of all this musical activity in Paris and the provinces is preserved today in the family archives. We know that composers who were invited to Chimay would write music specially for these private gatherings.

Of course, we also have to include in the private concerts during the Empire those that were held at the Tuileries by order of the emperor, especially the ones held each year on 15 August, his name day. The exact programs have been preserved in the *Archives Nationales*, as well as the accounts for each concert. Primarily vocal music was heard at these concerts, especially extracts from French operas for soloists and choirs. But I found an 1806 program that included the Symphony in C Major by Gossec. The number of performers is impressive: no less than 200 musicians (singers and instrumentalists) of whom 126 came from the opera and 94 had been brought in from outside. No other concerts in the capital used such large numbers at that time, except perhaps for performances at the Opéra itself.[70]

Empress Josephine also gave concerts once a week at Malmaison, featuring the very best artists of Paris. Mademoiselle Avrillon wrote a page in her *Mémoires* devoted to these exquisite evenings, which were probably more refined and exclusive than the big official court concerts and reserved a special place for chamber music:

> The best talents vied with each other on their various instruments: Dupont on his bass, Naderman on his harp, Tulou with his flute, Duvernoy with his horn. Baillot made his violin sing, and Paër accompanied the singers on the piano. There were quartets and quintets followed by singing. These concerts were held in the Little Gallery, and we went into the adjoining Main Gallery to hear these delicious sounds. The empress always asked me if I had been to the concert and if I had listened to the music. Of course I never missed them. It was at one of these concerts at Malmaison that I heard Garat sing for the last time, who was perhaps the cleverest singer who has ever existed. This was almost his swan song, and his voice had already lost much of the range that I had heard earlier—but what purity of technique, and what lovely expression he gave to everything he sang![71]

Discussion of the musical salons of the day would not be complete without saying a word about the romance, a musical form that was extraordinarily successful from the end of the Old Monarchy up to the July Monarchy. The romance is more or less equivalent to our modern songs, which can be heard on every street corner, but it is also the ancestor of the *mélodie*, by which I mean that it is more or less the only musical form that was both popular and aristocratic. It is universal in its simplicity and often sentimental naivete. The romance sings of love, especially of unhappy love.

Just before 1789, influenced by Rousseau, the romance (of which some remarkable examples can be found in the comic operas of the period, especially by Grétry) was more or less limited to the expression of tender and plaintive sentiments such as the famous *Plaisir d'amour* by Martini. Couplets are separated by a refrain, and there is a prominent vocal line with simple harpsichord or pianoforte accompaniment. During the Revolution, the romance was not heard so much (although there were historical romances, which were very close to patriotic songs), but after the Directoire, they reappeared better than ever. Over the following forty years several thousand were published in France. Anyone clever enough to cash in on the trend composed them, from the very best composers to the most mediocre. Blangini was one of these, but so was Garaudé, a singing teacher who states in his *Méthode* published in 1809 that the romance was "not so easy to sing as one would think." Everybody hoped for a salon success. Women also tried their luck, and certain poetesses wrote the words for them. In 1815 the *Journal de Paris* awarded "the award for the best romance" to the young Marceline Desbordes-Valmore. All sorts of people became composers, including Queen Hortense. She adored romances, and wrote some herself, or at least she wrote the melodic line and prudently left the accompaniment to her music master, the composer Plantade. Professional singers became the darlings of Paris salons and were paid enormous sums to interpret a few romances. The fascinating and talented Garat was among them and was just as much at ease singing for Marie-Antoinette as for Josephine. The romance was a very intimate musical form, but even so Garat sometimes gave in to public demand and performed them at concerts, such as at the Feydeau theater. He also occasionally composed them himself. His romances are all characteristically tender and passionate.

Henri Gougelot has written a definitive work on *La Romance Française sous la Révolution et l'Empire* (French Romances during the Revolution and the Empire) in which he defines different trends and different styles in the romance, reflecting changes of taste in French society at the time. There are pastoral romances, featuring shepherds and shepherdesses; fantastic romances, which are more like ballads; and lyrical romances, in which the poet expresses himself in the first person. This last category includes all the romances written for the verses of Anacreon, whose works translated by the Hellenist scholar Gail had made this ancient Greek poet fashionable in Paris. We even see Gossec, Le Sueur, Cherubini, and Méhul writing romances on these ancient Greek texts! One of the poems set to music was Anacreon's ode *To My Lyre,* which inspired Schubert himself to write a very beautiful lied.

During the Empire, the troubadour style took over the romance. The Middle Ages were fashionable thanks to Millevoye's poetry. They captured people's imaginations during these early years of the romantic period, and poets were inspired by any heroic gesture of Charlemagne or Alfred the Great. The *Journal de l'Empire* of 3 June 1813 wrote of this infatuation:

Troubadours are very fashionable at the moment. Our theaters love to depict their prowess in war, gallantry, and poetry. Our writers of romances love to choose them as the subject of their songs. Thanks to them the sweet voices of our beautiful ladies accompanied by chords on the harp or the piano, or the cracked voice of a song maker with his out-of-tune hand organ—they all celebrate the glory of these ancient bards from Provence or Aquitaine, whether in the salon or on the street corner.

The simplicity of the accompaniment was one of the reasons for the success of the romance, as it is hardly ever descriptive but merely supports the melody with a few chords or arpeggios. Amateur performers could almost always accompany themselves, either on the pianoforte, the harp, or the guitar. Rousseau had already noted in his *Dictionnaire* under the entry "romance" that any instrumental accompaniment too heavy actually weakened this feeling of tenderness that the romance evokes. All that was needed, he says, was "one true clear voice with good pronunciation, singing simply." We can understand that the romance found its most fertile ground in the salons where fashionable ladies could, without too much trouble, get the easy success they were looking for, while giving free rein to that nostalgia and gratuitous melancholy that so often marked this generation.

The Restoration in 1814 had a definite effect on the activities of the large public concerts in Paris. The government temporarily closed down the Conservatoire, which also put a stop to the students' public recitals that, thanks to François-Antoine Habeneck, had become one of the important centers of musical life in Paris. The arrival of the king completely upset the life of the salons and the whole musical activity that had developed under the Consulate and the Empire. Society had to pause a moment, no doubt, before it could reorganize itself and find the stability necessary for music to be practiced again. Edouard Fétis, whose father had witnessed all these changes, said so expressly: "the music societies were especially disorganized, as were the public concerts at the beginning of the Restoration. Political circumstances brought with them such disorganization that the arts were powerless to combat it."[72]

So it was with good reason that the *Journal de Paris* deplored the fact in 1818 that there was no longer any "permanent music society" in the capital, at least for large symphonic concerts. It is true that the Conservatoire, newly reopened in 1817 under the name of the Royal School of Music, had very timidly tried to reinstate the tradition of student recitals. This time they were no longer concerts at all, but very much public exercises, as fragments of tragedies and classical comedies alternated with the performance of musical works. About twenty of these "concerts" took place between 1817 and 1825, and Mozart's symphonies were featured several times (especially the Symphony in G minor), as well as Beethoven's First Symphony and the Overture to *Fidelio*.

From about 1818 to 1820, apparently, Paris society did reorganize itself fairly quickly, and public concerts began sporadically to reappear. In March 1821 the *Miroir des Spectacles*[73] announced: "Do you like concerts? You can find them everywhere." And indeed, Eastertime did permit the annual organization of so-called *Concerts spirituel* in the leading Paris theaters, where just about everything was performed except religious music. Mozart and Beethoven were played about as often as Rossini, Paër, or Paisiello, to the extent that the press began to complain that these so-called French concerts had eliminated absolutely all music by French composers; this was at the beginning of the Rossini vogue in Paris. The programs and financial accounts of all these concerts are preserved in the Opéra archives. There were usually four of them during Holy Week. In 1822, for instance, there was a performance of a Beethoven overture and the *Benedictus* from his Mass in C Major, Mozart's Symphony in G minor, and several Haydn symphonies,[74] with the young Moscheles at the piano.[75] In 1824, Mozart's *Ave verum* was on the program with several extracts from the Mass in C and Beethoven's First Symphony. In 1826, Beethoven's First Symphony was on the program again, with the Overture to *Fidelio*. These were the only performances of Beethoven's symphonic works in Paris between 1814 and 1828.[76]

Apart from the *Concerts spirituel*, a famous artist of the time, usually an instrumentalist, might ask for the use of the concert hall at the Louvois theater to give a benefit concert. The Bohrer brothers did this in 1818, Moscheles and Spohr in 1821, and Romberg in 1823. In 1824, thirteen-year-old Franz Liszt arrived in Paris with his father and asked for the use of the hall for a benefit concert for himself.[77] On 11 February, the Baron de la Ferté, who was director of the Royal Theaters, gave permission to the Opéra director, "on condition that Monsieur Liszt plays at one of the spiritual concerts." So on 12 April 1824, Liszt's name appears on the program of the first spiritual concert of the season, for "a piano concerto" and "an improvisation on the piano." Young Franz's father had arranged the programs with Habeneck, who was director of the Opéra at the time. The following year, on 22 January, Liszt again received authorization to play, but the Administration gave its opinion that "it is inconvenient to program these concerts too frequently." Considering the small profit that was made by some of the musicians, the Baron de la Ferté considered that "it would be better not to disturb the usual practice of the Royal Academy of Music" and that in general the royal establishments "should avoid as much as possible any community of interests with private persons."[78]

I will not go into detail about the big concerts—private, of course—that were given at the Tuileries every year on 25 August, Saint-Louis's feast day. The programs are all preserved at the *Archives Nationales*[79] and show that they were appallingly mediocre, entirely devoted to the work of "official" French composers such as Catel, Le Sueur, Berton, and Persuis. However, worth noting are the various efforts to set up regular public concerts in Paris from 1825 onward, including, for instance, an amateur concert at the winter Tivoli in the rue de Grenelle-Saint-Honoré.[80] There, the composer Mathurin Barbereau, winner of a grand prix de Rome, and the violinist Tilmant both made their first appearances as conductors. This short-lived society did not make much impression on musical life in Paris, and neither did the *Musical Athenaeum* society that was set up just before the Revolution of 1830 by the composer Hippolyte Chélard, also a first Rome prize winner.[81] But even if they made no lasting impression, these tentative attempts do indicate a degree of activity in an effort to shake off the torpor of the early years of the Restoration.

The foundation in 1828 of the *Société des concerts du Conservatoire* is, however, an important event in the history of French music, and its history has been extensively studied. It flourished throughout the nineteenth and early twentieth centuries due to the exemplary quality and originality of its programs. It was established with the considerable help of Habeneck, a brilliant musician who played an important role during the Empire as the head of the Conservatoire students' public exercises. Over the years, he had grown more and more enthusiastic about Beethoven's music, and he was able to introduce Beethoven's name on the program at the *Concerts spirituel* that were put on at the Opéra during the Restoration. He was greatly helped by the Director of the Conservatoire, none other than Cherubini, when he tried to revive the old system of public exercises. Their efforts were successful, and on 15 February 1828 the Minister of State, Sosthène de la Rochefoucault, expressed the wish to "retrieve for this school (the Conservatoire) the reputation that it had previously gained by its public exercises." He issued a decree that from now on every year there would be "six public concerts beginning at the latest on the first Sunday of March." The new concert society's president was Cherubini, and Habeneck was Vice-President and Conductor. The orchestra was made up of present and former pupils of the Conservatoire together with their teachers.[82]

The first concert was held on 9 March 1828 and began symbolically with the *Eroica* Symphony. We have some interesting memoirs written by the violinist Eugène Sauzay, a pupil and son-in-law of Baillot, who was a member of this orchestra from the start. He describes the atmosphere during what he called the militant years of this society:[83]

> Those of us who were members right from the start had to be pretty courageous. Only with difficulty could we put together this admirable selection of works in which everything was new, both in spirit and form. We rehearsed three times a week, from nine o'clock to midday or sometimes one o'clock, without lunch, with no heating, in that damp, cold room, which is well heated today. We may not have been exactly martyrs to art, but we were certainly brave and hard-working artists.

The second concert on 23 March was entirely devoted to Beethoven. It was there that Baillot played Beethoven's violin concerto for the first time in Paris: "I can still see my dear master," writes Eugène Sauzay, "sitting at his desk and working on that violin part which is so very different from Viotti's concertos!" The fourth concert, on 27 April, was entirely given over to the works of Mozart.

Little by little, this society was to open up the great works of Beethoven, Weber, and Mozart to the astonished Parisians. It played a decisive part in introducing German music into France in the nineteenth century, which at the beginning gave rise to difficulties with the old French masters, most of whom had spent their lives much too wrapped up in themselves and had practically no knowledge of contemporary German music. But for the young artists of the 1830 generation, these totally new concert programs opened up horizons that they had not dreamed possible. It was a shock, but a beneficial one, for the public, which mostly consisted of the leaders of the young romantic movement. The enthusiasm of the young intellectual élite of the time focused on the name of Beethoven much more than on that of Haydn or Mozart. Sauzay wrote:

> We only dreamed of the Choral Symphony and of Beethoven's last quartets. We were young 1830 revolutionaries, we forgot Mozart and Haydn because we were so entirely taken up by this music that went so well with the new ideas . . . . The public who followed us was just as eager to listen as we were to perform. After each concert

we would be surrounded, congratulated; people we did not know would come up to embrace us. In the amphitheater you could see enthusiasts who had denied themselves dinner in order to pay their two francs for a seat.

In his *Mémoires,* Berlioz recounts at length his own enthusiasm as a neophyte of Beethoven's great masterpieces. One day he managed to persuade his old master Le Sueur to come to one of the concerts, where Beethoven's Symphony in C Minor was to be performed. His account of this event is famous and has become a sort of symbol of the time. Le Sueur was dumbfounded:

Ouf! Let me out, I need air. It's extraordinary! It's marvelous! This has so moved me, troubled me, upset me, that when I left my box I wanted to put my hat on, and I thought I could not find my head! Leave me alone, I'll see you tomorrow!

The next day Le Sueur had recovered his calm, and in spite of yesterday's strong impression, he was much more reserved: "Even so, one should not write music like that!" "Don't worry, dear Master," replied Berlioz, "there will not be much like it."

Compared to the Directoire, the Consulate, and the Empire, a fundamental change took place after the Restoration. The violinist Pierre Baillot set up a series of public concerts exclusively for the performance of trios, quartets, and quintets. Until then, chamber music had been only for the privileged society, but now it was to leave the salons and become accessible to everyone. Of course, it would be quite wrong to imagine that after 1815 the Paris salons were no longer interested in music. On the contrary, as soon as society had reestablished itself, customs were resumed, and there were any number of private circles where instrumental or vocal music was performed just as it had been in the past. Often a professional such as Baillot would play together with a group of good amateurs. In her *Mémoires,* the Countess d'Agoult makes a distinction between modest salons "where music is cultivated with taste" and those where it was "merely a convenience." It appears from her writings that in some of the great salons of the Restoration, musical concerts were put on just for show, and the artists were there only "in a secondary capacity," rather like performing animals:

For instance, if one wanted to put on a good concert, one would go to Rossini, who would charge a rather modest fee, 1500 francs,

if I remember correctly, to organize the whole thing, including program and performance, so that the hosts need not be troubled by
problems of choice or the tedium of rehearsals, and so on.

Obviously this newly rich bourgeois society, which was becoming more
important every day, was beginning to develop a certain snobism as far as
music was concerned. They liked it not for itself but for its so-called social
significance. And the best artists of the time were prepared to go along with
this masquerade. At a time when composers were beginning to find their
independence by escaping from the tyranny of private financial support, the
performers, for their part, continued to be tied to the whims of bourgeois
society. Countess d'Agoult implies this in her comments:

> The great maestro (Rossini) would sit at the piano all evening, ac-
> companying the singers. He usually added a virtuoso instrument
> player, Herz or Moscheles, Lafont or Bériot, Naderman, the best
> harpist, Tulou, the king's first flutist, or the wonder of the musical
> world, little Liszt. They would all arrive together at the appointed
> time, by a side door, would all sit together round the piano, and
> then all leave together, after having received the compliments of
> the host and of various musical dilettantes. The next day Rossini
> would receive his salary and it was thought that that was enough,
> for them and for him.

Clearly every salon was not like this. After the first Restoration, for instance, the violinist Baillot wrote to a friend: "Every fortnight we meet to
play quintets at General Dessolle's house." He compares these sessions,
which were "art," to his lessons, which were his "job" and which enabled
him to repair "our previous disasters." It is certain that the influence of Baillot's personality contributed a great deal to the expansion of the chamber
music repertoire in Paris to works that the public did not yet know. He had
been familiar with the quartets of Mozart and Beethoven and also Haydn
and Boccherini since the beginning of the century. In fact he had "discovered" Beethoven's quartets in 1805: "we have had two Beethoven sessions,
and we are very satisfied with them."[84]

With his unique experience and knowledge of a repertoire which he
knew to be exceptional, Baillot decided to organize public concerts consisting exclusively of chamber music. He set up a subscription system, and the
first concert was held on 17 December 1814 at 16 Rue Bergère. Twelve

concerts were planned for the first year, but this number was soon reduced and from 1829 on remained at four a year. Admission was six francs per concert, which was about the same as for one of the big Paris concerts at the time. It is true that the subscribers were almost all aristocrats, or at least wealthy enlightened amateurs. These concerts went on until 1840, almost until Pierre Baillot's death. Much has already been said about the historical importance of these music sessions, especially by Joël-Marie Fauquet in his remarkable work on *Les Sociétés de musique de chambre à Paris de la Restauration à 1870* (Chamber Music Societies in Paris from the Restoration to 1870). Arthur Pougin, writing in 1872, already saw in Baillot "the true founder of chamber music concerts that for some years now have been so popular in Paris."

For the inaugural concert, the ensemble, which consisted of Baillot (first violin), Guynemer (second violin), Tario (first viola), Saint-Laurent (second viola), Delamare (first cello), and Norblin (second cello), performed three quartets, two by Haydn and one by Mozart (K. 575), and three quintets, two by Boccherini and one by Beethoven (No 7, opus 29). These are the four composers who were played most often until 1830, along with Baillot himself, who often had the ensemble perform his own chamber music works, and Viotti, as well as a few other composers. Reicha from 1823, Onslow from 1824, Hummel from 1825, and Cherubini from 1829 sometimes appeared on the program, but the main names were always Haydn, Mozart, Boccherini, Beethoven, and Baillot.

There were few true connoisseurs at first, about 150 to 200 people. But the success of these sessions encouraged Baillot from 1830 on to organize exceptional concerts in the large Saint-Jean room at the city hall, which could hold 700 people. Nothing of this kind had ever before been seen in the history of concert-going in France.

These public chamber music concerts had a determining influence after the Restoration and aroused interest in a whole new repertoire. In 1821, for example, the press announced that starting in mid-January, lovers of instrumental music could meet every Sunday in the foyer of the Favart concert hall. There they would hear Reicha's quintets and, on 25 March, Beethoven's septet.[85] All these concerts were attended by a public of real connoisseurs who no longer came to hear new works for the first time, but to hear them again and again, to get to know them and to compare different interpretations.

This was an élite public, a small group of initiates, not just as far as their social origins were concerned (the list of subscribers that has been preserved leaves no doubt about that), but also in their refined taste, which made them a microcosm inside the contemporary musical scene. These new dilettantes were quite different from those who, at exactly the same period, were gathering round Rossini in the Théâtre italien, but their attitude was fundamentally the same in that they refused to be interested in contemporary French music, which simply did not satisfy their thirst for new aesthetic emotions. And this was also the time when Choron's historical concerts[86] were having a tremendous success. Some people were looking for a breath of fresh air in the unknown past, others were looking for it outside of France's borders, but in either case, the basic attitude was the same.

These connoisseurs, the modern spirits of their time, were amazed and overjoyed to discover the new repertoire. Only one name, that of Schubert, was missing from the programs, even after 1830. Proof of this can be seen in these lines written by Fétis in 1827 after one of Baillot's chamber music sessions:

> Our great violinist had the opportunity to display his talent with such varied and delicate nuances and such colossal dimensions that the whole audience breathed admiration and enthusiasm for the entire two and a half hours, and at the end one heard only the words: "Perfect! Sublime!"[87]

In fact it is remarkable to note that from 1815 on, thanks to Baillot's concerts, the public began to be interested in questions of interpretation. They began to wonder if each composer had a particular style. They began to understand that Mozart should not be played in the same way as Beethoven, nor Handel like Boccherini, but that each composer has his own manner (or even several over different periods of his life) and that the performer has to understand this if he is to play in a way that is historically accurate. This was a new idea that the French critics had not realized up until now. This accounts for Framery's very penetrating judgment of Baillot, found in his *Encyclopédie méthodique* (1818) under the entry *Soirées musicales*:

> His intention in setting up these sessions was to give a course in ancient and modern music from Corelli up to our own time. . . . The allegro, the adagio, the presto do not just have meaning in an absolute sense, but each of these pieces, whether it belongs to Corelli, Geminiani, Tartini, Handel, Boccherini, Haydn, Mozart, Beethoven, or Monsieur Baillot himself, has its own chronological

color that is different and indicates the name of the author and the date it was written.

Only very incomplete information for this period on concert activities in provincial France exists, so it is not really possible to describe what musical life outside Paris would have been like. It is known that a number of local provincial societies flourished throughout the eighteenth century: Musical Athenaeums, *Sociétés d'émulation*, and the like, would meet regularly so that the musicians, who were mostly "enlightened amateurs," as they were called, could give a concert. It is true that in some places the Revolution temporarily put a stop to this, but is seems that very quickly (from 1795 on) music began to be practiced again in a great many medium-sized towns.

For instance, in Amiens, the music society existed in name only when the Revolution broke out. Yet on 18 March 1795, a declaration was made to the Council by a group of music-loving citizens who had once met every ten days at the house of one of their members at Rue de Metz to give concerts. Evidently a real need was felt to start up chamber music sessions again after the storm:

> The arts of pleasure and of utility are brothers and support each other mutually. They are all children of liberty, and it is therefore good, now that the Reign of Terror is over, that their enjoyment can safely be resumed. It is with this certitude that a few music lovers and artists of both sexes believe that they may meet together on certain days to continue to cultivate these arts, before the eyes of their parents and a few friends.[88]

Taking up music again was often recommended at this time as the best means of forgetting the dark days and getting rid of the nightmare. So when a new public society tried to set itself up in Amiens a few months later (early 1796), the municipality addressed these words of encouragement to the organizers:

> We are pleased to see that you intend to rekindle our taste for the fine arts and to resuscitate a society that used to practice them with distinction. The community was proud of its music society, foreigners came to admire its concerts, and before the advent of liberty, we used to find there a perfect example of true civic equality,

urbanity, and all those pleasures that made it so attractive. We greatly regret that the vandalism that has made all France groan should also have destroyed the concert hall where your predecessors used to meet, and all its decorations. But you will be able to repair these losses.[89]

At Lille, which had been so rich in concert societies up until 1789 (just before the Revolution, the famous *Concert de Lille* counted no less than six hundred subscribers), the Revolution had silenced all musical activities, and the first public concerts did not come back until 1798. A government official confirms this: "the concerts degenerated little by little and were finally reduced to nothing, in spite of the efforts of a few zealous amateurs who several times sought in vain to save them."[90] It was the same story in Lyon, which had to wait for the Directoire before the musical matinées that had been suppressed during the Terror could be reorganized. For a while, music for the revolutionary fêtes, which were mostly performed in the open air, replaced concerts, although they obviously were aimed at a much larger public. Similarly, at Bordeaux, concerts lasted until 1792, but then the Terror broke up the *Académie des Arts*. Both unemployed former chapel masters and their musician colleagues made a living primarily from private lessons. The only town where I can find anything about musical activity in concerts under the Terror is Rouen. Thanks to Boïeldieu, several large concerts were organized there from January to August 1793. They featured the violinist Rode and the singer Garat, who had fled to Rouen precisely to avoid the Terror in Paris. A concert was even programmed for 21 January, but it was canceled at the last moment and rescheduled for the following week because, according to the local newspaper, "Rode is indisposed."

In Nantes, public concerts ceased in 1793, and music went into hiding in private salons. There is evidence of a private salon performance of *La Volière*, Boccherini's quintet with two cellos, featuring Rode as first violin and Baudiot as first cello.[91] Later, during the Directoire and the Empire, both Mozart's and Haydn's quartets were performed in the salons of rich citizens of Nantes, whose names have been preserved.

Under the Directoire, local societies were re-established everywhere. At Bordeaux, for instance, a *Lycée littéraire et philharmonique* was set up in 1796. It was directed by Blanchard, who was first violin at the Grand Théâtre, and by Dacosta, a vocal and instrumental music teacher. The first concert was held on 24 May 1797, with a program very much like those of the large Paris concerts. A Haydn symphony was followed by a clarinet concerto, a viola concerto, and a harp concerto, some French and Italian vocal music, and a pianoforte sonata by Steibelt. However, the musicians were almost all unknown. They were local celebrities, "distinguished amateurs," but posterity has not retained their names.[92] From the time of the Directoire on, musical life seems to have come alive again and, thanks to the efforts of some wealthy families, concerts could be organized again at Versailles (from 1799), which had been deprived of music since the Revolution. Here "the best artists in Paris" played Haydn and Mozart to great applause.[93] It was at this time that the town of Lyon was also reorganizing its musical matinées. In 1803, a brilliant period began in Lyon, when some of the best Paris artists came to give concerts. Symphony concerts that featured professionals and amateurs alike were held at the Hôtel du Nord until 1820. After that date they were held in the foyer of the Grand Théâtre. Under the Restoration, musical meetings of great quality were also organized in the Prefecture, at the initiative of the Count de Brosse, who was Prefect of the Rhône.

In a town the size of Lyon there must have been a large number of other associations that were more or less short lived. The Rhône Departmental Archives[94] contain a petition addressed to the Mayor of Lyon on 8 December 1812, and forwarded by him to the Prefect. The signatories (about fifty of them)

> propose to set up a concert of amateurs which will meet every Sunday from ten o'clock to midday. They request the temporary use of a room in the City Hall. The first concerts to be set up in Lyon were given in the City Hall and were then transferred to a building in the Place des Cordeliers. It was built at the amateurs' expense, yet it was sold during the Revolution as a communal property.

There are not enough documents left today to be able to estimate precisely the extent to which local music societies existed in the main provincial centers up until 1830. Certain towns seem to have had a lot of difficulty getting themselves out of the quagmire of the Revolution. This was the case for Béziers where, under the old Monarchy, the musicians of the Saint Nazaire cathedral and the collegiate church of Saint-Aphrodise, with the Chapter's permission, used to take part in instrumental and vocal concerts held in the City Hall. Alex Bège wrote in the introduction to his *Mémoires du compositeur Guibal du Rivage* that, as far as Béziers was concerned, "between 1790 and 1810 we found nothing but occasional music, mostly music for civic events."[95] It was not until the Restoration that well-known artists from Paris returned to visit Béziers, and when they did, public attendance often was poor. Proof is an anecdote by Guibal du Rivage. It involves the violinist Lafont, who had given immensely successful concerts all over Europe and had for six years held the position of solo violinist at the emperor's court in Saint Petersburg, and the cellist Max Bohrer, who also had an international reputation thanks to the concerts he had given together with his brother, the violinist Antoine Bohrer:

> The famous Lafont knew that I was at Béziers and wrote me an extremely pleasant letter from Toulouse, asking me, as a friend and as a pupil of the same teacher (Kreutzer), to organize everything for a concert that he wanted to give while he was passing through town, and asking me to play with him the lovely sinfonia concertante, which had been dedicated to me by the immortal author of *Paul et Virginie* and *Lodoïska*.
>
> Everything was ready at his arrival, which I had been careful to announce on posters. Alas! He made the fantastic sum of 125 francs, after expenses. After the concert, I took him home to offer him some refreshment. He threw himself on a sofa in my living room, tired and humiliated at having had such a small audience— he who, every time he gave a concert in the largest concert halls in Paris, always had had the satisfaction of seeing them entirely filled with his admirers! He kept on repeating to me this phrase that weighed so on his heart: "My dear friend, when we see each other again in Paris I will remind you that the first violinist of the Emperor of All the Russias and of the King of France once played at Béziers for 125 francs."
>
> Bohrer, the cellist, was treated even worse than M. Lafont, since for his pains he only received 45 francs, which he disdained to take, but requested me instead to give it to one of the city's poor houses, which I did after he had left.
>
> Fortunately, there are several towns in provincial France where great artists do get satisfaction when they come.[96]

In the dull musical life of the provinces, there were nevertheless some names that did contribute to the development of music in a particular region. Franz Beck, for instance, settled in Bordeaux for nearly fifty years before his death in 1809. And Alexandre Guibal du Rivage himself, who came from Béziers, was a violinist and composer and pupil of Kreutzer, Catel, and Méhul; he was a fervent admirer of Haydn, Mozart, Spontini, and Beethoven, and contributed greatly to the development of local music in his home town whenever he was there, even though he is forgotten today. During the Empire, he set up an instrumental ensemble called the *Cercle Harmonique* and a free music school.

Even a little town like Douai was extremely active musically under the Empire and the Restoration, thanks to Luce-Varlet, a local man who had had an excellent musical education at the Paris Conservatoire (violin, harmony, and counterpoint) but chose not to stay in Paris, as most other young provincial talents did. He preferred to return to his native town to organize its musical life. He set up orchestral concerts and quartet sessions in which he played first violin. Research is going on at the moment into the musical life of this small provincial center, and it may turn up some surprises. The local newspaper *La Feuille de Douai* announced on 2 Nivôse year X (23 December 1801) that "the music lovers of this town, wishing to do all in their power for the citizens' pleasure, propose a subscription to ten concerts that will be held during the months of Nivôse, Pluviôse, Ventôse, and Germinal." A the same time, a local patron named Magin got together an orchestra "of the grandest kind, which will consist of eight violins, basses and bassoons, two clarinets, two horns, two serpents, and a fife." In November 1803 a Mozart symphony was performed in Douai, and on 9 December 1806, Luce-Varlet conducted Mozart's Requiem at Saint-Pierre for a ceremony to commemorate the dead heroes of Austerlitz. On 8 February 1812, *La Feuille de Douai* reports that a concert of amateurs was to be held that same day, "in Mr. Magin's drawing room, Rue Saint Éloi." The program was very similar to the Paris programs of the time, including a concerto by Viotti, a sinfonia concertante for two clarinets, vocal music, and so on. It also included "Beethoven's great symphony" cut in half, with one half performed at the beginning of each half of the concert. Would this have been the *Eroica* Symphony, which had been performed in Paris for the first time only the previous year? Of course it is impossible to know under what conditions this symphony could have been performed, but I certainly had not imagined up to now that some provincial centers could have such immediate access to foreign masterpieces that Paris was only just discovering. During the Restoration, Douai also received visits from some of the best musicians of the time: Baillot in 1815, Spohr in 1820, and Mazas in 1828.[97]

Bassoonist Camille Mellinet (a printer by profession) has left some interesting memoirs about music in Nantes. Around 1825 to 1828, important musical evenings took place in the salons of a certain Monsieur Larivierre, where great artists played who were passing through the town, along with young professionals: "sometimes, we even tried out some pieces of modern operas before they had been performed in the theater." An example was the hunters' chorus from *Robin des bois* (Robin Hood, the adaptation *Der Freischütz*).

Nantes was also the first town after Paris where Reicha's quintets were played. Our chronicler has left the following account of the quintets for wind instruments and the effect they produced:

> I cannot describe how delighted we were, who until now had only had those sterile quartets churned out page by page from mangled opera themes. Now at last we had some real music that could hold its own next to Haydn and Mozart's quartets, and which no longer obliged us to blush before the old lovers of string music.[98]

In spite of all their efforts, some of these performances by local orchestras may have been rather too ambitious. Haydn's *The Creation*, for instance, was performed for the first time in France at Lille, on 3 November 1800 (before Paris),[99] and three years later this gigantic work was performed in Caen at the *Abbaye aux Hommes*.[100] The Lille Music Society, conducted by Ambroise Fémy, was particularly active under the Consulate, giving no less than fifteen concerts during the 1801–1802 season. The programs were exactly the same as for a large Paris concert, with Haydn symphonies, sinfonie concertante, instrumental and vocal music. The same type of concert program was advertised at Orléans (including the mandatory Haydn symphony and Kreutzer's violin concerto) in February and May 1804. In 1810, Mozart's symphonies were presented at Bordeaux, "as they are performed at the exercises of the Paris music Conservatoire." In Saint-Brieuc, a much smaller town, a competition concert was given on 29 January 1803 by "a very large orchestra." One wonders about the quality of such ensembles.[101]

Castil-Blaze violently criticized what he called the "dreadful performances" of provincial orchestras, which he attributed to four main causes: lack of ambition, too few rehearsals, the force of habit, and the fact that they had never heard performances by the big Paris orchestras. It may well be true that, for someone who had heard the Rue de Cléry or the Conservatoire concerts, performances by provincial groups sometimes seemed pathetic. "As for Haydn's symphonies, don't mention them. You are lucky if you can recognize them." The composer Guibal du Rivage[102] knew what he was talking about, since he had heard many big Paris orchestras as well as local groups. He goes on to describe provincial concerts as a whole:

> One thing that is really bad is the makeup of the orchestra. The balance almost always is bad between high and low instruments and between strings and wind. There are almost always too few basses and too many violins, horns are rare, and oboes practically nonexistent. The viola part in almost all orchestras is given over to one or two old fools and amounts to nothing. Since there is no balance between the different sections, the effect can only be bad. In the provinces they don't even know how important it is to consider the size of the place where the brass will be playing, and to use only a suitable number, or else to make them play softer if there are too many, or to increase the volume if there are not enough of them. If the conductor is nothing but a time-beater, he will not be able to coordinate his orchestra to bring about a perfect blend. If he is a cold type, he will conduct dully and freeze his audience. If he has never been out of earshot of the church bell of his village, he will certainly never have the qualities necessary to imagine, to indicate, and then to obtain the different effects that would make his performance a success. And they are too often willing to admit real beginners, or even eccentrics. Beginners can sometimes be useful, if their parts are simplified for them, but eccentrics, never. Apart from the fact that they disorganize everything, they are almost always extremely bad musicians.

However, it is probable that there were exceptions, and also that, as exchanges between Paris and the provinces became more frequent over the years, some large French towns may have had good quality orchestras. From 1802 on, the Orléans amateur orchestra was able to recruit sixty musicians. A contemporary journalist wrote: "This is one of the most complete orchestras of this type that it would be possible to put together, even in a large city."[103] Toward the end of the Restoration, Caen also possessed an orchestra of sixty musicians conducted by the violinist Joseph Gravrand, a pupil of Baillot and conductor at the town theater. He also conducted a concert of the *Société Philharmonique* in Calvados on 16 March 1827. The program was an exact copy of the Paris concerts. Besides the Haydn symphony and the Viotti violin concerto, a new piece was also performed, the Overture to Rossini's *Siège de Corinthe*.[104] At this time, there were also two large symphony orchestras in Nantes: the Philharmonic Society, which was made up of amateurs reinforced by professionals as needed, consisting of about fifty-five musicians that played symphonies by Haydn, Mozart, and Beethoven; and the *Société Marivaux*, which specialized in symphonies and overtures for large orchestras. When these two societies got together, as reported by the local press, they formed a group of about one hundred players, and in 1830 they performed "two magnificent pieces by Beethoven and Hummel."[105]

Even in a town as large as Lyon, Beethoven's name remained largely unknown to music lovers until 1820. On 20 December, the *Cercle Harmonique*, a group of amateurs conducted by the violinist and composer Alday, performed the Overture to *Prometheus*. In March 1824, the musicians of the *Orchestre du Grand Théâtre* accompanied Beethoven's violin concerto. A member of the old Lyon family named Mocker was the soloist. The first symphony of Beethoven's to be played at Lyon was the *Pastoral* on 7 February 1830. The day after the *Eroica* was performed for the first time in 1833, the critic in *Courrier de Lyon* admitted ingenuously: "We are not yet civilized enough to be able to digest pieces of this size." The first time the Ninth Symphony was to be heard in Lyon in its entirety was 27 March 1907![106]

Many provincial towns did not succeed in organizing music societies until the last five years of the Restoration. The task depended on the initiative of artists who had received a good musical education in Paris; they then spread the taste for and knowledge of music throughout the French provinces. This happened in Arras, for instance, where Antoine Glachant, an excellent composer, was untiringly active from 1812 onward. In 1828, he managed, with the help of the mayor, to set up a Philharmonic Society of sixty-five musicians.

Musical life in the provinces between 1789 and 1830 certainly benefited greatly from artists on tour who were passing through. From the end of the eighteenth century on, instrumentalists and singers traveled over the whole of Europe, from Brest to Saint Petersburg, and even went to America. While they were traveling they did not mind stopping over in some very small towns. For provincial people who did not travel much, this was a unique opportunity to hear famous stars and to appreciate the talent required to be able to perform on the international stage.

The violinist Baillot was one of these touring musicians, and on 28 April 1803, he gave a concert in the Salle de la Redoute at Caen. In early June 1804, two of the best Italian cellists of the time, the Fenzi brothers, gave a series of concerts at Lyon. They performed some of Romberg's works, among other things, and some Italian airs were sung by the wife of one of them. This high quality trio had enormous success.[107] One of the Fenzi brothers also went to Lille in November 1807, where he presented himself as "first cellist of the King of Tuscany." In January 1805, the town of Bayonne was thrilled to hear the singer Isabelle Colbran, Rossini's future wife. At the same time, the Portuguese pianist Bontempo gave a concert in Bordeaux.[108] Garat and artists like him traveled over the whole of France and Europe. He shows up everywhere, always applauded and celebrated as the messenger bringing the latest novelties from Paris. The greatest violinists of their time, Kreutzer, Rode, and Baillot, also traveled a great deal of the time. The clarinetist Dacosta was born in Bordeaux and decided to travel to Paris where, as we know, a brilliant career awaited him. In 1797 he started the journey from Bordeaux to Paris, accompanied by a friend who was a pianist. They took three months to get to Paris because, Fétis explains, "they stopped in all the smallest places to give concerts."[109]

It would probably be dangerous to draw hasty conclusions from these few events. As I have said, there are still no documents available that would give us an overview of musical life in the provinces. It is probable that additional information would indicate that the situation varied from one province to another. And certain towns of little importance may have been favored because they happened to be situated on the routes the artists traveled to go on their international tours.

However that may be, it seems that concert societies were fairly numerous in the provinces during the time we are studying. It is surprising to discover how many amateur groups existed in such a range of places, excluding the years between 1793 and 1796, when many of them disappeared temporarily. Instrumental music was certainly practiced far more widely than it is today. Those players were understandably eager to form ensembles. If they were not always able to achieve more than an honest mediocrity, this should not be held against them. Their efforts at the turn of the century are what kept the provinces from becoming a musical wasteland.

Chapter 6

Instrumental Music

Eighteenth-century aesthetic and philosophical values had an impact on the course of French instrumental music. Throughout the century, music had been considered to be an imitative art, like literature and painting. The idea of imitating nature, which goes back to Aristotle, was taken up by most of the thinkers of the Enlightenment. In their desire to establish a kind of symmetry and correspondence between literature and the arts (for the most part entirely artificial), many of them followed Abbé Du Bos in defining music as an imitative art whose function was to reproduce nature. By "nature" they meant the physical universe as well as the world of the passions. However, by considering music as a language that must, like spoken language, have meaning, they clearly limited its field of interest. Du Bos wrote that the listener is at fault if when judging a piece of music he does not determine first and foremost "how well the song imitates the sound it is supposed to be imitating" or to what extent it is "suited to the meaning of the words." Batteux, Morellet, Rousseau, Lacépède, and Diderot—*mutatis mutandis*—all held to this theory. Diderot believed that "a song is a succession of pleasant sounds because it awakens our sentiments or reminds us of aspects of nature." The inevitable corollary of this definition is "music that neither paints nor speaks is bad." These ideas foreshadow the opposition in the following century to what was called "pure music." We hear this quite clearly when a sensitive man such as D'Alembert says, "All this purely instrumental music, with no form and no purpose, speaks neither to the spirit nor to the soul, so that we have to ask, like Fontenelle: 'Sonata, what do you want of me?'" Such extremely cut-and-dried positions at times strongly affected French music at the turn of the eighteenth century. Quite a number of composers allowed themselves to be influenced by principles that were often defined by literary people rather than by musicians, and they turned away from instrumental music to concentrate their creative abilities on all forms of vocal music, especially opera. Le Sueur, whose productive period spanned half a century (1780–1830), was the most representative of their attitude. He was the one most influenced by Rousseau's thinking, remaining faithful to it throughout his life. In a series of volumes that he brought out just before the Revolution, Le Sueur at length developed the theory of imitation in music. Among the 114 pieces that comprise the catalogue of his complete musical works, there is not one piece of symphonic or instrumental music. As far as he was concerned, music was music only if it was vocal. For him, words were essential, indeed, practically indispensable for music.

A book by Lacépède, *La Poétique de la musique* (The Poetry of Music, 1785), which came out just before the Revolution, also subscribed to these ideas. Lacépède was a naturalist and a future Chancellor of the *Légion d'Honneur*. He was a mediocre composer, but he was fascinated by music and liked to be thought of as an expert. *La Poétique de la musique* is 730 pages long; its title already makes it quite clear that the author considers music to be significant only as a language. Of these 730 pages, 710 are devoted to examining all the different forms of vocal music: tragédie lyrique, tragédie pastorale, church music, cantatas, songs, and so on. The chapter devoted to the symphony and the concerto is just thirteen pages long; duets, trios, quartets, and sonatas are dealt with in only six pages. The sonata itself is generously given the following few lines, which show quite clearly that the author simply did not want to deal with the subject: "Music is sometimes written for only one instrument. If the composer wishes to do this in order to show off his artistic dexterity, if he wishes to combine difficult passages with touching expression in order to demonstrate the musician's talent, in short, if he wants to compose a sonata, then he will know well enough what is expected of him from what has already been indicated."

The pages that deal with the symphony are quite obviously written with vocal music in mind. It is almost as though, from this aesthetic point of view, the symphony is, by definition, missing something. Instead of looking for its originality, there is a constant attempt to define the symphony by comparing it to something else, something that is not there and, by its very nature, never will be. "However bright the colors of a symphony, it is easy to see that they can provide only vague images." The composer must paint with energy and seek "to compensate with brighter colors and a larger number of images for the pleasure given by a specific representation." Each of the three movements should be worked out like a grand aria "with one or several voices seeking to express various emotions." The whole should be conceived "like three great acts of a theatrical piece," and should amount to "a kind of drama."

It was during this same period that the symphony became recognized as an art form and was perfected by Haydn and Mozart. It is, therefore, surprising to hear a music specialist still obstinately analyzing it in strictly literary and dramatic terms, as though completely ignorant of the musical work (harmonic or thematic) that is involved. He speaks of each movement as though it were an act of a tragédie lyrique divided into several scenes. "It should contain great variety, marked contrasts, and that growing warmth that is the soul of all drama." Nowhere in this text do we find any more precise thoughts on form. It is as though the structure of a movement in a symphony depends on some sort of superimposed, pre-arranged literary argument that gives it a picturesque superficiality rather than on internal, purely musical necessities. Lacépède goes on to say that different families of instruments should be used to set up "a sort of dialogue" (and the word *dialogue* is used advisedly here). An instrumental solo is considered to be a monologue, and when the instruments are played together, they "form a sort of scene with several different characters." I think it is important here to note the systematic use of certain highly significant words such as "a sort of dialogue," "a sort of scene," as though the symphony did not have a status of its own and as though it were somehow less than perfect when compared to tragédie lyrique.

Lacépède assessed chamber music using the same parameters and saw it as a supplementary ornament to a country idyll, with the voices of the instruments as "tender lovers who lie at the feet of their adored ones on flowered lawns." But all this sentimental phraseology, with its end-of-the-eighteenth-century overtones and its conventional descriptions of gentle

nature, contains advice given to composers of chamber music that is exactly
the same as that given to symphonic composers:

> These works . . . should be divided in the same way into three
> pieces, each with a different character, and should, as far as possi-
> ble, be given a dramatic form that is charming. One should be able
> to recognize an emotional sequence and some sort of interesting
> action. There should be a beginning, a middle, and an end, with
> developments, some sort of plot, and an outcome, or to put it
> another way, those who perform it should be able to follow all the
> parts of a drama in which they participate.

I could cite many similar quotations. I thought it important to deal at some
length with all of these theories that the eighteenth century left as its
heritage to the following generations: in spite of the blossoming of romanticism and the appearance of a new aesthetic, the ideas of the Enlightenment,
from a strictly musical point of view, have weighed more heavily on posterity than has sometimes been thought. For quite some time, the French continued to be rather wary of symphonic and chamber music. Even Berlioz, in
spite of the *Symphonie fantastique*—or perhaps because of it—went to the
trouble of discussing the theory of imitation in music in two long articles
published in the *Revue et Gazette Musicale* by Fétis in 1837. And Stendhal's
almost exclusive passion for vocal music and his lack of interest in all forms
of "pure" music make him a true disciple of Lacépède, at least on this point.
I found the following reference in his correspondence: "A certain Romberg
bored us terribly the other evening with his cello, but La Camporesi sang
"Quelle pupille tenere" by Cimarosa divinely, I thought."[1] Stendhal let his
imagination go in *La Vie de Haydn* and indulged himself with the following
dream:

> I have often thought that the effect of Haydn's and Mozart's sym-
> phonies would be greatly enhanced if they were played in a theater
> pit and if well constructed pieces of scenery representing the main
> ideas of the different movements were presented on stage. A beauti-
> ful decor representing a calm sea and an immense pure sky would,
> I think, enhance the effect of a Haydn Andante, which describes
> tranquil happiness. There is no doubt that music is the vaguest of
> the arts and is simply not descriptive by itself.[2]

Speaking of the performances in 1811 of Haydn and Mozart symphonies at the Conservatoire concerts, a critic in *Les Tablettes de Polymnie* wrote:

> One often forgets that these are only instruments that produce such magical effects upon the soul that it is drunk with sweet sensations. It is as though one were transported to the theater to see an opera where all human passions are depicted with such truth that only can produce strong emotions.[3]

These evaluations, all so strangely uniform, provide us today with some firsthand information about the history of taste. It helps us to understand the reactions of the French public toward symphonic music and chamber music at the turn of the century. More importantly, knowing the guiding principles helps us understand the content of the repertoire.

Curiously enough, these aesthetic principles did not prevent the French symphony from developing enormously during the whole of the eighteenth century. Barry Brook's exhaustive work on this subject[4] has given us sufficiently eloquent statistics, and although, in the history of French symphony, Gossec certainly holds first place at the end of the old Monarchy, he was by no means the only symphonic writer of his time. Barry Brook has listed about eight hundred symphonies written from 1730 to 1789, an extraordinarily large number that does not even take into account unpublished works composed by local celebrities in the provinces. For the period 1778 to 1789 alone, 110 French symphonies are listed, but from 1790 onward, the pace of production diminished dramatically. From 1790 to 1829 the number of French symphonies published went down to fifty-seven. Thirty-seven were published in the decade between 1790 and 1800, and very few were actually written by composers of French birth. It seems quite clear that the old-fashioned productions of the Monarchy stopped short with the beginning of the Revolution, and most French composers of the time turned away from this type of music where they could no longer make an impact. However that may be, on 26 September 1796, *Annonces, affiches et avis divers* published the following laconic item: "Sixty symphonies by well-known authors such as Pleyel, Haydn, Stamitz, Cambini, Guénin, and Filtz. All these symphonies bound and sold at a fourth of the price marked." It is astonishing to find Haydn's name in this list. Considering the concert programs in Paris and the provinces from 1795 to 1810, Haydn's symphonies were at an unprecedented level of popularity. The Paris public was certainly listening to symphonies just as much as before, as is clear from the enthusiasm that Haydn inspired. Moreover, around 1801, a clan of "*dilettanti* Mozartiens" was formed to champion the symphonies of their idol. Even more remarkable is that all the best French composers of the 1790s seemed to lose interest in the symphony as a form even though it had by no means lost favor with the public. Gossec, "the father of the French symphony," and younger composers such as Méhul, Le Sueur, Catel, Cherubini, and Berton, whose careers more or less began with the French Revolution, all seemed to turn away from the symphony even though it was a form that might have brought them considerable success.

How can this be explained? It may well be true that all these young men—and Gossec, too—had put their talent to the service of the Revolution, but this would not have caused them to turn away from the symphony except for ideological reasons. Perhaps a composer of Revolutionary music felt that it would look bad to use a musical form that evoked the wealthy eighteenth-century salons where it had been so popular. It is even more difficult to understand considering that after 1795, there was an increasing number of symphony orchestras in Paris and the provinces that were soon enlarged by the arrival of graduates from the newly formed Conservatoire. Whereas La Pouplinière had to hire clarinets, horns, and trombones from Germany to fill his orchestra with capable players, French orchestras now were able to recruit excellent wind instrumentalists from among the Conservatoire graduates. Choron, who rarely praised any French institutions, nevertheless expressly states in his *Dictionnaire historique* (1810):

> One thing that cannot be too highly praised in France is the excellence of the symphony orchestras. They are not only far better than the Italians, who are not good in this respect, but also far better than the orchestras in Germany, where instrumental music is held in such high esteem. This fact is even admitted by the most nationalistically minded foreigners.[5]

As far as French composers are concerned, it seems clear that their lack of interest in this type of music was at least partly influenced by the writings of the eighteenth-century theorists. This is definitely the case for Le Sueur, whose letters reflect a conscious decision on his part. People like Catel and Berton also turned chiefly toward vocal music. Méhul was the only one who dared go into the ring and have his symphonies measured against those of Haydn and Mozart. Had it not been for the tremendous popularity of

Haydn's and Mozart's symphonies in Paris, one wonders whether he would ever have tried his hand at this repertoire. Were his symphonic works inspired by his desire to establish a name for himself and the French school among these foreign masters? It is quite likely that French composers were annoyed by Haydn's triumph in France, and later Mozart's, even rejecting them altogether. I will demonstrate this later on when we explore the various stages in which the German school penetrated French music.

Several contemporary statements, some by Méhul himself, leave no doubt about the French composers' reaction to the prevalence of the German school. On 23 November 1808, for example, *Le Journal de l'Empire* announced a new symphony by Méhul: "This famous composer is successfully pursuing the career that was opened up by the Haydns and the Mozarts. He is one of the pillars of the French school, whose name shines the brighter because of him." During the Empire, the Paris press did not hesitate to speak out against the hegemony of German symphonies. In March 1809, Suavo, the editor of the *Moniteur Universel*, wrote: "Ever since Haydn has taken over the orchestras of Europe as though they naturally belonged to him, very few other composers have tried out the symphony as a musical form, since it appears that he has already taken it to the utmost degree of perfection." Méhul himself wrote to thank the critic Suavo for having praised him in his articles and added in plain terms:

> Since I am a passionate admirer of Haydn's music, I recognized the danger of my undertaking, and I knew the public would greet my symphonies with a certain coolness. I intend to write some new ones for next year and I will try to make them good enough at least to win your respect and to accustom the public little by little to the idea that a Frenchman may follow in the footsteps of Haydn and Mozart.[6]

Two months later, following a concert at which one of Méhul's symphonies had been a brilliant success, a critic in *Le Journal de l'Empire* wrote:

> Monsieur Méhul is in the strange position whereby he has to overcome the ridiculous opinion of certain people who apparently would like to forbid any other musicians from writing symphonies, just because Haydn and Mozart have written such admirable ones. To do this he is obliged to surpass himself with every new production.[7]

In March 1810, *Les Tablettes de Polymnie* admitted that for many years "nobody has dared to aim as high as composing a symphony."

Much is known about Méhul's symphonies, thanks to the remarkable work of the English musicologist David Charlton.[8] He has been able to establish that Méhul actually wrote six symphonies (two of which are incomplete), a fact unknown up until now. The full orchestral scores have been reconstructed and were published in 1982 by Garland Publishing.[9]

Méhul's career began in 1797 with two performances of his symphony at the Feydeau theater on 28 January and 7 February. Only two movements have been preserved, of which the final Presto is in sonata form, somewhat in the style of Haydn. Curiously enough, in spite of a favorable press review—"a charming symphony by Méhul"[10]—the composer then remained silent for more than ten years. During this period, however, he was able to perfect his orchestral writing in the overtures of his operas, especially *Héléna* (1803) and *Gabrielle d'Estrées* (1806), but it was not until 1808 that he resumed writing symphonies. Over the next two or three years, he composed five symphonies; the last one apparently was never performed, and it is not known whether Méhul ever finished it. A manuscript of only the first movement is preserved in the Vienna library. Of the four others, two (in G minor and D major) were published by Méhul by 1809. They have been programmed from time to time at concerts and have even been recorded. They are both in the traditional four movements (Allegro, Andante, Minuet, and Finale). The Allegros are in sonata form, although the development is short and often based only on the first subject. The recapitulation seldom conforms exactly to the exposition, a sign that Méhul did not feel bound by the classical Viennese tradition and that he was influenced by the opera overture, the form of which is much looser than the sonata form. In fact, like Cherubini, Méhul developed some of his opera overtures much further than was the custom at the time. They were no longer just short introductions but true symphonic movements that could stand on their own. Most of these overtures can be related to sonata form but with some important modifications. However, I should be careful not to over generalize. The Viennese themselves, and Mozart even more than the others, often refused to be restricted by this form, even though, for them, it was probably much more fluid than later generations developing a theory for it believed.

The Symphony in G minor, in any case, was to have the privilege of crossing the border. It was engraved in Germany and performed in Leipzig several times after 1810; in 1842, Mendelssohn himself conducted it at the

Gewandhaus. In 1810 it was received by the German critics with some reservations. Its melodic fabric was weak, but it was considered a serious, carefully orchestrated work. They concluded that it was written "in the style of Haydn but freely adapted for the French."[11] It seems very significant to me that it was judged primarily with reference to Haydn. In 1838, when it was again performed in Leipzig, it met with greater success: "This is a beautiful work; it would be difficult for any French-born composer to duplicate it now."[12]

In France or in Germany, Méhul's symphonies always suffered in comparison to Haydn's, not to mention Mozart's or Beethoven's. In 1818, in the *Encyclopédie méthodique*, Momigny wrote of Méhul's symphonic output: "Méhul showed real talent in his symphonies, but he could only reproduce some of Haydn's effects because he used Haydn's colors without having his artistic creativity."[13]

It seems to me that these judgments betray an error of perspective. It is clear that without a distinctively French frame of reference, that is, without a contemporary national repertoire, the critics were more or less obliged —as they still are today—to base their judgment on the great German "models." The lovely Andante of the Third Symphony in C major, which is possibly the best of Méhul's slow movements, with its beautiful opening melody for strings, was simply qualified as being "Beethovenian in spirit"; the Andante of the Fourth Symphony in E major, which is also quite exceptional, with its opening fifty-six bars for cellos accompanied only by basses, is described by *Les Tablettes de Polymnie* as being "varied in the manner of Haydn." And yet the very originality of these pages may constitute their "Méhulian character." These works are still considered to be of interest today, not only to musicologists but also to performing musicians, which indicates that they must have real value. They have recently been recorded, and since other recordings are in preparation, thanks to David Charlton's research, the public will be able to judge for itself. Unfortunately, Méhul's symphonic output was too small to result in a specific "French style." He seems to have been an isolated phenomenon; he was remarkably gifted, but his works did not establish a trend. In spite of their success, the symphonies could not by themselves restore the great French musical tradition of the eighteenth century.

As a matter of fact, apart from Méhul, right up until 1830, there was little else. I should, however, mention the return of Gossec, the "father of the French symphony," who in 1809 at the age of seventy-five and after more than twenty years of silence, wrote his *Symphonie à dix-sept parties*

(Symphony for Seventeen Parts). This was the period when Beethoven's early works could be heard in Paris, and perhaps the old master was influenced by them as well as by Mozart, since his work seems to show greater vigor than did his symphonies written before the Revolution. There are many original ideas here, such as the minuet in C minor, which is written in the form of a fugue with its subject and its countersubject. This symphony has been shamefully neglected in the past and has never even been published. It has recently been performed with much fire and success at the festival of La Chaise-Dieu under the direction of Jean-Louis Jam. This work is bound to appear in the catalogues of major record labels.[14]

Cherubini wrote his *Sinfonia* in 1815 for the newly formed London Philharmonic Society, and the young Hérold wrote two symphonies during his stay in Italy in 1813 and 1814. These three works are practically unknown to today's French public;[15] they constitute the entire output of these French masters since 1789. Against the backdrop of this desert, Berlioz's colorful personality must have made an even greater impression. His arrival on the Paris music scene in 1830 with his *Symphonie fantastique* caused one of those sudden and unpredictable changes of direction that occur from time to time in the history of the arts. The preceding pages bear evidence that there had been no French symphonic tradition to speak of since 1785. Berlioz must have been tremendously impressed when he heard Beethoven's great masterpieces at the *Société des Concerts du Conservatoire*, as he indicates in his *Mémoires*. He had discovered a music that derived its original character, in his view, from the fact that its composer responded to his own deepest intimate demands and not, as was too often the case in those days, to what society expected. In Beethoven, Berlioz found a genius who said what he had to say as he wanted to say it, without being bothered by superficial considerations of popularity or fashion. This time, it was the artist who imposed his own tastes instead of submitting to contemporary ideas.

To a certain degree, Berlioz did the same. That is to say, he filled his work with all the fantasy of his imagination, derived from his readings (Goethe, Shakespeare, Chateaubriand), his love affairs (his passion for Harriet Smithson), and his romantic artist's dreams. When the *Symphonie fantastique* appeared in 1830, it was subtitled *Épisode de la vie d'un artiste* (Episode in an Artist's Life), and each of the five parts also had a subtitle. So in spite of appearances, the work is not free of a particular type of French tradition. At its first performance on 5 December 1830, conducted by Habeneck, Berlioz had programs distributed to the audience, so that they could follow "the musical aspects of different situations in an artist's life." In this he was certainly much nearer the eighteenth-century French theorists (about whom Le Sueur had lectured at length during his instruction) and Stendhal's ideas concerning instrumental music than he was to the great German symphonic composers, past or present. Thus I find the review that appeared in *Le Figaro* the day after the premiere of the *Symphonie fantastique* to be absolutely incorrect: "This is the first time that someone has tried to give precise meaning to instrumental music." On the contrary, the work is the direct result of an aesthetic tradition over a century old.

At subsequent performances, Berlioz changed his mind about the need to provide a program for the audience to follow, since "the Symphony (the author hopes) contains musical interest in itself, independent of any dramatic content." This is the whole dilemma of programmatic music and the symphonic poem, which preoccupied musicians during all of the nineteenth century and even the beginning of the twentieth. It is not for me to take up this question in this book, but I thought it would be useful to show that in certain aspects, nineteenth-century symphonic music is more firmly rooted in the preceding century than is sometimes thought.

Even so, the *Symphonie fantastique*, with or without its program, seemed quite revolutionary at the time. It was not like anything heard before. To begin with, almost none of its five parts corresponded to the traditional form of a symphony movement. Then there was the makeup of the orchestra: There were at least a hundred players, and the instruments employed—the two pairs of timpani requiring four timpanists, the ophicleid, the off-stage bells, and the "several pianos"—were unusual for this type of music. Berlioz's innovations opened the way for the nineteenth century in its search for new orchestral tone color. Its strange harmonies and its lyrical and fiery melodies told of the anguish and torment of the author's soul. Until then, perhaps, no composer had ever "opened himself up" in this way in his work. What he revealed was that he was a disciple of René, and the reference to Chateaubriand and the *mal du siècle* (the "century's uneasiness") was clear.

> The author supposes that a young musician, suffering from the moral ailment that a famous writer has called *le vague des passions* (the uncertainty of passion) sees for the first time a woman who seems to embody all the charms of the ideal being his imagination had dreamed of, and falls desperately in love with her.

This exaggerated lyricism and tumultuous expression of passion was enough to ignite the younger generation. The day after the performance, Fétis was rather reticent in his praise, declaring that this music "is more astonishing than pleasant" and that it "lacks charm," but the young lions of the romantic generation made no mistake when they greeted Berlioz as a leader. It was certainly not by chance that the creation of the *Symphonie fantastique* took place in 1830, the same year that saw the literary quarrel over Victor Hugo's *Hernani*.

However, the French symphony had since 1789 been in a long period of eclipse. As I have said, except for Méhul, there was no important symphonic composer. Furthermore, none of the masters of the French symphony of the eighteenth century, including Gossec, appeared on concert programs after 1789. The Baroness de Bawr was, therefore, not completely wrong when she wrote in her *Histoire de la Musique* published in 1823: "France has produced no writers of symphonies to compare with the Germans."[16]

Although the symphony may have temporarily disappeared as a genre, not all composers necessarily gave up symphonic writing. For a number of years, in fact, mainly during the Revolution and the Empire, a new fashion arose for descriptive pieces for orchestra that were sometimes called *symphonies à programme* and described a particular historic event, usually heroic or warlike, such as a siege or a battle. Needless to say, in spite of their title, these works had little in common with real symphonies. Military instruments, such as drums, cornets, and trumpets, were brought into the orchestra. The three- or four-movement design was rarely respected, and thematic content was close to nonexistent, as the composers simply put different picturesque elements together in any way they wished. One of the most famous examples is the *Bataille de Jemmapes*, a symphony for large orchestra by Devienne, an excellent flutist but a mediocre composer. It was performed in 1792 at the Feydeau theater. He kept to a three-movement structure and, possibly for the first time in the history of the symphony, used three trombones (even Beethoven did not introduce this instrument until his Fifth Symphony).

The work begins with three cannon shots and a trumpet call, followed by the *Marche des Marseillais*. Obviously the descriptive element is by far the most important, overriding any pretense of harmonic ingenuity. For instance, after a dominant cadence in A, Devienne jumps directly to a new phrase in F major. The Largo is very short; with its syncopation and numerous *rinforzandi*, it is probably meant to represent the groans of the wounded, while the final Allegro assai trumpets victory with a fanfare and also includes the two Revolutionary songs *La Carmagnole* and "Ça ira." Musically, none of this is of much interest, but this wave of *symphonies à programme* lasted until 1815. A number of *batailles* were also written for harpsichord or pianoforte: the *Bataille de Marengo*, the *Bataille d'Austerlitz*, and more. In July 1800, the Paris correspondent of the *Allgemeine musikalische Zeitung* admitted that he did not understand the French enthusiasm for this kind of composition. He added candidly: "In German, we have no name for it yet" and proposed as an equivalent translation the name *Historische Symphonie*.

In spite of the diatribes of eighteenth-century theorists and the often unfavorable judgments of contemporary critics, instrumental music had always held an important place in the concerts of the Old Monarchy, whether in public or private concerts. One has only to look at the programs of the Concert spirituel or the *Concert des amateurs* or to think of the musical gatherings at the home of La Pouplinière to realize that in addition to vocal or symphonic music, instrumentalists were also often featured as soloists. From 1760 on, forms such as the sinfonie concertante or the concerto became surprisingly popular. It was actually for a private concert at the residence of a well-known Paris family that Mozart composed his famous Concerto for Flute and Harp in 1778. People were used to hearing instrumental music at the end of the Monarchy, and the beginning of the Revolution did nothing to change this. On the contrary, the number of instrumental works published in Paris kept on growing until the beginning of the nineteenth century. The catalogs of Paris publishers blossomed with sinfonies concertantes, concertos, quintets, quartets, trios, duets, and sonatas; they must have included several thousand works. Such abundance proves that they must have been in great demand.

As in the past, many foreign composers continued to have their works published in Paris, especially since some of them lived there almost permanently. Even so, the production of purely French works continued to grow regularly until a profound change began to affect the evolution of musical forms and language. To reiterate what has been stated about the symphony: the leading French composers of the time began to neglect instrumental music, and their works disappeared from the publishers' catalogues. There is no doubt that composers such as Méhul, Cherubini, Le Sueur, Berton, and Catel were primarily interested in creating vocal music.

Though the great masters of the time no longer cultivated certain musical genres such as sinfonies concertantes, concertos, or chamber music, all forms of instrumental music continued to develop for two reasons in particular. First of all, the evolution and manufacture of certain instruments continued to be perfected (harp, flute, clarinet, horn). Secondly, many instrumentalists began to emerge, often of extremely high quality, who were not content to be mere virtuosos. These accomplished artists were looking for repertoire and often had no choice but to become composers themselves in order to fill the gap; many works for instrumental music composed between 1789 and 1830 were written by virtuoso players rather than composers. In the article entitled "Concerto," which forms part of his *Cours complet d'harmonie et de composition* (1808), J.-J. de Momigny expressed his regrets about this paradoxical situation, which was not restricted to France: "The problem for wind instruments is that the great composers cannot play them, and those who can are not usually great composers."

The opening of the Conservatoire in 1795 undoubtedly favored the development of the French instrumental school, for winds as well as for strings. Not only was it no longer necessary to bring wind players from Germany to fill the ranks of French orchestras, as had often been the case in the past, but French artists soon began to be deservedly well known outside their national borders.

Take the woodwinds for example. The famous virtuosos who were on the faculty of the Conservatoire when it opened and whose famous methods were published from 1800 left a vast body of works devoted to their instruments. They included A. Hugot, who in 1796, according to Fétis, was applauded for having given "the best performance on the flute ever heard up until now in France," and the oboist A. Sallantin, clarinetist X. Lefèvre, bassoonist E. Ozy, and hornist F. Duvernoy. These artists, who acquired their reputations as soloists in the last years of the eighteenth century (especially at the Feydeau theater), soon had their own disciples, ensuring a succession of musicians to fill the orchestral ranks. I shall spare the reader a tedious list of names; all of these musicians have been forgotten today, and yet they and their teachers were the chief composers of the new repertoire for wind instruments.

Many of them were extraordinarily prolific. X. Lefèvre composed no less than six concertos for clarinet, and several of his most brilliant pupils followed his example. Isaac Dacosta, who became first clarinetist at the Théâtre italien and then at the Opéra, also wrote four concertos. During this period, many other clarinet virtuosos, some of whom were foreign born, settled in Paris because of its musical prominence (Iwan Müller, J. B. Gambaro, Frédéric Berr, and others). Each of them also wrote countless works for the clarinet, published at the time by the leading Paris houses. Some, like Gambaro, even became publishers themselves. In fact, Paris remained one of the most active centers in Europe for the publication of instrumental music.

The same is true for every other great wind virtuoso of the time. They performed as soloists at concerts and almost all of them were principals in one of the leading Paris orchestras (Opéra, Théâtre italien, Feydeau theater, or Tuileries Chapel). Flutist and bassoonist François Devienne, for instance, died young in 1803 but still had time to write ten concertos for flute and four for bassoon, all published in Paris. The horn player Domnich, who was of German origin, made a brilliant career as soloist and teacher at the Paris Conservatoire and published three concertos for horn and orchestra. Another German horn player, Stich (who used the name Punto) published more than ten concertos for horn and orchestra in Paris; Frédéric Duvernoy, leading figure of the French school, published no less than twelve horn concertos. I have limited this inventory to concertos for wind instruments. Most of these composers also wrote sinfonies concertantes, quintets, quartets, trios, duos concertantes, and sonatas.

Another instrument that became especially fashionable at this time was the harp. At the end of the eighteenth and the beginning of the nineteenth centuries, the great technical improvements in its manufacture helped to make it popular in Paris and provincial salons under the Directoire and the Empire, and also in the orchestra, where it became more and more important.

In 1782, G. Cousineau, who was a professional harpist, instrument maker, and music publisher, invented a system that greatly improved the instrument. By adding a double row of pedals, it became possible to modulate and therefore to play the harp in any key, which had not been possible before. But the new playing technique was difficult and discouraging to amateurs. It was not until the Paris instrument maker Sébastien Érard came up with his ingenious invention that it became practical to use the harp in any key. By inventing the *fourchette* (fork) and then the *harpe à double mouvement* (1810), a mechanism that remains in use to this day, Érard "put the seal on his reputation as an instrument maker," as Fétis said. This new type of harp was such an incredible success that from 1811 to 1835 its inventor built more than three thousand of them, many of them richly decorated in the Greek style.

The harp was fashionable in all the salons where ladies vied with each other in charm and style if not always in talent, looking for success and the praise of their admirers as they displayed flattering, languid poses. For a number of years, pre-romantic aesthetics seemed to be focused on the harp; its nostalgic sound filled the soul with delicious melancholy. Countless literary references testify to this popularity. All the most fashionable ladies (Madame de Genlis, Queen Hortense, Madame Récamier) were harp players of greater or lesser talent. Myriad solo pieces and transcriptions appeared at that time: harpsichord pieces, selections from operas, popular comic operas, romances, all rewritten for the harp by arrangers who were quick to profit from this new vogue. The harp was also widely used to accompany romances, where it rivaled the piano or the guitar. This may have been the origin of a very simplified style of writing that made self-accompaniment possible for the amateur.

However, the harp was used not only in fashionable salons, but also occasionally in orchestras. Gluck was one of the first to use it in *Orfeo* (1762). In France, it appeared at the Opéra during the early romantic evocations of far-away misty Scotland. In his opera *Ossian* (1804), Le Sueur asked for twelve harps to accompany the songs of the Scottish bard! Catel in *Wallace*, Méhul in *Ariodant* and *Uthal*, and Boïeldieu in *La Dame blanche* also used the harp in an attempt to add local color. At the beginning of the nineteenth century, the harp was often used in duets with the French horn. Paisiello composed a dialogue for these two instruments in the music he created for Napoleon's coronation in Notre-Dame. They were also found at the Opéra in 1801, in the adaptation of Mozart's *The Magic Flute*, which the composer Lachnith presented to the Paris public under the title *Les Mystères d'Isis*. During the Empire, harpist N.-C. Bochsa wrote sinfonies concertantes for harp and horn. The blend of these two sounds was especially popular. Its sweetness made sensitive souls shiver with delight.[17] The harp took its place in the symphony orchestra in 1830 with the *Symphonie fantastique*, but the public was already long used to hearing it in recitals. One could probably list several dozen concertos for harp and orchestra— not to mention sinfonies concertantes—published between 1789 and 1830. The most famous is Boïeldieu's in 1800, but all the leading soloists of the time added countless works to the rich repertoire of their instrument. Among the most famous were the Italian F. Petrini, who lived in Paris; the Cousineaus, father and son; the Naderman brothers, who were also music publishers; and M.-P. Dalvimare, author of a great many pieces for harp and horn that he performed together with his friend, French hornist F. Duvernoy.

Examining the situation for stringed instruments, it is no exaggeration to say that between 1789 and 1830 the French school was going through one of its most successful periods, especially for the violin. Neither the violin nor the cello underwent any fundamental changes in design, but as was true for the wind instruments, the great virtuosos of the time composed their own repertoire and opened up new possibilities for their instruments by developing their techniques far beyond anything that was thought possible up until then.

At the end of the eighteenth century, the cello had finally asserted itself in regard to the bass viol. It was recognized as an instrument in its own right and used more and more frequently. Between 1800 and 1828, no less than ten cello methods were published, including that of Baudiot, Baillot, Levasseur, and Catel, which was the official Conservatoire method. Catel presented the cello as "an instrument that is still new, since very little solo music exists for it" and stated that there were "very few concertos." The first pages of the treatise clearly show the changing status of the cello: It was now beginning to be considered as a solo instrument. In his method, a distinction is made according to how the instrument is used: It is called a cello when it is used as *partie récitante* (singing part) and when it is used as "accompanying part, [it is] usually called bass."

The repertoire for cello may still have been relatively limited, but contemporary composers began to enlarge it. A few important performers and teachers who doubled as composers dominated this period: J.-B. Bréval, whose early compositions date from the Old Monarchy, and especially Jean-Louis Duport and his brother Jean-Pierre, also a cellist, who were the oldest of their generation. Both had traveled extensively abroad, particularly to Berlin, where they were first cellists at the Chapel of the King of Prussia, greatly enhancing the reputation of the French school. The two other great masters of the early nineteenth century were C. Baudiot and J.-H. Levasseur. They taught at the Conservatoire and had as their pupils most of the great cellists of the romantic period, including A. Franchomme, who was Chopin's friend and became well known around 1830. All these artists wrote a great deal of music for their instrument and were first-class virtuosos. Thanks to them, the cello began to rival the violin; they systematically developed their technique and composed collections of studies that are still in use today. Their concertos are full of difficult passages that the cello had hardly been thought capable of accomplishing before, since it was so often relegated to the role of bass accompaniment. This evolution took place not only in France; the situation in Germany was very similar. One of Germany's best virtuosos, B. Romberg, came to Paris—like many foreign artists—in 1801 and taught at the Conservatoire. He was often heard at Rue de Cléry and other leading Paris concerts, where he was a great success playing his own works, especially his concertos.

The violin school, however, was the most famous in France at the turn of the century, thanks to a few important figures who soon became well known throughout Europe. It is difficult to classify G. B. Viotti as a French musician. He was an Italian by birth and a cosmopolitan artist, although he did stay in Paris for several long periods and even held administrative posts; he was director of the Théâtre italien at the beginning of the Revolution and of the Opéra in 1819. In 1793 a Berlin newspaper called him "the greatest violinist in Europe," but by his own choice, he had a fairly short career as a soloist and played in public for only a little over ten years. Even so, this relatively short period spent on the leading European stages was enough to make him a model for many young admirers who were deeply influenced by him, both as a player and composer. Mozart knew Viotti and admired him, and his violin concertos were played in all the capitals of Europe at the end of the eighteenth century. At the Feydeau theater in 1791, Pierre Rode programmed two concertos by Viotti, his teacher (no. 17 in D minor and no. 18 in E minor). Baillot heard them and, much later, wrote the following glowing comment: "Only then did we hear the violin in all its beauty and eloquence, and Viotti's genius, like the sun, brought to life all the talent that has shone ever since." [18]

Around 1800, three performers greatly contributed to the reputation of the French in violin playing: Pierre Rode, Rodolphe Kreutzer, and Pierre Baillot. Only Pierre Rode was actually Viotti's pupil; the other two were his admirers. They knew him and sometimes even performed with him. In 1802 in Paris, for instance, Baillot replaced Rode and in his absence played Viotti's duos concertantes together with the Italian master. The day after the performance Baillot wrote:

> I have only one regret, and that is that my poor friend Rode was not with us to hear this good Viotti who has nourished us for so long and to whom we owe so much for opening up a route on which no one else would ever dare follow him. [19]

These leading figures of French violin playing had truly international careers. They were applauded whenever they went abroad, but they also learned new techniques there, met other great masters, and gained valuable experience.[20] Kreutzer had met with unheard-of success in Holland, Germany, and Italy, and his name was to be immortalized by Beethoven's famous dedication. But in 1800, the *Allgemeine musikalische Zeitung* regretted that Kreutzer had stopped composing instrumental music, at which he excelled, and had gone over to opera. "A love of novelty and the number of theaters in the capital have led astray those composers who used to write instrumental music." This did not prevent Kreutzer from going on to have a brilliant career as a violinist. He was violin solo at the opera beginning in 1801 and at Tuileries Chapel from 1802.

Meanwhile, Baillot had gone to Vienna in 1805 and there had the privilege of meeting both Haydn and Beethoven, who were not above receiving such a famous French artist. Baillot was struck by Beethoven's friendliness when they talked in a tavern in Vienna "although his portraits always show him to be so unattractive and almost fierce."[21] Unfortunately, the composer did not have the opportunity to hear the violinist play. After that, Baillot traveled on to Russia, where he divided his time between Moscow and Saint Petersburg, organizing symphony and chamber music concerts wherever he went, often accompanied by Boïeldieu, who then was *maître de chapelle* for the Russian Emperor. Rode was Viotti's favorite pupil and had also traveled a great deal throughout Europe ever since his youth. He met Boccherini in 1799 on a visit to Madrid; in 1803 Vihe played at Brunswick and made a great impression on Spohr. He then left for Saint Petersburg to take up the post of first violin for the Emperor's music. He stayed in Russia for several years, then returned to France before going on to Central Europe and Vienna. In December 1812 he had the honor of playing the premiere of Beethoven's Sonata for Piano and Violin (opus 96) in Vienna, accompanied at the piano by Archduke Rudolf.

These artists performed with success abroad but were by no means forgotten in Paris. During the Empire, the three main rivals were Rode, Baillot, and Kreutzer. Critics of the time loved to compare the way Rode and Baillot played and to identify ways in which they resembled each other. They found that the former played more sweetly but that the latter had more strength and fire. When Rode and Kreutzer performed a sinfonie concertante for two violins, which Kreutzer had composed, a German critic in Paris called him "the most accomplished violinist in Europe."

Baillot probably had a more impetuous temperament and burning desire than Rode.[22] I am struck when I read his correspondence and also his *Art du violon* (The Art of the Violin), which appeared in 1830, by the fact that the word "soul" appears so many times. "The violin is played not only with the fingers but also with the soul," he wrote. Baillot was more like Viotti, and may have gone even further; his romantic outlook and his concept of what an artist should be was actually fairly close to Beethoven and later to Berlioz.

> Suffering sharpens an artist's sensitivity and adds the delicious charm of melancholy. The very trials of adversity awaken his energy, exalt his imagination and confer upon him those sublime movements and strong ideas that are born of great obstacles and seem to spring from the heart of the storm.[23]

It can be seen that Baillot had a very complex personality on a moral and human level. He seems to have held generous and humanitarian ideals that were characteristic of pre-romantic utopia. He was gripped at times by a nostalgia for universal happiness as it is celebrated by the *Ode to Joy* in Beethoven's Ninth Symphony. Thus he wrote: "I would like all the people of the earth to be in harmony from one pole to the other and to sing a hymn of praise to the God they adore."[24] In 1805 Baillot acquired an excellent Stradivarius that all of his contemporaries said was of exceptional quality. In 1814, when he inaugurated the public quartet recitals that were to have such a brilliant future, his instrument easily dominated the other three by the beauty of its sound. After Baillot's death it passed through various hands until it came into the possession of Jacques Thibaud. It was destroyed in the plane crash that killed Thibaud.

Viotti, Kreutzer, Rode, and Baillot were the four most famous violinists, but there were also others who had brilliant careers before 1830. I ought to mention M. Mazas, a pupil of Rode, and F. Libon and J.-B. Cartier, both pupils of Viotti. In 1798, Cartier published masterpieces of the Italian violin school for the first time in France—music by Corelli, Pugnani and Tartini—a repertoire that he had probably acquired from his teacher, Viotti.

Everything I wrote concerning wind instruments, the harp, and the cello is just as true of the violin. No music for this instrument came from the leading composers of the time. Instead, a new repertoire was composed by the prestigious performers whose careers in Paris and Europe at the turn of the century I have briefly mentioned. Unfortunately, much new violin music was also written by many lesser talents. It is obvious that performers composed music primarily with their own technical capabilities in mind, and they would then try to exploit their abilities to the maximum. If one of these virtuosos happened to be a true artist who was also endowed with creative genius, then and only then could one hope for a masterpiece. Too often these instrumentalists did not receive proper training in composition and wrote with facile mediocrity. This explains why thousands of *airs variés* (airs with variations), potpourris, variations on a well-known theme, and fantasies for the most diverse instrumental ensembles fill up publishers' catalogues, and why sometimes it is difficult for the historian to distinguish the wheat from the chaff. Next, I will from a strictly musical point of view try to select the best works for every main genre of instrumental music and point out specific formal changes.

During the period from 1789 to 1820, a particular musical genre came into fashion, flourishing most brilliantly in Paris. It was extremely popular, though only for a time, and was known as the sinfonie concertante, or sometimes *concerto à plusieurs instruments solistes* (concerto for several solo instruments). In the sinfonie concertante, a group of instruments played opposite the orchestra and could therefore be compared in this respect to the baroque concerto grosso, but actually the similarities were only superficial. The sinfonie concertante differed from the concerto grosso in that it gave most of the thematic material to the group of solo instruments, and the orchestra was often reduced to the role of simple accompaniment. As time went on, the solo parts developed more and more into virtuoso parts. The sinfonie concertante was quite unknown before 1770 and had disappeared completely by 1830. From the start, the genre was mainly appreciated for its diversity. At the Easter 1771 *Concert spirituel, Le Journal de Musique* regretted the absence of virtuoso singers who could have performed sacred motets: "so we have to make do with concertos and sonatas, but sonatas are so insipid and depressing, and concertos are so long! We ought to replace them with sinfonies concertantes." The period of greatest production in this musical genre was at the very end of the Old Monarchy. Barry Brook has listed about seventy French composers who showed an interest in it between 1770 and 1830. They produced about 250 sinfonies concertantes. There has been practically no modern edition of these works until now. This gap has recently been filled in the United States, thanks to Garland's publication of the sinfonies concertantes of Viotti, Ozy, and

Devienne issued in full score, indicating that this repertoire is interesting from more than just a historical point of view.

The group of solo instruments in the sinfonie concertante can vary greatly, both in number (from two to eleven instruments) and in combinations. However, by the end of the eighteenth century, combinations of wind instruments tended to take the place of strings more often than not. A great many sinfonies concertantes were written at that time for flute, oboe, bassoon, and horn. Mozart himself led the way with his Sinfonie Concertante for Four Wind Instruments (K. 297) in Paris in 1778. In any case, there existed the greatest variety in the choice and combination of solo instruments. It was not uncommon to find two violins or two harps or two horns, and composers seemed to like to use instruments from different groups. For instance, Catel composed a sinfonie concertante for flute, oboe, French horn, and cello, which is now lost.

As I have already said, the introduction of instrumental classes at the Conservatoire had greatly encouraged the development of wind instruments in France, although it took time for the public to get used to hearing these new sounds, at least by soloists. In June 1809, when the German bassoonist Bärmann, first bassoon at the chapel of the King of Prussia, was heard in Paris, a critic was astonished to find such sweetness and charm coming from "such a rough instrument." He admitted that he preferred hearing wind instruments in the short solos of a Haydn or a Mozart symphony. Otherwise, he wrote, it is difficult to listen to a whole concerto for bassoon or flute without yawning.[25] On the other hand, the sinfonie concertante, with its contrasting sounds and intricate dialogues between soloists, had a picturesque side to it that the public loved. They found in it precisely the "many-sided conversation" that eighteenth-century French music lovers had been looking for in instrumental music. In his *Poétique de la musique*, Lacépède summed up this type of music in a few very well-chosen words. Its two only goals were virtuosity and pleasure:

> Some symphonies are expected to showcase all the talents of musicians whose playing is worthy of admiration, and to satisfy the listeners as much as possible. These are called concertos or sinfonies concertantes, depending on whether they feature a single instrument or several.

Reading these scores I am surprised to discover the sometimes vocal treatment of the solo instrument. For instance, Ozy's first sinfonie concertante for clarinet and bassoon contains a cadenza between the end of the Allegro and the beginning of the Adagio in which the two solo instruments converse or play together in thirds or in sixths, in a continually changing tempo. The writing already suggests some of the great vocal duets of the operas of Rossini, Meyerbeer, or Bellini:

The use of the sinfonie concertante to showcase solo instruments by imitating a vocal style perfectly illustrates the ideas developed by the eighteenth-century theorists. Lacépède, for one, gave this advice to the symphonic composer:

> He should write as though he were working on a great aria where one or more voices are seeking to express various emotions. He should then replace these voices by the first violin or by other easily distinguishable instruments. From time to time he should try to imitate the sound of the human voice, using instruments that have a sweet or touching sound and play in octaves.

The public's interest in the evocative dialogue of instruments in the sinfonie concertante coincided, probably consciously, with its taste for virtuosity. Just before the Revolution, the Chevalier de Meude-Monpas compared the sinfonie concertante to "a perpetual struggle," and he added jokingly: "It is like a high ladder with two sides, and the players are like two school boys who challenge each other as to who can climb the highest." [26] There was certainly no shortage of individuals who tried their luck at composing to exploit this gold mine. They came from everywhere, from the provinces and from abroad, to have their easy compositions played and published in Paris; the compositions were forgotten as soon as they were heard, but the composers sometimes enjoyed a fleeting notoriety. The press announced many of these new editions, leaving behind dozens of names that are otherwise completely unknown to us today.

Apart from the great contemporary instrumentalists I have already mentioned, there were two other important composers of sinfonies concertantes. Their careers were international, and though neither one was born in France, they were based in Paris and published the majority of their works there. They were the Austrian Ignaz Pleyel and the Italian Giovanni Cambini.

When Pleyel settled in Paris in 1795, he had already written most of his works, mainly symphonic and chamber music. In his time, he was as popular in Europe as his teacher Haydn, and he was often compared to him in contemporary writing. Rita Benton has compiled a complete catalogue of his works, a necessary tool for sorting out such a large number of works published in complete anarchy. No composer has ever been the victim of so much commercial fraud as Pleyel. After 1795, during his stay in Paris, his composing slowed down considerably. Because his music met with such a success all over Europe, he decided to become his own publisher and established an important business in Paris. Shortly afterward, he set up a piano factory and became the direct ancestor of the famous family of piano makers and performers whose name is still well known today.

The Italian Cambini was definitely not so talented as Pleyel, but he knew how to profit from the fashion of the day and how to introduce himself to important people at court, during the Empire as well as the Restoration. He was also incredibly popular in Paris, where he had already settled before the Revolution. He composed symphonic and instrumental works by the dozen (nine symphonies, eighty-two sinfonies concertantes, over a hundred quartets) and was a violinist of talent, though not a genius. Never equal to the great virtuosos of the day, he had to content himself with being a fashionable composer who continually turned out a repertoire of works for soloists and orchestras. Around 1800 he was one of the most performed composers in Paris. He understood that much of his public was looking only for light entertainment in music.

The sinfonie concertante never was somber music, never anxious or tense. In contrast to the concerto grosso, it was almost never written in a minor key. It usually had two movements and lacked the peaceful quality of a slow central movement. Instead, the two fast movements followed each other without a break, and the whole work was supposed to be gay and fun. If it ever did have three movements, the central one was always an Andante, hardly ever an Adagio, and the orchestra rarely intervened in any original or dramatic way. Instead, this middle movement most often called only for strings, oboes, and French horns and simply accompanied the soloists. Sometimes oboes and French horns were even indicated *ad libitum*, as in the sinfonie concertante "interspersed with patriotic songs" for two solo violins that Davaux composed in 1794, in which the interest was entirely concentrated on the two protagonists. Toward the end of its history—that is, at the beginning of the Restoration—it is true that the sinfonie concertante sometimes called for a larger number of players in the orchestra, proving that it had a clear influence on the evolution of the modern symphony orchestra. In 1816, Baillot composed a Sinfonie Concertante for Two Principal Violins (opus 38) in which he added to the orchestra two trumpets, two trombones, and timpani.

But these were extreme cases. When it was at the height of its popularity the sinfonie concertante had no ambition to rival the symphony. It corresponded at first to the taste of a certain society, a public who wanted to be entertained and for whom all forms of variety, beginning with variety of sounds, were a way to avoid monotony and boredom. Historically, it was one of the last manifestations of the *style galant concertant* of the eighteenth century. It was conceived both by and for the old social order, but its popularity was not at all affected by the Revolution. Symphony orchestras multiplied in Paris under the Directoire, the Consulate, and the Empire, and the sinfonie concertante remained one of the most popular musical genres, even though it was now attended by a very different public. This continuity of musical taste is rather remarkable. The sinfonie concertante remained in fashion until the end of the Empire and disappeared completely after 1830. During the romantic period, the solo concerto became the more popular genre. People no longer wanted to listen to a group of soloists having an amiable dialogue with the orchestra, which was a sort of transposition into art of the worldly conversation of the salons. Instead, they began preferring the dramatic solitude of the individual. In the concerto, where one soloist is pitted against the orchestra, one could see the dramatic struggle of human consciousness against an oppressive world.

The period that saw the development of the sinfonie concertante was no less rich in concertos. The same virtuosos who have been identified as composers of sinfonies concertantes also wrote solos for their own instruments. It would not be an exaggeration to say that in 1789 practically all the strings and woodwinds were used as soloists in front of the orchestra. I found a very precise account of the concerto's history written in 1791 by Ginguené in his article "Concerto" in the *Encyclopédie méthodique*:

> I have spoken only about violin concertos because they were the first and for a long time the only concertos, and because concertos written afterward for other instruments were based on exactly the same model. Instrumental playing has developed to such perfection that every instrument now wants to shine as a soloist. The harpsichord won this privilege early on and has kept it, or rather, has handed it on to the pianoforte. The flute, oboe, and clarinet have had their concertos for a long time now. There even exist some for the French horn and for the sad bassoon. I have heard Stamitz's nephew play viola concertos marvelously well. Cello concertos have made the reputation of more than one famous artist, and some have actually been composed for the double bass.

However, concert programs clearly show that the public was more interested in the sinfonie concertante than in the solo concerto, which was often criticized in the press for being boring and monotonous. In fact I was surprised to find, as late as 1808, such a knowledgeable theorist as J.-J. de Momigny expressing the following opinion in the article "Concerto" in his *Cours complet d'harmonie et de composition*—an opinion that shows the reserve felt by part of the Paris intelligentsia regarding the concerto:

> Concertos are good only when they are written for the violin, or possibly the piano. God preserve any good musician from being obliged to listen to a bassoon concerto, or one for the flute, clarinet, double bass, or Jew's harp, because it is sheer poison. The cello should be given only occasional solo phrases, and the same is true

for any wind instrument. . . . When I hear the solemn cello start turning somersaults when it ought to be letting me hear the majestic language of the gods or the voice of a tender father, it seems to me like seeing a bishop or a magistrate dressed as a harlequin, which is both senseless and scandalous.

In spite of this judgment, which was rather old-fashioned for the time, the number of concertos written during the forty-year period is still impressive. There must have been several hundred at least, not all of which, obviously, have been published. It was thought that all this music had been forgotten forever, but in our own time people have found it interesting again and are delighted to rediscover pieces that have probably not been played for over 150 years. Today, restoration to prepare full scores requires a lot of editorial work. At the time, orchestral scores were not published for concertos, symphonies, and sinfonies concertantes; almost all instrumental music (quintets, quartets, trios, or duets) was published in separate parts only. For concertos, the leader conducted either from the solo part, or from the first violin part with *tutti* or *solo* marked in as appropriate. [27]

The sinfonie concertante was typical of the eighteenth century and survived only a few years into the nineteenth, whereas the concerto was in full development at the dawn of romanticism. One genre looks back to the past, the other looks toward the future. This difference is very clear when we look at content and musical forms. The sinfonie concertante is full of eighteenth-century *galant* feeling and does not develop beyond that, whereas the concerto, when written by one of the masters, is in a period of complete transformation. In their hands the music became something more than mere entertainment, more than just a lovely play of undulating sounds. Sometimes concertos moved the listener with more solemn, profound sounds; composers put more into their music and gave it a much deeper significance. In other words, it is not the sinfonie concertante but the concerto that shows the first signs of the profound upheaval that led to romantic lyricism at the beginning of the nineteenth century.

Two concertos for clarinet and orchestra by X. Lefèvre have recently been published by Heugel. They date from 1800 to 1805 and are perfect examples of the type of French instrumental music written under the Consulate. Each concerto is in three movements: fast, slow, fast. The orchestra is still restricted to strings, two oboes, and two horns, but it has important passages and does more than merely accompany the often virtuoso part of the solo clarinet. These pages are indeed of better quality than hundreds of other instrumental pieces from the end of the eighteenth century. They are more intense and more colorful when illustrating a theme, emphasizing a chord, or introducing a sudden major-minor contrast in an Andante da capo. This type of concerto obviously does not compare with Mozart's Clarinet Concerto, which is its great ancestor, but it is quite interesting even so. A careful study of some of the many woodwind concertos from the early nineteenth century would certainly give a clue as to how the classical edifice began to crack at this pivotal moment in music history.

This evolution of musical language would be clearer if more were known about the history of the violin concerto between 1789 and 1830. This account is still waiting to be written and would take up an entire volume. So many scores were published that a quick overview must suffice for the moment. The number of violin concertos written by the four leading composer-virtuosos of the period alone totals seventy works: twenty-nine by Viotti, nineteen by Kreutzer, thirteen by Rode, and nine by Baillot. Therefore, it is possible to give only a general outline of the evolution of this musical genre.

These seventy violin concertos were the exact contemporaries of Beethoven's Violin Concerto (1806), but they lack its vast dimensions. It is interesting to note that the works became longer over the years, not because composers had more to say, but because the development of thematic material was perfected. This tendency could be found first in the Allegro first movements. In the case of those cast in sonata form, lots of new, varied elements were added to the development, often only for the sake of virtuosity.

Viotti's twenty-nine concertos are very good examples of this new tendency at the dawn of the nineteenth century. Originating in the *style galant* they go on to display a more personal, expressive manner. Viotti's phrases often suddenly become clouded with melancholy, and many of his concertos are written in a minor key. In contrast to sinfonies concertantes, concertos never omitted the slow movement. On the contrary, they frequently lingered over it with evident pleasure. There are moments of tenderness, regret, or melancholy. All Viotti's contemporaries were struck by this aspect of his works; Ginguené had already noted it in 1791, when he wrote: "the lovely Adagios were quite enchanting. The composer performed them with a perfection that has not been heard for a long time and restores to the concerto all its dignity." [28] It is quite exceptional in this period to find French critics being that sensitive to an instrumental Adagio. In his *Art du violon*, which came out forty years later (just after 1830), Baillot described the special nature of the Adagio in a violin concerto: "The violin is no longer an instrument, it is the voice of the soul. It makes an impression even on the least attentive listeners, going right to the bottom of their hearts and making them shiver." This desire to set up a dialogue between two souls is a complete turnaround from the musical aesthetics of the end of the eighteenth century. Now music's role was no longer to paint a scene or evoke a particular emotion. On the contrary, its message should be vague, irrational, emotive, inviting dreams. Probably the best illustration of this change is the marvelous adagio in E-flat major in Viotti's nineteenth concerto (the last one in his Paris period). This moving and lovely song has both sumptuous and sober moments, reminiscent of Beethoven's lyricism. Brahms also admired some of Viotti's concertos, finding that they had romantic sensitivity if not yet a characteristic harmonic language.

It would also be interesting to study these concertos from the point of view of the orchestra. Brass and percussion were already found in certain eighteenth-century works, but most often soloists were accompanied by strings, two oboes, and two horns. This traditional scoring rapidly grew after 1800, adding flutes, bassoons, clarinets (as in Viotti's nineteenth and twentieth concertos), sometimes trumpets, drums, and (in the last movement of the twenty-fifth violin concerto) even a triangle, which the composer asked to be played very softly each time the soloist came in. It was a definite step toward the romantic orchestra, and the composer's concept of the orchestra's role in relation to the soloist was also changing. There were now two equal partners, which could be united or opposed to each other, each preserving its own strong personality.

There is as yet no historical or musical study of the exact relationship between the Viennese and French violinists—including Viotti, of course—at the beginning of the nineteenth century. Viotti and Baillot certainly did not find their inspiration in the French tradition for the slow introduction (often in a minor key) that sometimes preceded the opening Allegro and gave to a whole work its dark and solemn tone. I rather think that our composer-violinists had borrowed this idea during their long visits abroad, especially in Germany. It was new for them, and they knew how to use it to advantage. A detailed history of the violin concerto in France during those forty years that saw such a decisive change would have to include the influence of Vienna on Paris.

The repertoire of chamber music for the same period is also extensive. Publishers' catalogues and press announcements of the day continually advertised new publications of duets, trios, quartets, quintets, and less frequently, sextets and septets. Instrumental combinations varied greatly. There were trios for two flutes and viola, for three guitars, for two clarinets and bassoon, and so on. For the period beginning with the Restoration, a rapid scanning of the *Bibliographie de la France* would reveal every new piece of chamber music published in Paris, many by foreign composers.

Thousands of these works were intended for private clients. There were few public chamber music concerts in France before Baillot started them in 1814. This body of music was intended for amateurs and had to be easy to play and pleasant to listen to. There were original scores—composed for a specific group of instruments—and about as many transcriptions, mostly of operas or popular arias, rarely of symphonies. The most unexpected arrangements can be found. Almost all the successful operas and comic operas gave rise to transcriptions of excerpts of several numbers, often including the actual overture of the opera. The scoring was reduced to two violins, two flutes, two clarinets, two bassoons, or even to solo guitar. A large number of Haydn's symphonies were transcribed as quintets, and several of Mozart's as septets. We should not laugh at this practice, for the idea behind it was to make these new works accessible to a vast public who never went to an opera or a concert. This practice, though well intentioned, quickly gave rise to abuse and filled chamber music catalogues with arrangements that are sometimes questionable, especially at the beginning of the nineteenth century. One of the first who started producing these arrangements systematically was a certain Abraham, a professor of music theory and clarinet in Paris around 1800; Fétis said that he was a "sort of musical laborer on salary with music publishers." He worked for them, arranging overtures and arias from the latest operas for absolutely any combination of instruments. His kind of work could probably be understood, but it is really difficult to see why Blasius, a conductor and a violinist, should have transcribed thirty-six of Haydn's piano sonatas for string quartet! Was it because there were more amateur string players than pianists? A.-L. Blondeau wrote about this practice in his *Histoire de la musique moderne*, published in 1847, and recalled that he himself had arranged twelve of Beethoven's piano sonatas as string quartets. He also arranged three trios by the same composer for piano, violin, and cello, and "the lovely Symphony in D" as a quintet for two violins, two violas, and bass. The transcriber apologized for the sacrilege, giving as a very questionable excuse the fact that Mozart and Beethoven themselves

provided this sort of arrangement for their own works. Since then, hundreds of pieces have been arranged [or "deranged"!] for all sorts of instrumental combinations. Even five-act grand operas have been arranged as quartets for two violins, viola, and bass. This practice turned into real speculation, a kind of commerce.[29]

We should not judge these strange arrangements and bizarre transcriptions too harshly, however, because they do demonstrate how many more people played musical instruments privately then than they do today. A German journalist staying in Paris during the Empire drew attention to an interesting comparison between French and German amateur practices at the time (*Allgemeine musikalische Zeitung*, 6 November 1811). He wrote that across the Rhine the pianoforte reigned supreme, but in Paris, many more music lovers played the violin, the flute, or even the cello than in Germany. This was not merely by chance, since the Germans were known to prefer full and rich harmony, but it did explain why so many orchestral works—operas and symphonies—that were arranged for piano in Germany could not be found in France; most French amateur musicians played other instruments. French publishers sold these instrumental arrangements easily and cheaply because there were so many more potential buyers than in Germany.

This explanation may or may not be valid, but it does explore the century-old conflict between melodists and harmonists from an aesthetic point of view. This conflict has already been described as symbolizing the basic difference between the French and German schools. As will be shown, there were plenty of pianofortes in France at the time, but they were more often used to play caprices, fantasies, variations, and potpourris of popular operatic arias than to play vocal or piano scores of the same operas.

Nevertheless, the chamber music repertoire includes thousands of works, and though they are of very little musical interest today, historians cannot just ignore them, because they reveal the extent of amateur musical practice. A serious study of styles and form should of course be based on examples of more original works rather than on this repertoire.

J.-J. Rousseau, who liked striking statements and did not mind contradiction, wrote: "There are no real quartets, or else they are worthless."[30] This peremptory judgment can be explained and even justified by his own aesthetic theories: Music is a language that should signify something. Only melody, with no need of harmony, can speak directly to the heart because melody imitates nature. Harmony may possibly be considered an auxiliary of melody but makes no sense on its own. With this in mind, then, the idea of making four instruments all speak together becomes absurd.

> In a good quartet, the parts should always be played alternately because in any chord there are only two parts at the most that sing and can be distinguished by the ear. The other two are just fillers, and fillers have no place in a quartet.[31]

In spite of this sweeping argument, instrumental quartets were tremendously popular in France at the end of the eighteenth century. It has been estimated that several thousand quartets were published in Paris between 1770 and 1800. About two hundred composers have been identified, both French and foreign, and many of the latter chose to have their works published in Paris. The sheer number of compositions proves without a doubt that there was an enormous demand for chamber music in private circles. Ensemble practice must have been intense, not only in the high-class salons of the upper bourgeoisie, but also in simple circles of families or friends at a more modest level.

Most of the collections of quartets that appeared in the catalogues of leading Paris publishers at the end of the eighteenth century (always in separate parts and generally in sets of six works by the same author) bear the title *quatuors concertants*. What was the special meaning of that title, almost always found in the French editions (Imbault, Sieber, Pleyel) but absent from the same works when published in London or Vienna? In many cases the publishers were probably the ones who systematically named every new quartet concertant for purely commercial reasons. The *Encyclopédie méthodique* of 1791 has a perfectly clear definition of the term by Framery: "A trio or a quartet is called *concertant* to distinguish it from those where there is only one principal part while the others merely accompany." Generally speaking, the four instruments of a *quatuor concertant* were equal, and none of them was merely "a filler," to use Rousseau's words. While the sinfonie concertante, which uses several virtuoso soloists, was having a great success in Paris, it was probably thought that it would be a good thing to title these quartets *concertants*, so that none of the players would feel that they were secondary and all would consider themselves virtuosos. Significantly, the word *solo* was sometimes written in the second violin part or the viola or cello part of a *quatuor concertant*, as a way to indicate which part should be most important at that moment, the equivalent of what was called *Hauptstimme* by the Germans.

In fact, not all quartets published with the title *concertant* actually corresponded to the definition of the term. Some of them were just pieces for solo flute or violin accompanied by three other instruments. But when the content actually matched the title, the style of French *quatuors concertants* was quite special, and it was quite different from that of the great Viennese contemporaries in any event. Although Haydn's quartets were very well known in Paris before 1800—they had been published by Sieber and Pleyel—they did not influence French composers very much. Like Mozart's quartets, they had the reputation of being difficult to play and were nowhere near as popular in Paris as his symphonies.

By contrast, Boccherini's quartets were repeatedly published in Paris and enjoyed great popularity in France around 1800. Many French composers preferred to use the Italian composer as a model. In fact, even before 1789, composers such as Davaux, Gossec, Dalayrac, Saint-Georges, and particularly Viotti, Cambini, and Pleyel had learned much from Boccherini's experience and popularity. From Madrid where he was living, Boccherini kept up a correspondence with Pleyel, who was one of the best composers in this style and was also a music publisher. The letters show the extent to which composers were ready to bend to the wishes and taste of their public. Pleyel published Boccherini's chamber music works, asking him to make them "short and easy." Boccherini was very well respected in his time as a composer of chamber music, and his reply dated 18 March 1799 is worth quoting here:

> In this case I shall have to say good-bye to modulations, thematic development, and so on. One cannot say much with a few words, and meditate even less. However, I will put up with it, for I understand that our poor *dilettanti* have trouble managing elaborate pieces because of the difficulty of the tempos and other factors. Well, I promise to satisfy you on this point, since commercial considerations demand it.

The composer reluctantly agreed to send "commercial" compositions to Paris, but he did try to salvage his reputation:

> As I do not wish to lose my reputation and the international fame that I had so much trouble to obtain, let us agree on one point. Whenever I write quartets or any other pieces, there will always be two as I like them and four as you like them. But you should not

forget that there is nothing worse than trying to tie a poor artist's hands, to set limits on his inspiration and imagination and subject him to conventions.[32]

This important letter clearly states the nature of the relationship between musicians and their public at the very end of the eighteenth century.

Quatuors concertants were written for all kinds of instrumental combinations. Some of them, of course, were traditional string quartets, others were woodwind quartets. For instance, the clarinetist Gambaro wrote several *quatuors concertants* for flute, clarinet, horn, and bassoon. A third category was a mixture of strings and woodwinds, called *quatuor à flûte* (flute and strings) or *quatuor à clarinette* (clarinet and strings). Actually, the flute or clarinet quartet was often only an adaptation of a traditional string quartet, intended for sale to certain amateur groups. In 1796, Catel wrote three quartets for flute, clarinet, horn, and cello. Even though *quatuors concertants* offered many different possibilities of instrumental combinations, the form itself did not provide much freedom or variety. They are rarely in more than three movements and are often limited to two (Allegro, Rondo). When there are three movements, the middle one is an Andante or an Adagio, sometimes in theme and variations form. Occasionally, the slow movement contrasts the major and minor modes, with a *da capo* in major. Most first movements are in sonata form: exposition, development, recapitulation. However the development is very short, reduced to the simplest harmonic transition and return to the tonic, instead of being extensive in order to explore all the possibilities of the theme presented in the exposition (as in works by Haydn, Mozart, and later, Beethoven). Themes are not really shared among the four instruments; instead, they have alternate entries, playing games of questions and answers with each other. It is more as though the four participants took turns in the musical conversation, as soloists. As each one takes up the theme, the other three stand back, although they are not reduced to mere fillers. There is a constant effort not to upset the balance by keeping the four soloists constantly in touch. At no point is there any intricate harmony underlying this dialogue between the four. On the contrary, the *concertant* style uses a clear and relatively emotionless language. Throughout thousands of pages of music, it is rare to find any latent tension, any fleeting anxiety or drama. Effects are rather obtained by the constant movement of each of four very individual parts, melodic lines endlessly crossing and re-crossing. It is a world that did not know—or pretended not to know—darkness or mystery. Hearing this music, the listener would think that there is nothing but grace, elegance, and joy on earth.

The end of the Old Monarchy by no means put an end to the production of *quatuors concertants*, which sometimes makes it difficult to date a particular series within a ten-year margin of error. Several foreign composers who lived in Paris and were considered French, like Viotti, Cambini, and Pleyel, were extraordinarily prolific. Pleyel himself composed about fifty string quartets that became extremely popular. His success was so great that plagiarists were able to publish a large number of spurious quartets under his name, and several of his string quartets were transcribed for other instruments. At the beginning of the nineteenth century, his works fell out of fashion just as Haydn and Mozart's began to grow in popularity. In 1808 J.-J. de Momigny had already admitted that thanks to Pleyel, "that charming composer," the public was able to appreciate Haydn and Mozart's quartets fifteen years earlier than they would have without him. Their works were "too learned to be appreciated" by a public accustomed to a much simpler style of chamber music.[33] Ten years later, when Pleyel's star was beginning to wane, Momigny took up this idea again, stressing the positive role that Pleyel had played in the evolution of French taste:

> His quartets were extraordinarily popular, which they deserved, as they were both charming and easy to play. Pleyel was neither deep like Haydn and Mozart, nor insipid like the cheap music that we sometimes used to hear forty years ago, but he was an inspired pupil of Haydn's and had enough science in him to be understood by the French and Italians. If he had been a deeper, more thoughtful composer, he would not have been able to make his mark at the time when his quartets appeared, since Haydn's were already far beyond the reach of most musicians.[34]

This fair and moderate judgment sums up exactly Pleyel's talent, well placed between the German and the French schools of the end of the eighteenth century.

The *quatuor concertant*, so appealing to French eighteenth-century taste, ended its career like the sinfonie concertante, at the dawn of romanticism. People began to get more interested in virtuoso playing, which made enormous progress, and some virtuoso-composers did not hesitate to jump on the bandwagon. I have already mentioned the extraordinarily high level of the French violin school around 1800. Kreutzer, Rode, Mazas, Baillot, and Lafont were all more or less contemporaries and all composed string quartets. As they were virtuoso violinists themselves, they naturally favored their own instrument. This gave rise to a type of quartet called *quatuor brillant*, where all the attention was focused on the first violin and its technical possibilities. In fact, most of these quartets were just accompanied solos. In the *Méthode de violon* written by Rode, Baillot, and Kreutzer for the Conservatoire, the definition of the string quartet clearly shows how virtuoso playing would, around 1800, reduce the vogue of the *quatuor concertant* and eventually cause its disappearance. The terms used in this text should be weighed carefully. They illustrate exactly the changeover from the aesthetic concept of the eighteenth-century *concertante* to a much more modern concept of virtuoso playing and of the instrument's expressive power:

> The quartet is a genre featuring a charming dialogue, not unlike a conversation between friends who communicate their feelings, their emotions, and their mutual affections. They may have different opinions that give rise to animated discussion. Each [instrument] develops it in turn. They then enjoy following the impetus given by the first, who leads by the strength of his ideas, and his influence is felt not so much in his brilliant playing as in his persuasive and gentle expression.

During the Restoration, the young romantic generation began to prefer works where they could applaud the virtuosity of famous artists. Paganini's enthusiastic reception in Paris (when he appeared there in 1830) is well known. Baillot was astounded by Paganini's brio but had some reservations even so. He seemed to feel that the Italian virtuoso was going too far, as though he had parted with the herd and lost contact with his brothers: "In his hands the violin becomes a separate instrument, and the artist has stepped beyond limits." It is true that romantic genius did isolate individuals from the rest of society and made them both "powerful and solitary."

In this new idea of the quartet, the first violin dominated the other partners. In his public chamber music sessions, Baillot was known to stress this hierarchy by playing standing up while the three others remained sitting down. He is the best representative of this type of early nineteenth-century string quartet, together with his friends Kreutzer and Rode, each of whom wrote about fifteen of them. The influence of the French school spread abroad—as I have said, these violinists were great travelers and were able to export their own works—and music lovers in other countries were attracted by their sheer virtuosity. It is most revealing that in his *Violin-Schule*, which dates from 1830, Spohr established a distinction between what he rather naively called *véritables quatuors* (true quartets, obviously referring to the quartets of Haydn, Mozart, and Beethoven) and *quatuors brillants*:

> There is today a type of quartet in which the first violin performs the solo and the other three just accompany. These are called *quatuors brillants*, and their purpose is to give the solo player an opportunity to show his talent in small circles or salons. . . . When a true quartet is performed, all four instruments are absolutely necessary for the composer to express his ideas, and the first violin should not try to outshine the others. On the contrary, he should blend with them and be subdued whenever he does not have the principal part.

The *quatuor d'airs connus* (quartet based on well-known tunes) or *quatuor d'airs variés* (quartet with theme and variations) were like the *quatuor brillant* only insofar as the first violin had the melody while the three other instruments just accompanied. Virtuoso playing was out. These genres were not intended to give the virtuoso an opportunity to be admired for his technique but simply served the pleasure of amateurs wishing to play popular melodies together, mostly arrangements from well-known operas or comic operas. The thousands of editions published after every great success in Paris played a very important role in spreading opera all over France.

For the most part, composers who made these numerous quartet transcriptions were plain, good instrumentalists and no more. Typical is J. B. Gambaro, who settled in Paris in 1814 where he held the post of first clarinetist at the Théâtre italien. Immediately after Rossini's works were performed with success at this theater, Gambaro arranged them for instrumental quartets: two violins, viola, and cello; or flute, violin, viola, and cello. Gambaro also set himself up as a publisher, and his quartets sold well. He did not limit himself to Rossini but transcribed other successes from the Théâtre italien, such as works by Mozart and Paër. This is how chamber music arrangements popularized operas and even symphonies. Gambaro also published as quintets (flute, two violins, viola, and cello) Weber–Castil-Blaze's *Robin des bois* and twenty-four of Haydn's symphonies arranged by the German violinist J.-P. Salomon, who added "a piano accompaniment *ad libitum*." This is a typical example of the countless transcriptions that were made throughout the nineteenth century and at the beginning of the twentieth century as well: chamber settings for the most varied instrumental combinations published with a piano-conductor score.

During the Restoration, thanks particularly to Baillot's public chamber music concerts, Parisians were able to hear a number of quartets by foreign composers who had settled in Paris and, influenced by Haydn and Mozart, tried to get away from the fashion of quartets for solo violin with accompaniment. An example of this is Cherubini's first quartet, which was composed in 1814 but was not played until 1826. It is a work written by an experienced composer, not just a virtuoso instrumentalist, as its solid contrapuntal work shows. The introduction of a scherzo, which was absolutely new in Paris at the time, shows the influence of the German school and of Beethoven in particular. This was Cherubini's first attempt at a quartet, already late in his career, and he did not return to it until the end of his life, after 1830. Another example is Anton Reicha, Czech by birth, who lived permanently in Paris from 1808 on. He became professor of counterpoint and fugue at the Conservatoire in 1818. He wrote a great deal of chamber music, including a piece for ten instruments (five strings and five woodwinds), an octet, about thirty quintets, and over twenty quartets. In Vienna he had been Beethoven's friend for a number of years. His chamber music is remarkable, more for its rich harmonic language than for the quantity and charm of its ideas. Modern audiences would rediscover him with interest and probably with pleasure. Several of Reicha's quartets and quintets have been published and recorded over the last few years. These works were not well known by the general public of the time, but they marked a clear change in orientation in the history of French chamber music: they were influenced by the German school and took practically nothing from the French tradition. A pupil of Reicha's was G. Onslow, a Frenchman of English extraction, living in Paris. He, too, composed a large body of chamber music, including thirty-five quintets with two cellos and thirty-six string quartets. After 1824, Baillot at times included Onslow's works on his programs. Many of these works were not actually composed or published until after 1830, especially by Breitkopf and Härtel. They were no longer intended to be played by amateurs. Onslow composed them in the isolation of his provincial retreat, steeped in the tradition of Haydn and Mozart— much more than Beethoven, whom he did not appreciate. Onslow's quartets are of better quality than similar works by French composers of the previous generation, and along with Reicha's quartets, they inaugurated a new stylistic period in the history of the genre. The string quartet was no longer considered mere entertainment nor a pretext to show off instrumental virtuosity. Austere and serious, it came to represent the most profound musical thoughts. Its beauty rested, in Paul Valéry's words, in "its form and its construction of a separate intuitive order."

In trio and sonata compositions, French chamber music at the beginning of the nineteenth century was seriously behind the German school. There was hardly anything to compare with Haydn's trios for piano, violin, and cello, for instance, and certainly not with those of Mozart, Schubert, and Beethoven. The continuous tradition was still very strong in France, and the sonata for a solo instrument with piano accompaniment hardly existed as yet. In 1800, Baillot defined the violin sonata in these terms:

> It is a kind of concerto, without the accompaniment, giving artists the opportunity to show off their strengths and resources and to be heard alone, with no support, no rest, and no help other than that of the bass accompaniment.[35]

It is a fact that all instrumental methods published by the Conservatoire between 1800 and 1815 included a few examples of sonatas, all for two parts. The cello method, for instance, quotes three sonatas by Galeotti (an eighteenth-century Italian composer) that are actually for two cellos: cello solo and bass accompaniment. Most of X. Lefèvre's clarinet sonatas, Hugot's and Wunderlich's flute sonatas, and Ozy's bassoon sonatas are also written with a bass part. In the same way, works that were called trios were actually for two instruments and bass. Sonatas or trios in which the piano plays a part equal to the other instruments were not yet known. For instance, the flutist Hugot composed trios for two flutes and bass in which the second flute part could be replaced by a violin. Even after the Restoration, some authentic sonatas for piano and violin were published in a very unorthodox way, showing that their new concept had not been understood. In 1820, for instance, the Paris publisher Carli came out with an edition of Mozart's sonatas for piano and violin with the title *Sonatas for Pianoforte with Violin Accompaniment*. The violin score was published separately for the violinist, which was obvious enough, but what seems absurd to us today is that the piano score did not include the violin part, as though it could have been played by itself. Similarly during the same period, Beethoven's sonatas for violin and piano were published in two separate booklets, one for the violin and the other for piano alone.

A long time would go by before the sonata as a duet or the trio in the modern sense would be customary in France. This explains the countless *duos concertants* (some even dating after 1800) for two violins, two flutes, two clarinets, and so forth, or trios for two violins and bass, two flutes and bass, two clarinets and bass, and so on. It is difficult to establish the exact date when the sonata or trio with original piano accompaniment became the norm. It should be noted that many of the sonatas of the time are now published with a piano part that is an elaboration of the bass part; it is provided by the modern publisher and is not part of the original composition. X. Lefèvre's sonatas for clarinet and piano are an example.

The first sonatas for cello with piano accompaniment appear to be those by G. Onslow published in 1822. For their violin counterpart, I found Baillot's Opus 32 (1820), which corresponds exactly to the modern definition of the sonata for piano and violin. While reading it, I was struck by the mediocrity of the piano part and wondered whether this may be one of the reasons why the French school waited until around 1800 to adopt the sonata or trio for solo instruments and piano. For the most part, composers of instrumental music were virtuoso soloists rather than professional composers. It was easy for them to write a part for their instrument and a bass part to fit below it, but for a musician who was not a pianist, it was much more difficult to compose an idiomatic piano part. Characteristically, in the aforementioned sonata by Baillot, the middle movement, Adagio, is by far the most interesting. The violin sings superbly (the modulations are abrupt but unusually beautiful), but the piano part amounts to very little, which is not unusual in an Adagio. By contrast, the lackluster piano part in the two fast movements spoils the whole work. A proper dialogue between the two instruments, including a shared thematic development, may be expected but is not forthcoming.

It is a pity that the few really good composers of the period should have systematically favored vocal over instrumental music.

> The pianoforte is the most frequently used of all the instruments. It is preferred over the harpsichord because it can express sounds as loud or as softly as required and imitate all the subtleties of other instruments, which is quite impossible with the harpsichord.

When Jean-Louis Adam wrote this opening phrase in his *Méthode de piano du Conservatoire* in 1804, he could not possibly imagine the extraordinary popularity that his instrument would have during the nineteenth century.

The displacement of the harpsichord by the piano, between 1770 and 1800, was a decisive step. The history of the pianoforte in France has recently been retraced in detail by Adélaïde de Place. From the first pianoforte built in 1760 (the first public appearance of the pianoforte in Paris was on 8 September 1768 at the Concert spirituel) to the romantic piano of the 1830s, she describes almost year by year the successive inventions that brought about this metamorphosis.

Writings of the time prove that as soon as the pianoforte was invented, its importance became obvious. Replacing the principle of the plucked string (as in the harpsichord) with a string struck by a hammer (as in the pianoforte or, as it was sometimes called, *clavecin à marteau* or hammered harpsichord) enabled the performer to express nuances. In 1785, *L'art du faiseur d'instruments de musique et de lutherie* (The Art of the Instrument Maker) pointed out the advantages of this new technique: "A harder or softer pressure of the fingers determines the loudness or softness of the sound. Thus harpsichordists can now express their feelings."

I will skip here all the advances and setbacks of this instrument from 1789 to the romantic period. However, I must mention the research and achievements of the father of French piano makers, Sébastien Érard, whose name I have already mentioned in connection with the harp. He was born in Strasbourg but settled in Paris in 1768 and began to make musical instruments. With the help of his two brothers and later his children, he soon found himself at the head of a large factory. The German composer Reichardt, who stayed in Paris for a time in 1802, visited the Érard establishment and left a vivid description of his stay in this large bourgeois residence that was bustling with activity: the making of instruments, the execution of hundreds of orders from abroad, the marketing of music scores, and so on, in addition to a great deal of amateur music making and social life. In richly decorated apartments that were filled with paintings, the members of the family received the elite of the artistic society of the time and were keen chamber music enthusiasts. A few years later one of Sébastien Érard's daughters married the composer Spontini.

During the Revolution, Sébastien Érard went into exile for a while in England and opened a workshop in London where, in 1794, he took out a patent for his invention of the *escapement*. As soon as he returned to Paris at the end of the revolutionary unrest, he took up his research again. Meanwhile, Ignaz Pleyel had opened his publishing firm in Paris in 1795, and in 1809 began his own piano manufacturing business. This gave rise to much fruitful competition between Pleyel and the Érard brothers and forced the rivals to improve continuously on their inventions and pursue their research to perfect the instrument.

From 1800 on, the history of the Érard firm is characterized by numerous improvements in piano making: the extension of the keyboard from five octaves to six and even six and a half; the increased number of strings; the invention of the grand piano and various hybrid models, many of which were never developed. With the invention of what was called the double escapement mechanism in 1822, Érard's reputation reached its peak, and the pianoforte took another decisive step forward. With this new mechanism, a note could be repeated as often and as a rapidly as needed, so that the most daring high speed runs were possible, as well as nuances in the attacks. This was so revolutionary, after thirty years of research, that it brought about changes in both the types of music that could be composed for the piano and in virtuoso playing. The piano as a romantic instrument was born.

No other instrument at the time had evolved so far in less than half a century, and this rapid progress in its development and increased possibilities of expression contributed a great deal to its popularization. From 1800 onward, the piano as a modern polyphonic instrument, compared to the harpsichord, became fashionable throughout France and Europe. When the Conservatoire first opened in 1795, it had only six harpsichord classes, but this was soon remedied; by 1797 piano classes were introduced and soon replaced the harpsichord classes altogether. In 1822, Cherubini, who was director of the Conservatoire at the time, complained about the large number of piano students who were becoming a real problem. Like the harpsichord, the piano was useful for composers, but it was better because it was more expressive. According to the pianist J.-L. Adam, composers "can try out their compositions and hear all the parts of the orchestra," while amateurs "can discover different musical effects that they want to try out." This unique advantage, according to the *Journal de Paris* in 1805, "has made it so popular that wherever the musical arts are cultivated and honored, there are few salons that do not have a piano."[36] Interest in the new instrument was not limited to Paris; the main provincial cities soon attempted to obtain the newest Paris models. I found the following advertisement in the *Bulletin de Lyon* of 24 December 1803:

> Citizen Garnier, bookseller, purveyor of musical scores and instruments, located Place de la Comédie No. 18, announces to all music lovers that during his last journey to Paris he made a considerable

acquisition of pianofortes, both upright and grand, simple and ornate, made by the Érard brothers. It is clearly evident that these instruments have achieved a high degree of perfection in the quality of their tone and the solidity with which they are built. The pedals in the form of a lyre are a new mechanism which is sure to please. Prices are those of the Érard brothers, in spite of the transportation costs and accident insurance.

At first, however, the piano did have its detractors, mostly among critics who were hostile to modern art. Some refused to consider it as anything other than an accompanying instrument. When the composer G. Lemoyne put on a concert for two pianos in January 1804, the *Correspondance des professeurs et amateurs de musique* criticized his temerity: "One piano in a concert has always been cruel and soporific, but two are quite unbearable." Voltaire, who saw the beginnings of the pianoforte, wrote that it was "a boilermaker's instrument in comparison to the harpsichord." At the beginning of the nineteenth century, the critic Géoffroy was always a fervent defender of the classical school, and his grumbling reactions are quite typical. He was in favor of nationalistic art (he hated the Mozart fashion) and said that the piano had no right to be heard as a solo instrument. Its use should be limited to that of a modest accompanist, and a piano concerto with orchestral accompaniment seemed to him to be a heresy. He often wrote in this vein for the *Journal de l'Empire*. The day after a Paris concert by Dussek in 1810, he wrote that even an extraordinarily talented player "would not change the poor nature of the piano." There was no hope for it; this was "an instrument to help a composer in his work, excellent for accompanying a singer, quite proper in a chamber music salon, but totally out of place on a large stage or in a big concert where every instrument that accompanies the piano is worth more than it is itself." In 1812, the same criticisms were made after a concert by the young Hérold, who had recently received a first prize for piano at the Conservatoire. The critics listened "with great satisfaction and interest, although the piano really has no place in a concert." [37]

The first French masters of the piano made themselves known very early on, as much by their careers as teachers and composers as by their activities as concert artists. The two most famous names at the very beginning of the nineteenth century were Jean-Louis Adam, the father of the composer Adolphe Adam, and Hélène de Montgeroult, both teachers at the Conservatoire and both authors of a pianoforte method. The former was

originally from Northern Alsace and had a good knowledge of the harpsichord repertoire and of the German and Italian pianoforte composers:
C. P. E. Bach, J. S. Bach, D. Scarlatti, Mozart, and Clementi. He helped
make these works known in France, not only by playing them himself but
also by having his students study them. He was the author of the *Méthode
du Piano du Conservatoire* of 1804, and he published as an appendix two
fugues from J. S. Bach's *The Well-Tempered Clavier*, which had just appeared
for the first time in Paris in 1801. Hélène de Montgeroult, born Countess
of Charnay, had been taught by Hüllmandel and Dussek before becoming a
friend of Viotti, who advised her in her career. She was the first woman
before 1800 to hold the post of professor at the Paris Conservatoire. Like
her colleague J.-L. Adam and all the virtuoso players of her generation, she
composed a great many works for her instrument, mostly sonatas for solo
piano.

In spite of these famous names, one must concede that the French
piano school during the Consulate and the Empire never attained the international reputation of the violin school. Marie Bigot, one of the most gifted
young French pianists of her generation, left Paris in 1804 for personal reasons and settled in Vienna. There she was able to benefit from Haydn and
Beethoven's advice, whose works she played. Upon her return to Paris in
1809, she introduced a vast repertoire (including J. S. Bach and, of course,
Mozart) in the artistic circles of the capital, most of which was still largely
unknown in France. Unfortunately she was obliged to concentrate on
teaching. and she died before she was able to obtain the public recognition
she deserved.

During the first years of the nineteenth century, Paris welcomed foreign
virtuosos, some of whom settled for a while in the capital. The equivalent
of a modern recital did not as yet exist, so when pianists appeared in public,
they usually played one or two sonatas, a concerto, or perhaps the solo part
of a sinfonie concertante on a program that always included symphonic and
vocal music.

In 1801 the Portuguese J.-D. Bontempo arrived in Paris, but he was
only mildly appreciated as a player, and his sonatas appeared to the French
press to be "more intellectual than pleasing." His music was admired, but it
was "not thrilling." By contrast, the Austrian Joseph Wölffl—a pupil of
Haydn, Leopold Mozart, and perhaps Mozart himself—was considered to
be fascinating. He was one of the best European pianists of his time. In
1798, he won a piano competition in Vienna in which his opponent was
Beethoven. In 1801, a year marked by so many important musical events,

he decided to settle in Paris. The *Journal de Paris* of 2 December 1801 called him "one of the most astonishing performers ever to have been heard on the piano." However, the most famous of the foreign pianists in Paris at the time was the Czech composer Ladislas Dussek, who settled permanently in Paris in 1806 and became Talleyrand's concert master. Until his death in 1812, he often performed in Paris concerts. Fétis, who often heard him, wrote:

> People still remember the extraordinary impression he made in 1808 at the concerts given at the Odéon by Rode, Baillot, and Lamare. Until then the piano had not been much appreciated at these concerts, but under Dussek's hands it eclipsed everything around it. This artist's broad and grand style, his way of making the instrument sing even though it has no sustained sound, and the neatness and delicacy of his playing, all contributed to a triumph the like of which had never been seen.[38]

The press was unanimous in its praise of Dussek's talent, and he was considered to be the best pianist in France at the time. His playing was admired because it came both from the heart and from the head and because of "his sovereign calm, the assured attitude of his whole being when he plays."[39] The *Allgemeine Musikalische Zeitung* of June 1809, while deploring the lack of really good piano players in Paris, considered that Dussek's presence would be salutary in correcting the public's bad taste as a result of its exposure to another German virtuoso, D. Steibelt from Berlin.[40] Steibelt had his moment in the sun during the Directoire because some of the most fashionable women of the time were his pupils, beginning with Hortense de Beauharnais. He returned to Paris during the Empire and settled there in 1805 to publish a great many caprices, rondos, and fantasies for piano. A German newspaper stated:

> All the pianoforte teachers of France, and especially in Paris, imitate Steibelt's style and make it even worse by adding their own mistakes. They have discarded the lovely music of Haydn, Mozart, Beethoven, Clementi, Cramer, Dussek, and Hummel to throw themselves body and soul into charlatanism and bad taste that are paramount in most of Steibelt's works. In Germany they would never believe how detestably the pianoforte is played at the moment in Paris by those who wish to be in fashion.

One year later, the same periodical was still deploring the lack of good French pianists in Paris: "They do not have here, for this instrument, a single great talent such as Beethoven, Hummel, or Cramer."[41] Sure enough, when Dussek died in Paris in 1812, the press compared him to Cramer, who was a great success in London at the time.

Another pianist, also of German origin, was a very young man when he began his career in Paris during the Empire. His name was Frédéric (originally Friedrich Wilhelm) Kalkbrenner, who greatly benefitted from the teaching of Clementi and Hummel. After a long stay in London, he returned to settle permanently in France in 1824, where he was very successful both as a performer and as a teacher. To him goes the credit for having trained Marie Pleyel, one of the most gifted Frenchwomen of her generation and the first woman in the romantic period to have made a career as an international virtuoso. In ten years' time the repertoire and the technique of piano playing had evolved considerably. Mechanically, the instrument was continually being perfected and revealed possibilities that would not have been dreamed of a few years earlier. The most gifted young people of their generation took maximum advantage of these possibilities, and became, so to speak, the founders of the modern piano school. Ignace Moscheles is a good example; he was heard in Paris for the first time in 1821. Fétis wrote that his appearance on the Paris stage "was the signal for a transformation in the art of piano playing." Other examples were Franz Liszt, who gave his first concert in Paris in 1824 at the age of thirteen, and of course, the young Frédéric Chopin in 1831.

Although no actual documentation exists, it would be possible to retrace the technical progress of the piano through a careful study of the numerous piano methods published from the end of the eighteenth century until 1830. Starting with the enormously successful *L'art de toucher le pianoforte* (The Art of Playing the Pianoforte) by B. Viguerie in 1795, all subsequent teaching manuals naturally emphasized the problem of touch, which is quite different from the technique used to play the harpsichord. In his *Méthode de piano du Conservatoire*, Adam wrote "only with a delicate touch can one produce lovely sounds," and Hélène de Montgeroult recommended "pressing down hard on the note after it has been played in order to prolong the vibration." There was something completely new to study here, and even to this day, touch is probably the most difficult thing to teach on the piano. Sometimes this technique of touch was compared to vocal technique. For example, in *La première année des leçons de pianoforte* (The First Year's Piano Lessons) 1802, J.-J. Momigny instructed the beginner to "touch each note with appropriate delicacy. Touch is accent, and it is by touch that the pianist imitates the inflections of the voice that punctuate and give expression to speech." To achieve this, Momigny recommended what we would now call relaxation of the arms: "It is the keyboard and not the arm that should support the hand, since absolutely no force should be used when touching a note. If the fingers are tense or stiff or if the whole body is not absolutely relaxed, this will cancel out the real action, making it less easy and less effective." In their method that appeared in 1797, Pleyel and Dussek were already giving much the same advice when they recommended "avoiding lowering the head, rounding the back or contracting the chest by the shoulders, which should always be lowered."

As can be seen, so-called modern teaching has invented nothing new. It is obvious that as soon as the pianoforte was born, it was played badly, with serious technical errors. These errors came precisely from the fact that this new instrument made all the nuances of *pianissimo* and *fortissimo* possible, and the temptation was great to achieve powerful effects by force. In his method, Adam wrote scathingly of players who "bang with all their might on the keyboard to play *forte* or *fortissimo*," when the same effects could be achieved much more easily by totally relaxing the arm and carefully controlling the touch. It sometimes happened that the pianoforte became the victim of a player who was simply tyrannical. Andreas Streicher was a musician himself and the son-in-law of the famous Austrian piano-maker, Andreas Stein. His *Observations on the Way of Playing, Tuning, and Maintaining Pianofortes* (Vienna, 1801) contains an amusing description of one of those piano-destroying monsters who can still be found today but who finds the modern Steinway more difficult to conquer. I will quote him here describing a scene that he witnessed all too often:

> Preceded by his reputation as "an extraordinary pianist, such as had never been heard before," this musician entered the room and sat down (or rather, threw himself) at the piano. The very first chords he played were so loud that the audience wondered whether he was deaf, or if perhaps he thought they were. The movements of his body, his arms and hands all seemed to try to indicate that what he was doing was very difficult and terribly hard work. Then he started to warm up and to treat his instrument like a man thirsting for vengeance who has just got hold of his worst enemy and was slowly torturing him with cruel delight until he died. He wanted to play *forte* but as he had exaggerated the sound from the beginning,

it was impossible to increase the noise any more. So he banged on the instrument till the ill-treated strings went out of tune, and some of them suddenly broke and flew into the audience, who recoiled and covered their eyes to save themselves from these projectiles. Then there came a note that was marked in the score *sforzando*! Thank heavens, the hammer managed to resist, and the string, too. But what a grating noise it was, and how it wounded the ear! This pianist transformed fire and passion into unchained fury, but as soon as he had to express tender feelings, his playing turned cold. He exaggerated all sentiments, so that he made his pianoforte scream and shout when he tried to express suffering. The keys and hammers suffered from his banging till they were nearly paralyzed, whenever he had to play fast or joyful passages.

The instruments built at the end of the eighteenth century were not sufficiently robust to be able to hold their own in a concerto against an entire orchestra. This was one of the reasons why piano makers of that period were always looking for ways to develop the piano's power. It is probably for this reason that the music of the period was played with a certain restraint that modern instruments do not require, which may be regrettable. For instance, I was struck to read in the same document by Andreas Streicher some advice for the performance of concertos, especially Mozart's:

> The pianoforte should be placed several feet nearer the audience than the orchestra. Only the violins should be placed right behind it. The double basses and the wind instruments should be placed much further back, the former in front and the latter behind.

And further,

> In spite of all the rules, pianists, when playing a concerto would be well advised to wait a half a beat or even a whole beat before attacking, so that the sound of the orchestra has time to die away and let them be heard quite clearly as soon as they start their solo.

Anyone studying early piano repertoire should keep in mind these considerations concerning the instrument for which the music was written.

The first generation of composers who wrote music for the pianoforte were active before the Revolution, around 1770. They were mostly organists (Jean-François Tapray, Nicolas Séjan, Claude Balbastre), but some were harpsichordists, such as Nicolas-Joseph Hüllmandel. Étienne-Nicolas Méhul was another very young musician with a very promising future who took an interest in the new instrument. He published two collections of three sonatas each, in 1783 and 1788, before becoming more attracted by a career as an opera composer and abandoning the piano repertoire.

During the Revolution, several collections of sonatas for pianoforte appeared in 1794 and 1795. They were composed by Jean-Louis Adam and Louis Jadin, who were both quite well known before 1789. Boïeldieu who, like Méhul, was also interested in the pianoforte at the beginning of his career, made his debut in 1795. Though usually better known for his operatic works, he published a dozen sonatas between 1795 and 1810. Two other well-known figures emerged at this time: Ferdinand Hérold and Alexandre Boëly. Hérold was just nineteen years old in 1810 when he won first prize at the Conservatoire for the performance of an original piano sonata dedicated to his teacher, J.-L. Adam. Several other volumes followed during the next few years before Hérold turned to an exclusively operatic career. A. Boëly also began in 1810 with the publication of his *Deux Sonates pour le forte-piano*, and he remained faithful to the instrument for the rest of his life.

This rather dry list of names shows in a curious way how piano music seems to have somehow served as a practice ground for the three important composers of the period (Méhul, Boïeldieu, and Hérold), all of whom subsequently turned to opera and comic opera. It appears as though composers could not divide their activity between vocal music and instrumental music, and the former eventually won out.

For the most part, the works for piano by these young composers were sonatas, the favored genre until around 1820. Right around that time, Momigny commented: "The sonata is most suitable for the harpsichord and for the pianoforte, which is able to play three or four parts at a time. This is why the sonata chiefly developed on this instrument."[42]

Most of these sonatas were in two or three movements, the latter type (with a slow middle movement) being by far the most common. The scherzo was practically unknown in French piano music at that time, even though it was then being developed by Beethoven. I found only one example of it by J.-L. Adam (1810). A rather clumsy definition of the scherzo given by Castil-Blaze shows how unfamiliar the French were with this form at the beginning of the nineteenth century. For Castil-Blaze, the scherzo was "quite often a minuet, but in a stranger sort of form than the usual minuet."[43] The fast first movement of the piano sonata was almost always in sonata form, with the development growing more and more important. Several examples can be found (as we have already seen in one of Méhul's symphonies) in which the order of the themes is inverted in the recapitulation. The slow movement was almost always in a key closely related to that of the opening allegro and was most often in a ternary form, whereas the last movement was usually a rondo in order better to showcase the talent of the virtuoso soloist.

Until 1800, sonatas were still given ambiguous titles such as *Sonate pour le forte-piano ou le clavecin* (Sonata for the Pianoforte or the Harpsichord) for commercial reasons. Nonetheless, a specific style of writing for the piano, very different from the harpsichord style, began to develop quite rapidly at the end of the eighteenth century. Progress in piano construction caused the "Sonata for harpsichord or pianoforte with violin or flute accompaniment *ad libitum*" to disappear after 1800, since the main purpose of this accompaniment was originally to double and strengthen the harpsichord that was often thought to be too weak. Composers were now able to use the new instrument's own possibilities: its nuances and special qualities of sound and expression. Melodic lines were progressively freed of all the ornaments that so encumbered them in pieces written for the harpsichord. Initially the accompaniment was often reduced to simple Alberti basses that supported a very simple melody sometimes reminiscent of the vocal style of romances or comic operas. Harmonies were elementary, and the use of the diminished seventh chord was practically the only dramatic effect used by the young composers of that generation, none of whom chose to use the expressive possibilities of chromaticism or counterpoint. Actually, such characteristics also apply to certain sonatas by Mozart himself. In French piano music of the end of the eighteenth century, the melodic gracefulness and restraint are never interrupted or darkened by a passing shadow, a feeling of mystery or unease. Here all is clear and without any great depth.

This excessively limpid style of composition was soon taken up by true pianists and composers who were keen to exploit all the new possibilities of this instrument. After 1800, Hyacinthe Jadin (Louis Jadin's brother) and especially J.-L. Adam transformed the piano sonata into an exercise of extreme virtuosity with parallel octaves, arpeggios, staccatos with both hands over the entire keyboard, chromatic scales, cadenzas, and so on. Keyboard music began to have a sound and brilliance that it had never had before; carried to extremes, its only interest was in its virtuosity. The public loved these noisy acrobatic demonstrations, but for the moment, unfortunately, they were not very interesting. Only a few years later, the great romantics were to give them quite a different meaning.

Alexandre Boëly, who published his first two sonatas for piano in 1810, began to take a very different direction. He was a pupil of the Austrian composer and pianist Ignaz Ladurner, who had been in Paris since 1788 and who was a great admirer of Beethoven. Thanks to him, young Boëly learned all the great German and Italian repertoire for keyboard: Bach, Frescobaldi, Haydn, Mozart, and later, Beethoven. Boëly was a mature and thoughtful composer right from the start, but he was overshadowed in his lifetime by brilliant and superficial virtuosos and remained relatively unknown. He was an original figure in French music during the first half of the nineteenth century (he died in 1858) and has recently been the subject of some university research. His works have been published in modern editions and some of them have been recorded. Interestingly enough, his music is both intellectual and inspired. At a time when Bach and Beethoven were still hardly known in Paris, Boëly grew up on their music and totally assimilated their ideas. His writing is linear, with a strong taste for fugues, and the dreamy and imaginative character of his music makes him one of the most authentic forerunners of French romanticism at the end of the Empire.

Although not as popular as its counterparts for violin or wind instruments, the piano concerto did exist at the end of the eighteenth century. The relationship between an instrument that was still new and had limited dynamics and the orchestra posed a problem from the start. We noted the kind of advice Andreas Streicher gave pianists who played Mozart's concertos. In fact, since the first pianos had a relatively weak sound, composers sometimes chose not to use a large orchestra but to limit the accompaniment to strings. After 1800, woodwinds appeared more frequently in the orchestra. In 1803, for example, L. Jadin published a Sinfonie Concertante for Two Pianos (Concerto for Two Pianos) with an orchestra consisting of clarinets, bassoons, and a French horn in addition to strings.

Like the sonata, the piano concerto appeared in a two- or three-movement form, but the critics soon began to complain that this design was just a pretext for displays of virtuosity, as in this example from the *Miroir des Spectacles*, January 1797:

Three successive movements full of difficulties and stunts that say nothing to the soul are difficult to digest. Would it not be possible

to reduce these musical statements to a single piece in which virtuosos could prove that they have successfully completed their studies
on their instrument? We think that everybody would benefit.

This comment shows that at the time the piano concerto was still a mere
technical exercise that conveyed no message from the composer. Unfortunately, there are not nearly so many piano concertos as concertos for violin
or wind instruments. Boïeldieu, Hérold, and Jadin produced very few—not
enough to fully realize the as yet unexplored potential of this form. In
1800, Mozart's piano concertos were practically unknown to the French
public and French composers.

Apart from the repertoire of sonatas and concertos, the pianoforte inspired artists to write many genre pieces designed to bring overnight success
in the salons. I have already described this music in the section on the symphony. Much of it that was in favor during the Revolution and the Empire
described historical scenes and battles, inspiring facile effects of musical imitation. The pianoforte, which is a polyphonic instrument, was well suited
to these childish games. For example, the pianist Dussek used music to tell
the story of Marie-Antoinette's death, and all the great imperial victories
were recounted in music, sometimes in several different versions. The most
painful and horrible scenes were used as subject matter for musical description in the worst taste for the benefit of the lovely ladies who listened to
them in the imperial salons. The famous *Grand Battle of Austerlitz*, also
known as the *Battle of the Three Emperors, an Historical Event Arranged for
the Piano* by L. Jadin, contains tragic scenes that even include screams of
the wounded. It finishes with two pages of *Ländler* that the author justified
as well as he could in the score: "The French make the musicians who were
taken prisoner play waltzes, and dance while rejoicing in this great victory
and the anniversary of Napoleon's coronation."

After 1800, a large number of short works for piano appeared, such as
fantasies, caprices, variations, and potpourris. Most often they were extremely trivial. No composer nor critic could have imagined what could
have flowed out of a fertile imagination when writing in a free style. Variations—often on fashionable opera tunes—seemed just an excuse for filling-
in whenever composers lacked inspiration, a kind of conversation when
they had nothing to say. I was astonished to find that even Castil-Blaze in
1828 had scathing things to say about variations, such a rich form that even
the greatest geniuses never used up its infinite possibilities:

Are musicians no longer able to compose a piece for performance? All they do is make variations that require absolutely no imagination. They take a theme invented by someone else and proceed to subject it to all the usual changes. First, simple eighth-notes and triplets, then arpeggios, syncopations, octaves, not to mention the Adagio in the relative minor and the *Tempo di Polacca*. Using their fingers and very little taste, musicians can fill up any space just by following the given motives.[44]

It is a fact that after 1801 *Les Mystères d'Isis* (*The Magic Flute*) was used by Steibelt for a set of variations that may have been the first example of the *air varié* for piano ever heard in France at the beginning of the nineteenth century. Other pieces of the same type followed, based on tunes such as *Au clair de la lune* or well-known opera tunes, but none of them shows any real originality. The great romantic style of theme and variations never took root in France.

With the exception of Boëly, the contribution of French composers between 1820 and 1830 to the piano repertoire was rather poor. The situation did not change until after 1830, with figures like Alkan and, of course, Chopin, whose decision to settle in Paris in 1831 is a turning point in the history of the piano in France. With Chopin, the piano experienced a true renaissance. During the first fifty years of its young life, the piano had undergone enormous growth and change, such as few other instruments had known before. From the frail pianoforte of the 1780s to the grand piano of the romantics, the time that had elapsed was short indeed. Fumbling, hesitations, and failures were inevitable, both in its construction and repertoire.

Yet it is also true that the contemporary German school, under identical historical circumstances, produced a vast repertoire of masterpieces for the new instrument. France, during these years of apprenticeship, had not yet lived up to her potential.

Chapter 7

Influence of the German School in France

ℜelations between France and Germany in the area of music have unfortunately not yet been studied in detail for the period between 1789 and 1830. They were probably closer than one has been led to believe, and a study would certainly help explain certain fundamental characteristics of the French mentality. One century before Wagnerism, the French staged an overt nationalistic movement against German music. A typical contradictory reaction from the French—encountered in previous chapters—was to be attracted to the great masterpieces that came from the other side of the Rhine and at the same time reject them.

It has already been shown that exchanges between the two nations were frequent, at least as far as performing artists were concerned. Actually, the great French composers did not travel much, apart from Cherubini, who stayed in Vienna from 1805 to 1806, and Boïeldieu, who went to Saint Petersburg. It is true that Haydn, Beethoven, and Schubert never visited Paris. Some lesser-known German composers did, however, establish themselves in Paris, sometimes for extended periods, and successfully wrote operas on French librettos. Steibelt, for instance, put on *Roméo and Juliette* at the Feydeau in 1793; Winter produced *Tamerlan* at the Grand Opéra in 1802,

315

and every German staying in Paris at the time turned out to show patriotic support to their fellow countryman. According to a critic, the Germans were amused by seeing French musicians so astonished at hearing "such remarkable instrumentation."[1]

The situation was different for performers. Instrumentalists in particular were always on the road, and this encouraged exchanges between the two countries. A study of instrumental music shows that most of the famous French soloists (Rode, Baillot, Kreutzer, Lamare) traveled throughout Europe, especially to Germanic countries. At the beginning of the nineteenth century, the pianist Marie Bigot settled in Vienna for several years, where she worked with Beethoven. Oboist G. Vogt, who followed Napoleon's armies and witnessed the battle of Austerlitz, also met Haydn and Beethoven in Vienna. Conversely, the best German players came to Paris to perform. Romberg was appointed to teach cello at the Conservatoire; pianists Steibelt, Wölffl, and Dussek, among the best of their generation, were great successes in every major Paris concert. J. F. Reichardt, who was formerly in Frederick II's service in Berlin and traveled throughout Enlightened Europe at the end of the eighteenth century, revisited Paris from 1802 to 1803 and went to every theater, concert, and musical salon. I have frequently quoted from his memoirs in this book.

All these artists helped establish contacts—which today would be labeled cultural—between France and Germany. They carried in their suitcases new scores that they played to their Paris friends. Dussek, for example, performed Bach and Mozart. The larger Paris publishers also played an important part in this cultural exchange. Heinrich Simrock, whose brother Nicolaus was a music publisher in Bonn, came to Paris in 1792 as an orchestral player. Appointed horn teacher at the Conservatoire, he opened a music shop in the Rue du Mont-Blanc in 1802. He became a sort of Paris agent for his brother and resold with a new title page some of the German editions published in Bonn. This helped Beethoven's works to become better known in Paris. On 8 October 1800 the *Allgemeine musikalische Zeitung* announced that the Paris publisher Pleyel had merged with the firm of Breitkopf and Härtel "for all German editions." One year later (31 August 1801), the *Courrier des spectacles* informed its readers that the same Pleyel had just begun the publication of "a complete edition of the works of Haydn." On 18 April 1804, the French publishers associated with the *Magasin de Musique*, which had been created two years earlier in Paris by Cherubini, Méhul, Kreutzer, Rode, Isouard, and Boïeldieu, wrote a letter to the famous Leipzig publishers Hoffmeister and Kühnel in response to some of their proposals:

> We are afraid of making a dangerous speculation if we buy the manuscripts that you have offered us. . . . Among foreign composers, only the works of Haydn, Mozart and Hoffmeister (for flute) are really in demand. Beethoven seems too complicated, too strange. He is really only appreciated here by music teachers. [2]

Recent work by A. Devriès and F. Lesure on Paris publishers has shed new light on the history of these exchanges. Thanks to inventories made when certain collections were sold and also to some of the publishers' catalogues, we do have a better idea which scores by German composers were available to French music lovers around 1800. Unfortunately, every edition listed has by no means survived, but the fact that a particular work is mentioned in a catalogue or an inventory does mean that it was, at a particular moment in time, available to specialists if not to the public at large.

For the French of the early part of the nineteenth century, Haydn was the most typical German composer, in spirit as well as style. As has been seen, his works were performed in France by virtually every orchestra for any occasion. Sieber's catalogue from around 1815—a time when Hadyn's popularity was just beginning to wane—offers no less than sixty of the master's symphonies. Because of the widespread popularity of Haydn's work, the French hastily concluded that the German spirit was essentially symphonic and excelled in harmony rather than melody. This cliché was broadly circulated toward the end of the eighteenth century. In a leaflet published on 26 December 1800 (the day after the premiere of *The Creation* in Paris), Géoffroy naively oversimplified the issue: "the Italians and the Germans have each taken over one aspect of music, the two of which should never have been separated: harmony and melody. . . . On one side stands opera, on the other, symphonies." It should be noted that almost all of Haydn's vocal music was unknown at that time. Apart from his symphonies and *The Creation*, only a few quartets had been heard, since they were restricted to private performances up until 1815.

Prior to Haydn, German music was virtually unknown in France. To say that no one at that time had ever heard of Bach would not strictly be true, but J. S. Bach's sons were better known than he was, and only rare references to "Sebastian Bach" are found here and there. Cramer, writing in his *Anecdotes of W. G. [sic] Mozart* at the end of 1801, quoted a fragment of a jig by J. S. Bach, "father of the German fugue, whose profound works are practically unknown in Paris and which are an everlasting source and treasure of great and learned harmony." This text is quoted almost in its entirety by critic Ginguené in an article in *La Décade philosophique* of 1 December 1801. This was exactly the time of publication of the first French edition of *The Well-Tempered Clavier* (as announced in the *Courrier des spectacles* of 29 September 1801). No earlier French edition of Bach is known. His music was absolutely unknown to the general public and was for a very long time only studied by specialists. Pianist J.-L. Adam published two fugues in his *Méthode de Piano du Conservatoire* (1804), the first fugue from Volume One and the fourth fugue from Volume Two of *The Well-Tempered Clavier*, so he probably used them as studies for his class. Fétis wrote that when Malibran returned to Paris in 1819 with her family, "she was already playing J. S. Bach's pieces for harpsichord which Garcia loved so much."[3] It was also at this time that Organist A. Boëly introduced a few of the Leipzig cantor's fugues to a selected audience of initiates.

Following the article in Choron and Fayolle's *Dictionnaire historique*, much of which was simply lifted from earlier works by the German scholar L. Gerber, the first important writing about Bach that I know of is Framery's article entitled "Sonata" in the *Encyclopédie méthodique* (1818). Generally full of praise for Bach's "transcendent genius," Framery analyzed the *Six Sonatas for Harpsichord with Violin Obbligato* published in Zurich by Naegeli. His opinion, following the detailed analysis of the first movement of the Second Sonata in A major, is worth quoting:

> This model trio may open the eyes of those who have not pro-
> gressed beyond J.-J. Rousseau and think that besides the melodic
> line and its replica at the third, there is no other real voice. These
> sonatas are seldom played only because there are very few people
> who can perform or understand them. This type of music needs
> not only special performers but also a very special audience.

In any case, until 1830, Bach's music could not have had an impact on Paris musical circles and could not have had any influence at all on composers of the time. Only performers, mostly pianists, really knew some of his works for harpsichord and taught them to their students. Of course, the great monuments of his sacred music remained utterly unknown. Even Choron could not have introduced them to his public before 1830.

Things were somewhat different for Mozart and Beethoven. Mozart's music was introduced into France at a fairly late date, whereas Beethoven's music crossed the frontier much sooner than has been commonly thought. In fact, at the time of Beethoven's death in 1827, the Parisians had already been able to hear many of his works, at least in private concerts if not in public. A large number of works were published in Paris during the first quarter of the nineteenth century and prove an obvious interest in this "new" music on the part of both professional and amateur audiences.

The earliest mention of Beethoven's name in the French press was, to my knowledge, in the *Journal de Paris* of 22 Fructidor year VIII (9 September 1800), announcing the publication in Paris by Sieber of a *Sonate à quatre mains pour le clavecin ou forte-piano, oeuvre VI par Louis Vanbee-Thoven* (Four-Hand Sonata for Harpsichord or Pianoforte, Opus 6, by Louis Vanbee-Thoven [sic]). From this date on, more French editions appeared, but their existence is often known only through press announcements or publishers' catalogues. For instance, it is now known that in 1810 about forty of Beethoven's works were already available from the catalogues of the following Paris publishers: Sieber, Érard, Pleyel, and Simrock. It was possible to obtain piano music (in particular the *Appassionata* and the *Thirty-Two Variations on a Theme in C minor*), chamber music (sonatas for piano and violin, piano and cello, trios, and quartets), and the parts for the Second Symphony. The six quartets of Opus 18 were announced by Pleyel in September 1801. The *Correspondance des amateurs musiciens* of 17 March 1804 informed its readers of the recent publication by Simrock of "concertos, septets [sic], and quintets" by Beethoven.

Some hasty assertions that Beethoven's work remained unknown to Parisians for a long time should therefore be revised. Although it is true that this music was rarely performed in public concerts, it was quite widespread in private circles. In 1840 Habeneck, recalling memories of his youth (he obtained the first prize for violin at the Conservatoire in 1801), spoke of the quartet rehearsals of his early days:

> It must have been at least thirty-eight years ago that I first got to know some of Beethoven's quartets and played them with my friend Philipp and a few other people, without being particularly impressed. Soon after, we received the First and Second Symphonies, which we tried out with a small orchestra. Of all the

artists who heard us perform these works, only Méhul really liked
them. It was actually these symphonies that encouraged Méhul to
write similar ones of his own.[4]

The violinist Baillot wrote in a letter dated 13 June 1805: "We have
already had two sessions of Beethoven, with which we are very satisfied."[5]
So it was actually very early—only shortly after Vienna—that the musical
elite of Paris got to know the work of the young German master. Let us remember that in 1800 Beethoven was only thirty years old.

Since these piano and chamber music sessions were private, limited to a
few enlightened music circles in the capital, there was naturally no echo in
the press. It is therefore impossible to know what impression this music
made on the young French avant-garde or what influence it really had
on contemporary composers. The *Journal de Paris* gave its opinion of
Beethoven's music on 1 December 1804, one of the earliest critiques found
in the French press. The periodical announced the publication by Simrock
of a large number of works by the German composer (including fourteen
piano sonatas) and was pleased to add the following commentary:

> This young composer, the best harpsichord player in Germany to-
> day, has seen all the honors heaped upon Steibelt and is constantly
> working to wrest them from him. His music is both intelligent and
> graceful. Some amateurs criticize him for a lack of melody, but if
> they were able to study and play his works more proficiently, they
> would take back this reproach.

Thus it was by typically French standards, opposing *musique savante*
(scholarly music) and favoring *musique chantante* (singing music), that
Beethoven's music was first judged in Paris.

The first press reviews did not come until later, when Beethoven's symphonies were first included on French programs for public performances by
students of the Conservatoire: the First Symphony on 22 February 1807, the
Symphony in C minor on 10 April 1808, and the "Eroica" Symphony on
5 May 1811. These critiques do not express the point of view of the Paris
musical élite, but that of journalists, some of whom knew very little about
music. They were more accustomed to reviewing stage performances, where
the libretto and the production were more important than the musical score.

Their judgments were for the most part very conservative. Beethoven's
music seemed difficult and disconcerting. They were taken by the rich or-

chestral color but put off by the harmonies and themes, which seemed artificial and too intellectual to them. Sauvo, a critic writing in the *Moniteur universel* of 17 March 1809, reproached Beethoven for having "lost touch with his own genius in overly complex scientific combinations," and the *Tablettes de Polymnie* (March 1810) denounced the excess of "fugal imitation and counterpoint" in one of Méhul's symphonies, laying the blame on the success of Beethoven's symphonies at the Conservatoire:

> This is a dangerous example for musical art. The contagion of Germanic harmony seems to be creeping into the modern school of composition forming at the Conservatoire. They seem to think they can produce an effect by providing the most barbarous dissonances and by using all the instruments of the orchestra to make a din. Alas! The only effect is to break our eardrums while never once speaking to our hearts.

The public felt that the divide was deepening between the Germans, whose only concern was with intellectual research into harmony and instrumental possibilities, and the French, who above all wanted their music to describe simple feelings that appeal to the heart by means of lovely and charming melodies.

Thanks to the young Habeneck, who frequently directed the Conservatoire orchestra during this period, the Conservatoire became a kind of rallying center for the new French avant-garde. As will be shown, Mozart and Beethoven were received there with great enthusiasm. The *Tablettes de Polymnie* still wrote about the "danger to which young composers are exposed, who have adopted this school with an almost frantic enthusiasm." The press, in a clear show of nationalism, assured the public that performances by this orchestra were far superior to those of the Viennese orchestras of the time, a totally peremptory affirmation, although comparing the music-making in the two capital cities could have been made easier by the large numbers of French people flocking to Vienna, brought by the Napoleonic campaigns.

The French press, however, was not entirely negative. The same commentator of the *Tablettes de Polymnie* (20 May 1811), in spite of a few "Germanisms" that he found shocking, felt "compelled to admit that most of Beethoven's works are grandiose, original, and greatly move their audience." Two months previously, on 20 March 1811, an even more sagacious critique had appeared in the same newspaper. Using some colorful yet penetrating terms, the writer gave the public the benefit of his own personal impressions. This was the first time that the French press acknowledged the conflict that involved opposing factions in a furious quarrel over Beethoven's works.

> This composer, often strange and baroque, does sometimes shine with extraordinary beauty. Here he soars as majestic as an eagle, there he crawls along stony paths. One moment he fills the soul with sweet melancholy, the next he tears it apart with a heap of barbaric chords. I seem to see doves and crocodiles locked in together.

With the fall of the Empire, Beethoven's works for a while fell out of fashion in France. After 1815, the year when the Conservatoire and its concerts were closed down temporarily, references to Beethoven in the press were rare, although Baillot did program some of the composer's quartets in the public chamber music evenings he created in 1814. The music of the man whom Ingres called "a delirious Mozart" was probably most often performed in private Paris circles and in the larger provincial centers. In a letter to his friend Gilibert, written from Rome in 1819, the painter speaks of "the pleasure of playing together the divine quartets of Haydn, Mozart, and Beethoven." It is a fact that early on Ingres played first violin in the quartets of the German school, including, naturally, those of Beethoven. It would be interesting to know what enthusiastic or reticent reactions were felt in these private circles, through which Beethoven's works slowly but steadily became better known. In fact, his music was probably heard without the prejudice or the strange suspicion so characteristic of the official press of the time. Some contemporary newspapers seemed reluctant to admire music that set such a dangerous example. It is easy to detect, in many cases, a sense of guilt and a certain bitterness resulting from both secret admiration and the fear of letting go and being seduced. Exactly one century later the French press expressed precisely the same reservations, again about German music, but this time the dangerous seducers were Richard Wagner and Richard Strauss. The history of the musical relations between the two countries indeed reveals many unavowed feelings.

In 1818 the *Encyclopédie méthodique* described Beethoven as "Germany's greatest musician today," but while he showed "ideas of great talent, genius, and strange imagination," he was criticized for "letting slip from his pen so much that is arid or ungracious." The author of the article, too happy to have discovered a "mistake" in the finale of the *Les Adieux* Sonata, criticized Beethoven for "such artificial harmony that it exceeds the limits of music and is no longer real science but scholarly ignorance." Nothing can excuse such wanderings by a composer "unless he has become deaf." [6] The new *Société des concerts du Conservatoire* was created in 1828. As I have already said, it marked the true beginning of the introduction into France of all Beethoven's symphonic works under the direction of Habeneck. After hearing the Fifth Symphony at one of the Society's early sessions and being bowled over by it, old Le Sueur addressed his pupil Berlioz and expressed his tremendous admiration for the work, but added: "Even so, one should not make music like that!"

When Beethoven's music was first received in France around 1800, it was met with incomprehension or even hostility. At the same time, the introduction of Mozart's music gave rise to even more violent polemics that were tinted with obvious nationalism.

In contrast to Beethoven, Mozart's music had not become widely known in France during the composer's lifetime; yet to speak of a rediscovery of Mozart after his death in 1791 would not be true, since his name had never been forgotten in Paris. By the beginning of the nineteenth century, many French people must have remembered meeting him during his third (and last) stay in Paris in 1778. His music, however, was seldom played until 1800. An attempt to stage *The Marriage of Figaro* in French translation at the Grand Opéra in March 1793 failed. Admittedly, nearly all of Beaumarchais's original text had been added to Mozart's opera, which made the performance endless. The addition of spoken text in place of the recitatives customary at the Opéra shocked the entire press. The *Journal général de France* did speak of "Mozart's superb music, a distinguished artist who died a year ago in Vienna in the service of the Emperor," and the *Moniteur universel* (1 April 1793) prophesied: "This work is excessively long, but with many cuts it could be a success."

It is astonishing that Mozart's music should have been performed so seldom in Paris concerts before 1800, especially since an increasing number of editions of his works had appeared during the previous decade. A detailed chronology of their publication might bring some surprises. We know that Sieber had already brought out some symphonies (including the Symphony in G minor, K. 550, around 1796). Unfortunately, only bits and pieces survive today. Several concertos "for harpsichord or pianoforte" were published at the same time by Leduc, Boyer, and Naderman. Around 1796—it is sometimes difficult to date these old editions precisely—Imbault published some of the "Quintets for two Violins, two Violas, and Cello." Imbault also published some of the quartets, as did Pleyel and Sieber. Editions of the piano sonatas, though, are very rare before 1800. It is clear, however, that many foreign editions, especially those of J. André (in Offenbach) or Simrock (in Bonn), were circulating in Paris, increasing the connoisseurs' chances to hear and play Mozart's works in private gatherings. Surprisingly, I found a series of eleven excerpts from *Così fan tutte* that were rewritten for piano and voice and published in Paris around 1798 by Vogt in a bilingual French-Italian edition; this opera was not performed in Paris until 1809 at the Théâtre italien. There must be many such discoveries to be made in the chronology of the early publication of Mozart's operas in France. I have in my personal collection the (incomplete) orchestra material for the Overture to *Don Giovanni* published by Bonjour around 1795. Strangely enough, this work bears the unusual title of *Il Convitato di pietra,* the title of both Gazzaniga's and Gardi's operas on the same subject, instead of *Il Dissoluto punito.* This early edition may indicate that the Overture to *Don Giovanni* was already known in certain Paris circles before 1800, although I found no trace of it on the programs of contemporary public concerts.

The turning point of Mozart's posthumous career in France came in 1801. That year, several important events helped spread his reputation and place him at the center of conversation in Paris: the publication of the two earliest French biographies about him; the premiere of *Les Mystères d'Isis* (*The Magic Flute*), which had considerable success; and the effort to open a German opera house in Paris named the Mozart Theater.

The first of the two French biographies was by C. Fr. Cramer, a former professor of Greek at Kiel who had come to Paris to set up shop as a printer. An expatriate living in Paris, he translated a number of works from German into French. He drew from most of F. Rochlitz's articles on Mozart, which were published in the *Allgemeine musikalische Zeitung* from 1798 on, incorporating them into a little book. The sixty-eight-page study, entitled *Anecdotes sur W. G.* [sic] *Mozart,* appeared in Paris in August–September 1801. A few months later, the Paris editor Fuchs published a forty-eight-page booklet entitled *Notice biographique sur Jean-Chrysostome-Wolfgang-Théophile Mozart,* written by the Alsatian J. F. Winckler. The text had appeared a little earlier in *Le Magasin encyclopédique* and was, for the most part, a German translation. Winckler had taken his information from the pages on Mozart written by the German writer Schlichtegroll (in his *Necrolog*), published from 1790 on.

Although Rochlitz had known Mozart personally and Schlichtegroll had interviewed the composer's closest relatives, including his sister Nannerl, neither document is anything more than a collection of biographical anecdotes. This may have been the reason for their success. While Cramer's text was that of a devoted hero-worshipper, Winckler at least tried to retrace the story of Mozart's career. Naturally, both authors emphasized the child prodigy and his exceptional gifts. Both texts mention certain works for the first time—especially operas—that were virtually unknown in France, but neither reveals any real appreciation of Mozart's art in general. However that may be, these two brochures marked the beginning of the Mozart legend in France. These twisted, over-embellished, and facile anecdotes—including the mysterious commission of the Requiem, for instance—immediately began to circulate in Paris, as evidenced by the press of the time. Mozart became the composer people talked about. A very long article by Ginguené in *La Décade philosophique* of 1 December 1801 summarized Cramer's booklet and, for the French readers' benefit, filled in certain biographical and bibliographical gaps. This text gives a complete list, perhaps for the first time in France, of every Mozart opera, starting with *Mitridate*, which was performed in Milan in 1770.

Along with the biographies, the enormous success of *Les Mystères d'Isis* in August 1801 made Mozart's name famous. Looking at the repertoire of the Opéra at this time, it is clear how important this event was, no matter how scandalous this adaptation of *The Magic Flute* may seem to us today. This production is proof that the French public was able to hear large excerpts of the original music, in spite of all the changes made to Schikaneder's libretto and Mozart's score by the "arranger," Lachnith. Most composers and all the young avant-garde intellectuals and artists were enthusiastic about it. On the other hand, the conservatives, grouped around the official critic Géoffroy, were furious. There was even a nationalistic attempt to stop Mozart's music from being heard in Paris, but to no avail. It is no exaggeration to say that fifteen years before Rossini's debut in France, the first dilettantes of the nineteenth century were already carrying a banner for Mozart.

To make things even worse between "Mozartomanes"—to use the word that appeared in the contemporary press—and Mozartophobes, an attempt to open a German theater called the Mozart Theater was made in Paris in November 1801. In the article just quoted from *La Décade philosophique* on Cramer's *Anecdotes*, Ginguené announced to his readers:

These *Anecdotes* could not have been published at a better moment, when a new theater is about to open, under the auspices of this extraordinary man, to be almost exclusively devoted to presenting his masterpieces in their original version, masterpieces that up until then had been disfigured by inaccurate translations and unfaithful performances.

The story of this German theater in Paris has never been told in detail—a short, fascinating episode that ended in resounding failure. It was the very first attempt to introduce German opera, in particular *Singspiel*, to Paris audiences.[7]

The success of *Les Mystères d'Isis* in August 1801 drew attention to Mozart's operas and created a genuine curiosity about them. In this favorable atmosphere, a German company was brought to Paris in the fall of the same year. They had made a stop in Strasbourg the previous summer (from June to October 1801), where several of their productions had been successful, including *The Magic Flute* and *Don Giovanni*. The company's director, Haselmayer, was from Stuttgart. He hired several German star singers to build up his group before risking an appearance in Paris—namely, the bass Ellmenreich and two prima donnas, Madame Lang, also from Stuttgart, and Madame Canabich from Munich. Haselmayer was ambitious. First, he intended to occupy the Salle Favart for six months, which had just become available after the fusion of the two Opéra-comique companies, Favart and Feydeau. He asked to rent the hall for twenty performances a month, "offering to pay the sum of six thousand francs a month as well as the cost of the orchestra, lights, maintenance, guards, and so on." When the actors of Salle Favart refused these conditions, the German company had to fall back on the Théâtre de la Cité, located in Rue de la Barillerie, opposite the Palais de Justice. That hall, inaugurated in 1792, had been repainted and decorated. "At the front of the stage several boxes were made by dividing in half the large, existing ones." Quick to take advantage of the new Mozart fashion, the organizers changed the name from Théâtre de la Cité to Mozart Theater, since their ambition was to devote it "almost exclusively to that master's works."

This new theater was opened on 16 November 1801. A very select public (several ambassadors, literary figures, and artists) flocked to the Mozart Theater in spite of its rather unusual location. Most important events in Paris theater life at that time took place on the Right Bank, along Rue de Richelieu from the Palais Royal to the modern district of La Bourse (the Paris Stock Exchange). On the program was Mozart's *Die Entführung aus dem Serail* (The Abduction from the Seraglio), which of course had never been heard in its original version. According to newspaper sources that I was not able to verify, this opera had been performed a few times in French during the Revolution "at one of the small theaters newly built in the Palais Royal" (probably the theater of the Lycée des Arts, which was indeed located in the Palais Royal).

For this important premiere, only the singers were German. The French orchestra was conducted by Blasius, who had already led the orchestra at the Opéra-Comique and the *Académie de musique*. The press reviews listed the cast: Constanze was sung by Madame Lange, Blondchen by Mademoiselle Lügers. The male roles were taken by Walter as Belmonte, Hoffmann as Pedrillo, and Ellmenreich as Osmin. Ellmenreich was the male star of the company, which included at least a dozen more singers.

The success of the premiere was due to the etiquette and snobbery of the public rather than to their genuine enthusiasm. Apart from political and musical figures, we are told that the room "was filled with Germans and Jews." French singers could be identified by their worried expressions. They feared the potential rivalry of this newly arrived foreign company— this happened to be precisely the same time that the Italian opera buffa had just returned to Paris. They had "a look of consternation, different from the joyful expressions on the faces from the other side of the Rhine."

Even though "no one was satisfied by this performance," it was greeted with applause at the end. How can this reception be explained? According to the German critics, it was first and foremost due to the singers' mediocrity. The conductor and his orchestra, however, had great success right from the start of the overture. Except for the leading stars, the company was almost exclusively made up of artists from Frankfurt, and the French criticized it as being only the sixth best company in Germany, after Vienna, Berlin, Hamburg, Munich, and Stuttgart. It seems ironic today to find such a precise statement coming from a critic who had probably heard a German company for the first time in his life that very evening.

Walter, the young male lead, was accused of having a "weak and too pronounced counter-tenor" voice and of being a poor actor: "He seems rather like Don Quixote, with his airs and graces; he is a weak actor." After this attack, the critic adds "he is Jewish by birth." Selim the Pascha (an entirely spoken role) "leaves a lot to be desired and makes one wish for Brandt or Herzfeld, who played the role with such dignity in other theaters." This interesting judgment is evidence that German actors were already specializing in certain Mozart roles. As Osmin, Ellmenreich's acting was deemed overdone and exaggerated, especially in the drunken scene, "although this must seem quite natural to the good Germans." However, his basso profundo voice was much admired. Only Mademoiselle Lügers, the maid, was liked by all the critics. Constanze, the star of the company, received a mixture of criticism and praise. And yet, if there indeed was a Mozart tradition at the beginning of the nineteenth century, who better to represent it than Madame Lange, "a famous singer from Stuttgart"? Madame Lange was none other than Aloysia Weber, Mozart's own sister-in-law; the composer had been madly in love with her, and she inspired several great concert arias. At that time she was married to Joseph Lange, the artist and actor. Her biographers often fail to mention her single short stay in Paris. With only one or two exceptions, contemporary French critics, who would have loved such details about the Austrian composer to add to information derived from Cramer's *Anecdotes sur la vie de Mozart*, did not seem to know about this relationship. Many Mozart fans in Paris probably never found out the role this artist played in their idol's life.

Madame Lange's interpretation of Constanze received lukewarm comments. Her voice was found to be tired: "Her rare talent as a singer has been known for a very long time in Germany, but unfortunately it seems to be suffering a bit from its long-lasting fame" (Aloysia Weber had only just turned forty.) She was accused of producing "too much brilliance followed by notes that were too faint." Her voice sometimes seemed to "wander and her tone sound like that of a solo violin." The critics agreed that her vocalises in Constanze's grand aria were brilliantly sung but blamed her for singing out of tune several times during the marvelous *Ach, ich liebte*. Was it her fatigue or meanness that caused the critics to imply that her talent was better suited to the concert hall than to the stage?

Another criticism addressed to Constanze and Osmin was "their stiff and jerky acting." One critic asked "if this were a common fault of German actors, and whether they all had a habit of walking up and down on a straight line and gesticulating at a right angle." I must also quote this rather unkind criticism of Ellmenreich's performance of Osmin, as it indicates both a sentiment of superiority and a systematic desire to denigrate contemporary German art and culture: "He is an excellent buffoon, but he should remember not to overact the parts as much as he would in certain Germanic countries. Here he is dealing with quite a different audience." So the public, unable to judge for itself, was insidiously made to think of Germany as a vulgar, uncultivated place, where people were happy to watch mere slapdash intrigues at the opera. A few years later, fortunately, the works of Madame de Staël would put this right. For the moment the French press, as usual, was still more interested in the libretto than in the music and reacted to this German production with arguments that seem to come straight out of Saint-Évremond's writings on opera: "Our bad taste, said one critic ironically, wants plays, not canvases decorated with music."

Clearly, a major obstacle to the success of this attempt to introduce *Singspiel* to France was that most of the public could not understand German. German comic opera was similar to the French in that it contained much spoken dialogue and, unlike the Italians, the Germans had not thought it necessary to make available librettos in French at the entrance. But even in the sung passages, part of the audience was put off by the sound of the German language: "It will always be easier and more pleasant to speak and sing continuous vowels than groups of harsh, rough, grating consonants." For many Parisians who had never been to Germany, that evening's performance was their first contact with German singing, and they found the apparent roughness of the idiom shocking. One journalist even wrote: "None of our French prima donnas will ever want to bellow German words in a concert. They will always prefer to lisp Metastasio's harmonious verse."

Mozart's music did not succeed in capturing the interest of the French public, even those who were beginning to support his work. At the second performance, the theater was half empty, and no one came to the third. It makes one shudder today to think of Aloysia Weber in Paris singing *Die Entführung aus dem Serail* to an empty house. She left immediately afterward for Frankfurt, undoubtedly disappointed by her Paris failure.

Since Ellmenreich had also gone back to Germany, the company was left without its two stars but still had the courage to continue its series of performances. It performed *Das rote Käppchen* by Dittersdorf (1788) on 21 and 22 November, and *Das Neusonntagskind* by Wenzel Müller (1793) on 25 and 26 November. This *Singspiel*, presented under the French title *Le Visionnnaire* (The Visionary), did elicit some favorable comments: "At last the Germans let us hear a work that is worthy of their composers' reputation. . . . This is the sort of burlesque that makes you laugh out loud and is easy to understand just by its pantomime." The public liked the music. A duet was encored and the audience had the pleasure of hearing M. Rindler sing Viotti's *Polonaise* at the end of the last act, "thus announcing, as is the custom in Germany, the work to be performed the next day." The next production was a half-heroic, half-comic opera, *Der Spiegel von Arkadien* (The

Mirror of Arcadia) by Süssmayer (1794), Mozart's disciple. It was given on 29 November and 2 December and was reviewed in the following terms: "The wonderful musical score can only partly hide the imperfections of the German libretto." The last in this series of performances at the Mozart Theater was *Der Tyroler Wastel* by Johann Haibel (1796), presented on 30 November: "a detestable play as far as the plot is concerned, but the music can make you forget the poor pantomime."

After the repeated failure of each of these productions, the administrator of the company, Haselmayer, found himself in financial difficulties and actually skipped out of Paris, leaving the artists unpaid and in an extremely precarious position.

> For some obscure reason, he had agreed to very high fees for Monsieur Ellmenreich and Madame Lange. . . . That morning, before his departure had become known, Dittersdorf's opera *Doktor und Apotheker* (The Doctor and the Pharmacist) was still on the schedule. But at seven in the evening the musicians, artists, and public were all waiting in front of the doors because when the owner of the theater heard of Haselmayer's departure, he refused to allow the performances to continue.

In the end, the German artists desperately made a last ditch effort to set up an arrangement with the Italian artists of the Opera Buffa theater, who allowed them to use the Olympic theater where they had just moved themselves. The German company was scheduled to perform there three times every ten days. In the end they gave only one performance, *Das Braminenfest* (1790) by Wenzel Müller, on 6 December 1801. For that evening's performance they had to pay sixty livres, not to mention the considerable sums to be paid for the orchestra musicians and the rental of the costumes. "The German company's debut in this theater did not attract much of an audience" wrote one journalist, who added "the French want a play as well as music, and music alone is not enough for them." In any case the sets and the production were a disaster.

> The two rowboats that bring the Englishmen stopped very suddenly. Since those in them could not go forward, they jumped into the waves and made a lot of noise on the wooden floor with their feet. This staging mishap only provided extra ammunition to those people who do not attend this sort of event without prejudice.

So this was a new failure, and since the audience was just as scarce in the new theater as it had been in the Mozart Theater—many spectators had actually left after the first act—the German artists were completely ruined and had to request the French government to pay their trip back to their homeland!

Such was the sorry end to an attempt that might have been essential in the musical life of Paris. It exposed the French to a repertoire that they knew nothing about at the time. Mozart was the only name they knew, so these performances gave rise to interesting controversies in the press. One journalist foolishly wrote in the *Gazette nationale* that with the exception of about twenty selected operas of Mozart, Dittersdorf, Winter, and Müller, the Germans had nothing but translated versions of French or Italian operas. To this a reader replied in the same paper a few days later that "those composers whom he has cited, alone, have produced more distinguished operas than he is granting to the entire German nation." This was followed by an enumeration of all the composers unfairly left out: Weigl, Wranitzky, Süssmayer, Reichardt, Naumann, Zumsteeg, and many others "who are of such quality that nothing but envy could dispute or refuse them credit." With the possible exception of Reichardt, who in Paris could have known these composers in 1801? For composers of French comic operas there was plenty here to allow fascinating discoveries and enriching comparisons. In fact, included in the repertoire presented at the Mozart theater were some of the most popular specimens of contemporary *Singspiel*. *Das Neusonntagskind* by W. Müller, for example, had been performed five hundred times in the same theater in Vienna, starting in 1793. The French public knew hardly anything about the German musical scene except for Haydn and Mozart; unfortunately they were unable to take this opportunity to get to know the most representative works being performed in Vienna at the end of the eighteenth century. *Der Tyroler Wastel* (The Tyrolean Peasant) was composed on a text by Schikaneder, the librettist of *The Magic Flute*. Its composer, Johann Haibel, was Mozart's friend and became his brother-in-law posthumously by marrying Sophie Weber, Constanze and Aloysia's sister, in 1807. This opera had an enormous success when first performed in 1796 in Vienna, with sixty-six performances in less than a year. *Doktor und Apotheker*, which the Mozart Theater artists were planning to present to the Paris public, was the work of Mozart's great friend Karl Dittersdorf. In 1786, it even eclipsed for a time the success of *The Marriage of Figaro*. Clearly, Haselmayer's company tried to introduce Paris to the entire Viennese repertoire of German operas from Mozart's time.

At the very moment when Mozart was becoming famous, thanks to the two biographies that had just been written about him, there is something symbolic about Aloysia Weber's presence in Paris. We can well imagine that she must have been extremely upset by the cool reception she received, accustomed as she was to one triumph after another. Did she have the time to frequent Paris artistic circles during her too-short stay? The answer to this question is unfortunately unknown, though no one at the time would have been in a better position to inform her contemporaries about her brother-in-law. She was the only one who could have corrected the errors that were beginning to slip into his biography. Better yet, she had worked under his direction and interpreted his works. For example, she had sung the role of Donna Anna in the first Viennese production of *Don Giovanni* in May 1788. She could have been a great firsthand source of advice and opinion for the French musicians and performers who were beginning to be fascinated by Mozart's music, Unfortunately, they did not realize the advantage of having in their midst this foreign company that had introduced them to *Die Entführung aus dem Serail.*

The *Gazette Nationale*, which of all the newspapers was most favorable to the Germans right to the end, did have the courage to make the following observation:

> It is astonishing that people have not even shown any curiosity—in a city that is so in love with anything new, where so many foreigners come from so many different parts of Europe, where musical taste has made astonishing progress, and where composers both need and presumably desire to study foreign styles.

The German language was probably the real obstacle to *Singspiel* becoming established in France. But even without always understanding the texts, Paris critics declared themselves shocked by the platitudes and sometimes the vulgarity of certain librettos. In the plot of Müller's *Das Neusonntagskind,* they saw "a farce that even our street theaters would have felt unworthy of them." And yet neither the Italian opera buffa nor the French comic opera of that time really offered anything much richer dramatically. The French were equally severe with the Italians who had just come back to Paris in that same year (1801). They found their librettos just as meaningless: "The Germans used dreadful texts and they were not successful. Italian works are often just as feeble, but at least their language is softer and more familiar to us."

Beyond these more or less justified criticisms, which strangely enough were hardly ever concerned with the music itself, there remained, clearly more powerful than anything else, the fear of seeing French art smothered by foreign productions. Was this the unconscious defensive reflex of a nation that suffered from the absence of an unchallengeable and unchallenged musical leadership, or was it simply the expression of a morbid desire for absolute supremacy in everything? This rivalry with foreign schools could originally have been the result of perfectly good and honest intentions, but one cannot help but wonder, reading the following excerpt from *La Décade philosophique, littéraire et politique* of 11 December 1801, a kind of epilogue to the sad adventure of the Mozart Theater in Paris:

> If, during the days when the powers of Europe were allied together against France, they had succeeded in dismembering her and sharing the pieces, the best way they could have found to install themselves in the conquered areas would have been to enforce there their customs, language, religion, and art on the scattered remains of our own, which they would have overthrown and destroyed. But when, on the contrary, thanks to its genius and glory, our country has risen to prosperity and our institutions and our art compel us to become again the model and envy of our neighbors, is it not strange that some people should try to force us French to abandon our own masterpieces and to submit us to shapeless barbaric spectacles where one cannot understand a word and indeed would be even more embarrassed if one did?

A journalist who signed his articles L.C. thought that he would make an impression by formulating the following wish—perhaps addressed to the First Consul—that strangely resembles the Emperor's own decrees a few years later:

> It is about time that the Government decided to restrict the growing number of establishments of this type [the Mozart Theater]. Surely they are the obvious cause of the scarcity of good art by making it so easy to produce such a flood of bad art.

To end this list of press reviews, I shall quote an excerpt from the *Journal des Débats* of 24 November 1801—perhaps by Géoffroy. Its cynicism reveals not only a heightened sense of nationalism but also total ignorance of the conditions necessary for the development of contemporary opera:

> The Italians cross the Alps and the Germans cross the Rhine to bring us their music. Unfortunately for them we already have plenty of our own; it is like bringing wood to a forest or water to a river. . . . We don't want people of talent, but people with cash. As long as foreigners come in with plenty of cash we shall ensure that we have enough talent available for their money, and so we shall not have to go get it from our neighbors. . . . When we have a theater like Feydeau, who needs the *Théâtre de la Cité* [Mozart Theater]?

Thus a real controversy arose in 1801 around Mozart's name. A "Mozartophobe" who is completely forgotten today, composer and violinist Michael Woldemar, tried to drag the great composers of the time into his quarrel: "When are we going to have operatic patriotism?" he demanded in the *Courrier des Spectacles*. Le Sueur, an ardent defender of French art, refused to be drawn in and published in the same paper a noteworthy reply addressed to Woldemar. He took Mozart's defense and professed to be shocked by the attempt to denigrate Mozart in order to raise French composers up to his level. In Mozart he saw

> an extraordinary composer, one of those prodigies that Nature hardly ever produces. . . . Mozart may have been born in Germany, but his talent has made him a citizen of the world. . . . His melodious language has no limits, it is universal. In London, Vienna, Saint Petersburg, Madrid, Rome, or Paris his music will always speak to the heart, and people's hearts the world over will understand it.[8]

The Conservatoire increased the number of performances of Mozart's works at its public student concerts. Under Cherubini's direction, the Conservatoire orchestra gave the Paris premiere of the Requiem on 21 December 1804 at Saint-Germain l'Auxerrois. The orchestral score appeared soon after, in 1805, also thanks to the Conservatoire. It contained an important preface written by the critic Sévelinges that was full of praise for Mozart. The French found some new information in this text, mostly borrowed from *Mozart's Life* published in Prague in 1798 by Niemetschek. It was at this time that the symphonies began to appear more often in the programs of the leading Paris concerts. For a long time they were not attempted in their original form because of their technical difficulty, and several arrangements were made of them that were supposed to make them easier to play. The Italian composer G. B. Cimador published a number of Mozart's symphonies in Paris, for a sextet of two violins, two violas, bass, and double bass, with flute *ad libitum*. These arrangements distorted the original works, but they did allow them a wider circulation among music lovers. I note in passing that the symphonies chosen for this publication were some of his most famous—including the last three—which proves that as early as the beginning of the nineteenth century, wise choices were being made about his enormous output.

This enthusiasm may not always have been entirely straightforward. The *Allgemeine Musikalische Zeitung* pointed out in February 1805 that "those who are always talking about Mozart often don't even know a single note of his works. Why is the Requiem not performed a second time? Why do we never hear the piano concertos? People want nothing but anecdotes." Several more years went by before a deep and genuine interest in Mozart developed. In 1805 the Paris Opéra for the first time produced a French version of *Don Giovanni*. Unfortunately, the music had been "revised" by Kalkbrenner; the libretto had been rewritten as a heroic opera rather than a dramma giocoso. Ballets were added and the production was sumptuous: in the finale, furies flew through the air and the stage was drenched with a rain of fire. The French singers were not very used to this type of music, but the piece had a certain success nevertheless and was well supported by Mozart's fans. Still, in four years it was performed only about thirty times. Géoffroy wrote:

> There is too much music in *Don Giovanni*. There are so many choruses, and they are so full and so loud that the audience is crushed, so to speak, under the weight of all that harmony. . . We have too much taste to be able to bear all these complicated parts. We only like what is simple, natural, and touching. There is really nothing else that is good and beautiful in music.[9]

As was seen earlier, it was thanks to the artists of the Théâtre italien in Paris that three Mozart operas were heard during the Empire in their original, Italian version for the first time. They were *The Marriage of Figaro* (1807), *Così fan tutte* (1809), and *Don Giovanni* (1811) and were repeated several times up until 1815. These performances were for the most part successful, in spite of the implacable dislike of some conservatives, like Géoffroy, who predictably remained hostile to Mozart. Writing in the *Journal de l'Empire* of 24 March 1810 he stated:

> As soon as a new work or a revival of Mozart's is announced, musicians all over this vast capital city, almost all members of the Germanic clan, start to sing canticles in honor of Mozart in every good Parisian home, and their religious zeal will not stop until they have persuaded every husband, wife, and daughter to go and see the new masterpiece of the God of music.

Fétis, who was much more open-minded, wrote about *The Marriage of Figaro:* "This masterpiece began a reform of musical taste in France and introduced the charms of lovely melodies augmented by richer harmony and instrumentation to a people who were ignorant of that art."[10]

The first act of *La Clemenza di Tito*, also first produced at the Théâtre italien in May 1812, aroused immense boredom in the Mozartophobes. Géoffroy demanded:

> Who is to blame? I shudder when I must name the guilty party. *Horresco referens*: should I say it? And if I do, what will the Conservatoire say? The author of this boredom which has been taking hold for some time and which is gaining citizenship in our concerts, the guilty one is Mozart.[11]

This systematic rejection for reasons that were not musical was made worse by the fact that critics during the Consulate and the Empire were hardly ever musicians who could otherwise have helped public taste evolve more rapidly. In a letter of 11 April 1801, the day after a concert given by Madame Grassini in Paris, the violinist Baillot wrote ironically: "Haydn and Mozart were no match for the charming productions of Nasolini and Zingarelli. The *-i's* [the Italian clan] overshadowed the *-arts* [the Mozart clan], you'd better believe it."[12] Even the German faction sometimes seemed to back down before particularly difficult works, such as the Symphony in G minor performed by the Conservatoire students in 1810. Naturally, Géoffroy grumbled that "in spite of the virtues of the key of G minor, this is a very boring symphony for those who have to listen to it because it is nothing but a vain jumble of difficult and confusing harmony, with no melodic theme, no tune to it, no inspiration."[13] But there were some more interesting comments, such as Framery's analysis of the symphony in the *Encyclopédie méthodique*, which ran to several pages. A cultivated musician and a connoisseur, he was full of admiration for this work that he judged to be "superb and worthy of its composer." But he noted nevertheless a number of "mistakes" that he considered unacceptable. This commentary certainly reflects the point of view of the French musical elite of the time. Mozart's symphonic music seemed difficult compared to Haydn's, which was then being heard throughout Paris. After all these thoughtless judgments it is a relief to find this comment on the "Jupiter" Symphony in the *Tablettes de Polymnie* (May 1810):

> This symphony is so rich in harmony and its effects are so scientific and complex that one can only grasp the orchestral details by paying exhaustingly close attention in order to have some idea of the mass of pictures that the composer wished to draw. Only a very small number of connoisseurs can understand the four-subject fugue at the end of this symphony.

This last statement remains true today for this symphony, which is so universally admired.

It will not be necessary to continue here in detail the chronology of the Paris premieres of Mozart's works. Their fame spread, not only in the capital city but throughout France, and official press opposition decreased after the Empire. During the Restoration, it was Rossini's turn to become the focus of conservative and nationalistic harangues. The rejection of Mozart and the type of passions his music aroused that began in 1801 seemed to foreshadow the quarrels that broke out fifteen years later over Rossini. None of the leading French composers of the time felt hostile toward Mozart, but this was not the case for Rossini. I think the reason is that in 1801 Mozart had already been dead for ten years, whereas in 1815 the young Italian genius took no pains to hide his ambition to conquer all Europe and may therefore have appeared as a dangerous rival.

None of the great contemporary German composers visited France during the Empire. Haydn probably intended to do so but did not because of his old age. After 1815, however, the climate of rising romanticism was more favorable to contacts with Germany; Spohr, Mendelssohn, and Weber, to mention only the most famous, did travel to France and stayed in Paris. According to Fétis, "the name of Weber had never even been heard in

France before 1816, in spite of our ongoing relations with Germany during the Empire." Yet after its premiere in Berlin on 18 June 1821, *Der Freischütz* rapidly became extremely popular in Paris and in the provinces from 1824 onward, despite mutilations by Castil-Blaze and the new French title of *Robin des bois*. From then on, the battle was won, and by 1830 German opera fascinated the elite of the young romantic generation. When in 1829 a German opera company returned to Paris, they were now received with enthusiasm. *L'Enlèvement du sérail, Fidelio*—its first performance in France —and *Der Freischütz* in its original version were presented at the Théâtre italien. But there had been many discussions and disagreements in order to arrive at this change in taste.

These were important reasons for the systematic opposition to Mozart by some of the French critics at the beginning of the nineteenth century. This was the very time when the classical style was going out of fashion. Such opposition could have been one more way for a certain public to oppose the rise of romanticism.

This quarrel was deeply rooted in eighteenth-century aesthetic theories about music. It was merely the final episode in the great debate that shook the Enlightenment period and had supporters of harmony and supporters of melody pitted against each other—the Rameau clan against the Rousseau clan, as it were. Some saw the spread of German music into France as a danger that instrumental music would come out of its traditional secondary role and submerge everything, even opera. Géoffroy wrote: "The development of instruments has been disastrous for melody. Our orchestras are killing our operas." Comparing Germany, home of harmony, and France, home of melody, was a cliché of contemporary musical criticism. This basic dichotomy obviously did not fully reflect the actual situation. As I have pointed out, in spite of the tendency of the best French composers to express themselves too exclusively in vocal music, instrumental music nevertheless had undergone an extraordinary development over the last forty years. Every day brought larger numbers of concert goers, and symphonies, concertos, and chamber music were more and more successful. Concert societies programmed at least as much instrumental as vocal music and reached an ever-growing public. Without going so far as to speak of the democratization of music, it can be said that compared to the eighteenth century, when music was still the privilege of aristocratic salons and high society, the Revolution managed to demystify concerts and opened them to a larger segment of society. This process began during the Directoire and continued into the nineteenth century during the Consulate. A lucid critic from the *Correspondance des amateurs musiciens* of 25 June 1803 noted this change:

> Those who go to concerts these days do so by choice rather than for personal display. This was not always the case before, as we may remember. Today people make music and listen to it for its own sake, to enjoy its charms. The prejudices of luxury have been conquered and ostentation crushed.

Instrumental music was becoming more and more popular, and not only music from Germany. Even at the Opéra, particularly from 1790 on, the role of the orchestra was growing thanks to the music of Cherubini, Méhul, and Le Sueur. Some people worried about this. For melody-lovers at the end of the eighteenth century, Grétry had been a sort of model. Just when Mozart's name was on everyone's lips in Paris, the *Mercure de France* of 23 October 1801 had this to say about Grétry's operas : " This scholarly [!] musician was clever enough to hide his science. He has not sacrificed melody to harmony nor drowned the human voice with pretentious instrumental noise." Madame de Bawr's anecdote recounted in her *Souvenirs* is significant here: Attending a performance of Cherubini's *Médée* in Grétry's company, she heard the old master bitterly declare on their way out: " You are young, my dear child; one day you will hear them beat time with cannon fire." Indeed, one of the most widespread criticisms leveled against Mozart at that time was that in his operas the orchestra was too rich, too busy, and that the wind instruments were too prominent.

It was only one step further to blame the bad influence of Germany in general for the obvious development of the opera orchestra and the symphony orchestra in France and in Italy at the time, and the step was quickly taken. I found this typical comment in a paper called *La Clef du Cabinet des Souverains* of 19 November 1801:

> That German noise, with its trombones, trumpets, drums, and tam-tam, has worked its way into Italian orchestras. Pergolesi must have turned over in his grave. In music, as in many other things, we should try to return to Nature and simplicity. Will France set the example in such a musical revolution?

The main argument of French critics against Mozart at the beginning of the nineteenth century can be summarized as follows: the development of the orchestra and of harmony, inspired by Germany, had as its consequence the disappearance of melody, which had been the only *meaningful* element in music capable of *imitating Nature* and speaking to the human heart. So we see that it was the late supporters of the Enlightenment's aesthetics who persisted in opposing Mozart's music in France. "German composers have concentrated on harmony, arias, instrumental works, and a full orchestra," wrote Géoffroy on 27 January 1808 about *The Marriage of Figaro*. One year later, on 6 February 1809, in his article on *Così*, he once more criticized Mozart, saying that he had a "special talent and rare aptitude for harmony," but concluding that

> if he had been born with the true spirit of his art, he would have opposed this humiliating and destructive revolution that could only favor mediocrity by corrupting the public taste with seductive and dangerous new styles. But instead he preferred to profit from the revolution himself and founded his glory on the corruption of this century.

It is, indeed, a fundamental change of aesthetics that took place after 1801 thanks to a broad section of the young French intelligentsia of the time. Admittedly, a few of these young people were diehard avant-gardists, ancestors of our modern snobs, who applauded because it was the fashionable thing to do, not because they understood much. But their role as a beneficial catalyst should not be underestimated. One must rise above these quarrels in order to understand what was really happening. Mozart's acceptance in Paris at the dawn of the nineteenth century marked the beginning of a new era for French taste. At the same time, the old classical aesthetics suffered a setback that was to prove fatal.

Surprisingly, on the side of Mozart's supporters, some of the critics were quite right, but unfortunately they remained anonymous. Far from believing, as the Italian poet Alessandro d'Azzia wrote, that "the period of improvement in instrumental music begins with the decline of vocal music,"[14] the more intelligent and intuitive minds understood perfectly well the importance and significance of what was happening. "These are inspired sounds, a supernatural language that can be understood only by the soul but cannot be put into writing," wrote the *Courrier des Spectacles* about the music of *Les Mystères d'Isis* on 29 August 1801. A few months later, in February 1802, the *Mercure de France* wrote the following comment about Méhul's *L'Irato*, an opera buffa pastiche that had just been staged in Paris:

"It would not be in vain for our French composers to take harmony lessons based on Mozart's music at the Opéra and Paisiello's music at the Théâtre des Bouffons." These words predict Stendhal's criticisms fifteen years later. Music was no longer considered an imitative art. Its purpose was to speak directly to the soul in a language that reason could not understand. Its kingdom began precisely where the power of words stopped. It opened wide the doors to mystery and the unknown.

In 1814, in the letter closing his *La Vie de Mozart*, Stendhal described in just these terms the Countess's melancholy in *The Marriage of Figaro*: "The feeling of the soul here can hardly be expressed and is probably far better painted in music than in words." Soon after, F.-R. de Toreinx, the first historian of French romanticism, assimilated the concept of romanticism to that of innovation (*Histoire du romantisme*, 1829). Under these circumstances it was only natural that the dilettantes of the early nineteenth century would have claimed Mozart as their own and that he would therefore be considered a "romantic" composer.

Afterword

An Evolution Without Revolution

$\mathcal{F}$ orty years elapsed between 1789 and 1830, with one revolution at the beginning and another at the end. These years were filled with a series of greatly varying regimes, bringing about tremendous political and social upheavals and convulsing society by exceptional violence. There was absolutely no continuity: a total break occurred each time a new system made a point of opposing the previous one. In short, there were forty years of chaos the likes of which had not existed in France for two centuries.

Was this period in the history of music also a time of musical revolutions? Clearly, the eighteenth-century styles disappeared. After having reigned supreme for a century, the grand motet made way for the Latin oratorio, which was born just before the French Revolution and became extremely successful throughout the nineteenth century. After 1815 the sinfonie concertante was on its way out. The *style galant*, so typical of Europe during the Enlightenment, was no longer fashionable in its decline. The *quatuor concertant*, trios, duets, and sonatas with bass accompaniment also gradually disappeared. And a new instrument, the piano, which could dialogue with strings and woodwinds on equal terms, was born. From 1830 on, a new generation of virtuosos reached unheard-of heights performing on this king of instruments, achievements that nobody could have imagined twenty years earlier. The young generation of 1830—that of Berlioz, Chopin, Bellini, and Meyerbeer—had practically nothing in common with the great masters that emerged at the end of the eighteenth century.

Yet the conditions under which these transformations came about seem extraordinary. There was no truly decisive step, no single-minded school of thought that can actually be said to have imposed itself. On the contrary, the change happened gradually, one might say almost furtively. The writings of the time give no trace of the slightest inclination toward iconoclastic revolt. The composers went on writing quietly on their own. New ground may have been broken, but it was never really fully explored. It is regrettable that some efforts were never followed up, such as Méhul's breakthrough in the symphony. Many composers were anxious to keep continuity with the past, and the respect they showed for their predecessors was perfectly genuine. This respectful attitude can often be detected in the works of French musicians of the time, and composers of opera or comic opera seemed naturally to refer to Gluck, Sacchini, Salieri, Piccini, or Grétry whenever they needed great models to shelter behind.

The new romantic generation of 1830 greeted Berlioz's *Symphonie fantastique* with terrific applause. On the night of its first performance they probably felt, and rightly so, that they were experiencing something quite exceptional. Yet its success did not create a scandal. The old French masters Cherubini, Le Sueur, and Berton, who were probably in attendance that evening, do not seem to have felt that war was being declared on them. In contrast to literary authors, musicians do not seem to have really wanted to shake the dust off the old wigs. There was no attempt at a total break, apparently no desire to provoke. And yet surely the *Symphonie fantastique* was just as extravagant as Victor Hugo's *L'Escalier dérobé* or *Le Lion superbe et généreux*.

Fétis's write-up of this work of genius in the *Revue musicale* the day after its first performance is absolutely typical of the refusal to admit that it is possible to break with well-established continuity:

> This symphony is really an extraordinary composition. There is clearly genius to be seen in the new effects, and two of the parts, *Un bal* (A Ball) and *La marche au supplice* (March to the Scaffold), show vast imagination. The work is individual in character and outside of the usual art forms, but in general, this music is more

astonishing than pleasant. It lacks charm, and although we have to admit that its author has great talent, we must regret that he does not use it in a way more in keeping with the purposes of art.

Nothing could be clearer. The eminent music critic may have praised "the genius of new effects," but only in order to point out that in going outside of "usual art forms," one risked losing one's way. This critical attitude is based on the idea that an artist cannot achieve success by going against tradition. On the contrary, it is by profound reflection on the masterpieces of previous generations and by an ever-increasing knowledge of the past that a musician can best hope to express his or her genius.

It can even happen that this reflection on one's own past and origins, which seems to me to be so characteristic of the artistic world in France at the turn of the century, could sometimes lead our composers to quite specious arguments that reveal much about their true mentality! They were trying to justify themselves, come what may, by invoking "the venerable and wise Antiquity," just as Boileau might have done a century-and-a-half earlier. For instance, Le Sueur, who was engrossed in Hellenistic ideas about music, claimed—without the slightest proof, mind you—to have found in Greek tragedy the equivalent of free recitative, strict recitative, and the modern operatic aria. After this piece of fake archaeology, he claimed naively to be surprised at the resemblance and concluded that nineteenth-century opera, with such a guarantee behind it, could only be on the right path.

This kind of intellectual exercise, which today we would call neurotic, is quite the reverse of a true historian's approach. However, it is very significant in that it reveals a terrible desire for self-justification and, perhaps, a need to deal with fear of the unknown self, which was then beginning to be felt. The unknown was rejected, and reassurance was sought by establishing continuity between past and present by inventing musical ancestors. Only in this way could one be sure that one was not the victim of a fatal error.

Le Sueur made his audience shiver when he first introduced *Ossian*, with its Celtic and Scandinavian mythologies, on the European opera stage. But he awkwardly attempted to integrate the occult powers of this mythology into the pantheon of Antiquity—Hebrew this time, rather than Greek —as if to exorcise them. In his religious music, in his *La Mort d'Adam* (The Death of Adam) whose marvelous final scene of apotheosis seems to foreshadow the last pages of Goethe's second part of *Faust*, he recommended that the artists interpret the scene "in the great Antique style."

This constant reference to Antiquity continued throughout these forty years, but the idea it invoked gradually changed. In Cherubini's *Médée* (1797) the tragic hero, alone with his destiny, is already agonizing over painful romantic dilemmas. The Antiquity depicted in *Médée* is no longer the same as in Gluck's *Iphigénie* or Sacchini's *Œdipe à Colone.* In Méhul's *Adrien* (1799), Spontini's *La Vestale* (1807), Le Sueur's *Alexandre à Babylone* (an opera composed at the end of the Empire but never produced on stage), and Spontini's *Olympie* (1819) can be seen the beginnings of the French style of historical grand opera—Spontini's *Fernand Cortez* (1809) is a superb example. The show, the pomp, the enormous numbers of performers, and the vast choruses came into use, dramatically and musically, to represent Antiquity in a more anecdotal way. The mythical element was exhausted in these great historical frescoes (already forerunners of the reign of Meyerbeer) as more and more local color was sought.

The neo-classicism of the Louis XVI period reached its final metamorphosis and died out gently at the dawn of a new era. There was no abrupt break between the Enlightenment and romanticism. Instead, the landscape changed gradually, as in a clever and discreet fade-out. It would make no sense to try to systematically oppose these two periods of French history, and I believe that the history of music provides a convincing argument against such an attempt.

The French Revolutionary Calendar

The French Revolutionary calendar was in effect from 22 September 1793 (which became 1 Vendémiaire) to 1 January 1806.

Revolutionary month	Modern-day equivalent
Vendémiaire	22 September to 21 October
Brumaire	22 October to 20 November
Frimaire	21 November to 20 December
Nivôse	21 December to 19 January
Pluviôse	20 January to 18 February
Ventôse	19 February to 20 March
Germinal	21 March to 19 April
Floreal	20 April to 19 May
Prairial	20 May to 18 June
Messidor	19 June to 18 July
Thermidor	19 July to 17 August
Fructidor	18 August to 16 September
Sanculottides	17 September to 21 September

Revolutionary year	Modern-day equivalent
I	1792–1793
II	1793–1794
III	1794–1795
IV	1795–1796
V	1796–1797
VI	1797–1798
VII	1798–1799
VIII	1799–1800
IX	1800–1801
X	1801–1802
XI	1802–1803
XII	1803–1804
XIII	1804–1805
XIV	1805–1 January 1806

Notes

Chapter 1

1. *Archives du département de Côte-d'Or*, notary's study Bouché, batch no. 2470.
2. Pierre, Constant. 1896. *L'École de chant de l'Opéra*. Paris.
3. *Archives nationales* (French National Archives, hereafter abbreviated as A.N.) AJ^{13}.1047.
4. On this topic, see: Pierre, Constant. 1895. *B. Sarrette et les origines du Conservatoire national de musique et de déclamation*. Paris.
5. Pierre, Constant. 1900. *Le Conservatoire*. Paris.
6. *Correspondance des professeurs et amateurs de musique*, 1 January 1803.
7. Pierre, Constant. 1895. *B. Sarrette et les origines.* . . . 186–187.
8. Pierre, Constant. 1895. *Le Magasin de musique à l'usage des fêtes nationales et du Conservatoire*. Paris. Rpt.: Minkoff, 1974.
9. Fortia de Piles. 1812. *Quelques réflexions d'un homme du monde sur les spectacles, la musique, le jeu et le duel*. Paris. 48.
10. Castil-Blaze. 1820. *De l'Opéra en France*, vol. 2. Paris. 310.
11. Simms, B. 1971. *Alexandre Choron (1771–1834) as a Historian and Theorist of Music*. Ph.D. Thesis, Yale University, New Haven, Conn.
12. Pierre, Constant. 1900. *Le Conservatoire*. Paris.
13. Pierre. 1900.

14. Simms, B. 1971. *Alexandre Choron.*
15. Fétis. "Choron." In *Biographie universelle des musiciens.*
16. Choron and Fayolle. 1810. "Introduction." In *Dictionnaire historique des musiciens.* Paris.
17. *Annonces, affiches et avis divers, 9 et 30 germinal an VIII* (29 March and 19 April 1799).
18. Grégoir. 1888–1891. *Souvenirs artistiques.* Brussels. 3: 110.
19. Pierre, Constant. 1900. *Le Conservatoire.* Paris.
20. Brévan, Bruno. 1980. *Les Changements de la vie musicale parisienne de 1774 à 1799.* Paris. 200.
21. Pujoulx, J.-B. 1801. *Paris à la fin du XVIIIᵉ siècle.* 64.
22. Lefebvre, Léon. 1908. *Le Concert de Lille, 1726–1816.* Lille. 49–50.
23. Cardavaque, A. de. 1885. "La Musique à Arras depuis les temps les plus reculées jusqu'à nos jours." In *Mémoires de l'Académie d'Arras.* 145.
24. *Archives départementales du Rhône.* T. 410.
25. *Archives départementales du Rhône.* T. 410.

Chapter 2

1. In Caen, for instance, Pizet was a composer of local reputation as director of concerts of the city and the Saint-Pierre church at the end of the Monarchy. He also composed a large number of patriotic hymns to be sung in various national celebrations. See: Fétis. Supplement to *Biographie universelle des musiciens.*
2. Ozouf, Mona. 1976. *La Fête révolutionnaire.* Paris.
3. Ehrard, Jean, and Paul Viallaneix. 1977. *Les Fêtes de la Révolution.* In *Actes du colloque de Clermont-Ferrand (juin 1974).* Paris: *Société des études robespierristes.*
4. Pierre, Constant. 1895. *B. Sarrette et les origines du Conservatoire national de musique et de déclamation.* Paris. 40.
5. Carlez, Jules. 1876. *La Musique à Caen de 1066 à 1848.* Caen.
6. Cotte, Roger. 1983. *Les Musiciens francs-maçons à la cour de Versailles et à Paris sous l'Ancien Régime.* State Doctoral Thesis, University of Paris-Sorbonne.
7. Jam, Jean-Louis. 1980. *Poésie et musique des fêtes révolutionnaires.* 3rd Cycle Thesis, University of Clermont-Ferrand.
8. Framery, N. E. Brumaire year IV (October–November 1795). *Avis aux poètes lyriques ou De la nécessité du rythme et de la césure dans les hymnes ou les odes destinées à la musique.* Paris.
9. Ehrard, Jean, and Paul Viallaneix. Op.Cit.
10. *Le Moniteur.* 6 April 1791.

11. *Révolutions de Paris.* April 1791. 667.
12. Genlis. Mme de. 1805. *Nouvelle Méthode de harpe.* Paris. 8.

Chapter 3

1. Bernier, P. 1977. *Actes du colloque de Clermont-Ferrand, 1974.* In *L'Opéra comme fête révolutionnaire.* Paris. 419–432.
2. Bernier. 1977.
3. Grégoir. 1888–1891. 3: 49.
4. Destranges, Étienne. 1893. *Le Théâtre à Nantes depuis ses origines jusqu'à nos jours, 1430–1893.* Paris.
5. A.N. AJ¹³. 52.
6. A.N. AJ¹³. 89.
7. A.N. AJ¹³. 73.
8. A.N. AJ¹³. 91
9. A.N. AJ¹³. 91
10. Destranges. 1893.
11. A.N. F²¹. 969.
12. *Tablettes de Polymnie.* 20 April 1811. 348.
13. *Tablettes de Polymnie.* 5 April 1811. 324–325.
14. *Tablettes de Polymnie.* 5 April 1811.
15. *Tablettes de Polymnie.* 5 April 1811.
16. Mongrédien, Jean. 1980. *Jean-François Le Sueur.* Bern. 664 ff.
17. Fayolle, F. J. M. Winter 1808. *Les Quatre saisons du Parnasse.*
18. A.N. F²¹. 969.
19. A.N. F²¹. 969.
20. A.N. AJ¹³. 94.
21. A.N. F²¹. 969.
22. A.N. F²¹. 969.
23. A.N. F²¹. 969
24. Paris. *Le Théâtre Feydeau et la rue des Colonnes (1791–1829).* In *100ᵉ Congrès national des sociétés savantes, Archéologie.* 1975. 255–273.
25. A.N. AJ¹³. 72. A decree dated 19 Ventôse year X (10 March 1801) determined how the company and the orchestra were formed. See also: Paris. *Réglemens pour l'Académie Royale de musique du 1ᵉʳ avril 1792.* 1792, to be compared, on this particular issue, to *Réglement pour l'Académie Impériale de musique du 1ᵉʳ vendémiaire an XIV* (23 September 1805). In 1792, there were still two serpents in the Opéra orchestra, but they no longer existed in 1805. Organological terms quickly evolved at the turn of the nineteenth century. In 1792, the bass section was made up of *10 basses et 4 contre-basses,* and in 1805, *12 violoncelles et 6 contre-basses.* A *Réglement de l'Opéra*

(5 May 1821), kept in the Bibliothèque Nationale, tells that there were two conductors leading the musicians, who then were *soixante-dix-sept concertans* (77 players).

26. *Almanach des spectacles de Paris pour 1815.*

27. *Allgemeine musikalische Zeitung.* 30 April 1817. 300.

28. *Allgemeine musikalische Zeitung.* 23 July 1800. 746.

29. Grégoir. 1888–1891. 3:101.

30. Grégoir. 1888–1891. 3:81–82.

31. On the contrary, future unmarried mothers were reduced to a minimum wage. A decree by the Prefect of the Palais de Luçay dated 9 Nivôse year XIV (30 December 1805) determined that "the wages of women employed by the Imperial Academy of Music who are unmarried or separated from their husbands will be reduced by half during the interruption of their work caused by pregnancy." A.N. AJ[13]. 72.

32. A.N. AJ[13]. 72. A few years later, at the beginning of the Empire, annual salaries of musicians and singers at the Tuileries Chapel ranged from 4000 and 1300 francs, respectively. For most of them, this was only a part-time occupation. As a means of comparison, the orchestra assistant—employed to move instruments, distribute orchestral parts, and so on—made 600 francs a year (*État des appointements des musiciens de la chapelle,* Vendémiaire year XIV [September 1805], from the author's collection).

33. A.N. AJ[13]. 46. Boxes AJ[13]. 52 and 67 also contain several files on Lays's claims and his blackmailing of the Opéra management—with a medical certificate as proof! On the exorbitant salary earned by this singer, see also the *Compte rendu au ministre de l'Intérieur par les citoyens Francoeur, Denesle et Baco, ex-administrateurs du Théâtre de la République et des Arts,* 31 Vendémiaire year VIII (22 October 1799). Beyond their regular salary and the fees paid to them for each performance, singers also received annual bonuses. For year VII (1798–1799), Lays's bonus was in the amount of 28,000 francs. The second highest-paid singer was the bass Chéron, at 11,000 francs.

34. A.N. AJ[13]. 112.

35. A.N. AJ[13]. 72. Also see *Réglement pour l'Académie Impériale de musique.* 1st Vendémiaire year XIV (23 September 1805). 48. Also 1792. *Réglemens pour l'Académie Royale de musique, 1er avril 1792.* Paris. 11. For those dates, they indicate slightly smaller royalty amounts.

36. A.N. AJ[13]. 1040.

37. A.N. AJ[13]. 72.

38. *Journal des Spectacles.* 4 Frimaire year X (25 November 1801).

39. See Chapter 7.

40. Paris. *Mémoires.* 1835. 4:323–324.

41. This is true in spite of the fact that there was a second female role, the Grande Vestale, which first introduced the voice of a mezzo-soprano, thus

completing the vocal quartet, a genre that became very popular in nineteenth-century opera, thanks especially to Verdi.

42. In June 1810 a reporter from the *Tablettes de Polymnie* wondered about the reason for the strange modulation "in Beethoven's manner" to the chorus leader's words *La vierge impure est honnie à jamais* (The impure virgin is banished forever): "Did the author want to emphasize the words and describe the impure Vestale being insulted by filling our ears with a dreadful jarring noise?"

43. 9 November 1803.

44. 30 June 1813.

45. Mongrédien, Jean. March 1980. *À propos de Rossini: une polémique Stendhal-Berton.* In *Stendhal e Milano, Atti del 14° congresso internazionale stendhaliano.* Milan. 673–693.

46. In Join-Dieterle, Catherine. 1981. *Les Décors de scène à l'Opéra de Paris à l'époque romantique.* Paris. Doctoral thesis. University of Paris-Sorbonne.

47. A.N. AJ¹³.112.

48. 10 October 1826.

49. Berlioz. 1971. *À travers chants.* Paris. 125.

50. Berlioz. 1971. 126.

51. A.N. O³. 1684.

52. Pougin, Arthur. 1891. Minkoff reprint 1973. *L'Opéra-Comique pendant la Révolution de 1788 à 1801.* Paris.

53. de Curzon, Henri. 1930. *Elleviou.* Paris.

54. *Allgemeine musikalische Zeitung.* 25 October 1809.

55. Pougin. 1891. *Les Spectacles de Paris, 1793.*

56. A.N. F⁷. 3491. On the Feydeau theater, see Mongrédien, Jean. 1980. *Jean-François Le Sueur.* Bern. 207–215.

57. A.N. F²¹. 1091 contains a curious letter from one of Feydeau's good female actors, Madame Verteuil, addressed to the Minister, Chaptal. She denounced the "treachery" of some of her colleagues who, without any attempt "to defend the common interest, secretly got together with a few artists from Favart. Thinking only of themselves, they declared unilaterally that they were the only Feydeau artists who could become shareholders in the new company."

58. 1820. *De l'Opéra en France* (On Opera in France). Paris. 1:30.

59. Preface of the score of *L'Irato.*

60. *Biographie universelle des musiciens.* Article "Berton."

61. Mongrédien. 1980. 264–265.

62. Grégoir. 1888–1891. 1:8.

63. Reichardt, J. F. 1804. *Vertraute Briefe aus Paris geschrieben.* 1:159.

64. Favre, Georges. 1945. *Boïeldieu, sa vie, son œuvre.* Paris.

65. Favre. 1945.

66. On this subject, see Gavoty, André. 1947. *La Grassini.* Paris. and Soubies, Albert. 1913. *Le Théâtre italien de Paris de 1801 à 1913.* Paris. Also, many unpublished documents concerning the re-opening of the Théâtre italien in Paris and its management by Mademoiselle Montansier can be found in the French National Archives, F[21]. 1111, 1112, 1116.

67. *Biographie universelle des musiciens.* Article "Nozzari."

68. Reichardt, J. F. 1804. *Vertraute Briefe aus Paris geschrieben.* 1:148.

69. *Allgemeine musikalische Zeitung.* 25 October 1809.

70. *Affiches, Annonces et Avis divers.* 18 Fructidor year IX (5 September 1801).

71. *Allgemeine musikalische Zeitung.* 9 September 1801.

72. d'Azzia, Alessandro. 1801. *Sur le rétablissement d'un théâtre bouffon italien à Paris.* Paris.

73. *Gazette nationale.* 16 Brumaire year X (7 November 1801). *Mercure de France.* 16 Frimaire year X (7 December 1801).

74. *Allgemeine musikalische Zeitung.* 21 August 1805.

75. *Allgemeine musikalische Zeitung.* 25 October 1809.

76. *Journal de l'Empire.* 6 November 1808.

77. Even before the Revolution, similar rivalry had arisen at the *Concert spirituel* between German singer Gertrud Mara and Portuguese singer Maria Francesca Todi and had given way to the war between "Maratists" and "Todists."

78. *Tablettes de Polymnie.* 5 November 1810.

79. *Allgemeine musikalische Zeitung.* 31 October 1811.

80. 5 July 1811.

81. *Tablettes de Polymnie.* 20 March 1811.

82. *Tablettes de Polymnie.* 5 November 1810.

83. *Correspondance des Professeurs et Amateurs de musique.* 28 May 1803.

84. *Correspondance des Professeurs et Amateurs de musique.* 28 May 1803.

85. *Le Moniteur* 17 July 1800.

86. Mademoiselle Avrillon. 1969. *Mémoires.* Paris. 196ff.

87. A.N. AJ[13]. 1129.

88. *Tablettes de Polymnie.* 5 February 1811.

89. On French writers' opinions of Paisiello, see Mongrédien, Jean. 1969. *Un compositeur oublié: Paisiello.* In *Revue des Deux Mondes* (November). 370–375. Also Claudon, Francis. 1979. *L'Idée et l'Influence de la musique chez quelques romantiques et notamment Stendhal.* Lille-Paris.

90. *Gazette de France.* 1 April 1817.

91. *Journal des Débats.* 3 February 1817.

92. *Gazette de France.* 14 May 1819.

93. *Journal de Débats.* 21 March 1821.

94. *Journal des Débats.* 25 November 1820.

95. *Biographie universelle des musiciens.* Article "Pasta."

96. See Mongrédien, Jean. 1980. *À propos de Rossini; une polémique Stendhal-Berton*. In *Stendhal e Milano, Atti del 14° congresso internationale Stendhaliano*. Milan. 673–693.

97. de Cardavacque. A. 1885. *L'Opéra en France, premières troupes lyriques à Arras*. In *Mémoires de l'Académie des lettres, sciences et arts d'Arras*. Arras. 106ff.

98. Barbé, J. J. 1908. *Théâtre à Metz*. Metz. and 1928. *Le Théâtre à Metz pendant la Révolution*. Reims.

99. Carlez. Jules. 1876. *La Musique à Caen de 1066 à 1848*. Caen. Mongrédien, Jean. 1980. *Jean-François Le Sueur*. Bern. 263. Destranges. E. 1893. *Le Théâtre à Nantes depuis ses origines jusqu'à nos jours, 1430–1893*. Paris.

100. *Bulletin de Lyon*. 30 Pluviôse year XI (19 February 1803).

101. Combarnous. V. 1927. *Histoire du Grand Théâtre de Marseille (1787–1819)*. Marseille.

102. *Archives municipales de Lyon*. R2. *Grand Théâtre*.

103. During the Empire wages rose constantly. In the provinces, journeymen earned very little, between one and two francs a day, depending on their local guild and working conditions. In 1791, engineers for the *Ponts et Chaussées* (Bridge and Highway System) in the Puy-de-Dôme made 2400 francs a year. In year VII (1798–1799), their salaries reached 4000 francs. At the same time, office managers' salaries went from 840 francs to 1200 francs. Sources: *Histoire sociale et économique de la France*. 1976. Volume 3. *L'Avènement de l'ère industrielle (1789–1880)*. Paris. 68ff. Chabert. A. 1949. *Essai sur les mouvements des revenus et de l'activité économique en France, 1798–1820*. Paris.

104. Lefebvre, Léon. 1901. *Histoire du théâtre de Lille*. Lille.

105. Grégoir. 1888–1891. 2:170.

106. Castil-Blaze. 1820. *De l'Opéra en France*. Paris. 2:254ff.

107. *Archives départementales du Rhône*. T 420.

108. Castil-Blaze. 1820.

109. *Archives départementales du Rhône*. T 415.

110. *Archives municipales de Lyon*. R2. Grand Théâtre.

111. 14 Fructidor year X (1 September 1802).

112. Destranges, E. 1893.

113. Rivière, A., and A. Jouffray, 1978. *Le Théâtre du Capitole (1542–1977)*. Toulouse.

114. Except where mentioned, all information provided in the following pages came from *Archives départementales du Rhône*. T 416. T 417. T 420. T 421. T 422. *Archives municipales de Lyon*. R2. *Grand Théâtre*.

115. Sallès. A. 1906. *L'Opéra italien et allemand à Lyon au dix-neuvième siècle*. Paris.

116. *Bulletin de Lyon.* 3 Floréal year XI (23 April 1803). 24 Floréal year XI (14 May 1803), and so on.
117. On this subject, see Chapter 3.

Chapter 4

1. Mongrédien, Jean. 1980. *Jean-François Le Sueur.* Bern. 51ff and 121ff.
2. Reichardt. 1804. *Vertraute Briefe aus Paris geschrieben.*
3. A.N. AJ¹³. 68.
4. 1967. *Revue de musicologie.* 2:137–174.
5. 5 February 1806.
6. On the history of this chapel, see Mongrédien 1980. 803ff.
7. Mongrédien, Jean. 1970. *La Musique aux fêtes du sacre de Charles X.* In *Recherches.* 10:87ff.
8. Head copyist at the chapel.
9. *Maître de chapelle* at Notre-Dame at the beginning of the nineteenth century.
10. Harpist and composer of the end of the eighteenth and the beginning of the nineteenth century.
11. *Maître de chapelle* at Notre-Dame from 1734 until 1748.
12. Article "Cherubini" in *Biographie universelle des musiciens.*
13. *Revue et Gazette musicale de Paris,* 10 June 1838.
14. *Revue et Gazette musicale de Paris,* 10 June 1838.
15. 4 July 1804.
16. *Correspondance des Professeurs et Amateurs de musique,* 30 Floréal year XII (20 May 1804).
17. *Tablettes de Polymnie,* 20 August 1811.
18. *Tablettes de Polymnie,* 5 December 1810.
19. Spohr. 1954. *Selbstbiographie. Kassel.* 2:131ff.
20. Article "Cherubini" in *Biographie universelle des musiciens.*
21. *Allgemeine musikalische Zeitung,* 30 August 1809 and 30 October 1811.
22. Motet *Confitebor,* dated 1770. Bibliothèque Nationale. *Musique.* Ms 7839.
23. Rousseau, Jean-Jacques. 1753. *Lettre sur la musique française.* Paris. 43.
24. Mongrédien 1980. 128.
25. Mongrédien 1980. 177–178 (note 87).
26. 23 Floréal year XII (12 May 1804).
27. Speyer, Edward. 1925. *Wilhelm Speyer, der Liederkomponist.* München.
28. Dr. Véron. 1853. *Mémoires d'un bourgeois de Paris.* Paris. 1:106.
29. Contrary to the practice of the time, this oratorio had its first performance in a provincial city, Lille, instead of Paris (3 November 1800).
30. Grégoir. *Souvenirs artistiques.* 2:125.

31. A.N. AJ[13]. 89.
32. *Allgemeine musikalische Zeitung*, 16 January 1805.
33. Grégoir. *Souvenirs artistiques.* 2:145ff.
34. *Allgemeine musikalische Zeitung*, 15 May 1805.
35. Grégoir. *Souvenirs artistiques.* 2:8.
36. 19 May 1804.
37. 10 Nivôse year XIII (31 December 1804).
38. Article "Chant" In 1808. *Cours complet d'harmonie et de composition.* Paris.
39. Mellinet, Camille. 1837. *De la musique à Nantes depuis les temps les plus reculés jusqu'à nos jours.* Nantes.
40. de Sonneville, René. 1958. *Un musicien de Bordeaux au XVIIIᵉ siècle: Franz Beck.* In *Revue historique de Bordeaux et du Département de la Gironde.* 101–105.
41. Carlez, Jules. 1876. *La Musique à Caen de 1066 à 1848.* Caen.
42. Guibal du Rivage, A. 1978. *Œuvres littéraires et musicales. Centre de documentation occitane.* Béziers.
43. Simms, B. 1971. *Alexandre Choron (1771–1834) as a Historian and Theorist of Music.* Ph. D. diss. Yale University.
44. Simms. 1971.
45. 1827. *Revue musicale.*
46. 1827. *Revue musicale.* 378ff.

Chapter 5

1. *Correspondance des Professeurs et Amateurs de musique*, 15 January 1803.
2. 14 November 1806.
3. 4 April 1812.
4. *De l'Opéra en France.* 2:334ff.
5. Pougin. Arthur. 1874. *Notice sur Rode.* Paris. 9.
6. Article "Concert." In *Dictionnaire historique des musiciens.*
7. *Journal de Paris*, 24 Pluviôse year VIII (13 February 1800).
8. *Le Courrier des spectacles*, 8 January 1797.
9. Article "Concert." *Dictionnaire historique des musiciens.*
10. *Le Censeur des journaux*, 18 and 30 January 1797.
11. *Allgemeine musikalische Zeitung*, 23 March 1803.
12. de Goncourt. E. and J. 1855. *Histoire de la société française pendant le Directoire.* Paris. 374.
13. Pierre. Constant. 1895. *B. Sarrette et les origines du Conservatoire national de musique et de déclamation.* Paris. See also Brook, Barry S. 1962. *La Symphonie française dans la seconde moitié du XVIIIᵉ siècle.* Paris. 392ff.
14. Pierre, Constant. *Le Conservatoire national de musique et de déclamation.*

Beginning in 1802, the *Correspondance des Professeurs et Amateurs de musique* also devotes a section to these concerts.

15. *Tablettes de Polymnie*, 20 July 1811.
16. Pierre, Constant. *Le Conservatoire national de musique et de déclamation.* 169.
17. Reichardt, J. F. *Vertraute Briefe aus Paris geschrieben*, 22 November 1802. 1:156.
18. *Allgemeine musikalische Zeitung*, 18 April 1804.
19. *Allgemeine musikalische Zeitung*, 21 June 1809.
20. *Allgemeine musikalische Zeitung*, 23 August 1809.
21. Article "Habeneck." In *Biographie universelle des musiciens.*
22. *Allgemeine musikalische Zeitung*, 18 April 1804.
23. Grégoir. *Souvenirs artistiques.* 3:22.
24. *Allgemeine musikalische Zeitung*, 10 February 1802.
25. In 1838, in an article praising Tilmant, conductor at the Théâtre italien, a reporter wrote: "He does not tire his audience by hitting the music stand with his bow, as the conductor of the Opéra or the Conservatoire so often does." In *Revue et Gazette musicale*, 4 November 1838.
26. *Réglemens du concert des amateurs de Paris arrêtés en assemblée générale le 15 Brumaire an VIII* (6 November 1799).
27. Lafond, Paul. No date. *Garat*. Paris. 216–217.
28. *Allgemeine musikalische Zeitung*, 14 January and 25 February 1801.
29. *Allgemeine musikalische Zeitung*, 9 March 1803.
30. 10 February 1802. Report dated 28 December 1801.
31. *Allgemeine musikalische Zeitung*, 9 March 1803 and 8 February 1804.
32. Reichardt. *Vertraute Briefe aus Paris geschrieben.* 2:32ff. Letter of 7 January 1803.
33. *Correspondance des professeurs et amateurs de musique*, 29 January 1803.
34. *Allgemeine musikalische Zeitung*, 6 September 1801.
35. *Journal général de la littérature de France*, 1800. 3:63 and 189–191.
36. *Allgemeine musikalische Zeitung*, 8 February 1804.
37. *Correspondance des professeurs et amateurs de musique*, 26 January and 30 March 1805.
38. *Correspondance des professeurs et amateurs de musique*, 26 January and 30 March 1805.
39. Lafond, Paul. No date. *Garat*. Paris. 216–217.
40. *Correspondance des Professseurs et Amateurs de musique*, July–August 1803, *passim.*
41. *Allgemeine musikalische Zeitung*, 24 August, 21 September, and 9 November 1803. 8 February 1804. January 1805. See also Grégoir. *Souvenirs artistiques.* 2:130.
42. *Correspondance des Professeurs et Amateurs de musique*, 5 January 1805.

43. *Revue et Gazette musicale de Paris*, 5 September 1839.

44. François-Sappey, Brigitte. 1978. "Baillot par lui-même." In *Recherches*. 18:202.

45. *Le Mercure de France*, April 1797. 105.

46. François-Sappey 1978. 177.

47. de La Laurencie, Lionel. *L'école française du violon*. 2:501ff.

48. Collections of this periodical are shared by both the Bibliothèque Nationale and the Bibliothèque de l'Arsenal. The first issue of the *Journal* is dated 15 April 1793, and the last *Annuaire* preserved is that of 1805.

49. *Le Mercure de France*, Frimaire year X (November–December 1801). 474.

50. Grégoir. *Souvenirs artistiques*. 2:21.

51. *Correspondance des Professeurs et Amateurs de musique*, 1805, *passim*.

52. *Annonces, affiches et avis divers*, 25 and 27 Germinal year VII (14 and 16 April 1799) and 11 Frimaire year VIII (2 December 1799).

53. *Journal de l'Empire*, 7 and 23 November 1808.

54. *Tablettes de Polymnie*, January 1810. 8–9.

55. In 1800, all three leading French opera theaters (Opéra, Opéra-Comique, and the Feydeau Theater) gave concerts. The most successful ones were Feydeau's: "The orchestra and the hall seemed to be better-suited for this kind of performance." (*Année théâtrale, almanach pour l'an IX*).

56. *Annonces, affiches et avis divers*, 6 Germinal year VII (26 March 1799).

57. *Allgemeine musikalische Zeitung*, 24 December 1800. See also Grégoir. *Souvenirs artistiques*. 3:43.

58. *Correspondance des Professeurs et Amateurs de musique*, 25 December 1802.

59. Grégoir. *Souvenirs artistiques*. 3:54.

60. François-Sappey 1978. 178.

61. Reichardt. *Vertraute Briefe aus Paris geschrieben*. Letters of 24 December 1802, 4 February 1806, 11, 26, and 29 March 1803, and 4 April 1803.

62. Monnais, Édouard. 1844. *Souvenirs de la vie d'artiste*. 302ff.

63. Blondeau, Auguste-Louis. 1847. *Histoire de la musique moderne*. Paris. 290.

64. Blondeau 1847.

65. *Correspondance des Professeurs et des Amateurs de musique*, 27 November 1802.

66. *Correspondance des Professeurs et Amateurs de musique*, 11 January 1804.

67. *Tablettes de Polymnie*, 20 March 1811.

68. *Tablettes de Polymnie*, 5 January 1811.

69. Fétis, Édouard. In *Revue et Gazette musicale de Paris*, 5 September 1839; and Fétis, F. J. Article "Cherubini." In *Biographie universelle des musiciens*.

70. A.N. AJ^{13}, 69, IV.

71. Mademoiselle Avrillon. 1969. *Mémoires*. Paris. 196.

72. *Revue et Gazette musicale de Paris*, 5 September 1839.

73. *Le Miroir des spectacles*, 20 March 1821.

74. A.N. AJ¹³, 113, II.

75. Moscheles had already given one concert the previous year (25 February 1821). A.N. AJ¹³, 112.

76. A.N. AJ¹³, 118.

77. A.N. AJ¹³, 114.

78. A.N. AJ¹³, 111, VI and 115, I.

79. A.N. AJ¹³, 110, 111, 113.

80. Elwart, A. 1860. *Histoire de la Société des concerts du Conservatoire impérial de musique.* Paris.

81. Elwart 1860.

82. Elwart 1860.

83. François-Sappey, Brigitte. 1974. "La Vie musicale à Paris à travers les mémoires d'Eugène Sauzey (1809–1901)." In *Revue de musicologie.* 55:159–210.

84. François-Sappey 1978. 127ff.

85. *Le Miroir des spectacles,* 21 and 24 March 1821.

86. See Chapter 4 on Sacred Music.

87. *Revue musicale,* 1827. 190.

88. Niquet, E. No date. *Les Anciennes Sociétés musicales d'Amiens.* Cayeux-sur-Mer. 25. In a Minkoff reprint. 1980. *La Vie musicale dans les provinces françaises.* Geneva. 4:287.

89. Niquet. No date.

90. Lefebvre, Léon. 1908. *Le Concert de Lille, 1726–1816.* Lille. 39.

91. Mellinet, Camille. 1837. *De la Musique à Nantes depuis les temps les plus reculés jusqu'à nos jours.* Nantes.

92. Céleste, Raymond. 1900. *Les Sociétés de Bordeaux: les sociétés musicales pendant la Révolution (1792–1800).* Bordeaux.

93. *Allgemeine musikalische Zeitung,* 14 January 1801.

94. *Archives départementales du Rhône.* T. 410.

95. Guibal du Rivage, Alexandre. 1978. *Œuvres littéraires et musicales. Centre de documentation occitane.* Béziers.

96. Guibal du Rivage 1978.

97. I owe these facts about Douai to the kindness of one of my students, Guy Josselin, author of a thesis entitled *La vie musicale dans le nord de la France au XIXᵉ siècle.*

98. Mellinet 1908.

99. Lefebvre 1908. 39.

100. Carlez, Jules. 1876. *La Musique à Caen de 1066 à 1848.* Caen.

101. *Correspondance des Professeurs et Amateurs de musique,* February 1803.

102. *Correspondance des Professeurs et Amateurs de musique,* February 1803.

103. *Correspondance des Professeurs et Amateurs de musique,* 18 December 1802.

104. Carlez 1876.

105. Mellinet 1908.
106. Sallès, Antoine. 1927. *Les Premières exécutions à Lyon des œuvres de Beethoven.* Paris.
107. *Bulletin de Lyon,* 13 Prairial year XII (2 June 1804).
108. *Correspondance des Professeurs et Amateurs de musique,* January 1805.
109. Article "Dacosta." In *Biographie universelle des musiciens.*

Chapter 6

1. Claudon, Francis. 1979. *L'Idée et l'influence de la musique chez quelques romantiques et notamment Stendhal.* Lille-Paris. 410.
2. *Vie de Haydn.* In collection *Les Introuvables.* 100.
3. *Tablettes de Polymnie,* 5 April 1811.
4. Brook, Barry S. 1962. *La Symphonie française dans la seconde moitié du XVIIIe siècle.* Paris.
5. Choron, A. 1810. *Dictionnaire historique des musiciens.* Preface.
6. Pougin, A. 1889. *Méhul, sa vie, son génie, son caractère.* Paris. 303.
7. *Journal de l'Empire,* 27 May 1809.
8. Introduction to *E. N. Méhul, Three Symphonies.* 1982. In *The Symphony, 1720–1840.* New York and Paris. Also *E. N. Méhul, Symphony no. 1.* 1985. In *Recent Researches in the music of the nineteenth and early twentieth centuries.* A.-R. Editions, Madison. Vol. 6.
9. For all symphonies published at that time, including those of Haydn, no conductor's score was printed, only orchestral parts. The conductor used the first violin part which sometimes indicated, in small type, entrances of other instruments when the violins were silent.
10. Courrier des spectacles, 28 January 1797.
11. *Allgemeine musikalische Zeitung,* 6 June 1810.
12. *Allgemeine musikalische Zeitung,* 7 March 1838.
13. Article "Symphonie." In *Encyclopédie méthodique.*
14. The manuscript is in the *Bibliothèque nationale,* under the reference Ms. 1432.
15. Hérold's two Italian symphonies have been published in the United States, as part of a collection devoted to *Symphonies in Europe from 1720 to 1840* (Garland Publishing). They were not available before and could not have had any influence in their time.
16. Baronne de Bawr. *Histoire de la musique.* 199.
17. See Chapter 4.
18. Baillot, Pierre. 1825. *Notice sur Viotti.* Paris.
19. François-Sappey, Brigitte. 1978. *Baillot par lui-même.* In *Recherches.* 18:127.
20. C. Lafont, a pupil of Kreutzer, was famous in France during the first 30 years

of the nineteenth century. He also travelled throughout Europe during his young years. In 1812, for instance, he competed with Paganini in Milan.

21. Baillot, R. "Baillot à Vienne." In *Le Ménestrel*, 2 October 1864.

22. *Allgemeine musikalische Zeitung*, 9 July 1800, 13 May 1801, 18 April 1804, 15 May 1805, and 21 June 1809. The paper repeatedly compared the three virtuosos of the French violin school of the time.

23. Baillot, Rode, and Kreutzer. *Méthode de violon adoptée par le Conservatoire. Au magasin de musique du Conservatoire.* Paris.

24. François-Sappey, Brigitte 1978.

25. *Allgemeine musikalische Zeitung*, 21 June 1809.

26. de Meude-Monpas, J.-J.-O. 1787. *Dictionnaire de musique.* Paris.

27. It should be noted that shortly before 1810, I. Pleyel published a series of Mozart's quartets and quintets in pocket scores under the title *Œuvres de Mozart en partitions.*

28. Article "Concerto." In *Encyclopédie méthodique.* Vol. 1.

29. Blondeau, A.-L. 1847. *Histoire de la musique moderne.* 303.

30. Rousseau, J.-J. Article "Quatuor." In *Dictionnaire de musique.*

31. Rousseau, J.-J. Article "Quatuor." In *Dictionnaire de musique.*

32. de Rothschild, G. 1962. *Boccherini.* Paris. 131–133.

33. de Momigny, J.-J. 1808. *Cours complet d'harmonie et de composition.* Paris.

34. Framery, Ginguené, and Momigny. 1797–1818. *Encyclopédie méthodique, musique.* Paris.

35. Baillot, Rode, and Kreutzer. *Méthode de violon adoptée par le Conservatoire.*

36. *Journal de Paris*, 25 January 1805.

37. *Journal de l'Empire*, 20 and 24 March 1810, and 25 April 1812.

38. Article "Dussek." In *Biographie universelle des musiciens.*

39. *Allgemeine musikalische Zeitung*, 30 October 1811.

40. *Allgemeine musikalische Zeitung*, 21 June 1809.

41. *Allgemeine musikalische Zeitung*, 21 February 1810.

42. Article "Sonate." In *Encyclopédie méthodique.*

43. Favre, G. 1953. *La Musique française de piano avant 1830.* Paris.

44. Article "Variation." In *Dictionnaire de musique moderne.*

Chapter 7

1. *Allgemeine musikalische Zeitung*, 9 June and 6 October 1802.

2. Lesure, François. 1980. "Les premières éditions françaises de Beethoven, 1800–1810." In *Gedenkschrift Günter Henle.* München. 326–331.

3. Article "Malibran." In *Bibliographie universelle des musiciens.*

4. Prod'homme, J.-G. 1927. "Les débuts de Beethoven en France." In *Beethovens Zentenarfeier.* Vienna. 116–122.

5. François-Sappey, Brigitte. 1978. "Baillot par lui-même." In *Recherches*. 18:179.

6. Framery and Momigny. 1818. Article "Sonate." In *Encyclopédie méthodique*. Paris.

7. I borrowed the substance of the following pages from various reports published in newspapers of the time, namely: *Journal de Paris* (Brumaire, Frimaire year X), *Journal des Débats* (Brumaire year X), *La Clef du cabinet des Souverains* (Brumaire year X), *La Décade philosophique, littéraire et politique* (Frimaire year X), *La Gazette nationale* (Brumaire, Frimaire year X), *Le Courrier des spectacles* (Brumaire, Frimaire, and Nivôse year X), *Allgemeine musikalische Zeitung* (October 1801, February 1802), *Journal des Luxus und der Moden* (December 1801, January and March 1802).

8. *Le Courrier des spectacles*, 18 Fructidor year IX (5 September 1801). At the same time Méhul stated that he considered Mozart "one of the greatest musical geniuses of all times." (*Allgemeine musikalische Zeitung*, 17 March 1802).

9. *Journal de l'Empire*, 19 and 20 October 1805.

10. Article "Berton." In *Biographie universelle des musiciens*.

11. *Journal de l'Empire*, 5 May 1812.

12. François-Sappey, Brigitte 1978. 202.

13. Grégoir. 1888–1889. *Souvenirs artistiques*. Brussels. 3:172.

14. d'Azzia, Alexandre. 1801. *Sur le rétablissement d'un théâtre bouffon italien à Paris*.

Bibliography

I. Manuscript Sources

French National Archives
    Series AJ^{13} (Archives of the Opéra)
    Series O^2 and O^3 (House of the Emperor and House of the King)
    Series F^{21} (Decrees by the Censorship Commissions)
Diocesan Archives of Paris
    Registers of the Debates of the Saint-Roch Manufacture
Archives of the *Société des Auteurs et Compositeurs dramatiques* (SACD), Paris
    Librettists' Registers (1794–1796)
Archives of Notre Dame Museum
    Registers of the Debates of the Chapter (Empire and Restoration)
Rhône Departmental Archives
    Series T (Grand Théâtre and *Théâtre des Célestins*)
Municipal Archives of Lyon
    Series R^2 (Grand Théâtre).

N.B.: Pierre Baillot's unpublished letter mentioned in the Preface is in the author's personal collection.

Additional manuscript sources include the Peyrot File in the Music Section of the *Bibliothèque nationale*, which contains very valuable references to the press at the end of the eighteenth century.

II. Printed Sources

A. The press

Press articles constitute the bulk of my printed sources. Considering the vast number of articles, I necessarily had to be selective in my research. Many interesting discoveries remain to be made.

During the period 1789–1830 the only strictly musical periodicals that existed were as follows:

Allgemeine musikalische Zeitung (beginning in 1798)
Correspondance des Amateurs musiciens, then *Correspondance des Professeurs et Amateurs de musique* (1802–1805)
Tablettes de Polymnie (1810–1811)
Revue musicale by Fétis (from 1827)

Other periodicals consulted include the following:

Annonces, affiches et avis divers
Annuaire du Lycée des Arts
Bulletin de Lyon
Le Censeur des journaux
Chronique de Paris
La Clef du cabinet des Souverains
Le Courrier des Spectacles
La Décade philosophique, littéraire et politique
La Feuille de Douai
Frankreich (This review is a gold mine of information on Paris life during the Directoire and the Consulate. It was published in Altona. The only issue preserved in France is at the Strasbourg National and University Library, reference D 119822)
Gazette de France
Gazette nationale ou le Moniteur universel
Journal de l'Empire
Journal de Paris
Journal des Débats
Journal des Luxus und der Moden

Journal du Lycée des Arts
Mercure de France
Le Miroir des spectacles
Le Moniteur universel
Petites Affiches de Lyon
La Quotidienne

Most of the articles (feuilletons) written by Géoffroy on the Opéra, the Opéra-Comique, and the Théâtre italien were published in the *Journal des Débats* and the *Journal de l'Empire* and have been gathered in his *Cours de littérature dramatique* (1825 edition, Volume 5).

Much can be learned by consulting the various *Almanachs* that appeared, most of them annually, since the Monarchy. Unfortunately, some of those collections are incomplete: *Almanach national, Almanach impérial, Almanach royal, Almanach des spectacles de Paris,* and so on. A lot of information can be found there, year after year, on concert and opera houses, singers and musicians, frequency of performances, and more.

B. General writings

Agoult, Marie, Countess of. 1877. *Mes souvenirs*. Paris.
Azzia, A. d'. Year IX (1801). *Sur le rétablissement d'un opéra bouffon italien à Paris*. Paris.
Bawr. Madame de. 1853. *Mes souvenirs*. Paris.
Berlioz, Hector. 1968. *Les Grotesques de la musique*. Paris: Léon Guichard.
_____. 1971. *À travers chants*. Paris: Léon Guichard.
_____. 1972. *Correspondance générale*. Volume 1 (1803–1832). Paris: Pierre Citron, ed.
_____. 1973. *Evenings with the Orchestra*. Chicago. Trans. of *Les Soirées de l'orchestre*, Paris.
_____. 1974. *New Letters of Berlioz, 1830–1868*. Westport, Connecticut: Greenwood Press.
_____. 1990 *The Memoirs of Hector Berlioz*. 3rd edition. London.
_____. 1991. *Mémoires*. Paris.
Blangini, F. 1834. *Souvenirs*. Paris.
Blondeau, A.-L. 1847. *Histoire de la musique moderne*. Paris.
Castil-Blaze. 1820. *De l'Opéra en France*. 2 volumes. Paris.
_____. 1832. *Chapelle-musique des rois de France*. Paris.
_____. 1855. *L'Académie impériale de musique de 1645 à 1855*. Paris.
_____. 1856. *L'Opéra italien de 1548 à 1856*. Paris.
Choron, A., and F. Fayolle. 1810. *Dictionnaire historique des musiciens*. 2 volumes. Paris.

Coup de fouet (Le) ou Revue de tous les théâtres de Paris. Year XI (1803). Paris.

Fétis, F.-J. 1860–1881. *Biographie universelle des musiciens.* 10 volumes. Second edition revised by A. Pougin in 1884. Paris.

Framery. Ginguené. Momigny. 1791–1818. *Encyclopédie méthodique-Musique.* Paris.

Grégoir, G.-J. 1888–1889. *Souvenirs artistiques.* 3 volumes. Brussels.

Grétry, A. Year V (1796–1797). *Mémoires ou essais sur la musique.* 3 volumes. Paris.

Guibal du Rivage, A. 1978. *Œuvres littéraires et musicales.* Béziers: Centre national de documentation occitane.

Martine. 1813. *De la musique dramatique en France. Paris.*

Momigny, J.-J. de. 1808. *Cours complet d'harmonie et de composition.* Paris.

Monnais, E. (also named Paul Smith). 1844. *Esquisses de la vie d'artiste.* Paris.

Pincherle, M. 1939. *Musiciens peints par eux-mêmes.* Paris.

Pujoulx, J.-B. Year IX (1801). *Paris à la fin du XVIIIᵉ siècle.* Paris.

Reglemens du concert des amateurs de Paris arrêtés en assemblée générale le 15 Brumaire an VIII (6 November 1799).

Reglemens pour l'Académie Royale de musique du 1ᵉʳ avril 1792. 1792. Paris.

Reglement pour l'Académie Impériale de musique du 1ᵉʳ Vendémiaire an 14 (23 September 1805).

Reichardt, J.-F. 1976. *Briefe, die Musik betreffend.* Leipzig. Translated by A. Laquiante. 1896. *Un hiver à Paris sous le Consulat (1802–1803).* Paris.

Russe (Le) à l'Opéra ou Réflexions sur les institutions musicales de la France. Year X (1802). Paris.

Scribe and Mazières. 1823. *Rossini à Paris ou le Grand Dîner.* Paris.

Sevelinges. 1818. *Le Rideau levé ou Petite Revue des grands théâtres.* Paris.

Speyer, E. 1925. *Wilhelm Speyer, der Liederkomponist.* Munich.

Spohr, L. 1954. *Selbstbiographie.* First published Kassel, 1860–1861; English translation London, 1865 and 1878.

Tiersot, J. 1924–1927. *Lettres de musiciens écrites en français.* Turin.

III. Bibliography

Alahaydoyan. 1970–1971. *Les Tentatives de renouveau du chant choral au début du XIXᵉ siècle en France.* Thesis, Free University of Brussels.

Baldensperger, F. 1925. *Sensibilité musicale et romantisme.* Paris.

Barbé, J.-J. 1908. *Le Théâtre à Metz.* Metz.

_____. 1928. *Le Théâtre à Metz pendant la Révolution.* Reims.

Barbier, P. 1982. *Spontini à Paris.* Advanced degree thesis, Rennes.

Bartlet, E. 1982. *Étienne Nicolas Méhul and Opera during the French Revolution, Consulate and Empire: a Source, Archival and Stylistic Study.* Ph. D. dissertation, University of Chicago.

_____. 1984. *A Newly Discovered Opera for Napoléon.* In *Acta musicologica.* 56. II. pp. 266–296.

Barzun, J. 1950. *Berlioz and the Romantic Century*. 2 volumes. Boston.

Benton, R. 1977. *Ignace Pleyel: a Thematic Catalogue of his Compositions*. New York.

Bouteillier. 1860–1880. *Histoire des théâtres de Rouen*. Rouen.

Boyer d'Agen. 1909. *Ingres d'après une correspondance inédite*. Paris.

Brevan, B. 1980. *Les Changements de la vie musicale parisienne (1774–1799)*. Paris.

Brook, Barry S. 1962. *La Symphonie française dans la seconde moitié du XVIIIe siècle*. Paris.

Bruneau, A. 1901. *La Musique française*. Paris.

Cannone, B. *La réception des opéras de Mozart dans la presse parisienne (1793–1829)*. Klincksieck. 1991. Paris.

Cardevacque, A. de. 1885. *L'Opéra en France: premières troupes lyriques à Arras*. In *Mémoires de l'Académie des sciences, lettres et arts d'Arras*. Arras.

Carlez, J. 1876. *La Musique à Caen de 1066 à 1848*. Caen.

Céleste, R. 1900. *Les Anciennes Sociétés musicales à Bordeaux*. Bordeaux.

———. 1900. *Les Sociétés musicales pendant la Révolution (1792–1800)*. Bordeaux.

Charlton, D. 1973. *Orchestration and Orchestral Practice in Paris (1789–1810)*. Ph. D. dissertation, Cambridge University.

———. 1982. Introduction to *E. N. Méhul, Three Symphonies*. In *The Symphony (1720–1840)*. New York and London.

———. 1985. *E. N. Méhul, Symphony No. 1*. In *Recent Researches in the Music of the Nineteenth and Early Twentieth Centuries*. Volume 6. Madison, Wisconsin: A.R. Editions, Inc.

Claudon, F. 1979. *L'idée et l'influence de la musique chez quelques romantiques et notamment Stendhal*. Lille and Paris: Champion.

Combarnous, V. 1927. *Histoire du Grand Théâtre de Marseille (1787–1819)*. Marseille.

Curzon, H. de. 1930. *Elleviou*. Paris.

Daups, M. 1975. *Un instrument romantique: le violoncelle en France de 1804 à 1915*. Advanced degree thesis, Aix-Marseille.

Dean, W. 1967–1968. *Opera under the French Revolution*. In *Proceedings of the Royal Musical Association*. No. 94. London. pp. 77–95.

Deane, B. 1965. *Cherubini*. London.

Della Croce, V. 1983. *Cherubini e i musicisti italiani del suo tempo*. 2 volumes. Turin.

Destranges, E. 1893. *Le Théâtre à Nantes depuis ses origines jusqu'à nos jours (1430–1893)*. Paris.

Devriès, A., and F. Lesure. 1979. *Dictionnaire des éditeurs de musique français*. Volume 1, *Des origines à 1820 environ*. Geneva.

Ehrard, J., and P. Viallaneix. 1977. *Les Fêtes de la Révolution*. In *Colloque de Clermont-Ferrand, June 1974*. Paris.

Elwart, A. 1860. *Histoire de la Société des concerts du Conservatoire impérial de musique*. Paris.

Fauquet, J.-M. 1981. *Les Sociétés de musique de chambre à Paris de la Restauration à 1870*. Advanced degree thesis, Paris.

Favre, G. 1944–1945. *Boïeldieu, sa vie, son œuvre*. Paris.

_____. 1953. *La musique de piano avant 1830*. Paris.

Fleischmann, T. 1965. *Napoléon et la musique*. Brussels.

Fragapane, P. 1983. *Spontini*. Florence.

François-Sappey, B. 1974. *La vie musicale à Paris à travers les mémoires d'Eugène Sauzey (1809–1901)*. In *Revue de musicologie*. 60. p. 159–210.

_____. 1978. *Baillot par lui-même*. In *Recherches*. Volume 18. p. 127 ff.

_____. 1989. *Alexandre P. F. Boëly, 1785–1858*. In *Aux amateurs de livres*. Paris.

Gavoty, A. 1947. *La Grassini*. Paris.

Gomart, C. Undated. *Notice historique sur la maîtrise de Saint-Quentin*. In *Études Saint-Quentinoises*. Volume 1.

Goncourt, E. de, and J. de Goncourt. 1855. *Histoire de la société française pendant le Directoire*. Paris.

Gougelot, H. 1937. *Catalogue des romances françaises publiées sous la Révolution et l'Empire*. Melun.

_____. 1938. *La Romance française sous la Révolution et l'Empire*. Melun.

Guichard, L. 1955. *La Musique et les lettres au temps du Romantisme*. Paris.

Hellouin and Picard. 1911. *Un musicien oublié: Catel*. Paris.

Humblot, E. 1909. *Un musicien joinvillais de l'époque de la Révolution, François Devienne (1759–1803)*. Saint-Dizier.

Jam, J.-L. 1980. *Poésie et musique des fêtes révolutionnaires*. Advanced degree thesis, Clermont-Ferrand.

Julien, J.-R., and J. Mongrédien. 1991. *Œvres, pratiques et manifestations musicales sous la Révolution, 1788–1800*. Du May. Paris.

Jullien, A. 1884. *Paris dilettante au commencement du siècle*. Paris.

Lafond, P. Undated. *Garat*. Paris.

Landormy, P. 1944. *La Musique française de La Marseillaise à la mort de Berlioz*. Paris.

Lasalle, A. 1875. *Les Treize Salles de l'Opéra*. Paris.

Lefebvre, L. 1901. *Histoire du Théâtre de Lille*. Volumes 2 and 3. Lille.

_____. 1908. *Les Concerts de Lille (1726–1816)*. Lille.

Lesure, F. 1956. *L'œuvre de Mozart en France de 1793 à 1810*. In *Mozart-Jahrbuch*. Vienna.

_____. 1980. *Les premières éditions françaises de Beethoven, 1800–1811*. In *Gedenkschrift Günter Henle*. Munich.

Levy, J. M. 1971. *The Quatuor concertant in Paris in the Latter Half of the Eighteenth Century*. Ph. D. dissertation, Stanford University.

Locke, A. 1920. *Music and the Romantic Movement in France*. London.

MacDonald, J. 1968. *François-Joseph Gossec*. Ph. D. dissertation, University of Michigan.

Masson, P. M. 1934. *Les chants anacréontiques de Méhul*. In *Revue de musicologie, August–November 1934*.

Mellinet, C. 1837. *De la musique à Nantes depuis les temps les plus reculés jusqu'à nos jours*. Nantes.

Mongrédien, J. 1968. *La musique du sacre de Napoléon Ier*. In *Revue de musicologie*. p. 137–174.

_____. 1970. *La musique aux fêtes du sacre de Charles X*. In *Recherches sur la musique française classique*. Volume 10. p. 87–100.

_____. 1980. *Catalogue thématique de l'œuvre complète du compositeur J.-F. Le Sueur (1760–1837)*. New York.

_____. 1980. *Jean-François Le Sueur. Contribution à l'étude d'un demi-siècle de musique française, 1780–1830*. 2 volumes. Bern.

Monter, E.-M. 1866. *La musique et la société française sous le Directoire*. In *Revue et gazette musicale de Paris*. 27 May 1866 ff.

Niquet, E. 1896. *Les anciennes Sociétés musicales d'Amiens*. Cayeux-sur-Mer.

Ozanam, Y. 1974. *L'Académie royale de musique de 1815 à 1830*. Thesis, École nationale des Chartes.

Ozouf, M. 1976. *La fête révolutionnaire*. Paris.

Parker, C. P. G. 1972–1973. *A Bibliography and Thematic Index of Luigi Cherubini's Instrumental Music*. Ph. D. dissertation, Kent State University.

Pierre, C. 1895. *Le magasin de musique à l'usage des fêtes nationales et du Conservatoire*. Paris. Minkoff reprint 1974.

_____. 1895. *B. Sarrette et les origines du Conservatoire national de musique et de déclamation*. Paris.

_____. 1896. *L'École de chant de l'Opéra*. Paris.

_____. 1899. *Musique des fêtes et cérémonies de la Révolution française*. Paris.

_____. 1900. *Le Conservatoire national de musique et de déclamation*. Paris.

_____. 1904. *Les Hymnes et Chansons de la Révolution*. Paris.

Pistone, D. 1979. *La Musique en France de la Révolution à 1900*. Paris.

Place, A. de. 1978. *Le Piano-forte à Paris entre 1760 et 1822*. Advanced degree thesis, EPHE.

Pougin, A. 1874. *Notice sur Rode*. Paris.

_____. 1875. *Figures d'opéra-comique: Dugazon, Elleviou, Gavaudan*. Paris.

_____. 1889. *Méhul, sa vie, son génie, son caractère*. Paris.

_____. 1891. *L'Opéra-Comique pendant la Révolution de 1788 à 1801*. Paris.

Prod'homme, J.-G. 1927. *Les débuts de Beethoven en France*. In *Beethovens Zentenarfeier*. Vienna.

Reuchsel, M. 1903. *La Musique à Lyon*. Lyon.

Ringer, A. 1969. *Cherubini's Médée and the Spirit of French Revolutionary Operas*. In *Essays in Musicology in Honor of Dragan Plamenac*. Pittsburgh.

Sallès, A. 1914. *Les Représentations du* Freischütz *de Weber au Grand Théâtre de Lyon (1825–1914)*. Paris.

_____. 1927. *Les Premières Exécutions à Lyon des œuvres de Beethoven*. Paris.

Saloman, O. 1970. *Aspects of Gluckian Operatic Thought and Practice in France: the Musico-Dramatic Vision of Le Sueur and Lacépède (1785–1809) in Relation to Aesthetic and Critical Tradition*. Ph. D. dissertation, Columbia University.

Schemann, L. 1925. *Cherubini*. Stuttgart.

Schwarz, B. 1950. *French Instrumental Music between the Revolutions: 1789–1830.* New York. (This volume was being revised and was not available for consultation.)

Selden, M. J. S. 1975. *The French Operas of Luigi Cherubini.* Ann Arbor: University Microfilms.

Servières, G. 1914. *Épisodes d'histoire musicale.* Paris.

Simms, B. 1971. *Alexandre Choron (1771–1834) as a Historian and Theorist of Music.* Ph. D. dissertation, Yale University.

Snyders, G. 1968. *Le Goût musical en France aux XVIIᵉ et XVIIIᵉ siècles.* Paris.

Sonneville, René P. de. 1958. *Un musicien de Bordeaux au XVIIIᵉ siècle: Franz Beck.* In *Revue historique de Bordeaux.* pp. 101–115.

Soubies, A. 1910. *Le Théâtre italien au temps de Napoléon et de la Restauration.* Paris.

_____. 1913. *Le Théâtre italien de 1801 à 1913.* Paris.

Streicher, A. 1982. *Quelques observations sur la façon de jouer, d'accorder et d'entretenir les forte-pianos.* Translated into French by Hubert Bédard and Félia Bastet. Paris.

Suskin, S. 1972. *The Music of C. S. Catel for the Paris Opera.* Ph. D. dissertation, Yale University.

Ternes, H. 1980. *Die Messen von Luigi Cherubini.* Bonn University.

Tiersot, J. 1908. *Les Fêtes et Chants de la Révolution française.* Paris.

Veen, J. van der. 1955. *Le Mélodrame musical de Rousseau au romantisme.* The Hague.

_____. 1980. *La vie musicale dans les provinces françaises.* Volume 4. Geneva. Minkoff reprint.

Wangermée, R. 1972. *François-Joseph Fétis, musicologue et compositeur.* Brussels.

White, C. 1957 *Giovanni Baptista Viotti and His Violin Concertos.* Ann Arbor: University Microfilms.

_____. 1985. *Giovanni Battista Viotti (1755–1824), A Thematic Catalogue of His Works.* New York: Pendragon Press.

_____. 1992. *From Vivaldi to Viotti: A History of the Early Classical Violin Concerto.* Philadelphia: Gordon and Breach.

Wild, N. 1980. *Les Théâtres parisiens entre 1807 et 1848: la législation, les salles, les administrations, les structures musicales.* Paris. Thesis, EPHE.

Willis, Stephen C. 1975. *Luigi Cherubini: a Study of his Life and Dramatic Music, 1795–1815.* Ph. D. dissertation, Columbia University.

Winton, D. 1982. *French Opera.* In *The Age of Beethoven, 1790–1830.* New Oxford History of Music, Volume 8. Oxford.

Zsako, J. 1975. *The String Quartets of I. Pleyel.* Ph. D. dissertation, New York University.

Index of Names

Abraham, music teacher, 290
Abrantes, Laure, Duchess of, 76
Adam, Adolphe, 303
Adam, Jean-Louis, 22, 23, 300, 302, 303, 304, 306, 307, 309, 310, 318
Adrien, Martin-Joseph, 19
Agoult, Marie, Countess d', 247, 248
Albret, Henri d', 63
Albret, Jeanne d', 63
Alday, composer and violinist in Lyon, 209, 258
Aldobrandini, Prince, 181
Alembert, Jean le Rond d', 175, 262
Alfred the Great, 242
Aliprandi, Vincenzo, 122, 123
Alkan, Charles Morhange, alias, 313
Anacréon, 242
André, Johann, 324
Anfossi, Pasquale, 110, 111
Angoulême, Duke of, 63
Angoulême, Duchess of, 183
Anthony, James R., 160

Arioste, Ludovico, 97, 104
Aristotle, 261
Armand, Anne-Aimée, 68, 163, 165, 172
Auber, Esprit, 63, 64, 87, 88, 106, 240
Aubert, Abbé, 26
Avrillon, Mademoiselle, 125, 241
Azzia, Alessandro d', 112, 113, 114, 117, 340

Bach, Carl Philip Emanuel, 198, 304
Bach, Johann Sebastian, 29, 171, 174, 193, 201, 304, 311, 316, 317, 318
Baillot, Pierre
    on Beethoven, 279, 320, 322
    cello methods of, 277, 296
    concertos, 288, 299
    at the Conservatoire, 22
    on German music vs. Italian, 336
    on musicoragicomania, 226–227
    at French premiere of Mozart's Requiem, 189
    and Paris salons, 235, 236, 240, 241

[Baillot, Pierre]
 and public concerts, 239, 247–250,
   255, 259, 290, 298, 305, 322
 quartets, 295
 and Rode and Viotti, 278, 280, 289
 at Rue de Cléry concerts, 233
 sinfonia concertante, 285
 sonatas, 300
 as teacher, 180, 246, 257
 as traveling musician, 316
 at Tuileries Chapel, 165, 166, 183
Balbastre, Claude, 309
Bandi, Giorgi-Brigida, 110, 111
Baour-Lormian, Pierre, 55
Bara, Joseph, 53
Barbereau, Mathurin, 245
Barbier, painter, 211, 237
Barbier-Walbonne, Madame, 211, 220, 237
Barère, Bertrand, 37
Barilli, Luigi, 119
Barilli, Marie-Anne, 119, 121, 122, 240
Bärmann, bassoonist, 282
Barron, 235
Batteux, Abbé Charles, 261
Baudiot, Charles, 173, 233, 252, 277
Bawr, Baroness de, 126, 272, 339
Beauharnais, Count Hortense de, 181, 305
Beaumarchais, Pierre-Augustin Caron de,
   138, 140, 323
Beck, Franz, 141, 194, 254
Beethoven, Louis van, 319
Beethoven, Ludwig van
 Les Adieux, 323
 Appassionata, 319
 and Bigot, 304, 316
 and Bontempo, 304
 on Cherubini, 187
 Christ on the Mount of Olives, 201
 concertos, 246, 288
 Fidelio, 84, 93, 102, 244, 338
 and French opera, 100, 108, 117
 and Guibal du Rivage, 255
 interpretation of, 250
 lyricism of, 289
 and Méhul, 269
 Missa solemnis, 185–186

 never visited Paris, 315
 and piano, 305, 306, 309, 311
 Prometheus, 216
 quartets, 297, 294, 297
 quintets, 249, 290
 reception in Paris, 245–249, 270, 317,
   319–323
 sacred works, 244
 and scherzo, 298, 309
 septet, 249
 sonatas, 279, 290, 299
 symphonies, 216, 244, 247, 272,
   280, 320
 Thirty-two Variations on a Theme in
   C minor, 319
 and trombone, 272
 unknown in Lyon, 258
Bège, Alex, 253
Bellini, Vincenzo, 78, 80, 107, 120, 134,
   138, 283, 344
Belloy, Cardinal Du, 191
Benton, Rita, 284
Bereyter, Angelina, 119
Bériot, Charles de, 248
Berlioz, Hector
 and Baillot, 280, 323, 344
 on Beethoven, 247
 on Boïeldieu, 105
 and Branchu, 69
 on Cherubini, 186, 187
 Damnation de Faust, 76
 Enfance du Christ, 103, 184
 on the fugue, 176
 on Gluck, 102
 and Le Sueur, 171, 184, 323
 respect for predecessors, 51
 on Rossini, 86, 87, 137
 sacred music, 48
 on sacred music concerts, 201
 Sardanapale, 114
 on Spontini, 83
 Symphonie fantastique, 264, 270–272,
   276, 344
 on theory of imitation, 264
 on Tuileries Chapel, 170, 183
Bernier, Nicolas, 160

Berr, Frédéric, 275
Berry, Duke de, 65
Berthélemy, J.-S., 78
Bertin, Jean-Honoré, 189, 191
Berton, Henri Montan
    Aline, reine de Golconde, 104
    comic operas, 53, 90
    as composer, 53, 63, 232, 245, 344
    Le Délire, 104
    Montano et Stéphanie, 95, 97, 104
    La Nouvelle au camp, 54
    Les Rigueurs du cloître, 139
    and Stendhal and Rossini, 85, 136
    and the symphony, 266
    Virginie, 85
    and vocal music, 273
Bianchi, Francesco, 111, 121
Bianchi, singer, 124
Bigot, Marie, 304, 316
Bigot de Préamneu, 26
Blanchard, Henri, 252
Blanchard de la Musse, 56, 57
Blangini, Joseph, 63, 239, 240, 242
Blangini, Madame, 239
Blasius, Mathieu, 94, 226, 230, 290, 327
Blondeau, Auguste-Louis, 237, 290
Boccherini, Luigi, 235, 236, 238, 248,
    249, 250, 252, 279, 293
Bochsa, Nicolas Charles, 276
Boëly, Alexandre, 193, 309, 311, 313, 318
Bohrer, Antoine, 244, 254
Bohrer, Max, 244, 254
Boïeldieu, François-Adrien
    and Baillot, 279
    Le Calife de Bagdad, 93, 105
    co-founder of *Magasin de Musique*, 316
    comic opera, 104–108
    composer, 63, 309
    concertos, 312
    La Dame blanche, 106, 108, 148,
    154, 156, 276
    Jean de Paris, 106, 108
    Ma tante Aurore, 105
    organized concerts at Rouen, 252
    Le Petit Chaperon Rouge, 151
    and Rossini, 136

    and Sainte-James, 154
    sinfonies concertantes, 276
    sonatas, 309, 312
    Les Voitures versées, 105
    Zoraïme et Zulnare, 95
Boileau-Despréaux, Nicolas, 345
Bonaparte, Jérôme, 239
Bonaparte, Louis, 184
Bonaparte, Lucien, 235
Bonaparte, Napoleon
    and ancient themes in opera, 53
    battle of Austerlitz, 316
    and Cherubini, 83
    commissioned musical works, 52, 180
    Consul for life, 55
    coronation of, 167, 168, 169, 172,
    276, 312
    and Desvignes, 191
    and *Fernand Cortez*, 59
    and Grassini, 112, 124, 127
    and *L'Irato*, 102
    and the Italian Opera, 118, 126,
    162–164
    love of Italian music, 123
    marriage of, 171
    military victories, 54
    and *Ossian*, 75
    and prizes for best opera, 51, 74
    and provincial theaters, 149
    and report on choir schools, 26
    and *Le Triomphe de Trajan*, 60
    and Tuileries Chapel, 125, 165, 166,
    180–182
    visit to Nantes, 56
Bonaparte, Pauline, 239
Bondy, de, prefect, 224
Bonet [de Treiches], Joseph-Balthazar, 163
Bonjour, L., 324
Bonneville, director, 150
Bontempo, João-Domingos, 233, 259, 304
Bordeaux, Duke of, 63, 167
Bordogni, Marco, 134
Boucher, singer, 154, 158
Boucher, Don Alexandre, 190
Bourbon, Duke of, 57
Bourrienne, Louis-Antoine, 235

Boyer, Charles-Georges, 323
Brahms, Johannes, 101, 187
Branchu, Caroline, 20, 24, 60, 68, 69,
    81, 82, 146, 163, 165, 172, 189,
    211, 223
Brandt, singer, 327
Breitkopf, publishers, 199, 298, 316
Brenet, Michel, 205, 206
Bréval, Jean-Baptiste, 224, 277
Brévan, Bruno, 31, 53, 54
Brongniart, Adolphe-Théodore, 117
Brook, Barry S., 265, 281
Brosse, Count de, 253
Bruillion, singer, 158
Brulo, Philippe, 150
Bruni, Antonio, 111, 114
Buisson, Émile, 238
Bülow, Hans von, 100
Burney, Charles, 197, 199, 200

Callas, Maria, 82, 134
Calvière, Guillaume-Antoine, 193
Cambini, Giovanni, 265, 284, 293, 295
Cammaille, M.-C., 212
Camporesi, Violanta, 264
Campra, André, 160
Canabich, Madame, 326
Candeille, Pierre-Joseph, 165
Carafa, Michele, 106
Carillez, Paul, 233
Carli, publisher, 299
Carnot, Lazare, 235
Cartier, Jean-Baptiste, 280
Castil-Blaze, François
    on choir schools, 26
    on concerts in the provinces, 148–149,
        256
    on Damoreau-Cinti, 69
    as historian, 143–145
    on instrumental vs. vocal music, 208
    on masses at the Tuileries Chapel, 163
    on Œdipe à Colone, 144
    on opéra-comique, 94
    on Paul et Virginie, 145
    Robin des bois, 108, 156, 157, 256,
        297, 338

    on the scherzo, 309
    as translator of operas, 86, 143
    on variations in music, 312
Catalani, Angélique, 113, 129, 130, 131
Catel, Charles-Simon
    L'Auberge de Bagnères, 103
    Les Bayadères, 74
    composer, 218, 245
    composer of comic opera, 104, 142
    composer of opera, 72, 75, 80, 136
    composer of overtures, 213
    composer of revolutionary songs, 45
    quartets, 294
    Sémiramis, 74
    sinfonia concertante, 282
    and symphony, 266
    as teacher, 195, 255, 277
    Traité d'harmonie, 23
    and vocal music, 273
    Wallace, 103, 276
Catherine the Great, 162
Céllerier, director of Paris Opéra, 55
Chalgrin, Jean-François, 118
Champfleury, Jules, 103
Champagny, J.-B. Nompère de, 149
Champein, Stanislas, 140
Charasson, director, 151
Charlemagne, 242
Charles X, 86, 88, 167, 169, 170, 182,
    184, 186, 191, 202
Charlton, David, 268, 269
Chateaubriand, François-René, Viscount of,
    84, 128, 202, 270, 271
Châtre, Duke of, 166
Chaussier, Hector, 212
Chélard, Hippolyte, 245
Chénard, Simon, 146, 231
Chénier, Marie-Joseph, 15, 17, 36, 40, 51
Chéron, Augustin, 44, 68, 145
Cherubini, Luigi
    Abencérages, 61, 62, 84
    Ali Baba, 84
    Anacréon, 84, 156
    and Berlioz, 344
    and chamber music concerts, 249
    co-founder of Magasin de Musique, 316

and comic opera, 90
as composer, 45, 53, 63, 72, 109,
    168, 172, 174, 218
as composer of lyrical romances, 242
at the Conservatoire, 16, 17, 27, 245,
    302, 334
Les Deux journées, 94, 99
Faniska, 84
Hymne à la Victoire, 38
influence on French music, 83, 96
Lodoïska, 92, 93, 97, 98, 100, 234
Médée, 20, 80, 93, 97, 100, 101,
    108, 339, 346
as music director, 47, 164, 189, 215
overtures of, 100, 206, 214, 268
quartets, 298
and Rossini, 136
at Rue de Cléry, 224
sacred music, 167, 168, 169, 174–175,
    176, 185–187, 195, 240
Sinfonia, 270
and symphonic works, 266
at Tuileries Chapel, 166, 168, 174,
    183, 185–187
in Vienna, 315
and vocal works, 273
Chimay, Prince de, 186, 240
Chimay, Princess de, 240
Chopin, Frédéric, 306, 313, 344
Choron, Alexandre
    on choir schools, 25
    on the decline of the organ, 193
    Dictionnaire historique, 26, 266, 318
    on Feydeau theater concerts, 209
    on Garat and Barbier-Walbonne, 211
    and historical concerts, 250
    as music publisher, 196, 197–203
    on straight-forward harmonies, 185
    as teacher, 28, 29, 30
Cicéri, Pierre, 88, 108
Cicero, 86
Cimador, Giovanni Battista, 335
Cimarosa, Domenico
    Artemisia, 127
    as composer, 117, 189
    Il Convito, 121

death of, 123, 162
as defender of melody, 99
I Due baroni, 111
Il Matrimonio segreto, 69, 113, 115,
    117, 119
opera buffa, 110
Gli Orazii e Curiazii, 127
and Paisiello, 128
at public concerts, 219
"Quelle pupille tenere," 264
and Rossini, 130, 136, 137
sacred music, 198
Le Sacrifice d'Abraham, 210
Clairville, Louise Rietti, 155
Clari, Giovanni, 200
Claudon, Francis, 89
Clementi, Muzio, 304, 305, 306
Clercx, Suzanne, 177
Clotilde, Augustine Malfeuret (stage name),
    73
Colbran, Isabelle, 134, 206, 259
Constant, professor of music, 33
Corelli, Arcangelo, 250, 280
Cornu, 190
Cortez, Fernand, 59
Cotte, Roger, 38
Couperin, François, 193
Couperin, Gervais-François, 193
Cousineau, father & son, 276
Cousineau, Georges, 275
Cramer, Carl Friedrich, 305, 318, 324, 325
Cramer, Johann Baptist, 213, 306
Crescentini, Girolamo, 69, 111, 124, 125,
    126, 206
Crétu, Madame, 146
Crivelli, Gaetano, 119, 126
Crucca, singer, 123

Dacosta, Isaac-Franco, 230, 252, 259, 274
Dalayrac, Nicolas, 53, 56, 93, 95, 104, 105,
    107, 139, 140, 142, 145, 148, 293
Dalvimare, Martin-Pierre, 172, 276
Damesme, architect, 114
Damoreau-Cinti, Laure, 69, 134
Daquin, Louis, 193
Daunou, Pierre, 31

Dauprat, Louis-François, 173
Davaux, Jean-Baptiste, 293
Debussy, Claude, 46
Delaforêt, A., 86
Delamare, cellist, 233, 249
Delannois, François, 214
Delisle, Michel, 150
Della Maria, Domenico, 93, 95
Dercy, Palat, alias, 76
Derivis, Henri-Étienne, 60, 68, 146, 165
Desaudrais, Boniface, 238
Desaudray, Charles, 229
Desaugiers, Marc-Antoine, 85
Desbordes-Valmore, Marceline, 242
Desperez, organist, 193
Dessolle, General, 248
Desvignes, Pierre, 168, 172, 190, 191
Devienne, François, 16, 66, 96, 139,
        210, 213, 272, 275, 282
Devisme du Valgay, Anne, 66
Devriès, Anik, 317
Diderot, Denis, 99, 175, 261
Dietrich, Madame de, 43
Dietrich, Philippe-Frédéric, Baron of, 43
Dittersdorf, Karl, 329, 330, 331
Doche, Joseph, 192
Domnich, Henri, 275
Donfried, Johannes, 197
Donizetti, Gaetano, 120, 134, 138
Du Bos, Abbé Jean-Baptiste, 261
Duchambge, Pauline, 240
Dufrêne, Joseph, 231
Dugazon, Louise-Rosalie, 92, 93, 94,
        105, 143, 145, 225
Dugrenet, singer, 158
Duni, Egido, 95
Dupont, bass player, 241
Duport, Jean-Louis, 277
Duport, Jean-Pierre, 277
Duprez, Gilbert, 68
Dupuy, Laurent, 12
Durante, Francesco, 168, 196, 198, 216
Duret, Anne-Cécile, 211
Duret, Marcel, 215, 218
Dussek, Ladislas, 234, 239, 303, 304,
        305, 306, 307, 312, 316

Duvernoy, Frédéric, 22, 66, 166, 172, 210,
        213, 224, 241, 274, 275, 277

Ehler, André, 72, 236
Elleviou, Jean, 93, 95, 105, 143, 146
Ellmenreich, Johann Baptist, 326, 327,
        328, 329, 330
Enghien, Duke of, 181
Érard brothers, 303
Érard, Sébastien, 275, 301, 302, 319
Érard sisters, 81
Esmenard, Joseph-Alphonse, 47, 58, 60
Esterházy, Princes, 111
Euripides, 97, 101, 127

Farinelli, Carlo Broschi, alias, 121
Fauquet, Joël-Marie, 249
Faust, 76
Fayolle, François, 209, 318
Fémy, Ambroise, 256
Fenzi, Victor and Joseph, 259
Ferlendis, Giuseppi, 233
Festa, Francesca, 119, 126
Fétis, Édouard, 226, 243
Fétis, François-Joseph
        on Abraham, 290
        on Baillot, 250
        on Berlioz, 272, 344
        Biographie universelle des musiciens, 190
        on Branchu, 69
        on Cherubini, 174
        on Choron, 29, 201
        on Crescentini, 125
        on comic opera, 108
        on Dacosta, 259
        on Dussek, 305
        on Érard, 275
        on Habeneck, 215
        on Handel, 202
        on Hugot, 274
        on Lays, 67
        on Mainvielle-Fodor, 133
        on Malibran, 318
        on Méhul and Cherubini, 99
        on Mozart, 336
        on Pasta, 134

on Nozzari, 113
on Rossini, 88
on Tuileries Chapel, 167, 170
on Weber, 337
Filtz, Anton, 265
Florian, J.-P. Claris de, 90
Focillon, Henri, 54
Fontaine, Pierre-François, 125, 165
Fontanes, Louis de, 47
Fontenelle, Bernard Le Bovier de, 72, 262
Forkel, Johann Nikolaus, 197
Fortia de Piles, Alphonse de, 25
Fouché, Joseph, 181
Framery, Nicolas, 13, 40, 250, 292, 318, 337
France, King of, see Philippe-Auguste and Louis XII
Franchomme, Auguste, 277
Franck, César, 184
Franconi brothers, 60, 72
Franklin, Benjamin, 43
Frederick II, 221, 316
Frescobaldi, Girolamo, 311
Fridzeri, Alexandre, 232
Fuchs, publisher, 324

Gabrieli, Giovanni, 48
Gail, Jean-Baptiste, 240, 242
Gail, Sophie, 240
Galeotti, Stefano, 299
Galli, Filippo, 68
Gambaro, Jean-Baptiste, 275, 294, 297
Garat, Pierre-Jean
    biographical summary, 211–212
    as composer of romances, 242
    and The Creation, 187–188
    at the Feydeau theater, 207, 209, 210–212, 237
    as instructor at the Conservatoire, 19, 20, 28, 68, 133
    at the Paris Opéra, 28, 69
    at public and private concerts, 223, 240, 241, 252
    on tenor Lazzarini, 113
Garaudé, Alexis de, 131, 242
Garcia, Madame, 121

Garcia, Manuel, 68, 119, 120, 131, 133, 134, 240, 318
Gardel, Marie, Madame, 73
Gardel, Pierre-Gabriel, 44
Gardi, Francesco, 324
Garland, publisher, 281
Garnier, bookseller, 302
Garnier, François, 236
Gavaudan, Jean-Baptiste, 147
Gavaudan, Madame, 147
Gaveaux, Pierre, 93, 95 142
Gaviniès, Pierre, 238
Gazzaniga, Giuseppe, 324
Gebauer, François, 166
Gebauer, Michel, 230
Geminiani, Francesco, 250
Genlis, Stéphanie-Félicité de, 46, 276
Géoffroy, Julien-Louis, 68, 79, 84, 207, 303, 317, 325, 333, 335, 336, 338, 340
Gérard, François, Baron, 211, 237
Gerber, Ludwig, 318
Gervais, Charles-Hubert, 160
Gilbert, 322
Ginguené, Pierre-Louis, 286, 288, 318, 325
Giroust, François, 160, 168, 169, 229
Glachant, Antoine, 32, 258
Gloria, Mademoiselle, 121
Gluck, Christoph Willibald
    Alceste, 146, 156
    Armide, 66
    and Berton, 85
    composer of opera, 51, 72–73, 79, 80, 83, 84, 89, 96, 109, 219, 227, 344
    De Profundis, 194
    and Hoffmann, 97
    Iphigénie en Aulide, 53, 146, 147, 156, 210, 346
    Iphigénie en Tauride, 54, 68
    music compared to opera buffa, 123
    Orfeo, 145, 155, 276
    and ornamentaion, 122
    and psychological truth in librettos, 99
    and revolutionary songs, 39
    and role of orchestra, 100
    roles sung by, 24, 67
    and theory of true expression, 101, 102

Goethe, Wolfgang von, 43, 270, 345
Goldoni, Carlo, 115
Gossec, François-Joseph
    and Boccherini, 293
    box at Conservatoire, 214
    composer of arias, 189
    composer of *hiérodrames*, 160
    composer of lyrical romances, 242
    composer of revolutionary songs, 39,
        266
    founder of the *Concert des Amateurs*, 205
    Hymne à la Liberté, 15
    Hymne à l'Être Suprême, 38
    Marche funèbre, 213
    Marche lugubre, 45, 46, 191
    at National Music Institute, 14, 16
    Offrande à la Liberté, 44, 52
    O Salutaris, 168
    Principes élémentaires de musique, 22
    and Royal singing school, 17
    symphonies, 240, 265, 266, 269–270,
        272
    on *Uthal*, 102
Gougelot, Henri, 242
Gounod, Charles, 89, 184
Grandpierre, Count de, 238
Granges de Fontenelle, 72
Grasset, Jean-Jacques, 114, 165, 219, 237
Grassini, Josephina, 69, 112, 123, 124,
        125, 126, 127, 326
Gravrand, Joseph, 257
Grétry, André
    Anacréon chez Polycrate, 72
    at Arras, 140
    and Auber, 106
    and Boïeldieu, 105
    La Caravane du Caire, 71, 72, 156
    Colinette à la cour, 156
    comic operas, 51, 53, 90, 95, 104,
        107, 108, 139, 241, 339, 344
    Elisca, 90
    Guillaume Tell, 90
    on Handel, 176
    as inspector of instruction, 17
    and Lays, 67
    Lisbeth, 90

Richard Coeur de Lion, 148
    and Sainte-James, 154
    Le Tableau parlant, 54
    and Vigée-Lebrun, 93
Grimm, Friedrich Melchior, Baron von, 69
Grisi, Giuditta, 134
Guénin, Marie-Alexandre, 230, 265
Guglielmi, Giacomo, 126
Guglielmi, Pietro, 114, 121, 126, 136
Guibal du Rivage, Alexandre, 195, 254,
        255, 257
Guichard, singer, 189
Guynemer, violinist, 249

Habeneck, François-Antoine, 215, 216,
        217, 222, 243, 244, 245, 270, 319,
        321, 323
Handel, George Frideric, 29, 174, 176,
        198, 200, 201, 202, 232, 250
Haibel, Johann, 330, 331
Halévy, Fromental, 83
Hardy, Madame, 30
Härtel, publisher, 298, 316
Haselmayer, director, 326, 330
Hasse, Johann Adolph, 123
Hawkins, Sir John, 197, 199
Haydn, Joseph
    arias of, 189
    and Baillot, 279
    and chamber music, 299
    as composer, 189, 305
    The Creation, 187, 188, 256, 317
    French response to, 331, 336
    and Guibal du Rivage, 255
    never visited Paris, 315, 336
    and piano works, 311
    and public concerts, 250
    quartets, 237, 238, 248, 249, 293, 295,
        297, 298, 322
    and Rossini, 136
    and Rue de Cléry concerts, 219, 221
    sacred works of, 168, 195, 196, 201, 222
    "The Seasons," 216
    and sonata form, 268, 269, 294
    "Spring Chorus," 216
    and style sévère, 174

symphonies, 19, 206, 207, 210, 214, 217, 220, 223, 225, 228, 232, 233, 234, 235, 244, 252, 257, 258, 263–267, 268, 282, 290, 297
  as teacher, 284, 304
  and Versailles, 253
  and Vogt, 316
Henri, singer, 154
Henri IV, 62, 63
Hérold, Ferdinand, 63, 106, 107, 108, 270, 303, 309, 312
Herz, Henri, 248
Herzfeld, singer, 327
Heugel, publisher, 287
Heurtier, architect, 91
Hoche, Lazare, 45
Hoffman, François-Benoît, 72
Hoffmann, singer, 97, 327
Hoffmeister, Friedrich Anton, 196, 317
Homer, 59
Homet, Abbé, 168
Hortense, Queen, 242, 276
Hugo, Victor, 79, 85, 202, 272, 344
Hugot, Anton, 274, 299
Hüllmandel, Nicolas-Joseph, 304, 309
Hummel, Johann Nepomuk, 249, 258, 305, 306

Imbault, Jean-Jérôme, 236, 292, 324
Indy, Vincent d', 201
Ingres, Dominique, 76, 322
Isouard. See Nicolo.

Jadin, Hyacinthe, 95, 310
Jadin, Louis, 236, 237, 309, 310, 311, 312
Jam, Jean-Louis, 40, 270
Jannequin, Clément, 200
Janson, Jean-Baptiste, 66
Jarnowick, Giovanni, 238
Jomelli, Nicolo, 123, 168, 194, 196, 198, 199, 203, 211
Josephine, Empress, 59, 62, 125, 241, 242
Josquin des Prés, 199, 200
Jouy, Étienne de, 59, 61, 62, 79, 81, 84, 88
Juliet, singer, 93
Jumentier, Bernard, 35, 194

Kalkbrenner, Chrétien, 72
Kalkbrenner, Frédéric, 189, 306, 335
Kellermann, François-Christophe, 44
Klopstock, F. G., 78
Kreutzer, Jean-Nicolas, 237
Kreutzer, Rodolphe
  Aristippe, 156
  co-author of Méthode de violon, 296
  co-founder of Magasin de Musique, 316
  composer, 53, 63
  concertos, 256, 288
  at French premiere of Mozart's Requiem, 189
  and Garnier, 236
  Lodoïska, 92, 98, 146, 234, 254
  music director, 47
  quartets, 295
  Paul et Virginie, 92, 254
  at public and private concerts, 207, 209, 225, 230, 240
  sinfonie concertante, 16, 233
  as teacher, 15, 195, 231, 255
  as traveling musician, 259, 279
  Le Triomphe du mois de Mars, 58
  at Tuileries Chapel, 165, 166, 183
  as violinst, 278, 280
Kühnel, Ambroise, 317

Lablache, Louis, 68, 134
La Borde, Jean-Benjamin de, 197
Lacépède, Étienne de, 50, 175, 261, 262, 263, 264, 282, 283
Lachner, Franz, 101
Lachnith, Louis-Wenceslas, 73, 189, 276, 325
Lacombe, Jacques, 160
Lacretelle, J.-C. de, 58, 63, 64
Ladré, singer, 43
Ladurner, Ignaz, 237, 311
Ladurner, Madame, 237
La Ferté, Denis-Pierre-Jean Papillon de, 13, 86, 166, 244
Laflèche, professor of music, 32-33
Lafont, Charles-Philippe, 228, 230, 248, 254, 296
La Harpe, Jean-François de, 128

La Houssaye, Pierre, 94, 210, 228
Lainez, Étienne, 67, 68, 145, 147, 148, 151
Lalande, Michel-Richard de, 160
Lamare, J.-M. Hurel de, 305, 316
Lamartine, Alphonse de, 79, 136, 179
Lange, Joseph, 326, 328
Lange, Madame, née Aloysia Weber, 327, 328, 329, 330, 331, 332
Langlé, Honoré, 231
La Pouplinière, Alexandre-Joseph de, 208
La Réveillière-Lépeaux, 41
Larivierre, Monsieur, 256
La Rochefoucault, Sosthène de, Viscount, 88, 245
Lasso, Orlando di, 197
Laurent, Émile, 130
Lavoisier, Antoine-Laurent de, 231
Lays, François, 19, 27, 67, 68, 70, 120, 145, 148, 165, 231
Lazzarini, Gustave, 113
L. C., 333
Lebrun, Charles, 219, 224
Le Brun, Louis-Sébastien, 165
Leclerc, Jean-Baptiste, 41
Le Duc, Alphonse, 323
Le Duc, Auguste, 198, 199
Lefébure-Wély, Antoine, 26
Lefebvre, chief copist of the Tuileries Chapel, 168
Lefèvre, Théodore, conductor, 94, 225, 230, 232, 233
Lefèvre, Xavier, clarinetist, 66, 274, 287, 299, 300
Legrand, Jacques-Guillaume, 91
Lemoyne, G., 303
Lemoyne, Jean-Baptiste, 53, 156
Lender, director, 31
Lenoir, Alexandre, 201
Lenoir, Nicolas, 64
Leo, Leonardo, 123, 196, 198
Léonard-Alexis, Autié, alias, 110
Lesage, Alain-René, 97
Le Sueur, Jean-François
    Accingere gladio, 164
    Alexandre à Babylone, 346
    Les Bardes, 66, 147
    and Beethoven, 247, 323
    and Berlioz, 344
    and Berton, 104
    Cantate religieuse, 171
    La Caverne, 92, 97, 100, 141
    Le Chant du 1er Vendémiaire, 47, 164
    composer of lyrical romances, 242
    composer of motets for Napoleon's coronation, 167
    composer of operas, 80, 90, 96
    composer of revoluionary pieces, 45
    education of, 12
    La Mort d'Adam, 74, 78, 79, 103, 345
    on Mozart, 334
    on music not always known, 197
    as music director, 165
    and neo-classicism, 72
    Oratorio de Noël, 184
    Oratorios du couronnement, 184, 185
    Ossian (Les Bardes), 74, 75–76, 78, 83, 102, 276
    Paul et Virginie, 92, 97, 145
    and Rossini, 136
    and Rousseau, 262
    Ruth et Booz, 103
    Ruth et Noémi, 103
    and sacred works, 161, 167, 168, 169, 173, 175, 177, 178, 179, 182
    and Scio, 93
    on space and sound in music, 48
    on symphonic vs. vocal music, 23–24, 262, 266, 273, 339
    as teacher, 15, 16, 17, 176, 183, 190, 271
    Télémaque, 92
    on the theory of imitation in music, 262
    Tu es Petrus, 164
    at Tuileries Chapel, 166, 168, 170, 180, 245
    Unxerunt Salomonem, 164, 185
    use of tam-tam, 46
Lesure, François, 317
Levasseur, Jean-Henri, 15, 66, 210, 277
Libon, Felipe, 206, 225, 280
Liszt, Franz, 108, 244, 248, 306
Loiseau-Persuis, see Persuis, Louis-Luc Loiseau de

Louis, Victor, 64
Louis XII, 62
Louis XVI, 27, 36, 50, 54, 64, 68, 91,
 110, 166, 187, 346
Louis XVIII, 61, 91, 110, 129, 166,
 169, 170, 182, 186
Louis-Philippe, 29, 167, 203
Luce-Varlet, C., 141, 255
Lügers, Mademoiselle, 327, 328
Lully, Jean-Baptiste, 221

MacPherson, James, 75
Madin, Henri, 160
Magin, Mr., 255
Maillard, Marie-Thérèse, 68, 69
Mainvielle-Fodor, Joséphine, 130, 133
Malibran, Maria, 68, 69, 119, 121, 134,
 318
Mandini, Paolo, 111, 113
Manent, Mademoiselle, 172
Marcello, Benedetto, 200, 201
Marchand, Louis, 193
Marcou, Pierre, 238
Marie-Antoinette, Queen
 (Madame Bonaparte), 42, 54,
 110, 171, 172, 211, 242, 312
Marie-Louise, Empress, 58, 127
Marinelli, Gaetano, 121
Martainville, Alphonse Louis, 212
Martin, Jean-Blaise, 93, 105, 143
Martinelli, Luigi, 123, 153
Martini, Giambattista, 197
Martini, Jean Paul Égide, alias
 Schwarzendorf, 166, 168, 169,
 172, 197, 241
Masaniello, orator, 87
Mayr, Simon, 122, 130
Mazarin, Giulio, Cardinal, 99, 109
Mazas, Jacques Féréol, 255, 280, 295
Méhul, Étienne-Nicholas
 Adrien, 72, 346
 Ariodant, 97, 99, 104, 276
 and Beethoven's symphonies, 320
 La Caverne, 92
 Le Chant de triomphe du 25 Messidor, 124
 "Le Chant du Départ," 15, 36, 148

Le Chant national du 14 juillet 1800,
 46–47, 164
 co-founder of Magasin de Musique, 316
 and comic opera, 90, 95, 96
 as composer, 45, 53
 at the Conservatoire, 16, 17, 38, 215,
 218
 Euphrosine et Coradin, 100, 139, 141
 Une Folie, 155
 Gabrielle d'Estrées, 268
 Héléna, 102, 155, 268
 Horatius Coclès, 53
 Hymne du IX Thermidor, 40
 and instrumental music, 339
 L'Irato, 102, 141, 340
 Le Jeune Henri (Méhul), 100
 Le Jeune Sage (Méhul), 139
 Joseph (Méhul), 51, 55, 93, 102, 103,
 141, 142, 146
 and lyrical romances, 242
 and pianoforte sonatas, 309
 and revolutionary songs, 41
 and sounds in music, 48
 Stratonice (Méhul), 93, 94, 97, 99, 139
 symphonic works, 232, 266, 267–269,
 272, 310, 321, 344
 as teacher of composition, 195, 255
 Timoléon, 139
 Le Trésor supposé, 107
 Uthal, 102, 276
 and vocal music, 273
Mellinet, Camille, 256
Mendelssohn-Bartholdy, Felix, 268, 337
Mengozzi, Bernardo, 210
Mestrino, Nicolas, 111
Metastasio, Pietro, 329
Meude-Monpas, J. J. O., Chevalier de, 284
Meyerbeer, Giacomo, 68, 79, 82, 83, 108
 [Mayer-Beer], 138, 283, 344, 346
Millevoye, Charles-Hubert, 242
Milton, John, 78
Mirabeau, Victor Riqueti, Marquis of,
 36–37
Mocker, soloist, 258
Molière, Jean-Baptiste Poquelin, alias, 92
Molinos, Jacques, 91

Momigny, Jérôme-Joseph de, 192, 269,
    274, 286, 295, 306, 307, 309
Mondonville, Jean-Joseph Cassanéa de,
    160
Monnais, Édouard, 237, 238
Monsigny, Pierre-Alexandre, 90, 95, 104,
    146, 148, 214
Montansier, Marguerite Brunet, alias
    Mademoiselle, 113, 117
Montbeillard, 236
Montesquiou, E. P., Count of, 126
Monteverdi, Claudio, 197
Montgeroult, Hélène, 18, 303, 304, 306
Monvel, Jacques Marie Boutet, alias, 148
Morandi, Rosa, 131
Moreau, Jean-Victor, General, 236, 237
Moreau, Madame, 237
Morel de Chefdeville, 73, 189
Morellet, Abbé André, 261
Moreth, pianist, 210
Morichelli, Anna, 110, 210
Mosca, Giuseppe, 123
Moscheles, Ignace, 244, 248, 306
Mozart, Leopold, 304
Mozart, Nannerl, 325
Mozart, Wolfgang Amadeus
    admirers of, 128, 255, 266
    La Clemenza di Tito, 113, 336
    concertos, 273, 288, 308
    Così fan tutte, 118, 120, 223, 324, 335
    Davidde penitente, 196
    defender of melody, 99
    Die Entführung aus dem Serail, 327,
        329, 332
    and Géoffroy, 303, 336
    Don Giovanni, 55, 111, 118, 120,
        147, 153, 211, 216, 223, 324,
        326, 332, 335
    and Gossec, 270
    impact on French music, 316, 317,
        319, 321, 323, 324, 325, 326,
    and Ingres, 322
    instrumental music of, 290, 299
    interpretation of his music, 250
    The Magic Flute, 66, 73, 96, 276,
        313, 324, 325, 326, 331

The Marriage of Figaro, 67, 108, 118,
        119, 120, 121, 122, 143, 153, 223,
        323, 331, 335, 336, 340, 341
    and Mozartophobes, 335
    and Mozart Theater, 331, 334
    music for operas, 107, 111
    and opera buffa, 117, 121, 122
    opposition to, 329, 337, 338, 339, 340
    and Papageno, 67, 96
    pianoforte music, 304, 305, 311, 312
    at public concerts, 244, 246
    quartets, 236, 237, 238, 248, 249, 252,
        293, 294, 295, 297, 298
    as romantic composer, 341
    and Rossini, 137
    sacred music of, 168, 187, 189, 190,
        191, 195, 196–197, 201, 203, 215
    sinfonie concertantes, 282
    sonatas, 310
    and style sévère, 174
    success in Paris, 79, 84, 135, 253, 267,
        332, 334, 337
    and Süssmayer, 330
    symphonic works of, 199, 216–220,
        232, 233, 256, 258, 263, 264, 265,
        266, 269
    and Viotti, 278
    and A. Weber, 328
Müller, Iwan, 275
Müller, Wenzel, 329, 330, 331, 332
Musorgsky, Modest, 185
Muti, Riccardo, 82

Naderman, François-Joseph, 168, 173, 230,
    234, 241, 248, 323
Naderman brothers, François-Joseph and
    Henri, 276
Naegeli, Hans-Georg, 318
Nasolini, Sebastiano, 121, 127, 211, 225, 336
Naumann, Johann Gottlieb, 331
Navoigille, Guillaume, 219
Néri, Mademoiselle, 121
Neufchâteau, François de, 235
Ney, Michel, 181
Nicolo, Isouard, alias, 104, 105, 141, 142,
    232, 316

Niedermeyer, Louis, 201
Niemetschek, Franz, 334
Norblin, Louis, 249
Nourrit, Adolphe, 68, 146, 165, 211
Nourrit, Louis, 68, 153
Nozzari, Andrea, 113, 115, 122, 123

Onslow, George, 249, 298, 300
Ouvrard, Gabriel-Julien, 235
Ozouf, Mona, 36
Ozy, Étienne, 22, 66, 213, 230, 274,
    281, 282, 299

Paër, Ferdinand, 63, 118, 123, 124,
    127, 130, 132, 166, 168, 180,
    225, 241, 244, 297
Paër, Madame, 123
Paganini, Nicolo, 296
Pain, Madame, 238
Paisiello, Giovanni
    The Barber of Seville, 111, 115
    compared to Rossini, 137
    as composer of duets, 128, 276
    as composer of opera buffe, 110,
        111, 117, 121, 123, 130
    as composer of sacred works, 163, 164,
        168, 169, 170, 172, 173, 189, 190
    La Frascatana, 128
    and Italian opera, 99, 109, 162
    La Molianara, 113, 115, 117
    and Napoleon, 124, 162, 168, 172, 276
    La Nina, 115, 116
    not a contrapuntist, 175
    La Passion, 190
    Il Pirro, 126–127
    Prosperine, 55, 163
    and public concerts, 219, 235, 244
    La Serva padrona, 153
    and Tuileries Chapel, 162–163,
        172, 173
    Zingari in fiera, 128
Palestrina, Giovanni, 29, 197, 199, 200,
    202, 203
Pasta, Giuditta, 70, 119, 131, 133, 134, 135
Pelet, Désirée, 147, 189
Pellegrini, Félix, 132, 134

Percier, Charles, 165
Perez, David, 198
Pergolesi, Giovanni Battista, 168, 196, 198
Périn, René, 212
Perne, François, 27
Persuis, Louis-Luc Loiseau de, 19, 52, 60,
    165, 166, 168, 245
Petrini, François, 276
Philidor, François-André Danican, 90, 95,
    159, 189, 205
Philipp, 319
Philippe-Auguste, King of France, 56
Picard, 117
Piccini, Nicolas, 13, 67, 72, 79, 83, 109,
    111, 115, 155, 156, 189, 219, 344
Pichard, Sébastien, 238
Pierre, Constant, 35, 38, 39, 42, 206
Pixérécourt, René-Charles Guilbert de, 58
Place, Adélaïde de, 301
Plantade, Charles-Henri, 167, 168, 169,
    170, 172, 173, 175, 177, 183, 242
Pleyel, Ignaz, 188, 236, 237, 238, 265,
    284, 292, 293, 295, 301, 307,
    316, 319, 324
Pleyel, Marie, 306
Ponchard, Louis Antoine Éléonore, 211
Poniatowski, King (Joseph), 190
Ponte, Lorenzo da, 110
Porro, Pierre-Jean, 191, 196, 197, 200, 201
Porta, Bernardo, 72
Portalis, Jean, 26, 192
Porto, Mathieu, 119, 131
Pougin, Arthur, 249
Pradel, Count De, 71
Prat, director, 150
Provence, Count of, see Louis XVIII
Prussia, King of, 82, 237, 277, 282
Pugnani, Gaetano, 280
Pujoulx, J.-B., 22, 32
Punto, see Stich, Jan Václav
Puppo, Giuseppe, 111

Rabreau, Daniel, 64
Raffanelli, Luigi, 111, 113
Rameau, Jean-Philippe, 23, 24, 29, 41, 52,
    72, 100, 123, 338

Récamier, Jeanne-Françoise, 276
Regnault, composer, 195
Regny, professor of music, 30
Reicha, Anton, 249, 256, 298
Reichardt, Johann Friedrich
    on concerts at Paris Conservatoire, 214
    on concerts at Tuileries, 179–180
    on Feydeau concerts, 209
    on French orchestras, 19
    and *Magasin musical*, 199
    on *La Maison à vendre*, 105
    on musical life in Paris, 221–222,
        236–237, 301, 316, 331
    on Paisiello, 163, 172
    psuedonym of, 35
    on Strinasacchi, 113
Rémusat, Count de, 71, 126
Rey, Jean-Baptiste, 66, 165
Richardson, Samuel, 115
Richer, singer, 189
Rindler, singer, 329
Robespierre, Maximilien de, 209, 231, 235
Rochefort, Jean-Baptiste, 66
Rocher, conductor, 158
Rochlitz, Friedrich, 324, 325
Rode, Pierre
    co-founder of *Magasin de Musique*, 316
    as composer, 288, 295–296
    concertos, 288
    at the Opèra-Comique, 233
    at public and private concerts, 235,
        236, 240, 252
    quartets, 235
    as traveling musician, 259
    as violinist, 66, 207, 209, 232, 278,
        279–280, 305
Rodolphe, Jean-Joseph, 28
Rohan, Princess of, 236
Rolandeau, Louise-Joséphine, 113
Romberg, Andreas, 236, 259
Romberg, Bernard, 236, 237, 244, 264,
    278, 316
Rome, King of, 58, 195; see also
        Bonaparte, Napoleon
Ronzi de Begnis, Madame, 133
Rosine, singer, 210

Rossini, Gioachino
    and A. Nourrit, 68
    The Barber of Seville, 85, 130, 132, 133,
        134, 143, 148
    Le Comte Ory, 88
    and concerts, 244, 247–248
    defended Italian music, 73, 130, 131
    Demetrio e Polibio, 131
    and *dilettanti*, 109, 136–137, 250, 325
    Guillaume Tell, 82, 89, 90
    and Hérold, 107
    L'Inganno felice, 132
    and instrumental music, 297
    L'Italiana in Algeri, 131, 133
    masterpieces, 69
    Moïse, 86, 87, 89
    Maometto secondo, 86
    Mosè in Egitto, 113
    and opera, 83, 86, 88, 106, 128, 283
    oppposition towards, 104, 337
    Otello, 85, 113, 153
    La Pietra del Paragone, 131
    and romantic movement, 129, 138
    and sacred music, 168
    Semiramide, 135
    Le Siège de Corinthe, 63, 68, 86, 138,
        148, 258
    and spouse, 206, 259
    and Stendhal, 85, 135–136
    Tancredi, 86, 131
    The Thieving Magpie, 153
    Torvaldo e Dorliska, 133
    Il Turco in Italia, 133
    use of baritones in operas, 120
    Il Viaggio a Reims, 88
    and Voltaire, 74
Rouget de Lisle, Claude, 36, 43, 44
Rousseau, Jean-Jacques
    and Boïeldieu, 105
    Le Devin du village, 156
    Dictinnaire, 243
    on French language, 39
    on French shouting, 69
    and Le Sueur, 262
    influence on the romance musical form,
        241

on music, 175–176, 197, 318, 261, 338
on quartets, 291, 292
settings, 107
Rousseau, singer, 146
Rousseau, singer (Opéra of Lyon), 154
Rousselois, Marie, 154
Roze, Abbé Nicolas, 22, 164, 168, 175, 179
Rubini, Giovanni Battista, 134

Sacchini, Antonio, 24, 51, 53, 67, 68,
    72, 79, 84, 109, 155, 214, 219,
    344, 346
Saint-Amans, Louis, 55
Saint-Aubin, Jeanne, 92, 105
Sainte-James, Madame, singer, 154
Saint-Évremond, Charles de, 329
Saint-Georges, Chevalier de, 227, 293
Saint-Laurent, violist, 249
Saint-Louis, King of France, 245; see also
    Louis XII
Saint-Pierre, Bernardin de, 232
Saint-Saëns, Camille, 201
Salieri, Antonio, 68, 72, 79, 109, 344
Sallantin, Antoine, 213, 230, 274
Salomon, J.-P., 297
Sarrette, Bernard, 13-19, 21, 37, 213, 214
Sarti, Giuseppe, 110, 111
Sauvo, critic, 321
Sauzay, Eugène, 246
Saxony, King of, 123
Scarlatti, Domenico, 304
Schikaneder, Emmanuel, 325, 331
Schleyermann, professor of piano, 56
Schlichtegroll, Adolf Friedrich, 324, 325
Schneitzhoeffer, Jean, 166, 233
Schubert, Franz, 242, 299, 315
Schumann, Robert, 108, 187
Scio, Julie, 93, 95, 146, 209, 211
Scott, Walter, 106
Scribe, Eugène, 87, 88, 106
Sedaine, Michel-Jean, 90
Ségur, Louis-Philippe, 187
Séjan, Louis, 193
Séjan, Nicolas, 193, 309
Seneca, 86
Sessi, Marianne, 127

Sévelinges, Charles-Louis de, 70, 334
Shakespeare, William, 270
Sieber, Jean-Georges, 220, 236, 292, 293,
    317, 319, 323, 324
Sievers, G., 183
Simrock, Heinrich, 316, 319, 324
Simrock, Nicolaus, 316
Singier, Alexis, 152, 153
Smithson, Harriet, 270
Solié, Jean-Pierre, 95, 142, 146
Sontag, Henriette, 69, 134
Speyer, Wilhelm, 180
Spohr, Ludwig, 173, 185, 239, 244, 255,
    279, 297, 337
Spontini, Gaspare
    and Branchu, 68
    and Count De Pradel, 71
    as director of Italian opera, 118, 120,
        126, 127,
    L'Eccelsa gara, 59
    Fernand Cortez, 59, 62, 67, 68, 82, 83,
        118, 148, 153, 346
    La Finta filosofa, 118
    and French grand opera, 79, 80, 82, 83,
        109
    and Guibal du Rivage, 255
    and Jouy, 61, 88
    Olympie, 68, 82, 83, 346
    Pélage, 62
    and spouse, 301
    La Vestale, 50, 51, 59, 60, 67, 79, 80,
        81, 82, 83, 84, 101, 118, 141, 147,
        148, 153, 156, 346
Staël, Germaine de, 329
Stamitz, Johann, 265, 286
Steibelt, Daniel, 93, 95, 155, 187, 227,
    236, 253, 305, 315, 316, 320
Stein, Andreas, 307
Stendhal, Henry Beyle, alias
    and Bereyter, 119
    on Esmenard, 60
    on Gli Orazii e Curiazii, 127
    and Italian music, 73, 115, 128, 136
    and music, 99, 117, 137, 271
    Racine et Shakespeare, 85
    on Tacchinardi, 120

[Stendhal, Henry Beyle, alias]
  La Vie de Haydn, 264
  La Vie de Mozart, 341
  La Vie de Rossini, 135, 136
Stich, Jan Václav, 275
Stockhausen, Karlheinz, 48
Strauss, Richard, 322
Streicher, Andreas, 307, 308, 311
Strinasacchi, Teresa, 113, 115, 123, 151
Suavo, editor, 267
Süssmayer, Franz, 330, 331

Tacchinardi, Nicolas, 119, 120, 127
Talleyrand, Charles-Maurice de, 181,
  235, 305
Tapray, Jean-François, 309
Tario, violist, 249
Tartini, Giuseppe, 250, 280
Tasso, Torquato, 59
Thibaud, Jacques, 280
Tilmant, Théophile, 245
Toreinx, F.-R. de, 341
Trahcier, 35
Tritto, Giacomo, 110
Tulou, Jean-Louis, 241, 248

Urhan, Chrétien, 166

Vacher, Pierre-Jean, 228
Vacherand, André, 35
Valeroy, Mademoiselle, 143
Valéry, Paul, 299
Vanbee-Thoven, Louis, see Beethoven,
  Louis van
Véron, Dr. Louis-Désiré, 183
Vestris, Auguste, 73
Viala, Joseph, 53
Viardot, Pauline, 68, 119
Viganoni, Giuseppe, 111, 113
Vigée-Lebrun, Élisabeth, 93, 219
Vigny, Alfred de, 79, 202
Viguerie, Bernard, 306
Villotteau, Guillaume, 231
Viotti, Giovanni
  as composer, 232, 249, 255, 258, 281,
    288, 289, 293, 295

  concertos of, 210, 288
  as friend, 304
  sinfonia concertante of, 228
  as director of Italian opera buffa theater
    in Paris, 110, 111
  as instructor, 209, 278, 279, 280
  as violinist, 280
Virgil, 59
Vogler, Abbé Georg, 201
Vogt, Gustave, 166, 316
Vogt, Frédéric-Daniel, 324
Voltaire, François-Marie Arouet, alias, 45,
  52, 74, 303

Wagner, Richard, 78, 83, 87, 102, 103,
  108, 322
Walter, singer, 101, 327
Weber, Aloysia, see Lange, Madame
Weber, Carl Maria von, 73, 74, 83, 103,
  107, 108, 156, 157, 246, 297, 337
Weber, Constanze, 331
Weber, Sophie, 331
Weigl, Joseph, 331
Westphalia, King of, see Bonaparte, Jérôme
Wiederkehr, Jacques, 225
Winckler, J. F., 324, 325
Winter, Peter, 56, 117, 315, 331
Woldemar, Michael, 334
Wölffl, Joseph, 206, 304, 316
Wranitzky, Paul, 331
Wunderlich, Johann, 299

Zingarelli, Nicola Antonio, 121, 125, 168,
  336
Zuchelli, Carlo, 134
Zumsteeg, Johann, 331

Index of Music

Abencérages (Cherubini), 61, 62, 84
Accingere gladio (Le Sueur), 164
Adolphe et Clara (Dalayrac), 105
Adoremus (Bertin), 191
Adrien (Méhul), 72, 346
Agnese (Paër), 132
Air savoyard (Mengozzi), 210
Alceste (Gluck), 146, 156
Alexandre à Babylone (Le Sueur), 346
Ali Baba (Cherubini), 84
Aline, reine de Golconde (Berton), 104
Alla riva del Tebro (Palestrina), 203
Alma Redemptoris Mater (Durante), 196
Anacréon chez Polycrate (Grétry), 72
Anacréon (Cherubini), 84, 156
Apelle et Campaspe (Ehler), 72
Aria (Handel), 232
Aria (Mengozzi), 210
Ariodant (Méhul), 97, 99, 104, 276
Aristippe (Kreutzer), 156
Armida (Jomelli), 211

Armide (Gluck), 66
Artemisia (Cimarosa), 127
L'Auberge de Bagnères (Catel), 103
Au clair de la lune, 313
Ave Maria (Rossini), 168
Ave, maris stella (Leo), 196
Ave verum (Mozart), 168, 196, 244
Le Avventure amorose (Tritto), 110

The Barber of Seville (Paisiello), 111, 115
The Barber of Seville (Rossini), 85, 130,
    132, 133, 134, 143, 148
Les Bardes (Le Sueur), 66, 147
Bataille d'Austerlitz, 273
Bataille de Jemmapes (Devienne), 272
Bataille de Marengo, 273
Les Bayadères (Catel), 74
La Belle Arsène (Momigny), 148
Le Berceau d'Henri IV, 63
Blanche de Provence (Berton, Boïeldieu,
    Cherubini, Kreutzer, Paër), 63

Boris Godunov (Musorgsky), 185
Das Braminenfest (W. Müller), 330
La Buona figliuola (Piccini), 115

"Ça ira," 42, 43, 146, 148, 273
Le Calife de Bagdad (Boïeldieu), 93, 105
Cantate religieuse (Le Sueur), 171
La Caravane du Caire (Grétry), 71, 72, 156
Le Carillon national (Ladré), 43
La Carmagnole, 42, 43, 273
Carré (Stockhausen), 48
Castor et Pollux (Rameau), 128
Castor et Pollux (Winter), 56
La Caverne (Le Sueur), 92, 97, 100, 141
La Caverne (Méhul), 92
Chant de guerre pour l'armeé du Rhin (Rouget de Lisle), 43
Le Chant de triomphe du 25 Messidor (Méhul), 124
"Le Chant du Départ" (Méhul), 15, 36, 148
Le Chant du 1er Vendémiaire (Le Sueur), 47, 164
Le Chant national du 14 juillet 1800 (Méhul), 47, 164
Chimène (Sacchini), 53
Christ on the Mount of Olives (Beethoven), 201
La Clemenza di Tito (Mozart), 113, 336
Cleopatra (Nasolini), 127
Colinette à la cour (Grétry), 156
Complainte de Madame Elizabeth, 42
Complainte de Marie-Antoinette dans sa tour, 42
Le Comte Ory (Rossini), 88
Concerto for Clarinet (Dacosta), 274
Concerto for Clarinet (X. Lefèvre), 274
Concerto for Clarinet (Mozart), 288
Concerto for Flute and Harp (Mozart), 273
Concerto for Piano (Dussek), 234
Concerto for Piano (Viotti), 210
Concerto for Piano and Harp (Dussek), 234
Concerto for Orchestra (X. Lefèvre), 287

Concerto for Violin (Baillot), 288
Concerto for Violin (Beethoven), 246, 288
Concerto for Violin (P. Carillez), 233
Concerto for Violin (Kreutzer), 288
Concerto for Violin (Rode), 288
Concerto for Violin (Spohr), 239
Concerto for Violin (Viotti), 210, 288
Le Congrès des rois (Grétry, Méhul, Cherubini, Dalayrac, Kreutzer, Berton), 53
Il Convitato di pietra (Gardi), 324
Il Convitato di pietra (Gazzaniga), 324
Il Convito (Cimarosa), 121
Così fan tutte (Mozart), 118, 120, 223, 324, 335
The Creation (Haydn), 187, 188, 256, 317
Credo (Cherubini), 185
Il Curioso indiscreto (Anfossi), 111

La Dame blanche (Boïeldieu), 106, 108, 148, 154, 156, 276
Damnation de Faust (Berlioz), 76
Dardanus (Sacchini), 54
Davidde penitente (Mozart), 196
Le Délire (Berton), 104
Demetrio e Polibio (Rossini), 131
De Profundis (Gluck), 194
De Profundis (Mozart), 196
Les Deux journées (Cherubini), 94, 99
Dialogue de la tigresse Antoinette avec la guillotine, 42
Dido (Piccini), 155, 156
La Distruzione di Gerusalemme (Zingarelli), 121
Doktor und Apotheker (Dittersdorf), 330, 331
Don Giovanni (Mozart), 55, 111, 118, 120, 147, 153, 211, 216, 223, 324, 326, 332, 335
Le Duc d'Aquitaine (Blangini), 63
I Due baroni (Cimarosa), 111

L'Eccelsa gara (Spontini), 59
Elisca (Grétry), 90
Enfance du Christ (Berlioz), 103, 184
Enfant chéri des dames (Devienne), 96

Die Entführung aus dem Serail (Mozart), 327, 329, 332

L'Espoir réalisé, 58

Euphrosine et Coradin (Méhul), 100, 139, 141

Falstaff (Verdi), 106

Il Fanatico per la musica (Mayr), 130

Faniska (Cherubini), 84

Faust (Goethe), 345

Fernand Cortez (Spontini), 62, 67, 68, 82, 83, 118, 148, 153, 346

La Fête de la Paix (Saint-Amans), 54

Fête de la Victoire, 56

La Fête de Mars, 57

Fidelio (Beethoven), 84, 93, 102, 244, 338

La Finta filosofa (Spontini), 118

Une Folie (Méhul), 155

Fra Diavolo (Auber), 106

La Frascatana (Paisiello), 128

Der Freischütz (Weber), 73, 107, 156, 256, 338; see also *Robin des bois*

I Fuorusciti di Firenze (Paër), *130*

Gabrielle d'Estrées (Méhul), 268

Gianni Schicchi (Puccini), 106

Gil Blas (Lesage), 97

La Ginevra di Scozia (Mosca), 123

Gloria delle armi, 124

Grand Battle of Austerlitz (L. Jadin), 312

Griselda (Paër), 225

Gruppen (Stockhausen), 48

Guillaume Tell (Grétry), 90

Guillaume Tell (Rossini), 82, 88–90

Hécube (Granges de Fontenelle), 72

Héléna (Méhul), 102, 155, 268

Les Horaces (Porta), 72

Horatius Coclès (Méhul), 53

Hymne à la Liberté (Gossec), 15

Hymne à la Victoire (Cherubini), 38

Hymne à l'Être Suprême (Gossec), 38

Hymne des Marseillais (Rouget de Lisle), 43, 44; see also "La Marseillaise"

Hymne du IX Thermidor (Méhul), 40

L'Inganno felice (Rossini), 132

Iphigénie en Aulide (Gluck), 53, 146, 147, 156, 210, 346

Iphigénie en Tauride (Gluck), 54, 68

L'Irato (Méhul), 102, 141, 340

L'Italiana in Algeri (Rossini), 131, 133

Jean de Paris (Boïeldieu), 106, 108

Jeanne d'Arc (Carafa), 106

Jeanneton prend sa faucille, 42

Le Jeune Henri (Méhul), 100

Le Jeune Sage (Méhul), 139

Jeunesse trop coquette, 42

Joseph (Méhul), 51, 55, 93, 102, 103, 141, 142, 146

Judas Maccabeus (Handel), 201

Lakmé (Delibes), 75

Léonore (Gaveaux), 93

Lisbeth (Grétry), 90

Litanies de la Vierge (Durante), 168, 196, 216

Lodoïska (Cherubini), 92, 93, 97, 98, 100, 234

Lodoïska (Kreutzer), 92, 98, 146, 234, 254

The Magic Flute (Mozart), 66, 73, 96, 276, 313, 324, 325, 326, 331; see also *Les Mystères d'Isis*

La Maison à vendre (Dalayrac), 93, 105

Maometto secondo (Rossini), 86

Marche funèbre (Gossec), 213

Marche lugubre (Gossec), 45, 46, 191

Marguerite d'Anjou (Meyerbeer), 108

Marie (Hérold), 107

The Marriage of Figaro (Mozart), 108, 118, 119, 120, 121, 122, 143, 153, 223, 323, 331, 335, 336, 340, 341

"La Marseillaise" (Rouget de Lisle), 36, 45, 52, 148, 194; see also *Hymne des Marseillais*

Mass (Beethoven), 244

Mass (Paër), 168

Mass (Regnault), 195

Mass (Roze), 179

Mass (Zingarelli), 168

Masses (Cherubini), 168, 174, 186, 187, 240
Masses (Desvignes), 190
Masses (Haydn), 196
Masses (Jomelli), 196
Masses (Le Sueur), 173, 178
Masses (Martini), 168
Masses (Mozart), 244
Masses (Paisiello), 163, 168, 172
Masses (Plantade), 168, 172
Ma tante Aurore (Boïeldieu), 105
Il Matrimonio segreto (Cimarosa), 69, 113, 115, 117, 119
Médée (Cherubini), 20, 80, 93, 97, 100, 101, 108, 346
Messiah (Handel), 201, 202
Michel-Ange (Nicolo), 141
Miltiade à Marathon (Lemoyne), 53
Miserere (Jomelli), 168, 199
Miserere (Leo), 199
Misericordia Domini (Mozart), 196
Missa ad fugam (Palestrina), 199
Missa pro defunctis (Jomelli), 199
Missa solemnis (Beethoven), 185–186
Mithridate (Racine), 99
Mitridate (Mozart), 325
Moïse (Rossini), 86, 87, 89
La Molinara (Paisiello), 113, 115, 117
Montano et Stéphanie (Berton), 95, 97, 104
La Mort d'Adam (Le Sueur), 74, 78, 79, 103, 345
La Mort d'Orphée (Beck), 194
Mosè in Egitto (Rossini), 113
La Muette de Portici (Auber), 64, 87, 88, 148
Les Mystères d'Isis (Mozart), 66, 73, 74, 148, 276, 313, 324, 325, 326, 340; see also *The Magic Flute*

Das Neusonntagskind (W. Müller), 329, 331, 332
La Nina (Paisiello), 115, 116
Norma (Bellini), 83, 134
La Nouvelle au camp (Berton), 54

Œdipe à Colone (Sacchini), 53, 68, 84, 144, 146, 148, 153, 155, 156, 346
Offertory (Haydn), 222
Offrande à la Liberté (Gossec), 44, 52
Olympie (Kalkbrenner), 72
Olympie (Spontini), 68, 82, 83, 346
Ombra adorata (Crescentini), 206
Oratorio de Noël (Le Sueur), 184
Oratorios du couronnement (Le Sueur), 184, 185
Gli Orazii e Curiazii (Cimarosa), 127
Orfeo (Gluck), 155, 276
O Salutaris (Gossec), 168
Ossian (Les Bardes) (Le Sueur), 74, 75, 76, 78, 83, 102, 276
Otello (Rossini), 85, 113, 153

La Paix (Paisiello, Cimarosa, Guglielmi, Mozart, Winter), 117
Pamela (Richardson), 115
Le Passage de la mer Rouge (Giroust), 168, 169
La Passion (Paisiello), 190
Paul et Virginie (Kreutzer), 92, 254
Paul et Virginie (Le Sueur), 92, 97, 145
Pélage (Spontini), 62
Le Petit Chaperon Rouge (Boïeldieu), 151
Philippe et Georgette (Dalayrac), 146
Pie Jesu (Desvignes), 168, 191
La Pietra del Paragone (Rossini), 131
Il Pirro (Paisiello), 126
Plaisir d'amour (Martini), 241
Le Pré aux clercs (Hérold), 107
Preciosa (Weber), 108
Les Prétendus (Lemoyne), 156
La Prise de Jéricho (Cimarosa, Haydn, Mozart, and others), 189
Le Prisonnier (Della Maria), 93, 95
Prometheus (Beethoven), 216
Proserpine (Paisiello), 55, 163

Quartets (Beethoven), 297
Quartets (Boccherini), 238, 293
Quartets (Catel), 294
Quartets (Cherubini), 298
Quartets (Gambaro), 294

Quartets (Haydn), 238, 293, 295, 297
Quartets (Mozart), 238, 293, 295, 297
Quartets (Onslow), 298
Quartets (Pleyel), 238, 295
Quartets (Reicha), 298
Quartets (Rode), 235
"Quelle pupille tenere" (Cimarosa), 264
Quintets (Beethoven), 249
Quintets (Boccherini), 235, 249, 252
Quintets (Onslow), 298
Quintets (Reicha), 298

Raoul, sire de Créqui (Dalayrac), 146
Requiem (Berlioz), 48
Requiem (Cherubini), 187
Requiem (Cornu), 190
Requiem (Haydn), 222
Requiem (Homet), 168
Requiem (Jomelli), 168
Requiem (Mozart), 168, 187, 190, 255
Richard Coeur de Lion (Grétry), 148
Les Rigueurs du cloître (Berton), 139
Robin des bois (Weber & Castil-Blaze), 108, 156, 157, 256, 338
Le Roi et le Pèlerin (Foignet), 141
Roland (Sacchini), 53
Roméo et Juliette (Steibelt), 92, 96, 126, 155, 315
Romeo e Giulietta (Zingarelli), 92, 125
Rose et Colas (Monsigny), 146
Das rote Käppchen (Dittersdorf), 329
Ruth (Franck), 184
Ruth et Booz (Le Sueur), 103
Ruth et Noémi (Le Sueur), 103

Le Sacrifice d'Abraham (Cimarosa), 210
Salve Regina (Pergolesi), 196
Samson (Handel), 201
Sardanapale (Berlioz), 114
Sargines (Dalayrac), 56
Saül (Cimarosa, Haydn, Mozart, and others), 189
"The Seasons" (Haydn), 216
Semiramide (Rossini), 135
Sémiramis (Catel), 74
Septet (Beethoven), 249

La Serva padrona (Paisiello), 153
Le Siège de Corinthe (Rossini), 63, 68, 86, 138, 148, 258
Sinfonia (Cherubini), 270
Sinfonia Concertante (Baillot), 285
Sinfonia Concertante (Catel), 282
Sinfonia Concertante (Davaux), 285
Sinfonia Concertante (Devienne), 210, 213
Sinfonia Concertante (L. Jadin), 311
Sinfonia Concertante (Mozart), 282
Sinfonia Concertante (Viotti), 228
Sinfonia Concertante (Wiederkehr), 225
Sonata *Les Adieux* (Beethoven), 323
Sonata *Appassionata* (Beethoven), 319
Sonata for Piano (Cramer), 213
Sonata for Violin and Piano (Baillot), 300
Sonata for Bassoon (Ozy), 299
Sonatas for Cello and Piano (Onslow), 300
Sonatas for Clarinet (X. Lefèvre), 299, 300
Sonatas for Flute (Hugot), 299
Sonatas for Flute (Wunderlich), 299
Sonatas for Harpsichord and Violin (Bach), 318
Sonatas for Piano (Adam), 310
Sonatas for Piano (Beethoven), 299
Sonatas for Piano (Boëly), 311
Sonatas for Piano (Boïeldieu), 312
Sonatas for Piano (Bontempo), 314
Sonatas for Piano (Hérold), 312
Sonatas for Piano (L. Jadin), 312
Sonatas for Piano (X. Lefèvre), 300
Sonatas for Piano (Mozart), 299, 312
Sonatas for Piano (Steibelt), 253
Sonatas for Violin (Beethoven), 299
Sonatas for Violin (Mozart), 299
La Sonnambula (Bellini), 134
Der Spiegel von Arkadien (Süssmayer), 329
"Spring Chorus" (Haydn), 216
Stabat Mater (Haydn), 168
Stabat Mater (Josquin des Prés), 199
Stabat Mater (Palestrina), 199
Stabat Mater (Pergolesi), 168
Stabat Mater (Zingarelli), 168
Stratonice (Méhul), 93, 94, 97, 99, 139
La Sylphide (Schneitzhoeffer), 233

Symphonie fantastique (Berlioz), 264, 270–272, 276, 344
Symphonies (Beethoven), 216, 244, 247, 280, 320
Symphonies (Cambini), 265
Symphonies (Gossec), 269–270
Symphonies (Guénin), 230, 265
Symphonies (Haydn), 207, 210, 217, 220, 223, 228, 244, 257, 265, 297
Symphonies (Méhul), 232, 267–269
Symphonies (Mozart), 199, 216, 244, 255
Symphonies (Schneitzhoeffer), 233
Symphony (Filtz), 265
Symphony (Pleyel), 265
Symphony (Stamitz), 265

Le Tableau parlant (Grétry), 54
Tamerlan (Winter), 315
Tancredi (Rossini), 86, 131
Tartuffe (Molière), 156
Te Deum (Notre-Dame, 1791), 13
Te Deum (Haydn), 222
Te Deum (Le Sueur), 167
Te Deum (Martini), 168
Te Deum (Paisiello), 168
Te Deum (Plantade), 167
Télémaque (Gardel), 92
Télémaque (Le Sueur), 92
Le Temple de la gloire (Rameau), 52
Il Testamento (Farinelli), 121
The Thieving Magpie (Rossini), 153
Thirty-two Variations on a Theme in C minor (Beethoven), 319
Timoléon (Méhul), 139
To My Lyre (Anacreon), 242
Torvaldo e Dorliska (Rossini), 133
Toute la Grèce (Lemoyne), 53
Traité d'harmonie (Catel), 23
Le Trésor supposé (Méhul), 107
Le Triomphe de Trajan (Persuis), 52, 60, 61
Le Triomphe du mois de Mars (Kreutzer), 58
Les Trois Sultanes, 145
Tu es Petrus (Le Sueur), 164
Il Turco in Italia (Rossini), 133
Der Tyroler Wastel (Haibel), 330, 331

Unxerunt Salomonem (Le Sueur), 164, 185
Uthal (Méhul), 102, 276

"Veillons au Salut de l'Empire," 52, 148
Vendôme en Espagne (Auber & Hérold), 63
La Vestale (Spontini), 50, 51, 59, 60, 67, 79, 80, 81, 82, 83, 84, 101, 118, 141, 147, 148, 153, 156, 346
Il Viaggio a Reims (Rossini), 88
La Villanella rapita (Bianchi), 111
Virginie (Berton), 85
Les Visitandines (Devienne), 96, 139
Vivat (Roze), 164
Les Voitures versées (Boïeldieu), 105
Vous gentilles fillettes (Jumentier), 36

Wallace (Catel), 103, 276
The Well-Tempered Clavier (Bach), 304, 318

Zampa (Hérold), 107
Zingari in fiera (Paisiello), 128
Zoraïme et Zulnare (Boïeldieu), 95